526.99

D0554326

Fort Nelson Public Library
Box 330
Fort Nelson, BC
V0C-1R0

OCT - - 2005

THE RATTLESNAKE

by the same author

TOBACCO IN HISTORY: THE CULTURES OF DEPENDENCE

CONSUMING HABITS: DRUGS IN HISTORY AND ANTHROPOLOGY
(editor, with Paul Lovejoy and Andrew Sherratt)

THE STORY OF TAXOL: NATURE AND POLITICS
IN THE PURSUIT OF AN ANTI-CANCER DRUG (with Vivien Walsh)

USEFUL BODIES: HUMANS IN THE SERVICE OF MEDICAL SCIENCE
IN THE TWENTIETH CENTURY (editor, with Anthony McElligott and Lara Marks)

The Rattlesnake

A Voyage of Discovery to the Coral Sea

JORDAN GOODMAN

faber and faber

Fort Nelson Public Library
Box 330
Fort Nelson, BC
V0C-1R0

First published in 2005
by Faber and Faber Limited
3 Queen Square London WC1N 3AU

Typeset by Faber and Faber Limited
Printed in England by Mackays of Chatham plc, Chatham, Kent

All rights reserved
© Jordan Goodman, 2005

The right of Jordan Goodman to be identified as author
of this work has been asserted in accordance with Section 77
of the Copyright, Designs and Patents Act 1988

A CIP record for this book
is available from the British Library

ISBN 0–571–21073–2

2 4 6 8 10 9 7 5 3 1

For Dallas

Contents

Illustrations

PLATE SECTIONS Imperial College, Library Archives and Special Collections, 4 (HA/HM R1), 16, 28, 31 (HA/HP71); Mitchell Library, State Library of New South Wales 1 (PXC 281, f.115), 2 (PXC 281, f.2), 5 (PXC 281, f. 60), 6 (PXC 281, f.85), 7 (PXC 281, f.110), 8 (PXC 281, f.6), 9 (PXC 281, f.11), 10 (PXC 279, f.8), 11 (PXC 281, f.59), 13 (PXC 281, f.29), 14 (PXC 281, f.50), 15 (PXC 281, f.25), 18 (ML 1348), 20 (PXC 279, f.48), 22 (PXC 281a, f.8), 23 (PXC 281, f.66), 26 (PXC 281, f.84), 27 (PX*D82, f.23), 30 (PXC 281, f.96), 32 (ML 848), 33 (PX*D82, f.40), 34 (PXC 281, f.92); National Library of Australia, 12 (pic-an2838490), 21 (pic-an58633330), 29 (pic-an5576198); National Maritime Museum, Greenwich, 35 (HTN69, f.47).

CHAPTER HEADS Mitchell Library, State Library of New South Wales, 2 (PXC 281, f.1), 3 (PXC 281, f.10), 4 (PXC 281, f.22), 6 (PXC 281, f.116), 10 (PXC 281, f.106), 11 (PXC 281, f.82; artist Owen Stanley); National Library of Australia, 5 (pic-an6065555; artist Augustus Earle), 8 (pic-an20826282; artist Emile Lasalle), 9 (pic-an8008807; artist Walter G. Mason), 12 (pic-an3016731; artist Edward W Brooker); National Portrait Gallery, 1 (NPG 918; artist Stephen Pearce).

Prologue

On 15 August 1834, in fine weather, the Charles Eaton *struck so violently on Great Detached Reef that the rudder and keel were torn off and the ship totally lost. The nearest European settlement was 1,500 miles away.*

Five sailors immediately commandeered one of the boats and rowed away, leaving everyone else stranded.

Nothing more was heard of the fate of the Charles Eaton *until 12 October 1836, more than two years after the shipwreck, when the* Isabella, *a colonial schooner, arrived in Sydney. On board were John Ireland, the cabin boy of the* Charles Eaton, *five-year-old William D'Oyly and seventeen skulls.*

It was one of the worst shipwrecks in Australian history.

Thirteen passengers joined the Charles Eaton *in Hobart Town on 9 July 1834. The ship arrived in Sydney on 13 July, where seven passengers disembarked. The rest, Captain Thomas D'Oyly, his wife Charlotte and their two sons, George aged seven and William aged two, a Bengali nurse who cared for them, and a barrister remained on the ship for the next leg of its voyage. Thomas D'Oyly, who had just celebrated his thirty-eighth birthday, was a captain in the Bengal Artillery. He was from a distinguished family who had long and close connections with India. D'Oyly had been on sick leave in Hobart Town for about a year and was returning to Calcutta to take up a new post as Commissary of Ordnance in Agra.*

The Charles Eaton *left Sydney on 29 July 1834, following a course for Surabaya, at the eastern end of Java, where the D'Oyly party planned to disembark for the final leg of their journey back to Calcutta. The ship's master sailed northwards into the Coral Sea, outside the Great Barrier Reef, as did other commanders of merchant vessels plying between Australia and Asia at this time of the year. He would need to pass through the reefs using one of several possible entrances in order to change course to the west, sailing through the Torres Strait and beyond to Java. To navigate one of these highly dangerous entrances the master relied on the most up-to-date information available, a rough drawing by Captain Samuel Ashmore, a Sydney master-mariner and shipowner, showing the routes that various ships had taken between 1815 and 1830 up the Australian coast in the neighbourhood of Great Detached Reef. It was a far cry from an Admiralty chart. It did not show the entire reef system in the area, nor did it have any depth markings except on the tracks themselves.*

Experienced mariners like Ashmore, who knew their way around the area and had their favourite entrances, would have found the drawing adequate, but for mariners unfamiliar with the complicated hydrography, it was an entirely different story. Getting it wrong meant certain disaster.

PART ONE

CHAPTER I

London
1846

From his office on the upper floor of the Admiralty building in Whitehall Francis Beaufort controlled the charting of the world's seas. Beaufort believed passionately in British control and domination of the world's seas – not by gunboats but by charts.

Britain had been at peace following the end of the long and bitter Napoleonic Wars in 1815. Peace suited Beaufort. He feared not what preyed on the water's surface but what lurked below. He was the Hydrographer of the Navy, a position he took in 1829 at the age of fifty-five. The Hydrographical Office was established in 1795 for the purpose of making charts from information supplied by ships' officers and other sources.[1] By the time of Beaufort's appointment, however, the office had become pro-active. It now commissioned surveying voyages to acquire new information on coastlines, winds, currents, tides, depths, and navigational obstacles in order to produce accurate marine charts.[2]

Beaufort sent out his band of surveyors to every corner of the globe, to discipline the world's seas through charts and sailing directions.

The wreck of the *Charles Eaton* brought Beaufort face to face with one of the most treacherous and least known parts of the world. If the actual wreck wasn't enough to force action, the horrible fate of the people on the ship, as it came to be known in London and elsewhere, did.

Following a reported sighting of a white person on Murray Island, Sir Richard Bourke, the Governor of New South Wales, ordered Charles Lewis, commander of the *Isabella*, in June 1836 to sail to the island. There he found Ireland and the boy D'Oyly, happy and healthy, living as part of the island community.

On nearby Aureed Island, Lewis also discovered the remains of the less fortunate passengers and crew of the *Charles Eaton*. 'After searching all over the straits for this mysterious island,' he recounted,

> I at last found it, and saw no inhabitants there, having left the previous night when the ship hove in sight of their isle. I, however, found the skulls of the unfortunate people on the middle of the island, covered with a kind of shed and arranged near a place where they generally feasted on the dead. These heads of different people were placed round like the figure of a man, and painted with ochre. I observed long sandy hair on one of the skulls, also great marks of violence on all of them. Having satisfied myself of the truth of this detail, I set the whole of the house on fire, and also destroyed every cocoanut-tree in the place, which those savages generally exist on. I at the same time conveyed the skulls on board, and destroyed the skull-house.[3]

When they arrived in Sydney, William D'Oyly was placed in the care of a close friend of the D'Oyly family. The seventeen skulls, which the surgeon of an East India Company ship had pronounced as being European, were given a Christian burial in Sydney. John Ireland remained in the city for a few months and then left Australia on 11 March 1837 for London.

On 15 August, Ireland, after an incredible experience, was back in London. Though newspapers in Sydney, Canton and London had reported the *Isabella*'s gruesome cargo, Ireland's own story, which he told on 30 August at Mansion House, where he was summoned to appear in front of relatives of the deceased, filled in all the harrowing details of the fate of the crew and passengers of the *Charles Eaton*.

The Times picked up the story. A day or two after the five sailors made off without attempting to help the others, Ireland explained, the shipwrecked survivors managed to put together a sort of raft and the captain, some of the officers and the passengers left the ship in it. Five or six days later a second raft was made, and the rest of the ship's company, the other officers and Ireland left the ship. They drifted towards the Queensland coast. Upon reaching an island (later identified as Boydang), they were attacked and everyone was killed apart from himself. He related that he struggled for his life and that he was unexpectedly saved by one of his pursuers. His was not the only life that was spared. John Sexton, the other cabin boy, was also alive. Ireland provided gory details of how everyone else had been killed. 'Some had their brains dashed out, and others were stabbed, and the savages after they had stripped the bodies let them down with the tide, keeping all the heads, which they placed in a row before the fire. They ate no part except the eyes and cheeks.' He and Sexton, he stated, together with the heads of the unfortunate crew members, were taken to another nearby island where he was amazed to see Portland, Captain D'Oyly's Newfoundland dog, and George and William D'Oyly alive. George D'Oyly told Ireland that their raft drifted to this island and everyone, apart from him and his brother, had been killed. He saw his own mother being clubbed to death while she was holding his infant brother. His father was murdered in the same way. The four boys remained on this island for some time during which they saw ships passing by but were quickly hidden by the islanders. After a stay of three months, he recalled, John Sexton and George D'Oyly were taken away by one group of natives while he and William D'Oyly went with another. They went from island to island until one day, on an island near Aureed Island, they were visited and purchased by a group of Murray Islanders who took them to their home. One of them, a man called Duppa, took the boys under his care and there they lived until the *Isabella* arrived. The Murray Islanders, Ireland emphasized, treated him and William D'Oyly with kindness. While he was staying with Duppa, Ireland learned that both John Sexton and George D'Oyly had been murdered.[4]

No other shipwreck had been so widely and closely publicized. James Drew, almost anticipating this public exposure, was at the Mansion House meeting with John Ireland. His brother-in-law was one of those who had been murdered. He agreed that the atrocities committed in the case of the crew and passengers of the *Charles Eaton* were frightful. But recounting them would not put an end to them. He wanted, as he said, to 'press the necessity of the interference of the Colonial Government to prevent such horrible treatment as unfortunate people who were wrecked on these islands were subjected to'. What was required above all was 'to have an accurate survey taken of the coast, as the coral-reefs were forming islands every day, and intimidation should be held out to the chiefs of the savages to check their disposition to shed the blood of people whose colour differed from their own'.[5]

His was not the only voice clamouring for action. The newly formed Geographical Society, headed by its formidable President, Sir John Barrow, the Second Secretary to the Admiralty, and an acquaintance of Captain Charles D'Oyly's brother-in-law, had already put its weight behind a proposal to carry out a full and accurate survey of the Torres Strait.[6] The editor of the *Nautical Magazine*, Britain's most important and influential periodical on maritime affairs, echoed the Society's concerns.[7] Something had to be done to improve the charts and only the Royal Navy with its superior ships and state-of-the-art hydrographic techniques and instruments could tame these dangerous seas. The responsibility fell squarely at Beaufort's feet, but as he found out, charting the eastern coast of Australia and the Torres Strait would prove to take much longer than expected, and involved more ships than anticipated.

Beaufort was the fourth and longest-serving hydrographer in the naval service. He had already spent more time in the job than any of his predecessors and, more than any of them, had nurtured and honed the position in his own image. Born in Ireland, the son of a country parson of Huguenot descent, Beaufort entered the navy in 1787, at the age of fourteen, and spent the following twenty-five years in military service, mostly in the Mediterranean.[8] He was promoted to the rank of captain in 1810 and, with his first command, began surveying and drawing charts of the eastern Mediterranean. Despite the fact that his charts were generally considered the finest of their kind, Beaufort was not treated well by his superiors. They were mean when it came to money and promotion. He languished for fifteen years in the shadows of the Admiralty but during this time he actively sought out the company of Britain's greatest scientific minds. If his superiors, or their Lordships (strictly speaking the Lords Commissioners of the Admiralty, of which there were six), failed to acknowledge him, his scientific companions were showering him with recognition and accolades. He was elected to the Geological Society, the Royal Society and the Royal Astronomical Society.

When, in 1829, he was offered the post of Hydrographer, he knew he had arrived. Within two years, hydrography became a separate department of the Admiralty and Beaufort was responsible to the six Lords of the Admiralty directly. During his tenure in Whitehall, Beaufort was able to commandeer more ships for surveys and attract more money from Their Lordships than any other hydrographer before him. Admiralty charts had been made available for sale to anyone as early as 1825, a remarkable change from the previous policy when charts were guarded as state secrets. Beaufort strenuously pursued the new policy by increasing the number of charts published and their print run. Of some 50,000 Admiralty charts printed in the mid-1840s, the public bought half of them.[9]

Beaufort's relationship with his superiors was difficult. Surveying held an ambiguous position within the Admiralty. It was necessary, to be sure, but it was incompatible with military operations because of the fact that surveying vessels needed to reduce the numbers of guns they carried in order to make space for chartrooms, instrument rooms and the like. That Britain was at peace was, of course, no guarantee that threats would not occur.[10] To the Admiralty, each surveying ship represented one less fighting ship. Nurtured on decades of war, the Admiralty found it hard to adjust to peacetime.

One of the first ships Beaufort commissioned, and which signalled the kind of hydrographic service he had in mind, was HMS *Beagle* commanded by Robert Fitzroy with the responsibility of completing the survey of the southern extremes of South America. On board was the young Charles Darwin, whom Beaufort approved of as naturalist to the voyage.[11] As paymaster of these travelling naturalists, however, the Lords of the Admiralty were not as enthusiastic as Beaufort and made it as difficult as possible for him to get what he wanted. They were quite happy for the surgeon or the assistant surgeon to act as a natural history collector but for anything else Beaufort had to make out a case, and then, it was for a single individual, unlike the French (and also the American) expeditions of the same time where natural history was represented by a battery of specialists – botanist, zoologist and geologist.

*

Beaufort was not a mere mapmaker: he was also an explorer, an imperialist and, above all, a man of science, dedicated to the pursuit of knowledge of whatever kind and wherever it was. 'The harvest I look for', he told one of his surveyors, 'must be won in the Kingdoms of science and reaped in hydrographic fields.'[12]

He thought of surveying in a broad sense of scientific investigation and knowledge. To him, hydrography was not just a matter of knowing coastlines, ocean depths, currents, and so forth, but also included natural history, both of land and sea, geography and ethnography. To this end, he wanted survey ships to carry naturalists to make the necessary observations and collections to further that branch of knowledge and to fill the metropolitan, provincial and private museums with the exotic specimens of flora and fauna they encountered. He wanted discovery and exploration to be at the centre of marine surveys – Beaufort was one of the founding members of the Geographical Society.

Two stretches of water, however, eluded even Beaufort. One of these was the so-called Northwest Passage to the north of Canada. It was not for lack of trying. The search for the Northwest Passage had been a preoccupation since the late sixteenth century and, despite an enormous investment in people and resources over the centuries, a passage from east to west across the polar seas had still not been discovered.[13] A recent expedition led by John and James Ross had almost ended in tragedy and the 1835 voyage to search for them spent its whole time in the Arctic locked in pack ice. Determined to succeed at last, in May 1845, the Admiralty sent out the best-equipped expedition to date, led by Sir John Franklin, one of the country's most experienced Arctic explorers. After July 1845 they were never heard from again.

The other stretch of water was the Great Barrier Reef and the Torres Strait. Though not as daunting in physical terms as the frozen grey polar seas, the charting of this part of Australia lagged far behind that of other parts of the world. Unlike the polar seas, the Great Barrier Reef and the Torres Strait was a graveyard of ships. Islands, reefs, atolls, shoals and rocks were strewn throughout these waters and there were no existing charts that could guarantee a safe passage. Each voyage from Australia and the Pacific to China, India and Britain was a gamble.

The grisly fate of the passengers and crew of the *Charles Eaton* tormented Beaufort as these turquoise tropical and deadly seas haunted him. He was not alone in this nor the first to fear them. James Cook, in HMS *Endeavour*, in 1770, was the first European to sail between the Great Barrier Reef and the Australian coast but he was more interested in getting out of what he called 'The Labyrinth' than charting it.[14] Matthew Flinders tried to chart the area in 1802, but a combination of bad planning and a rotting ship put an end to his attempts. Phillip Parker King in 1819 to 1821 did a bit better. He made a running survey of the space between the coast and the Great Barrier Reef. This allowed him to outline a safe sailing track the length of what he called the Inner Route, but the space on both sides of the track remained unsurveyed. He did even less in Torres Strait through which he passed quickly and anxiously.[15]

King's was the last attempt to survey the Great Barrier Reef and the Torres Strait. Surveys of home waters, Africa, the West Indies and the Arctic were deemed more important and pressing than Australia. Beaufort expanded the geographic scope of his office by taking in the Mediterranean, South America and the Pacific, but he, too, did not pay Australia any attention, until, that is, the wreck of the *Charles Eaton* brought home just how impoverished that part of the world was in marine knowledge, and how dangerous were the waters surrounding it.[16] Relying on the kind of tracings people like Samuel Ashmore made available to merchant vessels gave Beaufort sleepless nights.

Beaufort responded to the call for action by commissioning a ship to return to Australian waters, for the first time in twenty years. And the ship he chose was HMS *Beagle* back from its surveying voyage with Fitzroy and Darwin. Beaufort placed John Clements Wickham in command of the ship. It left Plymouth in July 1837. Surprisingly, the Admiralty instructed Wickham to survey Australia's western and northern coasts, Bass Strait, another notoriously dangerous stretch of water, Torres Strait and the southern shore of New Guinea. Not a single word about the Great Barrier Reef.[17] The explanation probably lay in the fact that John Barrow at the Admiralty was now heavily involved in the thorny issue of a northern Australia settlement. The settlement, planned to be at Port Essington on the northern coast, to the west of the Gulf of Carpentaria, would not only thwart increasing territorial interest by the Dutch in the area, but would also act as a haven to shipwrecks. Though Phillip Parker King had surveyed the northern coast, it was felt that a more up-to-date hydrographic survey was needed. The northern coast, therefore, took precedence over the Great Barrier Reef.[18]

The *Beagle* spent over five years in Australia surveying the coasts. Though the ship sailed up the eastern coast of Australia, between the shore and the edge of the Great Barrier Reef, on two separate occasions, Wickham did not survey the area. The most he did was to correct some of King's earlier observations. In July 1839 the *Beagle* visited the island that King had supposed to be Boydang where some or most of the crew of the *Charles Eaton* had been killed. Lieutenant John Lort Stokes, it turned out, had seen William D'Oyly in Sydney and was moved by being at this location. He learned, incidentally, that D'Oyly had been saved from certain death because 'his helplessness excited the sympathies of an Indian woman [an Aureed islander], who snatched him from the arms of his murdered mother, and sheltered him within her own'.[19]

The Torres Strait and New Guinea surveys were left to the end of the voyage, but in the event these never took place. Missing out New Guinea proved to be a huge disappointment for everyone on the *Beagle*. Only a handful of Europeans had visited the island; and even fewer landed. As Stokes himself put it, all of the difficult and monotonous work of surveying was accepted because each tedious day brought them nearer 'the anticipated delights of discovery . . . from those hoped-for scenes of adventure on the unvisited shores of New Guinea'.[20] But it was not to be. The *Beagle* had run out of time and, in August 1842, John Lort Stokes, the ship's new commander (Wickham had left the *Beagle* because of illness in December 1840), received orders to return to England.[21]

The Great Barrier Reef had been overlooked in the *Beagle*'s surveying voyage and now Beaufort was determined to correct this glaring omission. Without waiting for the *Beagle* to return, late in 1841 Beaufort commissioned another ship, HMS *Fly*, to sail to Australia.[22] The ship's commander, Captain Francis Blackwood, received orders in March 1842 to head for the Great Barrier Reef. The instructions to Blackwood were unambiguous and echoed the tragic case of the *Charles Eaton*.

> Many of the vessels when weak-handed, in order to avoid the frequent anchorage necessary in the in-shore passage by what is called King's Route, stand out

to sea till an opportunity offers for making one of the narrow gaps in the Barrier Reef, through which they steer for the strait; and whereas several vessels have thus been lost there being no other guide to those openings than the casual observation of latitude, which is often incorrect, there being no land to be seen till entangled within the reefs, and no chart on which the dangers are correctly placed; we have therefore thought fit for the above reasons to have the Great Barrier Reef explored and to have those gaps surveyed, in order that some means may be devised for so making the most eligible of these openings that they may be recognised in due time and passed through in comparative safety.[23]

New Guinea was within 'the field of operations', but safe passages through the Great Barrier Reef and the Torres Strait were the main purpose of the expedition.[24]

HMS *Fly* left England in April 1842 and spent most of the next four years surveying an area of 1,000 miles in length and 170 in width.[25] Beaufort did not want anything to go wrong this time and kept reminding Blackwood of the importance of his work and the need to be extremely diligent. 'Do not hurry over the hidden dangers which lurk and even grow in that part of the world', Beaufort told him, reminding him that coral reefs were living organisms.[26] Beaufort emphasized the utmost need in getting this survey done, in particular in finding a good opening in the Great Barrier Reef, in the vicinity, if possible, of where merchant vessels were already entering. In any case, Blackwood was to concentrate on this one task and not to take his eye off his objective. New Guinea, Beaufort stressed, was a sideshow:

New Guinea you know is given to you as a matter of recreation after toiling at the Barrier Reefs out of sight of land – and though I look forward to your discoveries, these being useful as well as amusing, good for the health of your people from vanity, and likely to produce many interesting facts about that great island, yet I must remind you that it stands in the programme of your exploits entirely subordinate to the Barrier Reefs.[27]

Blackwood found the entrance he was looking for between Raine Island and Great Detached Reef in June 1843. Ironically, it was 10 miles north of the point where the *Charles Eaton* wrecked. In the following year, Blackwood returned and, with the help of a party of convicts and building materials from Sydney, erected a stone beacon, 5 feet thick and 70 feet above sea level.

Constructing the beacon and the strain of tedious, repetitive surveying work in the tropical seas under a blazing sun began to take its toll on the *Fly*. Blackwood first complained about the work in 1844 and, about a year later, in August 1845, wrote that he could no longer continue the survey. 'I will honestly confess', he wrote to Beaufort, 'I have had my share of as bitter and uninteresting a bit of work as ever came from the Hydrographic Office, and my zeal after three such years as I have had is evaporated ... all on board have had enough of the Coral Reef.'[28] He even hated his ship. Beaufort ordered the *Fly* home. Blackwood never got his vacation in New Guinea, never got to 'give fêtes to the Chiefs and flirt with the Papuan beauties'.[29]

Beaufort had his surveyed opening but the stretch of water between the coast and the Great Barrier Reef to the north of Rockingham Bay, near present-day Tully in Queensland, had still not been charted since Phillip Parker King. The Labyrinth was still untamed. New Guinea had hardly been touched.

Beaufort would not give up. The *Fly* arrived back in England in February 1846 but even before the ship was in home waters and before he had seen the charts, Beaufort launched his third attempt to map the Labyrinth. Blackwood was not the most experienced of surveyors, and Beaufort blamed Blackwood's lack of exposure to the rigours and tedium of hydrographic practices for his failure to complete the survey.

Beaufort was determined not to make the same mistake again. With commercial traffic increasing in the area and steam shipping certain in no time at all, the stakes of losing vessels in these uncharted, living reefs, shoals and rocks were growing enormously. To chart these dangers and put an end to their menace Beaufort needed a new ship and the best hydrographer he could find.

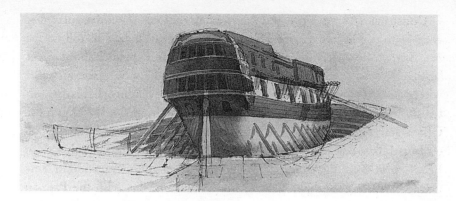

CHAPTER II

Portsmouth

1846

Beaufort knew that as long as there were gaps in the charts, ships and lives were at risk. He moved quickly to get a surveyor and a ship back to Australia.

Late in January 1846, Beaufort summoned Captain Owen Stanley to his office to discuss the survey. Thirty-five years of age and with a long and varied naval experience, Stanley's credentials impressed Beaufort. Just like Beaufort, he had developed an early and unquenching thirst for science and learned it in the navy, in classes and on board ship. As a young lieutenant, in recognition of his scientific skills, he was made a fellow of the Royal Astronomical Society, then of the Royal Geographical Society, and the Royal Society. His particular interest was terrestrial magnetism. He knew personally the leading scientific luminaries of the day, including Sir John Herschel, Colonel Edward Sabine, the Astronomer Royal George Biddell Airy, and Sir William Hooker.

Stanley came from a landed Cheshire family, his grandfather assuming the title of the 1st Lord Stanley of Alderley. His father, Edward Stanley, went into the Church (as did Beaufort's father), and spent thirty-two years as the Vicar of Alderley. Edward had a passionate love for the sea, natural history and drawing and painting. Edward Lear was a family friend and taught Owen drawing. In 1837, Edward Stanley was appointed Bishop of

First view of the *Rattlesnake*, Portsmouth

Norwich and in the very same year became President of the Linnean Society (the country's leading learned society for the pursuit of the study of natural history). In the previous year, Stanley had published a distinguished two-volume book on ornithology. The Bishop, a staunch member of the British Association for the Advancement of Science, held many scientific soirées at his residence.[1] Beaufort was a frequent guest.

Owen Stanley went into the Royal Navy at the age of fifteen, straight from naval college, the same year, in fact, that his elder cousin Isabella married the famous Arctic explorer, Captain William Edward Parry, a not insignificant development for the boy's future career. Short and stocky, Stanley may not have had the cut of a dashing young naval officer, but what he lacked in stature he made up for in experience and achievement. He had sailed with the greatest commanders of the time and had gone to virtually every corner of the world, including the Pacific and Australia. He had been on the coast of South America in the late 1820s and in the Straits of Magellan with Captain Phillip Parker King in HMS *Adventure*, sister ship to HMS *Beagle* on its first surveying voyage, and then with Captain John Franklin in the Mediterranean. Thereafter he sailed under the command of Sir George Back in HMS *Terror* to the Arctic in 1836 as scientific officer, in charge of the astronomical and magnetic instruments. A year stuck in pack ice, while the ship should have been surveying the adjacent channels and passages, gave Stanley the opportunity he needed to perfect his observational and drawing talents. In recognition of his achievements in the Arctic, he was given command, in 1838, of HMS *Britomart*, to accompany Sir Gordon Bremer to the remote tropical northern Australian coastline where they were instructed to establish a new British settlement at Port Essington. Surveying and scientific observations were not his only achievements, however. He also displayed useful diplomatic and linguistic skills when, in 1840, he took the *Britomart* to New Zealand where he was able to defuse a potentially explosive confrontation between Britain and France over property and settlement issues at Akaroa on the southern island, not far from present-day Christchurch.[2] After spending some time in Hobart where he enjoyed the company of the Governor, Sir John Franklin, and met and fell in love with his niece, Sophia Cracroft (who spurned his advances as she had those of many others before and after him), he returned to England in 1843 a hero.[3]

With his scientific interests and surveying experience, Stanley was as good as Beaufort's protégé. They belonged to the same scientific societies and Beaufort was a close friend of the family. Stanley embodied precisely what Beaufort wanted the hydrographic service to be: a broadly scientific organization, at the forefront of Britain's expansion, both territorial and intellectual.

But quite suddenly on his return and for no apparent reason, Stanley's life, which up to this point was full of adventure, promise and promotion, fell into inactivity. He was made a captain in September 1844 but no opportunities came his way. The only bright light in an otherwise dull horizon came in January 1845 when he was appointed Magnetical Officer to his old ship HMS *Terror* under the command of Captain Francis Crozier on Sir John Franklin's ill-fated expedition in search of the North-west Passage. In an abrupt change of heart, however, Stanley withdrew his name, possibly because he didn't want to serve under Captain Francis Crozier, a former rival for the love of Sophia Cracroft; or perhaps because he wanted his own command. Whatever the reason, he was thus saved from an appalling death.

Stanley did not hide his frustrations in being offered so little. He wrote to Beaufort on several occasions asking him to keep a lookout for a surveying position that would get him out of these doldrums.[4] In November 1845, he was offered the command of HMS *Blazer*, a dreary steam vessel surveying the equally dreary east coast of England and the North Sea. After the excitement of world-wide travel, being cooped up in a small ship frequently resting on the mud bottom of tidal rivers in Essex and Suffolk and gawped at by the locals was not how Stanley expected his naval career to flourish. Harwich, where the ship was stationed, Stanley simply hated, 'as wretched and dull as ever'.[5] He spent as much time as he could off the ship, at scientific gatherings in London and Cambridge, and at his father's home in Norwich, where he enjoyed the company of county society.

So, when Beaufort summoned him to his office for an appointment on 25 January 1846 to discuss the survey of the waters of Australia and New Guinea that were more familiar to Stanley than to any other surveyor in Britain, he was overjoyed.[6] But no sooner did it seem that his illustrious career was back on track than he was cast down again. Beaufort told him the devastating news that he was merely a back-up, not the first choice.

*

Beaufort wanted the formidable Captain Alexander Vidal to lead the survey to Australia. Vidal had had a long and distinguished career as a surveyor. He had been surveying for more than a quarter of a century and had been promoted to the rank of captain on the basis of one of the most strenuous and dangerous surveys ever undertaken, that of the African coast, between 1818 and 1825.[7] His latest survey, of the Azores and Madeira, had been completed in the previous year. Though he was now fifty-six years old (a surveyor in the prime of his life seen from the perspective of a seventy-two-year-old Beaufort), he had the kind of staying power that impressed Beaufort and so eluded Blackwood. Vidal seemed the perfect man for the job.

But when Beaufort asked him to take the survey he asked for time to decide. As the weeks rolled by Vidal seemed no closer to making up his mind. Stanley's future as a naval surveyor and captain, not to mention his personal life, waited on someone else's decision. Stanley became increasingly anxious, swinging between moods of depression and elation, as he tried in vain to anticipate Vidal's decision and make sense of the delay. Nothing that Beaufort did in hurrying Vidal along seemed to work. Both men knew, however, that Vidal had a real dilemma on his hands that justified his inability to take up the job. He had family responsibilities. His wife had died a couple of years earlier and he had been left in charge of a young family. Allowing himself to be separated from his growing family was something that Stanley, in the same situation, would have found intolerable – 'nothing would induce me to do so', he told his sister.[8]

February brought no answer from Vidal, and Stanley continued to get away from his ship as often as possible: busying himself with social engagements, trying to see Beaufort, and avoiding being consumed by the suspense which was even worse than being stuck in Harwich.

Then early in March Beaufort received a parcel containing charts, plans and views of the Azores and Madeira from Vidal. As he unrolled the bundle, Beaufort went into raptures of delight. He had never seen anything executed so perfectly and so precisely as these productions. 'They will be a lasting memorial of your unswerving devotion to a laborious, anxious, and highly responsible duty, and their Lordships may with pride refer to them in proof of their judicious selection of the surveyor.'[9]

Beaufort must have told himself that he was justified in thinking that Vidal was the right person for the job and now pressed him for the answer he hoped for.

Vidal's position at the top of the hierarchy of surveyors was assured if he would accept the invitation. He had to make up his mind and could delay no longer. After what must have been an agonizing period, Vidal finally decided to withdraw his name from the survey. He could not leave his children for a voyage to the other side of the world that would, even if everything went well, consume at least four years of his life. He put his family before his career.[10]

Stanley did not hear of Vidal's decision immediately and was kept in the dark until early April.[11] When he did learn that he would be leading the survey, he wasted no time in getting to the details of the voyage, beginning with the thorny issue of who would join the ship as naturalist, a process which, like Vidal's decision-making, would take months to resolve.[12]

In the mean time, there was another pressing matter, which now that Stanley was certain to be away from England and home for several years, had to be settled. On his return home from the Pacific and Asia in 1843, Stanley had met the seventeen-year old Anna Maria Boileau (Ama as she was always called), the eldest daughter of Sir John and Lady Catherine Boileau, highly prominent Norfolk gentry and intimate friends of his parents. Sir John was particularly active in the county's scientific societies: the two families could not have been better matched. Though the relationship appears to have begun innocently enough – Stanley was almost twice as old as Ama – over time and as they saw more of each other in Norwich and in London, their relationship became much more romantic.[13] Ama's mother, Lady Catherine, however, felt she was too young for a formal engagement, and though they were both in love with each other, they were to remain technically free, a state which Stanley himself believed should prevail and which Ama was resigned to accept.[14]

With his love life settled as best as it could be and the survey his, it was an exciting time for Stanley. He was to take command of a ship voyaging to a part of the world that he knew well and which, if surveyed properly, would make him famous, as well known as his predecessors Cook, Flinders and King. Thus established he would be in a position to marry, and once married and hoping and expecting to have a family, he would, like Vidal, be loath to leave them. As he told his sister Mary, he wouldn't dream of accepting any future foreign assignments 'four years hence'.[15] So for Stanley the voyage was not only an exciting opportunity, but he also saw it as his last chance for fame and fortune. If all went well, as he hoped it would, there was a very real possibility that Stanley would succeed Beaufort as the next hydrographer. So much, both personal and professional, hinged on the successful outcome of this voyage.

Everything was going well for Beaufort too. He even had the ship for Stanley. Its name was HMS *Rattlesnake* and just now it was anchored in Portsmouth harbour, not far from the dockyards, stripped of masts, rigging, sails and guns. At twenty-four years of age, it was an old ship, one of an obsolete class of frigates. The *Rattlesnake* had been bobbing at anchor for two years and was rotting away. John Edye, Chief Assistant to the Surveyor of the Navy, and keeper of the inventory of naval vessels, thought the ship had only four or five years left in it, even after a major refit.[16] This surveying voyage would see the ship out to the end of its useful life.

Beaufort was not put off by Edye's comments. Quite the opposite. He was overjoyed at the prospect. In his day he had seen many ships in all manner of states and saw the potential of this one for a tropical survey. In theory, Beaufort could have had his pick of naval vessels.[17] Ships in ordinary, as the navy called vessels such as HMS *Rattlesnake*, which were not in service, littered the harbours of naval dockyards from Plymouth to Chatham. Yet out of this large pool of possibilities, only a few ships met the requirements of the surveying service and it took a trained eye to spot a likely candidate. Beaufort immediately recognized the *Rattlesnake*'s potential. The ship was small with an overall length of 114 feet and designed to carry 28 guns. He was impressed that the *Rattlesnake* was 'high and airy', a not inconsequential feature of a ship destined to spend months toiling under a relentless tropical sun. He liked the size, a bit heavier than most survey vessels, to be sure, but at just over 500 tons the ship could carry a good complement of men and stores, another advantage seeing that it would be spending months far from a home port. And he also liked the fact that it had recently been a troop ship during the Opium War (1839–1842) in China.[18] This meant the ship had already been stripped of many small rooms on the upper and main deck, used for naval personnel, to make way for the open space where the troops were housed. This was a bonus. The refit might be quick as it would consist mostly of putting in rather than ripping out. He couldn't wait to get his hands on the *Rattlesnake*. A quick letter to Sir William Symonds, Surveyor of the Navy, clinched his prize.[19] He shared his enthusiasm for HMS *Rattlesnake* with Stanley and instructed him to design its refit for a surveying voyage. Stanley was given carte blanche.

Specially built survey ships did not exist. They were adapted from pre-existing relatively small naval vessels, usually frigates with few guns (fifth and sixth rate battleships as they were called in the navy), and other two- and three-masted vessels such as sloops, and brigs. Refitting ships from one kind of duty to another was a common activity in the Royal Dockyards. Although some of the details varied from ship to ship, in general, refits consisted of two stages. In the first, the ship was brought into dry-dock where the extent of the structural repairs, especially to the hull, could be assessed. The necessary repairs and structural changes to the decks, such as the siting of cabins, gunrooms, storage rooms, and the like, were made here according to the plans that were submitted to the dock-yard. In the second stage, the ship was moved out of dry-dock and moored in the harbour or basin alongside a hulk (a ship permanently out of service because of its poor state), where some of the ship's company lived while they completed the refit, rigging, painting and putting the final touches on the interior fittings. With that done, the ship's company moved into the ship itself and, once provisions, instruments and the like were loaded, the ship would be ready to sail. Portsmouth Dockyard, where the refit of the *Rattlesnake* would be carried out, had just refitted HMS *Herald*, a ship of the same class as the *Rattlesnake*, for surveying work.[20] A template, there-fore, existed and the hopes for a quick refit were realistic.[21]

Beaufort shared Stanley's optimism and early in May 1846, long before the ship would be ready to sail, he urged Stanley to draw up a list of offi-cers he wanted with him, before they might be appointed to other ships.[22] The *Rattlesnake* went into dry-dock in Portsmouth some time in late April or early May. This was when Stanley first saw the ship he was to com-mand. For the next few months, he shuttled back and forth between London and Portsmouth on the newly opened railway, supervising the work for which he had drawn up the specifications and making sketches of his very own ship, the first of many he would make throughout the ship's voyage.[23]

The new plans called for the construction of a large chart room at the rear of the quarterdeck replacing a number of cabins on the ship's previous design. The chart room, the largest single room on the ship, was 18 feet by 18 feet at its greatest width; to provide the maximum amount of direct light, it was crowned by a skylight, pushing almost 2 feet into the poopdeck above, directly over the drawing table in the centre of the room. Its size, position and design was a testament to the absolute centrality of surveying and chart-making on the ship. Beyond the chart room, on the quarterdeck, lay the cabins of the master and assistant surveyor and the small auxiliary boats. The Captain's cabin and those of his officers, personal steward and surgeon were to be on the main deck below the chart room, transforming the relatively open space which had characterized this part of the *Rattlesnake*'s previous layout. The berths and mess roon of the midshipmen and the assistant surgeon, together with storage rooms for the officers and mess tables for the crew, were placed on the lower deck. To provide maximum space, the *Rattlesnake*, it was agreed, would carry fewer guns than it was designed to have.[24]

Comparing the plans of the *Rattlesnake* as a surveying ship in 1846 with those when it was a troop ship in 1839, one can see why Beaufort felt that the refit would be straightforward. However, when the ship was lifted out of the water, the optimism started to dissolve. Upon closer examination, the *Rattlesnake* appeared to be 'more defective than was suspected and thus a much longer time would be necessary to make her worthy for the arduous service she was to be employed on'.[25] The years spent in China ferrying troops here and there followed by two ignominious years in the cold grey waters of Portsmouth harbour had taken a toll on the ship below the water line.

An early sailing date – September had been mentioned – now seemed out of the question. This came as a bitter disappointment to Stanley. He had been planning a major family outing, which would include his younger (by eight years) brother Charles (Charlie to his family) and his new bride Eliza, and his two sisters. Charlie had just been appointed Private

Secretary to Captain William Denison, himself newly appointed to the post of Lieutenant-Governor of Van Diemen's Land (Tasmania), and was expected to leave England in September to take up his new post.[26] Stanley had convinced him and Eliza to join the *Rattlesnake* in preference to another ship for the voyage out to New South Wales.[27] Eliza had set her heart on going out with Stanley partly because it would be a more comfortable voyage than on a merchant or emigrant vessel, and partly because she disliked children – the Denisons had five of them, all apparently spoilt.[28] But the delay in the *Rattlesnake*'s refit put paid to one part of Stanley's family party. Charlie and Eliza could not wait for the refit to finish and had no choice but to sail with Captain Denison on another ship.

His sisters, Catherine and Mary (twenty-five and thirty-four years old respectively), had no other pressing engagements so the delay did not affect his plans with them. Stanley had invited them to sail with him to Madeira. Catherine had been unwell and, as Madeira was a popular destination for Europe's and especially Britain's ailing rich, he hoped that a stay on this semi-tropical island would restore her health. As for Mary, Stanley was very close to her (they were only a year apart) and he welcomed any way of prolonging their time together. But Stanley was taking a gamble. He hadn't yet received his sailing instructions and didn't know where his first stop would be, though the chances were even as surveying ships typically called at either Madeira or Tenerife on their outward journey.[29] Stanley's father thought it was a good idea and gave it his full support. Stanley would need Beaufort's permission to take his sisters on the ship, but at the moment he had other things on his mind.

The disappointment over Charlie and Eliza did not dent Stanley's excitement and optimism about the voyage ahead.[30] Thoughts of his ship consoled him. 'It will be a satisfaction to know that I shall have an almost new ship under my feet', he told Jennie Herschel, the daughter of the astronomer Sir John Herschel, in June.[31] He was progressing with his list of officers with whom he was very satisfied, as he was with the dockyard workers whom he knew well. '[They] have from beginning to end been most civil and have given us every thing we have asked for ...'.[32]

On 22 September the *Rattlesnake* was finally commissioned. The same day, Stanley received a letter from Admiral James Dundas, one of their

Lordships, asking him if he would mind taking his friends, Mr and Mrs Courtenay, to Madeira.[33] Mind? He was delighted. Now he knew that Madeira was to be the first stop and all that stood between him and his plans was Beaufort's permission.

Two days later Stanley arrived in Portsmouth and took formal command of his ship.[34] He could now begin to enter his officers and crew on to the ship's muster and they could begin to receive full pay. According to the instructions he had just received from their Lordships, the *Rattlesnake* was to have a complement of 179 men, 31 more than he had been led to expect back in June.[35] These instructions were very detailed and gave the precise number of men Stanley would have in each rank, right down to the last able seaman and boy.[36]

Ever since Beaufort told him to start rounding up his officers, Stanley had been busy. He knew several of them personally and others had come with recommendations from fellow commanders. Robert Suckling, the first lieutenant, in his late thirties the oldest commissioned officer, '[a] steady good officer tho somewhat deaf', and the ship's master, John James Brown, 'a young and very shy man who speaks very little but gets through no end of work and promises very well in his time', were the first to appear.

A few days later, on 2 October, Stanley welcomed and entered on to the muster book his assistant surgeon, a young man named Thomas Huxley, 'a very good naturalist'. At just under 6 feet tall, Huxley, aged twenty-one, towered above the Captain. Both stature and background separated the two men. The sixth child of an impoverished schoolmaster, Huxley had had only two years of formal schooling. Though he was from a disadvantaged background Huxley had done well. He had decided on a medical career, which, aged sixteen, began as an apprentice to a doctor in the East End slums. At the age of twenty, after three years as a scholarship student at Charing Cross Hospital, he completed part 1 of the Bachelor of Medicine Examination brilliantly and was awarded the gold medal for physiology and anatomy.[37] He could not, however, afford to sit part 2, and was too young, by one year, to practise.[38] He was broke. A friend suggested the Navy as a way out of his problems: the pay wasn't bad and the service was known to foster scientific assistant surgeons. Without sponsors or patrons to aid him, he wrote directly to Sir William Burnett, Physician General of the Navy, to try and get an appointment. This bold approach worked and he was accepted into the Navy, but had to borrow money to buy his uniform. He took up residence in Haslar Naval Hospital in Portsmouth in April 1846 where the intrepid and experienced Arctic explorer and naturalist, Sir John Richardson, was in charge.[39] There Huxley waited for a commission.

Huxley was probably more comfortable staring down the barrel of a microscope than doing ward rounds. He wanted to be a scientist and one of the best ways of doing that, especially without private means, was to join the service, and particularly to sail on a surveying voyage where, since Beaufort took charge of the department, science was paramount. Joseph Dalton Hooker, the son of Sir William Hooker at Kew, had done precisely the same and was now making his name, independently of his father, as an expert on Antarctic, New Zealand and Tasmanian flora. Stanley, not surprisingly, knew Richardson well and asked him to recommend to him an assistant surgeon with a scientific bent. Richardson had no hesitation in recommending Huxley for the post on the *Rattlesnake*. Huxley was in the right place at the right time and Stanley held the key to his future. For Huxley, as for Stanley, there was a great deal riding on the success of the voyage.

Stanley and Huxley met in London on at least two occasions at which times Stanley introduced him to several of Britain's leading scientists in the burgeoning fields of zoology and marine biology, including Richard Owen of the Royal College of Physicians, John Edward Gray of the British Museum, Robert Grant of University College, London, and Edward Forbes, Professor at King's College and at the Geological Survey.[40] Stanley had the right man and Huxley was pleased with his boss, especially his scientific credentials and connections. 'He is a son of the Bishop of Norwich, he is an exceedingly gentlemanly man, a thorough scientific enthusiast, and shows himself altogether very much disposed to forward my views in every possible way.'[41] Stanley allowed him to bring as many books as he wished and gave him access to the drawing table in the chart room where he could read and work with his microscope.[42] Stanley's generosity notwithstanding, Huxley's warm feelings towards his commander would not last the voyage.

Following very close on the heels of Huxley was the third lieutenant and assistant surveyor, Joseph Dayman, in his early twenties, 'a very clever and intelligent person who went out with James Ross in the Erebus' and who had a very strong reputation in naval circles as a scientific man. Several days then passed without any appointments until 8 October when John Thomson, the ship's surgeon and Huxley's superior, appeared. Thomson, 'a young and clever man fond of botanical pursuits', was, in fact, thirty-one years of age and had been at sea, on various ships, as assistant surgeon since 1836. He had been appointed to his present post very recently, on 22 May 1846.[43] Though he had been at sea over a ten-year period, this was to be his longest voyage and time away from home to date.

Not long after his promotion, Thomson, on leave in Edinburgh, wrote to Stanley of his wish to be appointed to the *Rattlesnake*. In early June 1846, Stanley told Thomson that Sir William Burnett, the Physician General of the Navy, had agreed to the appointment and also invited him to London to meet Sir William Hooker, Director of the Royal Botanic Gardens in Kew, and other scientific men who might be useful to him.[44] Thomson obviously had an interest in botany (as he also had in the very new pursuit of photography) and while in Edinburgh he sought the help of Professor John Balfour of the Royal Botanic Gardens, Edinburgh, in preparing himself for the study of Australian flora.[45] Thomson's delight at his appointment must have been mixed. Voyaging to the other end of the earth meant leaving behind his sweetheart Mary. They married on 14 July 1846 and when he returned in 1850 it was to see his son for the first time.

George Henry Inskip, the second master, who had served under Stanley on HMS *Blazer* on the east coast survey, was the next to turn up and with him was John Ince, the second lieutenant, 'a fat laughing good humoured sailor who was out with Capt. Blackwood in the *Fly*'. But within a month he was promoted and chose to sail with another ship. A young officer in his twenties named Henry George Simpson took his place. Ince's promotion, Stanley cheerily remarked, meant that 'the New Guinea people will lose the chance of having a glorious feast which he certainly would have afforded them had he fallen into their hands'.[46] The purser also changed, the first choice being a man named James Little who told Stanley that a mistake had been made as he intended joining a different captain.[47] His place was taken by Frederick Brady, 'a very young man but intelligent and well up to his work'. He almost had his full complement of executive officers. 'As far as the Superior Officers go,' Stanley wrote to his cousin Louisa on 19 October 1846, 'I have every reason to be satisfied.'[48] He was still missing a fourth lieutenant, however. But no one could help him. 'Do you happen to know any aspiring young hero who would do for us?' Stanley inquired of Alexander Becher at the Hydrographical Office.[49] No luck and Beaufort couldn't help either.[50]

The midshipmen and naval cadets (youngsters as Stanley referred to them – few exceeded fifteen years in age) pleased him too. There were about sixteen of them; some were placed there because they were sons of friends of the family (Arthur Packe, seventeen years old, and Philip Ruffle Sharpe, fifteen years old, fell into this category) and others because they were sons of other captains.[51] They berthed in the gunroom. Huxley was with them, their 'caterer', living and eating with them, towering over them and, at twenty-one years old, more like an older brother than a messmate.[52] The youngsters were getting on well with rigging the ship and other preparations and they all had 'a turn for science'.[53] This was the first voyage for most of them.

On 21 October the Lords Commissioners of the Admiralty stunned Stanley with the first of several high-level intrusions. Throughout the months of the refit, there was an agreement, minuted several times, that the number of guns would be kept down to eight on the ship and four on the auxiliary boats. This alteration freed much valuable space and several of the officers' cabins were built where the unused gun ports had been positioned in the original design. Their Lordships had written to Admiral Sir Charles Ogle, in charge of the Portsmouth Dockyard, telling him to remind Stanley of the order concerning 'The State of Preparation for Battle of HM Ships employed on Surveying Service', namely, '. . . in every case to require that a surveying vessel shall be perfectly efficient and available, upon the shortest notice, as a man of war . . . '[54] The Admiralty was jittery: the British Government had received information of a build up of French ships in the Mediterranean.[55] But Stanley was a surveyor not a warrior. He agreed that 'some notice need be taken of the recent Admiralty order', but though he didn't know what exactly they wanted him to do, he felt strongly that their Lordships would understand that surveying ships could not act as fully armed battleships. It was not a matter of principle so much as a practical issue. 'If we are really to carry on surveying work we cannot exercise at General Quarters the same as other Men of War to say nothing of the effect of continued firing from the gun deck upon the Chronometers.'[56] Besides which, he argued, when surveying vessels were called upon in the past to prepare for battle, they did not disappoint: 'when the hour of need came we were not wholly unprepared'.[57] He left it with his superiors to sort out and got on with the job.

The *Rattlesnake* came out of dry-dock on 22 October 1846 and was moored alongside a hulk, where the some of the ship's company lived while the refit continued.[58] Stanley had been very closely involved in the early stages of the refit and now, with that phase over, he could relax a bit and look forward to the more individual aspects of the work, such as the rigging and interior fittings. The provisions were brought on board a week later. Twenty thousand pounds of what the navy called bread – a hard, flat cake, slowly baked from flour and very little water also known as ship's biscuit – together with flour, suet, raisins, peas, oatmeal, salt beef, salt pork, sugar, chocolate, tea, tobacco, soap, vinegar, lemon juice, ale and wine were put into the hold.

Stanley could now see the end in sight. He was overjoyed with his men. '[They] seem inclined to work and take an interest in the service we are to be employed upon . . . In short all as yet Couleur de Rose how long it may remain so time only can show,' he wrote to cousin Louisa on 4 November 1846.[59]

Not long, as it turned out. The very next day, their Lordships interfered, for the second time, in the plans by sending Stanley 'a most peremptory order' that the *Rattlesnake* had to be ready to sail by 20 November, whatever state it was in.[60] The ship had already had forty days spent on her refit and that, according to their Lordships, was more than enough. The *Rattlesnake* had outstayed its welcome in Portsmouth Harbour. 'I cannot conceive what makes them in such a violent hurry with the ship', Stanley wrote, 'as I do not think at this time of the year that two months is a very long time to fit a surveying ship out – there must be some thing behind the decrees I do not know.'[61] Stanley had planned for 30 November as the day the *Rattlesnake* would be ready for sea and 'all the arrangements had been made with reference to it'.[62]

Stanley was on the point of writing to their Lordships giving reasons why he should be allowed the ten days he had been banking on, when he received a note from Admiral Dundas to follow his original plans and to explain that he needed the extra time to test the scientific instruments used in the surveying work.[63] Admiral Sir Charles Ogle, commander-in-chief of the Portsmouth naval station, agreed he should write to their Lordships naming the 30 November and justifying the date with Dundas's suggestion. And that was exactly what he did.[64] Although Stanley admitted that it would not have been impossible to complete some of the work at sea, he was mightily relieved 'to get every thing as perfectly fitted as possible before leaving the Dock Yard which is the more necessary as it will be some years before we again have an opportunity of seeing one'.[65] The Admiralty must have accepted Stanley's story because they never mentioned the matter again. Why they pressed for an earlier date was never explained.

Stanley had not yet asked Beaufort's permission to take his own sisters to Madeira. Dundas's intervention in the sailing plans gave him the excuse he needed. He wrote to Beaufort about the whole episode and, at the same time, mentioned Dundas's request about the Courtenays as well as his own. Obviously Beaufort had to accept Stanley's request, as he could not possibly turn down Dundas's. A clever move and a very lucky break. The family party was set.

Once the confusion over the proposed sailing date was settled, Stanley faced another problem. He had not received the surveying instructions from Beaufort. Indeed no one, including Becher, his assistant, seemed to know the details.[66] Beaufort was away from his office and Stanley did not want to bother him with business even if he knew where he was. He was stuck in Portsmouth whatever.[67]

On 18 November, the naturalist John MacGillivray arrived in Portsmouth to join the ship. Stanley was away in London but the two men had already met on several occasions. Describing himself as 'little, ugly, red-haired and "tawny"', MacGillivray, twenty-eight years old, had just returned from a four-year surveying voyage to and around Australia with HMS *Fly* on which he had sailed as the private collector for the Earl of Derby, one of the world's most important private collectors of natural history specimens.[68] He was from a respectable background. His father, William MacGillivray, held the Regius Chair of Natural History at Marischal College, Aberdeen. Medical studies did not suit the young MacGillivray and he turned instead to the study of natural history. By the time he joined the *Rattlesnake*, he had already published a number of distinguished articles on the natural history of Scotland in the widely read journal *Annals and Magazine of Natural History* and on Australian natural history; and his abilities as a naturalist had come to the attention of the country's leading authorities in the field.[69] MacGillivray's instructions were to collect Australian and New Guinea flora and fauna for the Royal Botanic Gardens and the British Museum, but he also undertook to do some private collecting as well.

It was a great honour and a major achievement to be appointed the official naturalist to a surveying voyage. Besides getting the chance of seeing the world, the travelling naturalist was a highly respected member of the scientific community. MacGillivray was, in many ways, an obvious choice for this voyage. He had the experience of a long surveying voyage and knew the natural history of northern Australia better than anyone else, but like Stanley himself, he was not the first choice for the post. Indeed, there were several others, all eminent naturalists, whose names preceded MacGillivray's. Besides which, when the *Rattlesnake* was commissioned, MacGillivray was still at sea on HMS *Fly*, on its way home.

Ernst Dieffenbach had been the first name that went forward. Dieffenbach had served as the official naturalist to the New Zealand Company and had spent two years, between 1839 and 1841, in New Zealand. In 1843, he became President of the newly founded Ethnological Society and in the following year his German translation of Darwin's *Beagle* journal was published. Sir William Hooker recommended him to Beaufort.[70] Despite his close relationship with a number of leading British scientists, including Darwin and Charles Lyell, Dieffenbach was finding it difficult to find someone to sponsor him to join a scientific voyage. The period he spent with the New Zealand Company was fraught with controversy and this seemed to plague his progress. Hooker's recommendation was, therefore, a godsend.[71]

Stanley had been told that Dieffenbach was the top runner to join the survey back in April at one of Stanley's first meetings with Beaufort, but when Stanley heard the name, he refused to have anything to do with the man. He didn't like him: 'I shall try all I possibly can to prevent him coming as I am convinced he would prove troublesome . . . I told Capt. B I would much sooner have a person of a lower status in life who would not mind being told what to do,' he told his sister Mary in mid April.[72] It would have been unwise under the circumstances for Beaufort to have forced Dieffenbach on Stanley, and his name was dropped. Stanley suggested Joseph Hooker, Sir William's son, who turned down the offer because he had already planned an extensive tour of India.[73] Several months passed. Then Sir William suggested another of his favourites at Kew, Berthold Seemann, and he seems to have been acceptable, but at very short notice he was appointed to another ship.[74] The *Rattlesnake* still didn't have its naturalist.

Then, in late June, Stanley bumped into Francis Blackwood, the commander of HMS *Fly*, on a train between Portsmouth and Plymouth. Sitting next to him was MacGillivray.[75] The two of them had only been back in England since 19 June. That chance meeting convinced Stanley that MacGillivray was the right man for the job.[76] MacGillivray had hardly time to catch his breath before he was starting to pack for the next voyage. By early August, MacGillivray had been assured of the post but it took until the end of October before he heard officially from Beaufort that he was to be appointed.[77]

MacGillivray was highly spirited, adventurous and brilliant. He also had a bit of a reputation, amongst friends and family, for running up large debts at London taverns. He relished the voyage ahead and was to be paid £250 per annum for his troubles.[78] This voyage meant a great deal to him. Through it he would become the world's foremost expert on Australian natural history, certainly as far as fauna was concerned. And since New Guinea was in the Admiralty Instructions, he would also be the world's leading expert on that virtually unknown field. The next few years would also bring him in close contact with key figures in British natural history – men such as Edward Forbes and Sir William Hooker, not to mention the great ornithologist and collector, John Gould, whom he already knew from his time on the *Fly*. With all this behind him he could look forward to a top position in one of the institutions of natural history, such as running a national or provincial museum.

Stanley was extremely generous to MacGillivray as he was to Huxley. 'He is fond of naturalists,' MacGillivray told his friend James Harley in

Leicester. 'I shall have a large cabin – in fact the largest on the lower deck – with plenty of room for specimens – a table in the chart room for writing or skinning at – 2 assistants, and a botanical collector (a kind of gardener) under me . . . the Admiralty paying for all.' While the room he was promised materialized, the same was not true for his assistants. In the end he worked on his own but he was not on his own. Stanley's father had, in fact, placed a man named James Fowler Wilcox on the *Rattlesnake*, to collect specimens of natural history for the museums in Norwich and Ipswich, in which the Bishop took an interest.[79] Wilcox had worked for Bishop Stanley for several years as a groom and had expressed a wish to try his hand as a naturalist. Not having had any connection with the navy, Wilcox joined the ship as an able seaman, carpenter's mate, with a personal responsibility for Stanley's cabin.[80]

Though Stanley was not able to welcome MacGillivray on the ship, he was lucky to be in London on that day. Their Lordships were about to drop a bombshell in Stanley's path, the third of their unwanted, unsolicited intrusions. The earlier order about the ship's state of readiness for battle that Stanley had conveniently let his superiors handle reappeared in a frightening way. It began by the Secretary of the Navy asking why the *Rattlesnake* was not fully armed.[81] HMS *Rattlesnake*, as far as the Admiralty was concerned, was first and foremost a warship and, only incidentally, a surveying ship. It needed, therefore, to be armed accordingly. The Admiralty ordered Stanley to fit the vessel 'immediately with armament proper to her class'.[82] Just a few weeks before, Stanley was in high spirits about the shape of the ship and his relationship with the Admiralty. '. . . They have given us carte blanche in fitting her out – so that having only eight guns on the main deck, I have arranged all the officers' cabins and the Mess place there, the midshipmen occupying the gunroom below,' he told his sister Mary.[83] But now everything had been turned upside down. His cheerfulness changed to rage. The upheaval would be intolerable: 'all that had been done on board [would have to be] undone, an entirely new internal arrangement made, all the stores unshipped and it would have caused 6 weeks delay besides no end of trouble and expense.'[84] Beaufort must have been astonished at the audacity of this late order but did not object believing it 'to be founded upon consideration of Political necessity' and not to be interfered with.[85] Stanley, at the end of his patience with his superiors, cut his losses and marched straight into the Admiralty to present his case for not changing the arrangements. Beaufort did not leave his top surveyor unprotected. He discovered that the order was not founded on a specific political threat. He brought all the influence he could muster to convince his bosses they should rescind the order.[86] And it worked. Their Lordships backed down and, in a surprising change of position, ordered instead that the ship should have more provisions and boats than normal.[87]

That was as close as either man had come to a disaster. With that over, loading the ship continued as planned. Wine labels bearing the Stanley coat-of-arms were ordered; books, pictures and sofas for Stanley's cabin arrived; Stanley was given a dog as a present by his cousin Emmy; and a piano, which played Bohemian quadrilles, waltzes and much more besides, was hoisted on board.[88] A fiddler, 4 feet tall, and an accordion player, who was a stay maker but found that playing at parties earned him more money and who now wanted to see the world, joined the musical assembly.[89] Stanley had everything arranged just as he wanted for his comfort and for that of his sisters.

Stanley was pleased with himself, his self-confidence rising all the time. But he must have felt that the sooner he got away from their Lordships, the better. Once beyond British seas, he was well out of reach. It would take up to a year for letters to be exchanged.

The sailing date of 30 November was approaching rapidly and everyone was getting very excited. On Thursday 26 November, the *Rattlesnake* separated from the hulk and the men moved into what was to be their home for the next four or five years. Arthur Packe, the midshipman, began his journal that day with a description of the ship's layout. The arrangements pleased him: 'We have got a very nice mess place where in any other 28 gun Frigate the Lieutenants would have,' he recorded.[90] The next day, Stanley's mother, father and sisters arrived in Portsmouth. His parents came to bid their son farewell and to install their daughters on the ship for its first leg to Madeira. Robert Gale, Stanley's steward, had changed the Captain's cabins so that the sisters would have a dressing room and sleeping quarters and they seemed delighted with the result.[91] Mary and Catherine brought a special present for their brother, a set of dissolving

Annotated sketch by Robert Gale, the steward, showing the allocation of cabins
on board HMS *Rattlesnake*

views (also known as a magic lantern), something he badly wanted but could not afford once he had paid his bills and purchased two instruments, which the Admiralty had refused to buy for him. The magic lantern projected slides onto a screen in such a way that one view smoothly dissolved into the next one – hence its name. Stanley had asked his sister Mary to convince other family members to chip in to buy the apparatus from Carpenter & Westley, opticians of Regent Street.[92] 'This seems very like begging,' he told her, 'but I think it worth the chance from the influence it will give me over the natives.'[93] Family members came up with more than half the purchase price of £30.10 shillings: his father covered the rest.[94]

Stanley's father, the Bishop of Norwich, had prepared a big farewell sermon for the coming Sunday, the day before the *Rattlesnake* was scheduled to sail, but their Lordships had one more go at the schedule. On Saturday, 28 November, just before the sailing date, they ordered Stanley to proceed not to sea but to Plymouth where the ship was to receive treasure to be conveyed to British colonies: £50,000 for the Cape colony and £15,000 for Mauritius.[95] A further delay but this one Stanley did not mind too much for he stood to gain financially from it. Commanding officers made 1 per cent on the carriage of treasure beyond 1,800 miles – Stanley's share amounted to £650, about the same as his annual pay.[96]

The next few days were packed with activity. The Bishop gave a shortened version of his sermon on Sunday, leaving the longer one for the *Rattlesnake*'s departure from Plymouth. He joined the ship for its short trip. Mr and Mrs Courtenay embarked for their trip to Madeira, accompanied by 'an old sofa with blankets sheets towels pillows etc. piled upon it secured by a carpet over all'.[97] On Monday, 39 cases of instruments were loaded, including 28 chronometers, compasses and a number of devices for magnetical observations.[98] The same day, the *Rattlesnake*'s compasses were swung in order to compensate for any attraction they would have for the metal in the ship's construction. On Tuesday, Queen Victoria passed by the ship on the Royal Barge and the ship's company 'manned yards'.[99] The same day, Stanley, Dayman and Simpson, the ship's official surveyors, began to draw their survey pay (above and beyond their normal pay) at a rate of 21 shillings, 8 shillings and 5 shillings per day, respectively.[100] On Wednesday the pay clerks arrived to give the ship's company two months' advance pay and Stanley's sisters embarked. The next day Admiral Sir Charles Ogle inspected the ship and, in the afternoon, it set sail for Plymouth where it arrived the following day.

In Plymouth, Stanley received his orders from the Admiralty, revised to take account of the shipment of treasure to the Cape and Mauritius and signed by their Lordships, Sir Charles Adam and Admiral James Dundas.[101] The stops were Madeira, the Cape of Good Hope and

Mauritius, before the final destination, Sydney. Stanley had wanted to call at Rio de Janeiro as he thought it would be a good opportunity to check the ship's chronometers, but the sailing instructions did not include it.[102] Sydney was to be the *Rattlesnake*'s base for the planned series of voyages needed to complete the hydrographic survey of the Barrier Reef, the Torres Strait and the southeastern coast of New Guinea, including the Louisiade Archipelago.

The ship now had everyone on board apart from two other passengers – Captain Charles Denison, who had been appointed as aide-de-camp to his brother Captain William Denison (Charlie Stanley's superior) and was making his way to Hobart; and the Reverend Robert King who was making his way to Sydney to take up a clerical position near to his family home.[103] King was the son of Phillip Parker King, surveyor and businessman, with whom Stanley sailed on his first voyage to the Straits of Magellan in 1830. He could not have picked a better way of returning to Sydney:

> [It could not] possibly be more pleasant both as regarded the temper of the Captain and goodness of the ship, the number of her crew and the Society of her officers. The great saving in expense was also a consideration of much importance. And while the prospect of seeing so many new places, and which the ship would touch, and the scientific nature of the pursuits on board would add much to the interest of the voyage, the kindness in which the offer of the passage was made as an acknowledgement of kindness received from my Father made it entirely pleasant. [104]

Now it was the Bishop's turn to bless the ship. He had a huge audience listening to him on that cold Sunday afternoon on 6 December 1846. Edward Stanley, Bishop of Norwich, President of the Linnean Society, gentleman of science and father of the ship's Captain fought against the bitter wind from the southeast with a strained but direct voice. Choosing his text from Psalm 139, verses 6 to 9, the Bishop reminded his listeners of the parallels between life and a ship's voyage and rounded on those who viewed both as a result of chance. 'When I see worked out upon a chart a vessel's course,' he implored, 'telling with unerring certainty the precise track in which she has sailed, and at a given moment the very spot where she then is, and all this wonderful knowledge obtained by the regular movements of the stars and planets, I feel, and have often felt, that the very nautical observations of a day or a night are in themselves unanswerable proofs of the power and wisdom of the Almighty.'[105] Nothing, he repeated was to be left to chance.

> Unseen perils hover around you like angels of death. Everything points out the necessity of watchfulness and readiness for the call which may come upon you in a moment when you look not for it. Therefore, in bidding you farewell, I would as one anxious for your welfare, again say, Watch and be ready for ye know not the hour when your call may come.[106]

Bishop Stanley had already bade his younger son, Charlie, farewell. Now it was time to say good-bye to his naval son. All his children, apart from his middle son, Arthur, who would, in time, become the Dean of Westminster, were going to be away at the same time. As it turned out, Bishop Stanley saw his daughters safely return, but never saw the two voyaging sons again. Indeed, the whole scientific and artistic line of his family, embodied in Owen and Charlie, would be wiped out during the life of the voyage.

The next few days were spent adjusting the compasses and checking final details before departure. On Wednesday 9 December, under heavy protection, 35 cases of bullion bound for the Cape and Mauritius were carefully loaded into the *Rattlesnake*'s hold. The ship could now sail, but, just as it was about to leave, the gunner was found to be drunk and the *Rattlesnake* was forced to wait at the breakwater at the entrance to Plymouth harbour for him to sober up.[107] Finally, on Friday, 11 December 1846, almost eight months to the day since Stanley had been told of his appointment, and with a force eight wind behind and squally snow showers around them, the *Rattlesnake* ran out of Plymouth harbour for the heat of the tropics. The last word can be given to Huxley. No doubt, he was speaking for them all. 'Thank God! fitting out is at last over. We have no more caprices to fear but those of the wind – a small matter after having been exposed to those of the Admiralty.'[108]

The futures of Stanley, Huxley and MacGillivray rested critically on the successful outcome of the voyage. A surveying voyage was a major undertaking and chances like this, for surveyor, scientist and naturalist, were rare. Though its field of operation was the other side of the globe, the eyes of London were focused on the *Rattlesnake*. British science, geography and navigation, the cornerstones of British interests abroad, depended on the bounty that the ship would harvest.

Stanley had done his best to provide Huxley and MacGillivray with the most precious commodity on the ship – space. What he couldn't provide, or at least, what he couldn't guarantee, was time – the time to collect, to observe, to analyse and to report. Stanley was about as scientific a surveyor as existed in the service, but his prime, unconditional concern, was the survey. Everything, as Beaufort would remind him as he had reminded others, was subordinate to it.

Huxley, young and without experience in naval matters, would not have known what to expect from the voyage. MacGillivray had a better idea but he had been a passenger on the *Fly* not an Admiralty appointee. Both men, however, were to learn the hard way about life on board ship. Their aspirations would clash with those of Stanley.

There would be successes but also irreversible disappointments; more than one tragedy; and one quite remarkable chance encounter.

But all this was in the future. Sydney was many months away.

Right now there was the small matter of the wind.

PART TWO

CHAPTER III

A Taste of the Tropics:
Madeira and Rio de Janeiro, 1847

The wind may have seemed a 'small matter' to Huxley in anticipation, but in the event the effects were dire. As the *Rattlesnake* left Plymouth, its receding shores were gleaming white with thick snow; it was incredibly cold. Soon the fresh breeze became a howling gale and as the waves rose, the ship began to roll. As John Thomson, the surgeon, put it in a letter to his wife, 'the unseasoned retired finding themselves deadly seasick.'[1] Then the ship began to leak. The cabins on the main deck, including his own, were flooded to a depth of six inches. On the deck below it was even worse: 'there was a great flood of water working violently from side to side'. It was eighteen inches deep and bitterly cold, it engulfed everything; anything moveable – 'desks and gun cases and books' – was swept away. The plight of the young midshipmen particularly struck Thomson: 'nearly one and all of them were sick and so far gone as totally to disregard the destruction that was going on amongst their property.' It was a pathetic scene: the teenage boys, the oldest seventeen, just parted from their homes and families, too sick to try and save their few precious possessions from the sea they had so recently embarked on. The gale went on for four days during which time not only the human cargo suffered; the livestock they carried for fresh meat also had a terrible time, the ducks in particular 'died in bucketfuls'. It was an inauspicious start for the voyage, but gradually

Leaving Madeira, 26 December 1846

'the wind and seas slackened and the temperature became perceptibly milder'. The wind continued to blow strongly from the northeast, and the ship made 250 miles a day towards Madeira where they arrived on Friday, seven days after leaving Plymouth.

This dramatic account of the *Rattlesnake*'s first days at sea comes from Thomson's letter to his newly wed wife, Mary. It was his first letter to her since he departed on the *Rattlesnake*. Thomson began his naval medical career as an assistant surgeon in 1836 at the age of 22 and now, ten years later and recently promoted to the rank of surgeon, he was on his longest and most important assignment. He had never spent more than a couple of years on a single ship and, on that occasion, the vessel remained in home waters during its cruises.[2] Now he was going on a voyage that would certainly last four years and possibly more. He was already feeling the pain of separation from Mary. He kept rereading the letters she had sent him since leaving Edinburgh, all the while looking at a small photograph he had taken of her and stroking a lock of her hair she had given to him.

The voyage of the *Rattlesnake* was Thomson's first trip in charge of the health of a whole ship. He was not new to the tropics, having spent over three months at the naval hospital in Port Royal, Jamaica, five years earlier, but even so, on this voyage, as the ship's surgeon, he would have to deal with problems he had never encountered before in his naval medical career. But this was all in the future. Seasickness and, remarkably, several cases of frostbite, which appeared in the first few days of the voyage, were his concerns at the time but there was little he could do for these conditions except wait for the weather to change.

Not everyone suffered from seasickness, however. Reverend Robert King was one of those who escaped this most unpleasant experience. He put it down to the fact that he was 'the son of a sailor, born at sea and [had] crossed the line in three different voyages and having been round the world'.[3] He was, therefore, not surprised at his sea legs. He could not, however, so easily account for the good shape of the Captain's sisters, who had never been to sea, and applauded their mettle. '. . . They have been held up as a pattern to the whole ship's company', he wrote in his journal, 'as their spirits have not once failed nor have they experienced the least inconvenience from the motion of the vessel. This was the more singular as the first breeze we had was a gale and the ship is one which knows how to roll.'[4]

By Tuesday 15 December, four days after leaving Plymouth, the incidence of seasickness was much reduced and with the temperature rising and the wind dropping, passengers and officers began to emerge from their quarters and enjoy the changing conditions on deck. The ship's leak, however, was becoming worse. It was, of course, most inconvenient and uncomfortable for those who made their home on the main deck and the lower deck where the flooding was worst. MacGillivray found his cabin uninhabitable and many of his possessions ruined by the flood.[5] But it was not the present inconvenience that mattered so much as what it might forebode. The leak or leaks (no one was sure which while the ship made its way south to Madeira) smacked of bad workmanship in the Portsmouth Dockyard. Reverend King was quick to note that the fault lay entirely with the Admiralty for hurrying the ship out of dry-dock. Only when they reached Madeira could the carpenters assess the nature of the damage and the possibility of repair.

As the ship approached the latitudes of Madeira, the sea became smooth and the difficulties of the past days began to recede. On Thursday the *Rattlesnake*'s surveyors faced their first task, to ascertain the existence or not of what was called the Eight Stones, a group of rocks which voyagers since the eighteenth century had reported to the north of the island of Porto Santo as being a hazard to shipping.[6] The sea and the dangers that lurked were not constant. Sea levels changed, rocks subsided into the depths, and bearings were far from accurate. It all made for a very messy situation. The Eight Stones were particularly worrying as many ships from Europe heading towards southern latitudes passed through this area, and the rocks were marked on earlier charts. To erase their existence from charts was a task not to be taken lightly and every manner of evidence was garnered, including asking the fishermen of Porto Santo about their knowledge of the rocks.[7] The *Rattlesnake* was one in a long line of ships that had been asked to investigate the supposed position of the rocks. The naval vessels working on hydrographic surveys, such as HMS *Blossom* in 1825 and HMS *Beagle* in 1832 and 1837, failed to find the rocks. But the reports continued, nevertheless, and Beaufort had sleepless nights over these 'vigias', as the ocean dangers were called.

While looking for the rocks, the surveyors took the opportunity of using newly invented sounding equipment. They took various soundings,

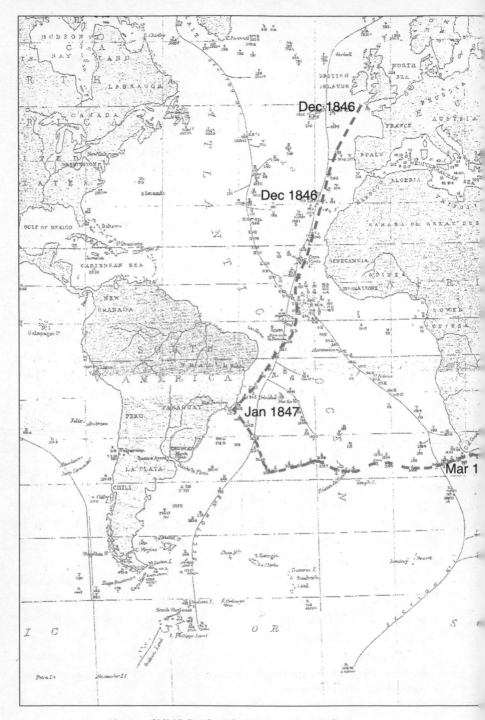

Voyage of HMS *Rattlesnake*, Portsmouth to Sydney

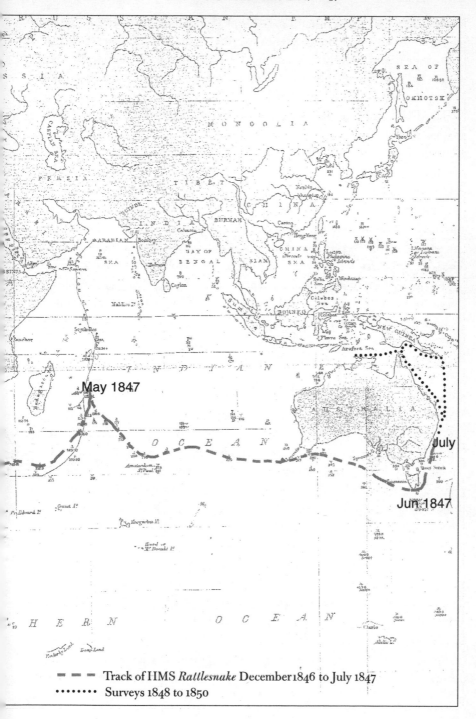

May 1847

July

Jun 1847

- - - Track of HMS *Rattlesnake* December 1846 to July 1847
.... Surveys 1848 to 1850

managing to reach a depth of 140 fathoms (840 feet), and reported that no rocks could be found. Stanley sent Beaufort a revised track over these supposed rocks and reiterated that no shoals were seen in the vicinity from the masthead, providing further proof that if the rocks existed they were not where they had been reported in the past.[8]

Reverend King was highly impressed by this, the ship's first survey, and his excited anticipation of a voyage full of scientific pursuits was amply rewarded. He recorded his delight in the form of a description of the sounding equipment in his journal entry for the day. The most commonly used equipment for measuring deep-sea depths – 100 fathoms or more – was fairly simple and consisted of a lead weight attached to a line of rope marked with knots for each ten fathoms. The *Rattlesnake*'s equipment, invented by the highly acclaimed nautical instrument maker, Edward Massey, did away with the fathom markers.[9] 'A clever device they have upon the lead', he wrote, 'to ascertain the depth to which it has reached. A large Archimedean screw with 8 wings is attached to the lead and moves round once in a fathom. Its motion is registered by two simple cogwheels moved by a small screw in the axle of the larger screw.'[10] This was an elegant example of Victorian engineering.

The *Rattlesnake* approached Madeira on its eastern end, rounding the Ponta de São Lourenço and proceeding on a westerly course, passing the village of Santa Cruz and heading for an anchorage in Funchal roadstead, so-called because, lacking a harbour, the Bay of Funchal offered only partly sheltered anchorages to vessels. Ironically, Captain Alexander Vidal, Beaufort's first choice for commander of the *Rattlesnake*, had drawn the charts guiding Stanley to his destination. As the ship approached, the beauty of the place, remarked upon by all British visitors to the island who committed their feelings to paper, deeply impressed its onlookers as the changing vistas came successively into view. It was so different from what they had left behind. '. . . We had a beautiful opportunity of taking a bird's eye view of the outline of the island', Reverend King noted in his journal. 'The day was beautiful. The summits of the hills were covered with clouds which added to the effect and the light showers as they passed gave us a constant succession of beautiful rainbows. One in particular being over a deep mountain gorge just as we anchored and continued there for nearly half an hour.'[11] The colours were vivid in a clear light: the greens of the vineyards, the gardens and the vegetation on the mountain slopes contrasted with 'the deep blue of the ocean, and the delicate white of the ever-changing clouds of mist which rolled incessantly along'.[12] John Thomson shared his delight with his wife Mary:

> The appearance of Madeira is beautiful from the sea as the land rises up abruptly from the sea without any level being interposed between the hilly ground and the beach the highest mountain extending to six thousand feet in height the whole surface is beautifully varied with knoll and ravine and on some occasions when the rainbow hung over a valley the scenery was enchanting. The appearance when you reach the shore is no less captivating all the houses in Funchal have their gardens and they are filled with the rarest flowers and richest fruits of the tropics.

Thomas Huxley, the assistant surgeon, remarked on the sublimity of the scene, impressed by the paradox of utter beauty and the violence from which it sprang. 'Nature is a true tragedian,' he noted, 'her most painful throes, her wildest struggles have all within them some element of beauty . . .'[13] Huxley, having grown up and worked in the world's largest city, felt liberated by the view. He had never before seen mountains and the sight of 'bananas, cactuses and the palm trees' whetted his appetite for southern latitudes.

The *Rattlesnake* dropped anchor in the afternoon of Friday, 18 December 1846, seven days after leaving Plymouth in angry seas. Within an hour of the ship's arrival, the pratique officer, whose job it was to declare the vessel free of disease and allow the company to disembark, and George Stoddart, the British Consul, were on board. On the shore a crowd of British residents and visitors had gathered to find out the latest news from home.

Madeira, a Portuguese possession, lies in the Atlantic Ocean at about the same latitude as Marrakech in Morocco, more than 300 miles to the west of the coast of North Africa and 300 miles to the north of the Canary Islands. It is a small, precipitous, highly mountainous and yet densely populated island. At the time of the *Rattlesnake*'s arrival, Madeira supported a population of around 110,000, of whom 25,000 lived in Funchal, the island's main town.[14] British interest in the island dates from the late sixteenth and seventeenth century, when British merchants first established themselves in the island's wine trade, but it was only in the latter part of the eighteenth century that Madeira became more than a commercial proposition. From that date onwards, increasing numbers of wealthy British visitors annually made a pilgrimage to the island seeking its curative qualities, swelling the numbers of Britons who had, by virtue of the wine trade, already made their homes there.[15] Madeira, or at least the area around Funchal, was 'anglicised to a greater degree than any other island that does not wear the British flag'.[16] Relations between the Madeirans and the British were, at best, ambivalent. A mere 300 British residents owned and ran most of the island's export economy and to many Madeirans they appeared to be taking over their island: the British were 'always tolerated but never much liked'.[17]

By 1846, Madeira's curative reputation was well established. The publication of Sir James Clark's *Medical notes on climate, diseases, etc.* in 1820, and now in its fourth edition, made Madeira a firm favourite for convalescence. Clark, an Edinburgh-trained physician with substantial royal connections (he was, at various times, personal physician to Prince Leopold of Belgium, the Duchess of Kent, and physician in ordinary at Queen Victoria's court), was a man whose words were held in high regard. As he wrote, 'there is no place on the continent of Europe with which I am acquainted, where the pulmonary invalid could reside with so much advantage during the whole year as Madeira.'[18]

A small industry had thus grown up around the annual visitation of some 300 British and other foreign pulmonary invalids seeking the beneficial effects of Madeira. Boarding houses, dispensaries, tour guides, resident physicians, and a regular steamer service from Falmouth had all sprung up in the past decade or two to meet the seasonal requirements.[19] Catherine Stanley was thus well advised by her brother Owen to spend the winter and spring in Madeira. She would be in good company.

Funchal presented a rich panorama of white houses, gardens, and churches rising up into the surrounding hills. It was strangely foreign; European, to be sure, but also more exotic than that. The roads of the town were very narrow, roughly cobbled and extremely steep. There were no wheeled vehicles and walking, for the British at least, appeared to be difficult. What struck most visitors was the odd and unique means of transport in the town. Three devices always elicited comment. One of these, the *carro de bois*, was a sledge, fitted with springs, a reclining seat – like a chaise longue – and an awning supporting a set of curtains, and driven by a pair of oxen when going up a road. The second device, called a *carro do monte* and used for going down an incline, was also a sledge on which was built 'a very short sofa, made of basket work, nicely stuffed and cushioned ... to which ropes are attached, and two men give the sledge a push, when by its own weight it runs down the hill, at a pace that is ... accelerated every moment, while the two men holding the ropes, and running at the top of their speed, keep pulling with all their might to prevent the sledge from going too fast'.[20] The other mode of transport was a palanquin, similar to ones used in Brazil and India but with its own, distinctive Madeiran qualities:

> It consists of a board just large enough for one person to sit on with the legs extended; one end is usually raised two or three inches for the seat, and cushioned, the rest is lined with a piece of carpet; a light iron railing about seven or eight inches high surrounds the whole, rising considerably higher at the seat end; it is suspended by an iron rod at each end from the pole, to which it is still further secured by stays. .... nearly all of them have a kind of roof, made of a slight iron frame, covered with oiled cloth, and curtains of the same material lined with chintz were coloured calico; in fine weather the curtains are rolled back. This machine is borne by two men, in the same manner as the ... hammock.[21]

Women, and those who, because of an infirmity, could not walk or ride, were carried in palanquins.

Captain Stanley's party left the *Rattlesnake* early on Saturday morning to visit the island's main attractions and enjoy the rounds of picnics, balls, dinners for which the British community was well known. Stanley's party was not just a family affair for it included, besides Catherine (borne in a palanquin) and Mary, Lieutenants Dayman and Simpson, Reverend King (almost family) and Captain Denison. Their first port of call was the home of the resident English Chaplain, the Reverend Richard Thomas Lowe, a man with an interesting secular vocation and an even more interesting and controversial (offensive to some) religious practice.

Lowe had come to Madeira in 1828 in order to improve his health and was appointed Chaplain of the English Church in Funchal in 1833, the Church itself having been recently built. He was a passionate naturalist and had already published a number of highly original pieces on Madeiran fauna (principally fishes) and flora.[22] He counted many contemporary influential scientists – William Hooker, Charles Darwin, Richard Owen and John Stevens Henslow – among his close correspondents. This was reason enough for the scientifically minded officers and passengers of the *Rattlesnake* to pay him a visit. But Lowe was also something of a maverick in this closely knit English community. Within a very short time of his appointment on the island, Lowe ran straight into trouble with the then British Consul, Henry Veitch, a long-time resident of Madeira and architect of the English Church.[23] The two men differed profoundly on their religious practices and orientations, Veitch holding to Low Church sympathies while Lowe was deeply influenced by the High Church leanings of the Oxford Movement. The dissension between the two broke out into ugly scenes, which lasted over a two-year period and were only ended by the dismissal of Veitch from his post by Lord Palmerston, the Foreign Secretary. Matters seem to have rested quietly for the next decade but flared up once again when George Stoddart, the British Consul who replaced Veitch, accused Lowe of offending a majority of the congregation and destroying the harmony of the resident English community by practising ritualism in his church.[24] About nine months before the *Rattlesnake*'s visit to the island, Lowe's stipend had been suspended and Stoddart made it clear that the only solution was for Lowe to go. Both parties in the argument turned to their respective superiors – the Foreign Office and the Bishop of London, respectively – for support.[25] This is how matters stood when Stanley's party descended on the Chaplain at breakfast time. A few months later Lowe was ousted but, far from leaving the island, he set up his own church in a room in a seventeenth-century Spanish mansion on a Funchal back-street and took the more devout parishioners with him.[26]

Whether the party was aware of the tension between Lowe and Stoddart is uncertain but if they were it certainly didn't bother them. Charlie and Eliza, Stanley's brother and sister-in-law, had paid a visit to Lowe just about a month before and nothing of Lowe's troubles had been communicated back to the family in England.[27] Aware or not of Lowe's circumstances, the party happily proceeded after breakfast to Stoddart's country residence, the Quinta do Bello Monte, one of the first foreign

quintas on the island and dating back to the 1760s, where they were entertained to lunch. Stoddart was a well-known local personality having been
in residence on the island for more than a quarter of a century.[28] In the
evening the party split up, the Stanleys proceeding to have dinner at the
home of the aunt of Arthur Packe, the seventeen-year-old midshipman –
Owen knew and had dined with Arthur's mother – while the others
returned to the ship.[29]

The resident British community was renowned for its hospitality to
British visitors.[30] The *Rattlesnake*'s officers were treated to an embarrass-
ment of attention. John Thomson remarked that the hospitality was
unbounded: 'invitations to dinners to evening parties and to picnics up
the mountains have been sent on board without number'.[31] Stoddart, the
British Consul, gave a ball one night, followed by a dinner the next.[32] The
Portuguese authorities threw a public ball in the *Rattlesnake*'s honour.[33]
Robert, the son of the ex-Consul Henry Veitch, invited a number of officers to his father's Quinta, the Jardim de Serra, at an altitude of over 2,000
feet, for meals and to stay the night, while James David Webster Gordon,
one of the island's most important wine traders, provided similar hospitality on another occasion.[34] Catherine and Mary Stanley had originally
planned to stay with the Reverend Lowe but that plan fell through. Instead
they were the guests of the Gordons and after the *Rattlesnake* departed
stayed at their country residence, the Quinta do Monte.[35] Considering the
British community was so small it is remarkable how many of the residents
were known personally to the *Rattlesnake*'s officers. Arthur Packe, the
midshipman, not only had his aunt there but also knew several other people who were living or visiting; Owen Stanley knew George Stoddart
(Stanley's parents arranged lodgings in London for the Stoddarts when
they visited in 1847) and the Gordons;[36] and John Thomson spent the
evening at the Veitch Quinta at which there were several guests known
personally to him. All of this made for a very cosy visit.[37]

Aside from the generous hospitality, the area around Funchal was famous
for its sights, particularly the Curral, which attracted its fair share of visitors. The Curral is a very large crater-like geological formation inland from
Funchal, close enough to the town to make it possible to ride to and from
it in a day.[38] Groups of the ship's officers visited the Curral. Some trips

were simple affairs, consisting of no more than a few people taking a horse ride out and back again, as did Arthur Packe, Thomas Huxley and the purser, Frederick Brady. Others were much more lavish affairs which included riding, picnicking, sketching, scientific observations and specimen hunting. This was how Owen Stanley organized his visit to the Curral, ensuring that not only were his sisters treated to the extraordinary views but that he and his officers were given the opportunity to measure the heights of the surrounding peaks, take measurements of magnetic inclination (the angle between the direction of the earth's magnetic field and the plane of the horizon) using the latest instruments, and sketch the scene; while John MacGillivray and others with a bent for natural history collected specimens.[39]

The Curral was a scientific phenomenon and opportunity. The surveyors, particularly Joseph Dayman, were anxious to measure the height of one of the peaks, Pico dos Bodes, using barometric readings, and to try out different recording devices to measure magnetic inclination.[40] John Thomson had only been ashore once since the *Rattlesnake*'s arrival and that was to dine at the Veitch residence in Funchal. Now he was thrilled when Stanley invited him to join his party on what was their second visit to the Curral. Thomson had already warmed to his commander. 'I have had great reason to be pleased with the treatment which I have received from Captn Stanley,' he wrote to Mary, 'he always listens with the greatest consideration to any recommendations from me in regards to the arrangements for the sick . . . indeed with a degree of kindness equal to that of Captain Robinson [Charles Gepp Robinson, Commander of HMS *Shearwater*, Thomson's previous commission] he conjures more prudence and common sense.'[41]

The Curral did not disappoint. Thomson described the view to Mary thus:

Yesterday was spent in a very pleasant excursion I was pressed into the service by Captn Stanley who would take no excuse from me we landed at nine o'clock Captn Stanley and two sisters the first Lieutenant and Purser Captn Denison and Mr King who are passengers Mr Veitch and myself and two youngsters [midshipmen] are being all provided with splendid horses except the ladies who were carried in palanquins we started off to have a sight considered the most beautiful and at the same time the grandest on the island and never was I more fully repaid for my trouble than on the present occasion. The place is called the Curral and is a gigantic valley in the form of a ravine with the summits of the hills rising around it to more than three thousand feet our road for about 10 miles lay along the side of the hills and we had to ascend to an altitude of upwards of three thousand feet before we descended again to the valley . . . after three hard hours we arrived at the spot and all of us were bewailing with disappointment that we had encountered so many difficulties to no good purposes when gradually the sun began to burst through the thick veil of mist in different points and in a quarter of an hour the whole lifted up like an immense curtain and displayed to our sight a view more grand and beautiful than any that I have ever beheld all of us were in raptures and exclaiming and descanting on the beauties of the spectacle. After partaking of a splendid repast and gathering a few plants and insects and plucking up a few land shells we remounted about three o'clock to find our way to Funchal.[42]

This was also MacGillivray's first opportunity to collect specimens for his patrons in London. The change in elevation, from sea-level to over 3,000 feet, provided him with a wealth of flora and fauna from which to sample. Madeira was, of course, not unknown to natural history: indeed, the Reverend Richard Lowe had done much to publicize its riches. MacGillivray had been to Madeira for a few days when he was on HMS *Fly* in 1842. On that occasion he collected nothing and, on this trip, he expected little in the way of novelties.[43] There were a few flowering plants and many butterflies to be observed but what caught his eye was the rich variety of ferns jutting out from the dripping rocks – 'the ferns', he remarked, 'would, to a botanist, have made ample amends for the small number of plants in flower.'[44] More of a zoologist than a botanist, however, MacGillivray, despite his belief that the area had been well picked over, did not go away empty-handed. Turning over stone after stone, he managed to obtain twenty-three species of land shells, at various elevations, which formed the nucleus of his collection.[45]

The Curral excursions occupied many of the days in Funchal. Science, picnics, sketching and sightseeing were a tiring combination. Christmas Day, by contrast, was less taxing. The ship's officers spent the day at the English Church and some also went to the Catholic Cathedral. Most returned to the ship in the evening while others, more privileged, retired to the Quinta do Monte, the residence of James Webster Gordon, for the festivities.

The *Rattlesnake* was ready to leave Madeira on the 26 December, just over a week since arriving on the island. The carpenters had been hard at work trying to repair the leak but the result of their work would not be known until the ship was at sea again. It was common knowledge on the *Rattlesnake* that if the leak continued, Stanley would have to take the ship to Rio de Janeiro for repairs, something that would please him since he had wanted to take the ship there when the itinerary was planned.[46] Stanley alerted his masters in London to this possibility in a letter to Beaufort written on the day of departure.[47]

For many of the ship's company, Madeira was their first view of a world outside Britain. It was foreign yet strangely familiar. While the landscape inspired feelings for the sublime and exposed the inadequacy of language to describe it, simple prejudices were not left behind. Both King and Huxley were deeply offended by the smell of garlic. '. . . The insufferable stink of garlicky humanity drove me out', Huxley remarked of his short stay at the Christmas Eve Mass in Funchal's cathedral. 'I consider that stink as one of the most remarkable circumstances in my travels.'[48]

For all that, the visit to Madeira was intensely pleasurable and the departure emotional. None knew, however, that some of the farewells were for ever. Owen Stanley was leaving his sisters and would never see either again. Arthur Packe bade his aunt and family farewell: 'I wished them good bye for the next five years and perhaps for ever.'[49] As it turned out, he never saw them again. Even King, though not leaving family and close friends behind, felt the sense of loss. 'Said adieu to our fair passengers,' he noted. 'Never were passengers followed by more universal regrets of those with whom they had sailed.'[50] At 3 p.m., after a final farewell to George Stoddart and James Webster Gordon, the ship weighed anchor and continued on its journey south.

No sooner had the *Rattlesnake* departed the Madeiran shores in calm seas than the leak erupted again. Whatever the carpenters did in Madeira had made no difference. Stanley decided then and there to head for Rio de Janeiro. It was the closest port en route where extensive repairs could be carried out. He would take the ship south towards the Canary Islands continuing on a southerly course carried by the northeast trade winds to the vicinity of the Cape Verde Islands, where he expected to meet the southeast trade winds for the run across the Atlantic towards the coast of Brazil.

Midshipman Arthur Packe was very relieved: 'We are not fit to go to sea at all,' he noted in his journal, 'much more to stop out 5 years. I think she will go down before that time is over.'[51] Stanley was satisfied that Rio would be his next port of call. He knew the city and the countryside around it well. He had first seen Rio when he was a sixteen-year-old midshipman on HMS *Ganges* and HMS *Forte* and then, a few years later, when he was serving on HMS *Adventure*. Several years later he was in Rio again, this time, at the age of twenty-seven years, in command of his own ship, HMS *Britomart*, on its way to Australia.[52] Altogether over this period he spent four or five months in the city. When not engaged on naval business, Stanley spent much of his free time exploring the countryside in the vicinity, sketching and painting a rich variety of subjects.[53] He must have been looking forward to yet another welcome spell of sketching in the brilliant light that awaited him. Besides satisfying his artistic ambitions, this unexpected detour also afforded him the opportunity to impress Beaufort even more by searching for the peak of a subterranean mountain off the coast of Brazil from Rio.[54]

But, right now, in the Atlantic, there was work to be done and the leak, the source of which remained unknown, had to be managed as best as possible. Thankfully, in this part of the ocean, the winds were light and the sea generally smooth. All that could be done was to keep pumping out the sea from the flooded hull.

As the *Rattlesnake* headed towards the equator, the air and water temperature began to rise and the sea changed. On 28 December, two days after leaving Madeira, the ship passed within sight of the island of Palma, the most westerly of the Canary Islands. Had it not been hazy, Mount Teide, the highest peak on Tenerife, the main island, would have been visible even from this distance. The air and sea temperature were now virtually the same at 67 degrees Fahrenheit. They were making excellent time. According to the readings that Arthur Packe recorded, the *Rattlesnake* covered, on average, 150 miles daily, though in a good wind, the figure could exceed 350 miles. New Year's Day found the ship less than a day's sail from the island of Sal, in the northeastern corner of the Cape Verde Islands, and just over 1,000 miles from the equator. 'One drum, one accordion and a whistle' heralded the New Year. The temperature now touched the low seventies.

Robert Gale, Captain Stanley's steward, began his journal on this New Year's Day. He recorded the details of the weather and the nature of the sea, but his thoughts were turned to his family and friends back home, praying to God that he would meet them again. Gale was twenty-nine years old and had known the Stanley family for seven years. He had been Stanley's cook on HMS *Blazer*. His present position as his steward was a promotion. Their relationship was fraught. They rubbed each other the wrong way. Stanley certainly thought that his steward fussed too much and acted in a self-important manner. 'He looks and talks very important and big,' Stanley had confided in Mary before the *Rattlesnake* left Plymouth, but he felt that once the ship was out to sea, Robert would settle down.[55] On this day, Gale also reflected on his superior with whom he had recently had some difficulty, but the worst seemed to be over: 'Captain behave better,' he remarked tersely in the first entry of his diary.[56]

This was also the first day that the towing net was used or, as Reverend King put it so eloquently, the beginning of 'a season of pleasure'.[57] The marine towing net was similar to but heavier than the ring net used to catch butterflies and other flying insects.[58] It was a makeshift but very efficient device. The kind used by the *Rattlesnake*'s company consisted of a bag made of coarsely woven cotton fabric, about 2 feet deep, the mouth of which was sewn around a hoop just over a foot in diameter. The net was towed astern of the ship, in its wake. The rope attached to the hoop was either fastened to the ship or simply held in the hand. As the ship ran along, the net scooped marine life from the surface and just below it.[59] An easier but generally less productive way of using the net was simply to throw it over the side when the ship was stopped and haul its contents on board.

What was so exciting about the towing net experience was that most of those on board the ship had never before seen these marine creatures alive and certainly not in the northern waters. And they were extraordinarily weird. The net yielded such denizens as *Ascidiaceae*, or sea squirts, so-called because they filter water and shoot jets of it, *Porpita*, a brightly coloured, jellyfish-like creature, consisting of a central disc surrounded by

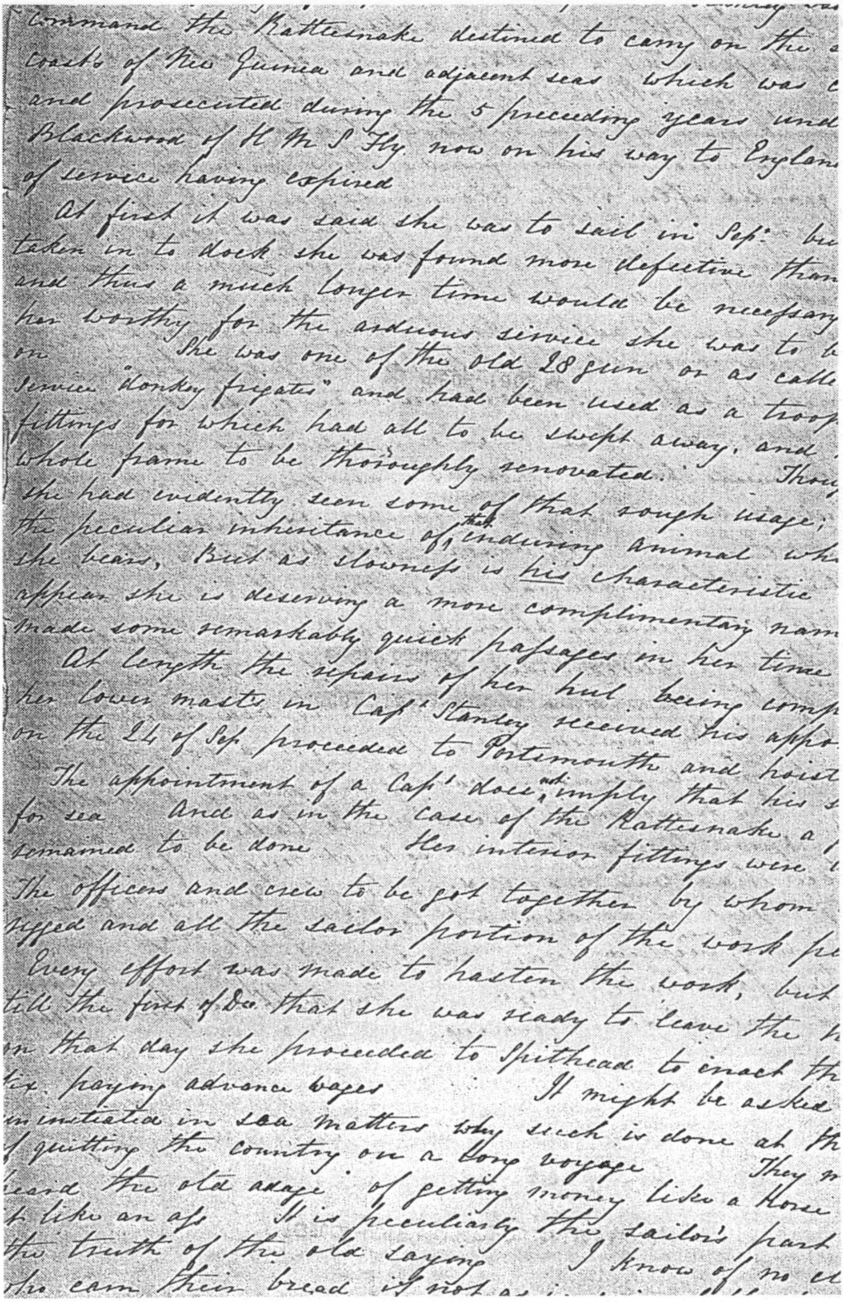

[Handwritten journal page, partially legible]

command the Rattlesnake destined to carry on the
coast of New Guinea and adjacent seas which was
and prosecuted during the 5 preceding years und
Blackwood of H.M.S. Fly now on his way to England
of service having expired

At first it was said she was to sail in Sep. bu
taken in to dock she was found more defective than
and thus a much longer time would be necessary
her worthy, for the arduous service she was to b
on   She was one of the old 28 gun or as called
service "donkey frigates" and had been used as a troop
fittings for which had all to be swept away, and
whole frame to be thoroughly renovated   Thou
she had evidently seen some of that rough usage
the peculiar inheritance of that enduring animal wh
the bear, But as slowness is his characteristic
appear she is deserving a more complimentary nam
made some remarkably quick passages in her time

At length the repairs of her hull beeing comp
her lower masts in Capt Stanley received his appo
on the 24 of Sep proceeded to Portsmouth and hoist

The appointment of a Capt does at imply that his s
for sea   And as in the case of the Rattlesnake a
remained to be done   Her interior fittings were
the officers and crew to be got together by whom
rigged and all the sailor portion of the work pe

Every effort was made to hasten the work, but
till the first of Dec that she was ready to leave the
on that day she proceeded to Spithead to enact th
tix paying advance wages   It might be asked
in initiated in sea matters why such is done at th
of quitting the country on a long voyage   They
heard the old adage of getting money like a horse
like an ass   It is peculiarly this sailor's part
the truth of the old saying   I know of no e
who earn their bread if not as

A page from the journal kept by Robert Gale

masses of tentacles, and a number of small molluscs. Reverend King was overwhelmed by the harvest. 'I had not had any previous opportunity of examining the living animal', he remarked in his journal, 'and of course this I embraced with avidity.'[60] King preserved his haul in salt water for as long as he could and admired God's creation.

Thomas Huxley also peered into the pelagic bounty and though he saw the same gelatinous creatures as King, he saw much more than that. Three weeks into what would be a very long voyage, Huxley was about to embark on his scientific career, his first intellectual challenge. He knew precisely what he wanted out of the voyage. Not for him collecting, classifying and naming. 'My memory is not sufficiently selective of these facts to give me any hope of attaining profound systematic knowledge,' he reflected.[61] He wouldn't waste the opportunity of a scientific voyage naming species and filling in specimen tags giving time and place of collection. This, he noted wryly, 'is far better done by those who sit in museums at home'.[62]

He had worked out very carefully that 'the study of the habits and structure of the more perishable or rare marine productions [is] most likely to be profitable' and provided himself with a task list of which marine animals he should concentrate upon and which kind of analysis he should perform.[63] The very nature of his fresh specimens, he believed, lay at the minutest scale visible only with a microscope. Before joining the ship, Huxley had splashed out a month's wages on a microscope.[64] But this was no mere pastime, no intellectual game to stave off the inevitable bouts of boredom. Treasuring a copy of Lesson's natural history of the acalephes, or stinging jellyfish, and buttressed by his medical experience in dissection and histology, Huxley had set his sights no less on throwing himself into the great scientific debates of the time, jousting with the cream of Europe's scientific community.[65] The specimens were perishable, to be sure, but they would be preserved not in spirits but in the scientific papers and the accompanying detailed drawings he would produce as the *Rattlesnake* ploughed its way through the world's great oceans.

Thanks to Stanley, Huxley had already met select members of Britain's scientific elite and rubbed shoulders with others at the Southampton meeting of the British Association for the Advancement of Science before joining the *Rattlesnake*. These would prove to be useful contacts, especially Edward Forbes whom he had met and heard at Southampton, and who presented Huxley with a living specimen of *Amphioxus lanceolatus*, commonly known as the arrow worm, a marine animal with no heart and hardly a brain.[66] A strange vertebrate creature, but when Huxley examined a sample of its blood under the microscope, he found that it had all the characteristics of an invertebrate animal. Now, on the *Rattlesnake*, Stanley's generosity towards Huxley extended to the precious gift of granting him space to pursue his science, to use the chart room to 'read, draw, or microscopise at pleasure'.[67] But, as the only person on the ship with a microscope, Huxley's solitary moments of peering down the barrel into the minutiae below him were, at first, few and far between. 'Microscopy is a thing requiring a great deal of attention and quite incompatible with being bothered to show something pretty,' he confided in himself. Not to be cramped by onlookers and the devaluation of his precious scientific corner, Huxley schemed 'to show them nothing but "interesting" structures in wh. they can see nothing and of wh. they will soon become thoroughly tired and so leave me alone'.[68]

With a steady breeze blowing, the *Rattlesnake* continued to make headway. January 2 saw the ship pass between the islands of St Jago and Mayo in the southern section of the Cape Verde Islands. Huxley stood on the deck looking over the horizon for evidence of the fine red dust that Darwin had observed when he was here in 1833 but in vain.[69] Despite being so close to the islands, Stanley made no attempt to land, possibly because several months earlier there had been a particularly horrible outbreak of yellow fever on Boa Vista, an adjacent island.[70] Once clear of the Cape Verde Islands, their next sight of land would be the coast of Brazil. Now, with the islands behind them, they were in the warm Atlantic and fortunately benefited from the southeasterly trades and avoided being stuck in the doldrums. The next day, Sunday service was held under a blazing sky with the temperature reaching 84 degrees Fahrenheit, and they were still 750 miles north of the equator.[71]

Despite the trade wind, for the next week and more the *Rattlesnake* inched towards the equator, some days making as little as 40 miles headway. The weather alternated between bright clear skies and torrential rains but two things remained constant: the temperature and humidity both kept rising. It got too hot and uncomfortable for Robert Gale to retire to his hammock so he spent the night on the floor of his cabin. John Thomson commented on the 'sultry oppressive weather' and Thomas Huxley noted that the sick list had grown to more than a dozen, complaints about swelling of the feet and rheumatism, particularly among the younger crew, being most prevalent.[72] For relief, Stanley ordered the crew to bathe. A lower studsail was put over the port side of the ship between the mainmast and the foremast and raised so that it filled with sea water. According to the Reverend King, some sixty or seventy persons, crew members, midshipmen, a few officers and King himself included, jumped into the deep blue water from all parts of the ship's side.[73] To keep them on their toes, literally, Stanley also ordered the crew to dance to the piper's tune.

Despite the unpleasant weather, the scientific pursuits continued. Each day the towing net brought up a new harvest over which King, for one, waxed lyrically. Besides these surface creatures, the sea brought forth other inhabitants, indicative of the tropical waters, including dolphins, flying fish and sharks, one of which was caught and 'speedily shared among the men'. Huxley was at his microscope and MacGillivray, less than impressed by the contents of the net, took the opportunity of calm conditions to exercise his talents of spotting and shooting down interesting birds.[74] He often took one of the jolly boats, sometimes in the company of John Thomson. They had become close friends, particularly as they had much in common. Both men were Scots and educated in Edinburgh and shared an interest in natural history. MacGillivray also advised Thomson on his collection of Aberdeenshire shells, which he had brought with him. From the jolly boat, MacGillivray shot several species of storm petrels, also known as Mother Carey's chickens, one of which, *Thalassidroma Tropica*, was new to science.[75] MacGillivray skinned five birds and prepared them to be shipped to John Gould in London, when the occasion would arise.[76] On board the *Rattlesnake*, Thomson caught several flying insects including a locust, a dragon fly and a sulphur yellow coloured butterfly, all of which he added to his personal collection.[77]

Meanwhile, Lieutenant Joseph Dayman daily sounded to various depths with a register thermometer attached to the lead so that he could record the sea temperature at various depths, as compared with the surface temperature: at 400 fathoms (2,400 feet), for example, the thermometer registered 50 degrees Fahrenheit as compared to 80 degrees at the surface.[78] As for deep-sea soundings, these were not very successful. On the first attempt, the spun-yarn line of 2,500 fathoms split and the attached weight of 384 pounds was lost. On a later day, just above the equator, the line held but no bottom was reached.[79]

On 12 January 1847, the *Rattlesnake*'s noon position was 1° N 22°W. The equator would be crossed on the following day. Preparations for the ceremony of crossing the line were already under way as the cutlers were busy 'making razors'.[80] The ceremony was great fun for the crew for it was they who took over the ship by forcing all the officers, passengers, and remaining crew who hadn't crossed the line before to undergo a rite of passage. It was pure theatre, deadly serious and possibly dangerous. The precise details of the show varied from ship to ship and from time to time but certain features were fairly universal.[81] On the *Rattlesnake* the day, as recorded by John Thomson, went like this:

> Passed the Equator about 6 o'clock this morning. About 9 am Neptune's throne was erected and the sail was prepared for a bath to sauce all those who had never yet crossed the line. Breakspeare, the sailmaker, acted as Neptune, Coleman, the forecastle, as Amphytrite [his queen]. Amfield as Neptune's boy. Dick, Taylor and Whitewood were the bears and about 10 others acted as constables but the chief officials were Scott, the Secretary, Rowe, the ship's cook, Doctor, and Blake and Lord, the marines, Barbers. About 10 am Neptune . . . paid Captn Stanley a visit on the quarter deck and mentioned for what purpose he had come on board to initiate a great many to his dominions. His marine majesty was dressed in a fantastic manner and all his officials wore their peculiar uniform. His progress along the decks was attended with bucketfuls of water from the tops and the playing of the fire engine. Having been received by the Captn a glass of grog was ordered to Neptune and each of his officers of state and this over the real duties of the day commenced. In the first place a party of Constables secured all the unshaved on the lower deck and Neptune, his wife and boy became spectators of all that was to follow. The barbers and doctors were close by with their appropriate instruments and the bears were stationed in the bath. The physic consisted of pills and emetics. The composition of the pills was oatmeal and salt water and each pill was about 2 inches in diameter. The emetic mixture consisted of salt water and oatmeal and was contained in a bottle. The soap, which the barber used, was made of oatmeal,

black paint and cooks slush and the razors employed were pieces of old hoops, notched like a saw. The Secretary stood by and read from his list the names of who had to undergo the ceremony. My own name was the first on the list and accordingly when called two of the Constables laid hold of me and blindfolded and led me on deck to Neptune. In the meantime bucketfuls of water had been poured over me and the fire engine had continued to play upon me. When brought into Neptune's presence, he told his officers that I was a very good man that I was not sick and consequently that I required no assistance from the Doctor. Having been properly seated on a board which overhung the bath, at the order I was carted off into the bath and ducked. The same routine was gone through with by everyone else who had not previously been introduced to Neptune with the slight exception that those who were in any way disliked by the Ship's Company had their mouths filled with the Doctor's physic and their chins lathered over with the filthy preparation and scraped with the serrated razor and when overwhelmed into the bath were kept under water by the bears until they were nearly chocked. In the evening Neptune and his officers paid a visit to each of the messes and being liberally supplied with grog drank health and long life to all.[82]

King looked on in amusement at the whole spectacle. Of course, he had already been initiated, having gone around the world several times. As the eventful day approached, he noticed the different reactions in anticipation of those on board. Captain Denison appeared frightened and, whenever the ceremony was mentioned, quickly changed the subject. Huxley, by contrast, dismissed them as 'tomfooleries', and 'that the whole proceedings are childish and exceedingly absurd'.[83] King listened attentively to these admonitions and then chuckled to himself: 'alas! alas! childish or not his fate is sealed he is a doomed man.'[84]

Huxley, as it turned out, was third on the list, after Thomson and Denison. The others followed. Most of those in the gunroom, the midshipmen in particular, and nearly all on the lower deck, paid their respects to Neptune. Robert Gale got a drenching, too, but before he felt the pangs of humiliation, Philip Ruffle Sharpe, one of the midshipmen, soused Captain Stanley with a bucketful.[85] Luckily, he got away with it. MacGillivray, exempt from the proceedings like King, watched and did not seem to be moved one way or the other. Upwards of 100 of the ship's company, more than half of the total, received some sort of treatment that day.[86]

The next day the trade wind was blowing fresh and the ship returned to its normal business except that the ceremonies caused a swelling of the sick list. Huxley was appalled. There were twenty-two on the list with complaints of rheumatism, pleurisy and bruising. He vowed he would formally complain if ever he were made a surgeon.[87] Thomson knew that for most of those on the sick list the consequences of Neptune's day were not life threatening. But two of the ship's company were not so lucky. One teetered between life and death for several days and Thomson believed he would be an invalid from the experience for some time. James Dawkins, one of the carpenter's crew, however, was in an even more serious state and suffered terribly for several days before dying of severe bronchitis in both lungs. Both Thomson and King were with him towards the end of his life and both agreed that 'he died in a cheerful state of mind'.[88] The death was the ship's first serious setback and the funeral its second major ritual.

Thomson had never witnessed a burial at sea and was deeply moved by the experience. 'I can never forget that morning,' he wrote to Mary:

> the sun was shining in his glory, silvery masses of clouds were scattered on the horizon, all else in the face of heaven was clear and dazzling and the wide expanse of waters spread out around us of an inky blue save where the waves moving on their course had their tops broken presenting crests of snowy white. Captn Stanley read in an impressive manner the service . . . and the corpse previously placed by his own messmates in the starboard gangway on a grating and covered with the flag of his country was launched into its watery grave. Then was heard through the stillness a rough and jarring sound of the rope rubbing on the grating, afterwards a splash in the water and a gurgle and all was over and the ship sped on her course, and the spot of the poor man's grave was left unmarked for ever.[89]

The ship certainly sped. The *Rattlesnake* was now covering 200 miles per day. The towing-net was launched each day and the contents examined, recorded and analysed. King was pleased with his quarry but Huxley was less than impressed, hoping for a major catch: *Physalia*, the Portuguese man-of-war. Though they were spotted almost on a daily basis, these impressive creatures seemed to refuse to be caught in the net. And then, after much frustration, the towing-net came up with the goods. Huxley now concentrated all his efforts and experience on analysing the finest details. King, normally very inquisitive and knowledgeable about the contents of the net, knew what this meant to Huxley. Although King knew as much about *Physalia* as the next man and managed to convince Huxley to let him have a quick look down the microscope, he withdrew swiftly, allowing Huxley free rein. He knew he was in the presence of a master. 'For very remarkable discoveries of the singular anatomy of this pungent animal,' he remarked, 'I beg to refer to the learned works which will doubtless shortly appear from the talented pen of my amiable friend Mr Huxley.'[90] King's confidence in his friend would be well rewarded for Huxley soon realized that the accepted descriptions of *Physalia* and its place in the system of animals were muddled and that he could clarify them.[91] He was a happy man and any misgivings he may have had about his position on the ship – his accommodation and his messmates – which he had voiced earlier, now evaporated. 'We have been quite long enough at sea now', he reassured his mother,

> to enable me to judge how I shall get on in the ship, and to form a very clear idea of how it fits me and how I fit it. In the first place I am exceedingly well and exceedingly contented with my lot. My opinion of the advantages lying open to me increases rather than otherwise as I see my way about me. I am on capital terms with all the superior officers, and I find them ready to give me all facilities ... My immediate superior, Johnny Thompson [sic], is a long-headed good fellow without a morsel of humbug about him – a man whom I thoroughly respect, both morally and intellectually. I think it will be my fault if we are not fast friends through the commission. One friend on board a ship is as much as anybody has a right to expect.[92]

And so, with the *Physalia* bagged, dissected and discarded, the excitement of Neptune's show over and the tragedy of a young death behind them, the *Rattlesnake* made steady progress towards the Brazilian coast. On 21 January 1847, the ship was stopped about 80 miles from the coast to allow Lieutenant Dayman to make his final sounding before their destination. The weather was fine, warm and somewhat sultry. Two days later, at daybreak, the high rocky point of Cape Frio came into view and the run down the coast towards the harbour of Rio de Janeiro began. They had been at sea for almost a month and were still afloat, albeit leaking still.

Aside from Captain Stanley, few on board the ship had ever been to Rio de Janeiro and probably none had been there as often or stayed as long as he.

The impression for most was, therefore, the more dramatic. Huxley, for one, was lost for words, having, as he said, used them up in admiring Madeira, but Rio 'beats it into fits'.[93] Though he'd never been out of England before, he was sure that Rio 'contends with the Bay of Naples for the title of the most beautiful place in the world'.[94] MacGillivray, already by the age of twenty-five a well-seasoned maritime traveller and tropical expert, had never been to Rio before and was completely overwhelmed by the sheer scale of the beauty. Looking back on that day when the *Rattlesnake* slowly and quietly headed along the coast into the harbour of Rio, MacGillivray found words to express his emotions in a description he penned for the narrative of the voyage. It is uncharacteristically evocative for a man who was normally economical with his words: 'It exceeded my most sanguine expectations,' he confided.[95]

> The morning was beautifully fine, and with a light breeze scarcely sufficient to cause a ripple on the water, we were slipping past the high and remarkable promontory of Cape Frio, which at first appeared like an island. A long beach of glittering sand stretched away to the westward, and was lost in the distance; behind this a strip of undulating country, clad here and there in the richest green, was backed by a range of distant wooded hills, on which many clumps of palms could be distinguished. Few harbours in the world present a more imposing entrance than that of Rio de Janeiro. Several islands lie off the opening, and on either side the coast range terminates in broken hills and ridges of granite, one of which Pao d'Açucar, the Sugar Loaf of the English, rises at once near the water's edge to the height of 900 feet, as an apparently inaccessible peak, and forms the well known landmark for the entrance. Passing the narrows . . . the harbour widens out with beautiful sandy bays on either side, and rocky headlands covered with luxuriant vegetation. Here the view of the city of Rio de Janeiro is magnificent . . . Beyond the city the harbour again widens out to form an immense basin, studded with green islands, extending backwards some seventeen or eighteen miles further towards the foot of the Organ mountains, the highest of which attains an elevation of 7800 feet above the sea.[96]

John Thomson, too, was inspired into describing the luxuriant panorama, in a letter to his wife, remarking particularly on the vibrancy and variety of life in front of him: 'trees loaded with the rarest and most delicious fruits grow there fresh from the hand of nature. Life, animal and vegetable, is lavish here.'[97] Nature, as it expressed itself in and around Rio, certainly enthralled the *Rattlesnake*'s company, as it had Charles Darwin when he was there many years earlier.[98] Quickly, however, this emotion was challenged by something much more distasteful.

With its 200,000 inhabitants, Rio de Janeiro, the capital of an independent Brazil since 1822, was one of the largest cities in the Americas.[99] Brazil had enjoyed particularly close commercial and political ties with Britain for more than a century and a half, on account of the latter's relationships with Portugal, but now these ties were being strained. Stanley would now find a different Rio from the one he remembered, a city that was not as welcoming to British naval personnel as it had once been. The reason for the change was fairly recent.

Britain supported Brazil's independence from Portugal but this came with a price, namely that Brazil had to agree to declare the slave trade illegal, which Britain had done in 1807.[100] After much resistance on the Brazilian side and protracted negotiations to ease the way forward, the Brazilian authorities finally agreed to a treaty, ratified in 1827, to make the slave trade to Brazil illegal within a three-year period. Yet, despite the existence of the law, the slave trade not only continued as before but actually increased in volume, as planters sought increasing numbers of African slaves to produce highly desirable export crops (sugar and coffee) and as enforcement proved almost impossible. In 1846, the year the *Rattlesnake* began its round-the-world voyage, Brazil imported more than 50,000 slaves from Africa, more than twice the amount that had been imported in the years before the trade was declared illegal.[101] Against this backdrop of a rising tide of illegal slave trading, relationships between Brazil and Britain began to deteriorate as each side accused the other of meddling and stalling.[102]

In this period of the *Pax Britannica*, the Royal Navy played a major role in suppressing the slave trade by deploying squadrons on the west African coast, the Caribbean and South America.[103] But they had largely failed to curb the trade. Despite measures designed to extend British rights to search and detain suspected slave ships in the Atlantic, the trade continued to expand. Finally in 1845, the British Parliament passed the Aberdeen Act, which allowed British warships to seize suspected Brazilian slave ships wherever they were encountered. The Royal Navy had been using Rio de Janeiro as a strategic base for their own needs as well as for the larger design of expanding British interests in South America, Africa, India and Australia since the latter part of the eighteenth century.[104] Now, as it patrolled the Brazilian coast, the Royal Navy came in for the same anti-British sentiment that was already being directed at the British government.[105]

Rio was not the social whirlwind of Madeira. There were no breakfasts, lunches, dinners and balls, no evening entertainments hosted by the British Consul and the British merchant community. There was a curious disengagement with the city. Arthur Packe found so little to interest him that he spent most of the days on the ship. On the rare occasions he ventured forth, he didn't seem to do much and generally felt the city to be a disappointment, in marked contrast to his experiences in Madeira.[106]

The *Rattlesnake* had company in the harbour. Besides a number of Brazilian and Portuguese warships, there was a Dutch frigate and a British corvette, HMS *Curaçao*. There would be time for socializing but more pressing now was the leak, the reason the ship was there in the first place. The job, it turned out, was greater than first imagined and Stanley was fortunate in being able to call upon the assistance of the carpenters of HMS *Curaçao*. The source of the leak was found to be 'the bad fitting of the cistern round the rudder head in the after gunroom', and the choice of Rio for repairs was a wise one.[107] Stanley invited Captain William Broughton, the commander of the *Curaçao*, on board the *Rattlesnake* to thank him for his help. The two men hit it off immediately and for good reason. Broughton was a Cheshire man and his father was the famous explorer William Robert Broughton who accompanied George Vancouver on his epic voyage to the northwest coast of America in the 1790s. The two men got drunk, much to the annoyance of Robert Gale who complained that 'he abused me meanly'.[108]

While the repairs were being carried out, and without the demands of a hectic social calendar, the *Rattlesnake*'s officers and men of science set out to sample the luxuriance of nature. The public market, the public gardens and the Botanic Garden were there to be visited and specimens from them procured. MacGillivray thought the market worthy of any collector's trip. He happily purchased a wide variety of fish and molluscs, preserved and prepared them for shipment back to England.[109] In the gardens, the collecting parties, variously consisting of Stanley, Thomson, King, Brady, Simpson, Robert Gale and James Wilcox, helped themselves to plants, land shells and butterflies. Stanley took the opportunity of sketching Corcovado. Excursions into the Laranjeiras Valley and behind the city towards the Organ Mountains – a round trip of about 9 miles as recorded by Stanley's pedometer – yielded a number of birds, shot by Stanley and his two officers.[110] The specimens of shells and insects collected by Gale and Wilcox, together with the skins of the birds shot by Stanley, were placed in a box for shipment to London, to Stanley's father, for distribution to the museums in Ipswich, Norwich and Kings Lynn, of which he was a patron – the box arrived exactly a year later.[111] All in all, the *Rattlesnake* officers were astonished by the quantity and variety of the animal life that filled the air and covered the ground and they bagged as much as they could carry.

MacGillivray, the experienced professional naturalist, typically stayed away from such large collecting parties, preferring less social natural history excursions. Being in South America for the first time, he was anxious to increase the size of his collection. Birds, he complained, were scarce and, instead, he opted for butterflies which were numerous and extremely beautiful. On these rambles in and around Rio, MacGillivray invited Huxley to accompany him. They were a formidable pair, acutely examining the natural world draped in front of them. This was the first time they had been together in this way and were becoming closer by the moment. Their natural history excursions, Huxley divulged, were often pretence. 'Our investigations', he commented ironically, 'always took in the end a chemical turn, to wit, the examination of the nature and properties of a complex liquid called Sherry Cobbler.'[112] Sharing a meal of 9 pigeons and 18 sherry cobblers on one occasion must have done wonders for their bonding.

Country walks, however pleasant, were not really challenging enough for MacGillivray's skills as a collector. What he wanted to do more than anything else in Rio, as much for his as for Huxley's benefit, was to dredge. Dredging was serious business. It was the method then current to collect marine animals from the sea floor. It was a two-person job, one handling the boat and the other managing the ropes and lifting the dredge from the bottom. The kind of device typically in use at this time consisted of a bag made of coarse netting secured from a rectangular iron frame. This, sometimes referred to as the naturalists' dredge, was dragged along the sea floor scooping up whatever animals there were.[113] The contents of the dredge were examined by means of sieves, preferably three of them.[114] The dredge gave access to an otherwise hidden world and one that the collector could not visit. Scooped up in the dredge were molluscs that were alive (in contrast to the empty shells strewn over the beach) and most of which had never been seen before.[115]

The champion of dredging, indeed a name synonymous with the practice, was none other than Edward Forbes, the friend and colleague of both MacGillivray and Huxley, responsible, more than anyone else, for the establishment of the Dredging Committee of the British Association for the Advancement of Science in 1839.[116] Thanks to the members of this committee, including, besides Forbes, people such as Charles Lyell, the leading geologist of the time, John Edward Gray of the British Museum and John Goodsir, intimate friend of Forbes and soon to be Curator of the Royal College of Surgeons in Edinburgh, marine zoology, through dredging, became an extremely popular and highly respected scientific pursuit.[117] So keen was Forbes about dredging that he wrote a short four-stanza poem in celebration of this noble scientific act. A flavour of it can be had from the following selection:[118]

> Hurrah for the dredge, with its iron edge,
> And its mystical triangle,
> And its hided net with meshes set,
> Odd fishes to entangle!
> The ship may rove through the waves above
> Mid scenes exciting wonder;
> But braver sights the dredge delights
> As it roveth the waters under!
>
> CHORUS
> *Then a dredging we will go, wise boys!*
> *Then a dredging we will go!*
>
> Down in the deep, where the mermen sleep,
> Our gallant dredge is sinking
> Each finny shape in a precious scrape
> Will find itself in a twinkling!

They may twirl and twist, and writhe as they wist,
And break themselves into Sections;
But up they all, at the dredge's call,
Must come to fill collections!

MacGillivray had managed to bring a dredge with him but 'no sieves had been furnished by the dockyard', and although he combed the length and breadth of Rua do Ouvidor, the fashionable shopping avenue in Rio, he was unsuccessful in finding any.[119] At first the pair used their hands as sieves, a tedious job, but MacGillivray, true to character and experience, improvised for a better result.[120] Made of a 'wire-gauze meat cover and a curious machine for washing rice', the makeshift sieve worked perfectly.

The two naturalists dredged in Botafogo Bay, in the shelter of the Sugar Loaf, to a depth of up to 30 feet, having commandeered a boat, which was rowed by four African slaves. The contents revealed about 45 species of molluscs and starfish and polyps, 'some of which were new to science'.[121] But the greatest prize of all was a collection of *Amphioxus*, seemingly different in respects from the British species, an example of which Forbes had given to Huxley in London before the *Rattlesnake* sailed. MacGillivray was content with a superficial description and preserved a few in spirits, asking Forbes to pass them on to Professor John Goodsir in Edinburgh who had previously written a paper on the animal.[122] Huxley was, of course, not content with a superficial description. He now had a 'chance to expend his talents and ingenuity' and he did just that.[123] MacGillivray ensured that Forbes knew what Huxley was up to. In a letter to him, MacGillivray told Forbes that 'Huxley, with his usual industry and success, has been working away at it, and pointed out to me distinct hepatic and generative systems, neither of which Goodsir mentions.'[124] Huxley, for his part, thought that MacGillivray was an excellent ornithologist and collector, in spite of the rumours he had heard from his own brother-in-law concerning MacGillivray's abilities.[125]

Capturing and analysing *Amphioxus* was, for MacGillivray and Huxley, the achievement of the Rio visit. It was hard work. 'Dredging with the sun blazing away with tropical fierceness', he wrote to his friend James Harley in Leicester, 'was no joke.'[126] MacGillivray pointed to his 'apprenticeship' in Port Essington, northern Australia, on his last voyage in HMS *Fly* as the reason why he did not succumb to the 'undermining influences of a hot climate'.[127] Huxley, who also escaped the effects of the heat, remarked, with a logic contrary to MacGillivray's, that he attributed his good fortune to the little time he had spent in such conditions.[128]

Whatever the reason for their good fortune, others were not so lucky. Robert Gale was laid up for most of the Rio sojourn, apart from the very first days when he accompanied Stanley catching butterflies.[129] Thomson was ill as well and spent many days on board the ship. MacGillivray reckoned that there were many who were laid up and Thomson confirmed this.[130]

All the beauty of Rio notwithstanding, the conditions of the city appalled the *Rattlesnake*'s visitors. Many commented on what they considered to be the city's dreadful smell but what disgusted them most was the existence and practice of slavery. Brazil had been receiving slaves from Africa since the early part of the sixteenth century and as many as 5 million slaves had made the transatlantic journey over the previous three centuries.[131] Of the city's population, roughly 38 per cent were slaves.[132] Rio presented the greatest concentration of slaves in the Americas and perhaps in all of history. It was impossible, therefore, not to encounter enslaved people. African slaves performed all the manual jobs in the city and served as beasts of burden, but there was hardly an occupation in which slaves were not found.[133] Most of the *Rattlesnake*'s observers – Stanley was certainly an exception – had never witnessed slavery before as it had been abolished in all British possessions in 1833. Words could not capture their indignation at the scene.[134] John Thomson expressed his horror to his wife Mary. 'How miserable are its inhabitants here. In every quarter may be witnessed the most revolting results of slave dealing.'[135] MacGillivray didn't hold back either: 'It nearly sickened me', he told James Harley, 'to see [slaves] with iron collars and masks fastened behind by padlocks.'[136] Harsh words of disapproval and disgust were levelled at the Brazilians.

The repairs to the *Rattlesnake* took about a week and were completed on 1 February. MacGillivray, Huxley and Reverend King had a final fling at the shops along the Rua do Ouvidor, looking to buy presents and more shells for their collections. Stanley, meanwhile, had decided they were ready to sail and, in the evening, ordered that they would get underway at daylight for the Cape of Good Hope. At that announcement, 'nothing could equal the discontent and dissatisfaction of nearly everyone on board.'[137] Whether it had simply slipped his mind or whether he was so jittery about staying he didn't care, Stanley was about to commit an unpardonable act. He was about to leave Rio without the men's clothes that had been sent for washing. Possibly someone slipped off the *Rattlesnake* in a panic to tell the laundry to hurry up, because just as they were about to sail, a boat came alongside the *Rattlesnake* with the clothes. But they were not in a finished state – some were still dirty and others were still wet – nor were they all there: precious items were left behind.[138] Stanley was the most unpopular man on the ship.

Pieter Both Mountain at sunset, Mauritius

CHAPTER IV

The Bullion Run:
Cape Colony and Mauritius, 1847

There was something frantic about the rush to leave Rio. Not only were clothes overlooked, but so was one of the jolly boats (a small boat used as a utility tender) that had been sent on shore to collect fresh beef. The weather, by contrast, was languid. The morning was too calm for the ship to sail out of the harbour under its own power and, instead, it had to be towed out by the boats of the naval squadron. The result of all this was that the *Rattlesnake* had to hang around the entrance of Rio harbour while waiting for the beef delivery and a breeze. Stanley may have been tapping his fingers on the railings but MacGillivray and King, the one using a dredge and the other a towing net, grabbed the opportunity of calm water to sample the abundant marine life. MacGillivray struck lucky and hauled in a rare *Terebratula rosea*, a brachiopod also known familiarly as a lamp shell, from a depth of almost 80 feet, while King simply revelled in his catch – a dozen specimens of a species of *Hyalea* (a pteropod, another type of mollusc, sometimes called a sea butterfly), a *Medusa* and an 'infinitude of crustaceans'.[1]

Once the beef was on board, Stanley ordered the ship to search for a shoal that had been reported 24 miles to the west of the Sugar Loaf and which Beaufort had specifically asked Stanley to investigate.[2] Despite traversing the neighbourhood of this supposed rock for almost two days,

Pieter Both Mountain at sunset, Mauritius

taking soundings, watching for discolouration and breaking of the water, and other signs of the presence of an object, nothing lurking below the surface was found. Stanley knew, however, that Beaufort's singular anxiety was the lack of proof of existence of dangers and simply to report that no rock was found would give him no peace whatsoever. For what it was worth, Stanley remarked that he did see bands of discoloured water as he left the vicinity and these were caused by 'immense masses of a small species of Salpe most of which were dead. Such an appearance may have given rise to the report of a shoal existing in that neighbourhood.'[3] Stanley's report must have convinced Beaufort for he never mentioned the shoal again, though in other similar circumstances no amount of placation could comfort his anxieties.

With that task completed, Stanley now swung the ship away from the Brazilian coast in a southerly direction and, with a fair breeze on the port side, began making good progress across the South Atlantic. On Thursday, 4 March 1847, two days out of Rio, the ship was hove to (stopping the vessel by trimming and shortening the sails and pushing the helm downwind) for the first of many occasions to take temperature readings at two depths. Lieutenant Dayman was responsible for this operation. A line, with a thermometer attached at the bottom and at the halfway point, was lowered to a depth of nearly 2,000 feet (though the exact depth on each occasion varied around this number). The thermometers, invented by James Six in the late eighteenth century, were called self-registering because once they registered the minimum (or maximum) temperatures, a metal index that produced the readings became fixed until it was physically moved.[4] Thus, while the line was hauled in, the temperature readings on the two thermometers remained as they were when the line was at its fullest extent and, therefore, the readings at the two depths were accurate, assuming, of course, that the temperature decreased with depth.[5]

It had been standard practice for deep-sea temperatures to be taken on all Royal Navy surveying voyages since the time of Cook, and, indeed, on most surveying voyages sent by other nations. Some 35 surveying voyages had already collected deep-sea temperature recordings by the time the *Rattlesnake* set sail, and a not inconsiderable amount of data had been accumulating.[6] All of the data, including Dayman's, was being collected to feed the growing bank of observations in meteorology and geography;

and in the interest of drawing more accurate isothermal lines of the oceans, and making more sense about how currents, in particular, worked and how water in the open seas, in general, circulated.[7] While Dayman's observations shared much with those taken earlier, such as the depths chosen and the instruments used, in one respect his were unique. Never before had a surveying ship taken systematic observations of deep-sea temperatures in a west-to-east direction, both across the south Atlantic and, as it was planned, across the Indian Ocean.[8] On that Thursday afternoon, Dayman recorded that in the latitude of 26 degrees south (approximately 2 degrees to the south of Rio), the air temperature was 66 degrees Fahrenheit, the surface water temperature was 77 degrees Fahrenheit and the temperatures at 231 and 351 fathoms (1,400 and 2,100 feet approximately) were 60 degrees and 51 degrees Fahrenheit, respectively. It was a job well done.

The pleasure of a successful piece of science at sea was short-lived, however. While the ship was stationary, Stanley noticed a sealed bottle bobbing on the surface at the stern of the ship. Without delay he ordered one of the jolly boats to be lowered to retrieve the bottle. It was usual practice to send messages of impending sinking and shipwrecks from castaways by this method and Stanley lost no time in pulling out the paper from the inside of the bottle. When it was unrolled it read: 'H.M.S. *Rattlesnake* Feb 4 1847 we are sinking.' Once he got over the shock, Stanley, enraged by the sheer idiocy of the act, sought out the perpetrators. This did not take long. Their punishment was a flogging with 3 dozen lashes each, scheduled for the next morning at 11 a.m. The legal limit was one dozen lashes. It was a savage punishment.[9] It was the first hitch in what was until then a fairly smooth run. 'We are in danger enough without making a ridicule and a lie of it,' remarked Reverend King.[10] And that was the end of the matter.

This part of the voyage, sailing across the south Atlantic without landfall, not to mention without the sight of land, may have lacked the excitement and anticipation of the voyage to Rio, but from the point of view of science, it was a rich experience. Stanley was feeling good about the ship as a vessel of scientific enquiry. He praised his scientific men in letters to both Beaufort and Robert Were Fox, the inventor of the magnetic dipping needle, on the first occasion he had. Huxley, MacGillivray, King and Thomson, the band of *Rattlesnake* naturalists as they were coming to be, were embarked on their own lines of enquiry, sometimes on their own and sometimes in company. However solitary the pursuit, no one was ever alone on the ship. King, to take one example, while poring over the contents of his towing net and minutely observing the shape and structure of the *Medusa*'s tentacles, sought Huxley's opinion on the larger questions of specie variation and commonality.

Each day that the ship was hove to gave opportunities to do some science. MacGillivray was especially busy. During the ship's trek across the South Atlantic, MacGillivray watched the skies carefully for signs of bird life, and day after day he recorded his ornithological observations, providing a highly detailed account of the number of each species seen and the latitude and longitude of the event.[11] Whenever it was calm enough to be safe, MacGillivray lowered a boat to shoot specimens of the more interesting birds he had seen. These he skinned, preserved in spirit and boxed ready for shipment back to England, whenever it was possible. MacGillivray was highly adept at skinning birds, a very skilled and delicate operation, though many of the difficulties in preserving specimens had been ironed out by this time.[12] The problem of preserving the living colours of the birds, however, remained and in several cases MacGillivray had to provide a literal description to enhance the appearance of the specimen. In the box of specimens he prepared on this part of the voyage were several species of storm petrels, shearwaters and albatrosses.[13]

Out here in the South Atlantic, MacGillivray had to rely a lot on his own knowledge of bird species, attempting, on the one hand, to provide valuable information as to the geographical distribution of these exceedingly long-distance birds and, on the other hand, supplying just the right kind and number of specimens. We do not know which reference material he had with him, but we know that most if not all his knowledge was in his head. MacGillivray's guide to the birds of the South Atlantic skies, for example, was a paper by the inveterate bird expert, John Gould, which MacGillivray had clearly committed to memory. No one could but be impressed by the sheer perseverance of the South Atlantic birds in following the ship over thousands of miles. MacGillivray noted that a young albatross remained with the ship for 24 days during which time it had travelled over 2,500 miles; storm petrels, too, accompanied the ship for days and days on end.[14]

Firing at birds from a small boat in the open sea was not without its dangers. MacGillivray did not take chances and Stanley was cautious in letting parties out onto the sea, yet even though conditions had to be very favourable before such excursions took place, there was always a possibility of something going wrong. And indeed on 16 February, Shrove Tuesday, the jolly boat carrying a party of eight, including MacGillivray, Thomson and Captain Denison, was swamped as soon as it touched the water, and all three were thrown into the cold sea, desperately holding on to the craft that rolled over each time they tried to grasp it.[15] An attempt to lower another boat failed as it got entangled in ropes, and what should have been a minor incident began to look like a horrible accident. Thomson was clearly in the greatest danger as he was entwined in the ropes, one of which was around his legs and another wound itself about his head. By dint of violent thrashing and diving below the surface, he managed finally to free himself and swim to a life buoy some distance away. The others extricated themselves as best they could, and were able to swim away from the rolling craft and wait to be hauled from the sea. Many of the sailors in the boat were injured to a minor degree and one of the boys had his cheek cut through by the boat's hook. Apart from the injuries and the shock of being so close to a major disaster, and a royal soaking in the cold waters of the South Atlantic, the only permanent damage was the loss of the guns. MacGillivray's loss was perhaps the greatest since his had been bought for him by John Gould at one of London's finest gunsmiths. Later, in recounting the incident to Edward Forbes, MacGillivray could see its lighter side. 'My best gun,' he wrote, 'having none of the natatorial properties of the birds it was intended to destroy, went down to the realms of Father Neptune, where I can only hope it may prove useful in developing the "young idea" of the juvenile members of his family.'[16] Undaunted by this experience, MacGillivray continued his forays in the jolly boat and from the ship, shooting and skinning the interesting specimens that happened to come this way – 'a strange tern came aboard and was added to the collection.'[17]

The albatrosses, petrels and shearwaters also impressed Huxley. The albatrosses, in particular, reminded him of Coleridge's poem about the ancient mariner and the bad luck killing these 'easy and beautiful' birds brought; but this did not seem to worry anyone else as 'whole broadsides of small shot and rifle bullets are fired at them daily' from the *Rattlesnake* and the jolly boat.[18] Huxley remained focused on his invertebrates, having, like King, an almost insatiable passion for them. While many days yielded little in the tow net, there was always something for him to analyse. But the sea was rich and he didn't have to wait too long before the harvest satisfied his requirements. On 24 and 25 February, with the island of Tristan da Cunha behind them and the shores of Africa ahead of them, the sea swarmed with pelagic creatures which excited everyone in the boats towing nets. While they gloated over the *Salpae* with 'their large bladdery organs and the beauty and delicacy of their shells', Huxley's sharp eyes picked out specimens of *Physalia*, his pet invertebrate, the foundations of his excursions into the microscopic world and of his scientific career. '. . . I carried out the examination further. There is a month's work in it; but notwithstanding its complexity I hope in time to get a very complete account of its structure and even the forms through which its different organs pass.' But there was much more to it than this, for he was thinking about the unity of seemingly disparate species:

> At the same time I think I can already perceive that it will form a great link in the chain of Acalephae, at once explaining and explicable by many as yet isolated structures in the Diphydes, the Physophoridae, and even the Medusae. I feel half ashamed to put such a thought on paper but I have a feeling that by the more or less perfect manner in which this is worked out, my capacities for these undertakings must stand or fall, as at any rate it is a somewhat difficult investigation and not a bad test.[19]

Ideas were one thing but Huxley realized he needed to go through a great deal of biological material to establish his case and he also understood, only too well, the vagaries of nature and of the ship travelling through it:

> If Dame Nature will send me one every day I shall do, but if she sends me a thousand one day and none for a week afterwards I shall be done. This is the misfortune and difficulty in working at these animals in hot climates. You get a day's work out of your specimen and on the morrow he is rotten and have nothing to go on with although there were millions to be had the day before.'[20]

But Huxley was not the only one with the towing net and, thanks to King, the supply of *Physalia*, which certainly seemed to have dried up in the few days following the bountiful harvest, was back in full swing. On 1 March, King presented the budding scientist with some more young *Physalia*, 'which delighted Huxley beyond measure'.[21]

The passage across the South Atlantic was long. The weather was generally fine but the winds were frequently in an unfavourable direction. Despite the frustration at the ship being a bit off course, from time to time, it was not a tedious voyage. The science was good and even those, such as Midshipman Arthur Packe, who found his first shell attached to a jellyfish he had caught, now joined in the collection business.[22] Stanley clearly enjoyed himself watching his enthusiastic naturalists at work and provided all the help he could give. King benefited directly from Stanley's generosity when he ordered a new towing net to be made after several of the midshipmen, in a prank that went wrong because of their inexperience in handling the delicate device, lost the Reverend's towing net in a swell.[23] MacGillivray praised his captain's interest in his own work and looked forward to the same support when they got to Australia.

At daylight on 8 March 1847, three months after leaving Plymouth, and after 34 days at sea, the ship was within sight of Table Mountain and, with a freshening breeze behind them, the *Rattlesnake* turned in front of the Cape of Good Hope into False Bay, heading for an anchorage in Simon's Bay with Simon's Town at its head.

No one had a good word to say about Simon's Bay and the town. Thomson thought the whole place 'wretched' and the countryside around 'most wretched and barren'.[24] It was MacGillivray's third visit, having been here on HMS *Fly* in 1842 on its outward journey and 1845 on its return. He too disliked the place and hoped he'd never return.[25] Huxley was more expressive but the message was the same. 'I care not how long it may be before I see Simon's Bay again – so far as the town goes – for a more dull, dreary platitude never met my eyes. Nothing but officials, stall-keepers and Malays to be seen, and very few of these.'[26]

There was no doubting that this was a real comedown. Simon's Town was a small place with a population of less than 2,500.[27] In 1814, it became the sole naval station at the Cape after the closure of the base at Table Bay.

The town's main business was therefore servicing the docks and the ships that anchored there. It was a far cry from the bustling, exciting and exotic world of Funchal and Rio de Janeiro. Cape Town, the only delight in the area and about the same size as Funchal, was over 20 miles away and a hard day's ride, not a place to visit easily.

The Admiralty's original instructions to Stanley, drawn up at the end of November 1846, were to stop at Simon's Town for the sole purpose of being supplied with fresh water on the understanding that the *Rattlesnake* would be making a non-stop run to the Cape from Madeira. On the very same day, Beaufort, who never missed an opportunity to have his charts improved upon, instructed Stanley to remain there long enough to complete a survey of the bay begun, but not completed, by Captain William Owen and Lieutenant Alexander Vidal in 1822.[28] A few days later, the Lords Commissioners added an instruction to the effect that the ship should convey £50,000 in gold to the Cape Colony. As far as the Lords Commissioners were concerned that was all there was to do in Simon's Town. Their Lordships were probably ignorant of Beaufort's addendum, but equally, it seems, was he of their instruction to convey the money, a problem that almost undermined the relationship between Stanley and Beaufort.

The *Rattlesnake* anchored in Simon's Bay in the company of several other Royal Navy vessels, including HMS *Eurydice*, on its way to Mauritius, and HMS *President*, which had brought Admiral James Dacres to Simon's Town to take up his post as commander-in-chief of the station in succession to Rear Admiral Sir Josceline Percy.[29] Very soon after anchoring, the cases containing the gold were removed to a warship, HMS *Nimrod*, which set sail almost immediately for Algoa Bay in the eastern frontier of the Colony where the Seventh Frontier War was in full flow.

Since its settlement in the seventeenth century, the Cape Colony had expanded eastwards from Cape Town until, by the 1770s, it had reached the Bushmans River to the east of Algoa Bay. Dutch settlers began to occupy an area further to the east, the Zuurveld, between the Bushmans and Fish rivers during the 1770s, and as they did so, they encroached on traditional Xhosa lands and local tribal politics resulting in two major clashes, one in 1779–81 and the other in 1793. These, the first of the so-called Frontier Wars (also known as the Kaffir Wars), were followed by subsequent clashes through the nineteenth century as settlers continued to dispossess Xhosa lands, moving continuously to the east.[30] By 1834, the Cape frontier stood at the Keiskamma River and settler eyes were looking even further eastwards seeking to expand their territory to the Kei River and, in consequence, launching the sixth of the Frontier Wars.[31] This war proved unsuccessful for the British settlers. Xhosa autonomy was restored to the territory, which was temporarily renamed as Queen Adelaide Province. But the restlessness of colonial expansion could not be contained and another, the Seventh Frontier War (also known as the War of the Axe), erupted in March 1846 ignited by an incident involving a stolen axe and the freeing of a Xhosa prisoner.[32]

The Colonial Government in London, previously relying on the 'civilising' methods of missionaries to bring the Xhosa into the imperial net, now supported settler claims with military power. By June 1846, Sir Peregrine Maitland, Governor of the Cape Colony, had amassed a military force of 14,000 men, until then the largest British army in South Africa, against a Xhosa force estimated at between 8,000 and 15,000 men.[33] All of this cost a great deal of money. In London, the Treasury estimated that the seventh war against the Xhosa would cost £520,000 in the year to 31 March 1847 and a further £580,000 to 31 March 1848.[34] Stanley realized that his conveyance of £50,000 was 'a mere drop in the ocean' and he thought that war could last a long time, thanks partly to what we would now call the Xhosa's guerrilla tactics.[35] Aside from delivering his precious cargo (which was a nice little earner for him, thanks to his 1 per cent commission) and the effect the war had on raising the price of goods in the Colony, Stanley saw it of no great importance to him or to his mission. Besides which, as he wrote to Robert Were Fox, 'long before any change can take place we shall be far away from this.'[36]

Stanley's stay in Simon's Bay was, as it turned out, not as short as he had hoped. The survey, for one, was not simply a matter of improving on Owen's charts. As Stanley explained it to Beaufort, he found the charts he had been supplied with so needing of corrections that he decided to resurvey the bay. Under normal circumstances this would have taken a week to do, but the weather turned against him and his surveyors with heavy gales on most days so that the survey effectively took a month to complete.[37]

Despite the weather, time was not wasted, according to Stanley.

Niggling problems with the ship, more a matter of inconvenience than one of making the ship unseaworthy, were dealt with thanks to the help of the craftsmen from HMS *President*. And the work done in Rio to stop the leak was checked to ensure the problem would not recur. Between this and the surveying work, Stanley had little time left during the day. His evenings, too, were hectic, as he spent most of the time, aside from a couple of excursions to Cape Town, at Admiralty House, the official residence of Admiral Dacres.[38] Here he dined in company with the Admiral's two daughters whom the Reverend King thought 'lovely and elegant'.[39]

Whether others on the *Rattlesnake* saw the spell in Simon's Town as fruitful as Stanley is not entirely clear. Huxley, we can be sure, was glad of the break from the rigours and inconveniences of the sea, for he was on a mission to write up the results of his researches into *Physalia*. He told his mother as much in a letter he wrote to her from Rio, and now, in Simon's Town, and with nothing else to do, he finished his paper.[40] Huxley thought first of sending it to Edward Forbes and leaving it up to him to decide whether and where to have it published, but Stanley intervened and suggested that it should go to his father, who was also President of the Linnean Society.[41] Huxley was uncomfortable with this kind of patronage and thought that if it were to be published in the Society's prestigious *Transactions* it would not be because of its intrinsic value, but because the Bishop would promote it as a scientific product of his son's voyage. At any rate, whatever he felt about it, the paper was sent to the Linnean Society from Simon's Town in late March or early April and probably arrived in London sometime in August. Huxley only got word early in January of the following year, 1848, that the paper had arrived safe and sound, but it took another eleven months before the first part of it was read to the meeting of the Society by Bishop Stanley on 21 November 1848 and the second part a fortnight later; or, to put it another way, nineteen months had elapsed between the paper's despatch and its reading.[42] What Huxley would have made of the fact that the paper, 'On the Anatomy and Physiology of *Physalia* and its Place in the System of Animals', was attributed to a 'William Huxley, Esquire, Surgeon R.N.' we can only imagine. Here in Simon's Town, however, his mind was full of ideas about what he would do next, the 'grand project floating through my head', as he called it. Wherever the ship went for the next few years, he knew that the whirlwind of scientific investigations ahead of him would keep him busy. Without that, he told himself, he would 'go clean daft, shortly, in my present environment . . .'[43]

Huxley appeared to keep himself to himself, immersed in his own thoughts and work, ironically dismissing the stay in Simon's Bay – 'We remained in Simon's Bay until the 9th of this month [April] for the sole purpose so far as I can judge of being present at a ball given by the Admiral on the 7th', he wrote.[44] Cape Town didn't appeal to him. He preferred instead 'zoological foraging among the holes in the rocks on the seashore'.[45] That, as MacGillivray knew from previous experience, was a limited exercise since the area around Simon's Bay was, as he put it, 'extremely sterile and uninteresting'. His only enjoyable experience during the stay was a climb up Table Mountain where, at 2,000 feet, he found a freshwater crab in a rivulet.[46]

Others occupied themselves with whatever natural history pursuits they could find. John Thomson continued to look for shells to add to his growing collection and Arthur Packe teamed up with James Wilcox, Bishop Stanley's private collector, to shoot and stuff birds.[47] When the fun in that ran out, some of the officers turned to playing quoits on a barren plot of land. It was only Reverend King who, somehow, managed to keep his natural history interests bubbling, finding delight in the smallest specimen, even though surroundings bore 'a most singularly barren and desolate appearance, the want of large trees and the quantities of rock visible everywhere making it appear very wretched'.[48] No wonder that when Stanley reported to Beaufort how pleased he was with his scientific men and their natural history interests, he singled out King who 'seems to have more enthusiasm in the pursuit than any of them and is at work from morning to night'.[49]

There is a sense of marking time whatever Stanley's brave words. Cape Town did not seem to attract the degree of interest aroused by Funchal and Rio, though everyone who went there agreed it was beautiful, especially when seen from high up Table Mountain. The road to Cape Town from Simon's Town was more tedious than interesting, apart from the inn called Farmer Peck's whose reputation, partly owing to the pub sign, was well established in naval circles.[50] Even the ball given by Admiral Dacres was a bit of a disappointment because of the absence of sufficient female company. Midshipman Packe stayed away because he forgot to pack his kid gloves but he was actually glad he had missed the ball. It might have been a mere coincidence, but the *Rattlesnake*'s first desertion happened in Simon's Town several days before the ship left.[51] As MacGillivray remarked: 'We were all heartily tired of Simon's Town long before quitting it . . . The weather was too boisterous to be agreeable, the zoology of the place was already well-known, and we were tired of hearing the interminable 'Caffre War' dinned into our ears from morning to night as an excuse for high prices and various kinds of extortion worthy even of Sydney in its halcyon days of convictism.'[52]

On Saturday morning 10 April 1847, after almost a month's stay, the *Rattlesnake* weighed anchor for Mauritius, but no sooner were they free and on their way out of the bay than someone noticed that some washerwomen from the shore were still on the ship. According to Midshipman Packe, Stanley went into a 'most tremendous rage' and ordered them to be put on a rock in the bay. Fortunately for the women, a light vessel was closer than the rock, and that was where they found themselves unceremoniously dumped.[53]

Despite the heavy weather while the ship was at anchor, False Bay was relatively sheltered from the winds racing about the Cape. Once the *Rattlesnake* cleared the bay, however, the full force of the weather bore down on them. Seasickness, which had become a distant memory, returned with a vengeance, and even Reverend King who boasted of his sea legs on the run to Madeira, succumbed. The ship rolled violently through a heavy and 'confused sea'.

The passage to Mauritius took 24 days and everyone seemed to agree that it was a long and rough passage. Not that every day was difficult but the bad weather appeared relentless. In truth, the ship was going through a notoriously rough area and doing so during the tail end of the cyclone season, which generally lasted in these southern latitudes from December to April. Calm days were few and far between and only gave a short respite from the constant buffeting of the large waves. But science could not wait for ideal conditions. Three days out of port and the ship was hove to for differential temperature readings, continuing the work Lieutenant Dayman had begun on the passage across the South Atlantic. This continued irregularly over the next few weeks, whenever the sea moderated.[54] After 10 days at sea, Stanley began to look for a shoal, called 'Slot van Capelle', more than 1,000 miles to the south of the island of Madagascar. This proved difficult, as the seas were too rough to allow a careful examination. During a moment of calm, Stanley tried to take a sounding and found no bottom at 1,800 feet but the differential temperature readings were larger than expected, indicating, perhaps, the presence of shoal water.[55] But he didn't stay around to take a closer look, an omission that enraged Beaufort when he heard of it.[56]

Even in heavy seas, Stanley continued his scientific pursuits, measuring, for example, the height and length of waves, a topic of great interest to hydrography and meteorology alike.[57] One day he measured a wave 22 feet in height and over 300 feet in length.[58] Stanley's method for measuring the length and speed of waves was probably his own, whereas that for the height of waves was suggested to him by Mary Somerville, the foremost woman of science in nineteenth-century Britain: the methods became standard practice thereafter.[59] Calm days, when the ship was hove to, saw King, as usual, at his towing net collecting specimens of pelagic animals, which he shared with Huxley. The net yielded little of great value during the early part of the passage but then, towards the end of April, during a relatively calm day, King captured 'the thing of things', as he called it.[60] It was a species of *Physophora*, a jellyfish. King handed it over to Huxley for examination but King, himself, recognized that *Physophora* connected the two families of *Diphyidae* and *Physalia*, an idea that had been forming in Huxley's mind certainly since February. This specimen of *Physophora* became the basis of another paper that Huxley began to think of as a building block in his larger argument about the unity of the whole class of jellyfish he had been examining on the voyage.[61]

As the *Rattlesnake* approached Mauritius, it became much warmer and oceanic birds started to give way to tropical varieties. The ship narrowly missed a cyclone, which was brewing near the Madagascan coast, but the winds from it pushed the ship to the eastward. Even though land was sighted late in the day on Sunday 2 May 1847, the *Rattlesnake* had been blown sufficiently to the east that it had to round the island from the south which, while lengthening the time at sea, nevertheless made a very pleasing approach, rewarding those on board with a brilliant scene of a sunset in a clear sky set against the tall white sails of the vessel, the deep blue ocean below and the verdant land beyond. Two days later, after following the entire eastern coastline of the island, the *Rattlesnake* rounded Cap Malheureux at the tip, and began to beat for the harbour of Port Louis, on the northwestern side of Mauritius.

Stanley had been ordered by their Lords Commissioners of the Admiralty to proceed to Mauritius with £15,000 of silver coin. Survey ships, especially those bound for Australia, New Zealand and the South Seas, did not, as a rule, stop at Mauritius. The preferred route from the Cape of Good Hope was straight across the southern Indian Ocean, benefiting from the strong westerlies in these latitudes and stopping, perhaps, at the tiny uninhabited island of St Paul's Rock, before heading straight towards Cape Leeuwin, Australia's south-western tip. Mauritius, a volcanic island fringed almost entirely by coral, and lying about 500 miles to the east of Madagascar and on the same latitude as Rio de Janeiro, was off the beaten track, too far to the north. The last survey ship to visit the island was HMS *Beagle* with Charles Darwin on board in 1836, on its return voyage to England from Australia.

Back in London, and unbeknownst to Stanley, Beaufort's patience with his star surveyor was wearing thin. He had only heard once from Stanley since he departed Plymouth in December of the previous year, but it appeared that the letter, which took three months to reach Beaufort from Rio de Janeiro, had been mislaid or lost in the office.[62] He was particularly annoyed that Stanley had not reported the leak in the gunroom to the Secretary of the Admiralty in the official manner that was laid down in naval regulations covering matters relating to the seaworthiness of naval vessels.[63] In frustration, Beaufort turned to Stanley's father, asking him to tell his son to get in touch. On top of all this, Beaufort, as it turned out, did not know about Stanley's plans to go to Mauritius. Neither their Lordships nor Stanley told him before setting out on the voyage. Beaufort only learned about the side trip to Mauritius, but not the reason for it, in July from a letter Stanley sent to him from Simon's Town dated 9 April. Beaufort couldn't understand why Stanley was going to Mauritius and he told Stanley of his displeasure in an instant reply to him.[64] It was, however, only for the record, because, by the time he learned of his master's anger, Stanley had already been in Sydney for seven months. It was not until May of the following year, 1848, that Beaufort heard from Stanley why he had detoured to Mauritius.[65] Scarcely a state secret, their Lordships, nevertheless, never uttered a word to Beaufort about Stanley's conveying of bullion to Mauritius.

By the time the *Rattlesnake* arrived on the island, Mauritius had been a British colony for just over thirty years. Under British rule, Mauritius had become the empire's single largest producer of cane sugar and production grew in most years reaching a maximum in the harvest in the year before the *Rattlesnake*'s arrival.[66] While the sugar economy was booming, at least from the point of view of output, the island's monetary situation was in serious trouble. In particular, the amount of coin in circulation had been recently and severely depleted, leading to fears of crises in payments for goods and services, bank failures and merchant financial distress.[67] In addition, there were reports of specie hoarding and exporting. While Stanley's delivery of £15,000 in British coins was not going to solve the whole problem, it certainly helped in an emergency.

Mauritius had been ceded to Britain from France at the end of the Napoleonic wars in 1815. Thirty years of British rule had only begun to make a dent in what until then had been a successful French settlement, though they were not the first inhabitants of the island. The Dutch had preceded the French in the seventeenth century but had abandoned the place after a largely unsuccessful colonization. French culture and institutions had flourished in the eighteenth century and these were left largely intact under British rule.

While the Frenchness of Mauritius struck everyone – Reverend King called it 'very unEnglishlike' – it was the exceedingly cosmopolitan nature of the society, especially visible in Port Louis, which drew most comment. Because of its proximity to Madagascar and other islands of the Indian Ocean, its long history of slavery and the recent immigration of contract labourers from India and China following the abolition of slavery in 1834, Port Louis had become a vibrant mixture of cultures from the entire rim of the Indian Ocean. With a population approaching 50,000, or roughly one-third of the island's inhabitants, Port Louis was a bustling port with ships of every size and kind from throughout the Indian Ocean and beyond packed into its narrow harbour.[68] The town was no less crowded than the port, a veritable cauldron of humanity, packed into a site described by MacGillivray as resembling an amphitheatre, the backdrop of which was formed by the amazingly shaped mountains Pieter Both and Le Pouce.[69] MacGillivray couldn't remember seeing a more beautiful place nor, apart from Singapore, a more cosmopolitan one. 'The stranger landing in Port Louis,' MacGillivray remarked,

> stares at a Coolie from Madras with a breach cloth and soldier's jacket, or a stately, bearded Moor, striking a bargain with a Parsee merchant; a Chinaman, with two bundles slung on a bamboo, hurries past, jostling a group of young Creole exquisites smoking their cheroots at a corner, and talking about last night's Norma . . . his eye next catches a couple of sailors reeling out of a grogshop, to the amusement of a group of laughing negresses in white muslin dresses of the latest Parisian fashion, contrasting strongly with a modestly attired Cingalese woman, and an Indian ayah with her young charge.[70]

To match the variety of people on the streets, the Port Louis market was awash with produce, especially fish, MacGillivray counting up to 100 different species. The most beautiful he saw were *Labridae* 'of the most gorgeous colours'.[71] He was tempted to purchase a few but declined on the grounds, he felt, that even the most skilful taxidermists would not be able to retain the colours. He had to make do, instead, with purchasing a specimen of *Arca antiquata*, a variety of land shell, to add to his growing mollusc collection; and a look at a collection of 400 coloured drawings intended to illustrate a work on the island's ichthyology being prepared by Eliséc Lićnard, a leading Mauritian naturalist.[72]

Huxley was in raptures about this 'complete paradise', as he confided to his mother. Madeira and Rio weren't a patch on Port Louis. 'If I had nothing better to do, I should pick up some pretty French eve (and there are plenty) and turn Adam.'[73] The *Rattlesnake* had dropped its anchor in Port Louis harbour on Huxley's twenty-second birthday. He reflected on his time and his place:

> Twenty-two years ago I entered this world a pulpy mass of capabilities, as yet unknown and save by motherly affection uncared for. And had it not been better altogether had I been crushed and trodden out at once? Nourishing me up, was as though one should pick up a stray egg, unconscious whether dove's or

serpent's, and carefully incubate it. And here I am what a score of years in the world have made me – such a bundle of glorious and inglorious contradictions as men call a man . . . In the region of the intellect alone can I find free and innocent play for such faculties as I possess. And it is well for me that my way of life allows me to get rid of the 'malady of thought' in a course of action so suitable to my tastes, as that laid open to me by this voyage.[74]

Not everyone found Port Louis's foreignness enchanting. Arthur Packe certainly didn't. Though he found the island as beautiful as everyone else, he was appalled by Port Louis, 'a horrid nasty dirty town hardly anybody but French & niggers both of which I detest'.[75] Yet even Packe, so thoroughly xenophobic, had to pay homage to the doomed lovers, Paul and Virginia, by visiting their 'tombs' in the nearby village of Pamplemousses.

Pamplemousses, so-called because of the substantial planting of shaddock trees bearing the pomelo fruit by the Dutch in the seventeenth century, is located about eight miles to the northeast of Port Louis. At the time of the *Rattlesnake*'s visit, Pamplemousses was a small village consisting of several houses, a gleaming white church, a few coffee plantations and a Botanical Garden. Established in 1735, the gardens at Pamplemousses became under the guidance of Pierre Poivre, the colony's first royal intendant, one of the most important botanical gardens in the world during the eighteenth century and the major institution for the selection, acclimatization and propagation of tropical produce for the whole French empire.[76] But now, after decades of mismanagement and neglect, it was in a serious state of dilapidation.[77] For the budding naturalist with a taste for history, however, a visit to the gardens was obligatory, but even though MacGillivray went there and saw some magnificent trees, he felt it was a waste of time and concluded, 'that the title *botanical* had misled me'.[78]

The botanical gardens were not really much of a tourist site. The same cannot be said of the tombs of Paul and Virginia. These, also in a state of neglect, were, surprisingly perhaps, located in an overgrown, unkempt garden, at the back of a house owned at the time by an English mechanic whose expertise lay in repairing steam machinery used in sugar milling. Not the most sophisticated introduction to a story about two lovers that had been taking Europe by storm since it was first published in 1788.

To most outsiders, Mauritius was famous as the setting for the tale of the tragic lovers, Paul and Virginia, the fictitious creations of Jacques-Henri Bernardin de Saint-Pierre in the late eighteenth century. Outsiders learned of the island from Bernardin de Saint-Pierre and, to those tourists who set foot on the island, a visit to the natural sites mentioned by St Pierre and the tombs of Paul and Virginia was a must. (The dodo, another non-existing feature of the island, would not become part of the popular imagination until later in the century.) Indeed, it was such an important pilgrimage that 'Who that ever visits the shores of the Isle de France does not at once post to Pamplemousses, to satisfy the curiosity excited by that beautifully-written romance? If the voyager returns to Europe without this local knowledge, he is supposed to have seen nothing and is branded as little less than a savage.'[79]

The novel told the tragic tale of the idyllic infancy, childhood and adolescence of Paul and Virginia, two children of French mothers who found themselves, because of dire circumstances, living alone with their babies in close proximity in Mauritius in an uninhabited mountain valley to the east of Port Louis. The two mothers tilled their own soil and spun cotton, and as they grew older they found their lives becoming increasingly inseparable. Paul and Virginia grew up together like brother and sister, but by the time of their adolescence, began to be aware of more sexual feelings for each other. Virginia's mother, Madame de la Tour, had come from a wealthy family but had been disowned by them because she had married her husband in secret and without a dowry. Her aunt in Paris, one of those who had failed to support her in the past, now growing old and without a family of her own, offered to make her niece her heir on condition that she returned to Paris. Madame de la Tour was now too old and frail herself for this voyage but, on the advice of the Governor of Mauritius, who had been pressed by the aunt to act on her behalf, consented to let Virginia take her place and receive the inheritance. While recognizing the love that was growing between the Paul and Virginia and the pain that separation might cause them, Madame de la Tour, nevertheless, decided to separate the pair for the sake of their future happiness together. Virginia embarked for France secretly one morning against the protests of Paul and in spite of her desire to remain with him.

Virginia's stay in Paris proved to be a disaster. Her great-aunt tried with all her power to force Virginia to renounce her mother and the La Tour name and to become a countess bearing the name of her great-aunt's family. Virginia stoutly refused and her great-aunt reacted by disinheriting her and sending her back to Mauritius. Paul learned that the *Saint-Géran*, the ship bearing Virginia back to the island, had been sighted on the western side of the island and was lying at anchor in a very rough sea between the Ile d'Ambre and the coast. Paul, together with a number of settlers from the nearby district, rushed to the scene but no sooner had they arrived than a hurricane descended on the channel where the ship was anchored. Huge waves crashed over the vessel, each one tearing more out of her structure, forcing the ship further onto the reefs that protected the shore from the surging seas beyond and finally onto the rocks themselves. Paul threw himself into the water in a desperate attempt to save Virginia but each time he tried he was driven back by the power of the waves. He was now barely able to leave the shore, so dangerous the sea and so low his energy. The ship was fast breaking up and then, amidst the panic of the crew jumping into the foaming seas to save themselves, Virginia, her arms stretched towards Paul, appeared on the ship's stern gallery. One of the sailors, discarding the clothes that hampered his survival, begged her to follow his example by disrobing and following him into the surf but Virginia refused to undress in front of him and stayed on the ship. Within a moment, a huge wave came crashing down on the vessel, and Virginia was drowned.

Several days later, amidst a pile of debris that had washed up on the opposite, eastern shore of the island, in a place called the Baie du Tombeau, the body of Virginia was found. One of her clenched hands still held a tiny box, inside of which was Paul's portrait. She was buried near the church at Pamplemousses. Paul never recovered from the tragedy. He remained in a listless and shocked state. Nothing could console him. He died two months after Virginia and his body was laid to rest next to hers.

The novel was an instant success, the sales were spectacular and Jacques-Henri Bernardin de Saint-Pierre became a wealthy man. It went through countless printings in France and was translated into every major European language within a short time.[80] In English, the novel appeared in more than 20 separate translations and publications, several running to many editions and the most famous translation, which first appeared in 1795, was in its fifteenth edition when the *Rattlesnake* was in port.[81] But that was not all. The story of Paul and Virginia inspired songs, poems, plays, ballets and other musical entertainments, and scenes from their lives appeared on wallpaper, china and articles of clothing. It was impossible to avoid them, everyone knew the story.

There were many reasons for the book's success but one was that the story was set in a real place with real place-names. Armed with the book, or the memory of it, it would be possible to embark on a Paul and Virginia tour of Mauritius. Bernardin de Saint-Pierre lived in Mauritius between 1768 and 1770. So convincing was the story – a ship called the *Saint-Géran* did break up near the Ile d'Ambre, for example – that many who read the book must have been unsure whether it was fact or fiction. Huxley, for example, concluded that it was fiction based on fact and was convinced that 'Paul and Virginia were at one time flesh and blood, and that their veritable dust was buried at Pamplemousses in a spot considered as one of the lions of the place, and visited as classic ground'.[82]

Someone, at some time – it is not known who or when – decided that it would be a good idea to put up tombs to Paul and Virginia. They were certainly available for viewing in the mid-1820s. Lady Alfred Bartram, an early English visitor to the island, provided her readers with an interesting and less than romantic story about these tombs. She says that the tombs, which were made of red stone (and not Parisian marble), were built 'to gratify the eager desire which the English have always evinced to behold such interesting mementos'.[83] She further relates that the owner of the property, in whose garden the tombs are found, began his little enterprise with only one tomb, that dedicated to the memory of Virginia, but when visitors kept asking him to see Paul's tomb, he decided to erect one to his memory as well; hence the tombs of the tragic lovers. Lady Bartram also mentions that it was common practice for visitors to scribble over the tombs with their names, sentimental remarks and 'verses and pathetic ejaculations'.[84] Later visitors to the tombs also noted the visitors' additions to the site ('testimony to John Bull's invariable and inveterate habit of leaving a memorial of himself wherever he goes', as one writer put it), and remarked that it was also often the custom to break off a fragment of the tombs as a souvenir or take flowers or parts of plants that grew around as mementoes, and to pay sixpence for the privilege.[85]

A visit to the tombs required a whole day, the walk to and from

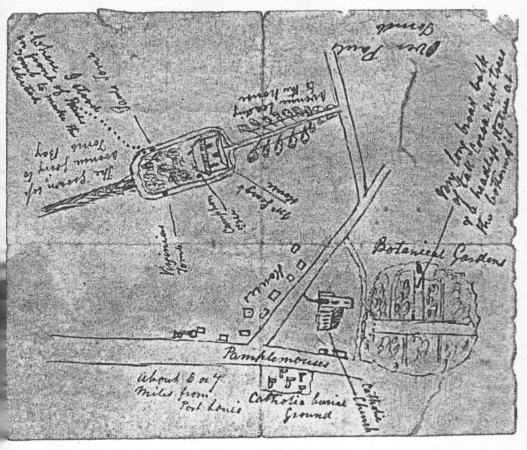

Robert Gale's map of Pamplemousses

Pamplemousses taking between four and six hours. Because of the heat, it was advisable to make the outward journey in the morning and the return in the early evening. From all accounts, the road from Port Louis to Pamplemousses was a delight in itself, bordered by tamarind and coconut trees and busy with people making their way to market. Finding the tombs, however, was not so easy. There were no signposts but locals knew where to direct the visitors. Huxley described the tombs as being 'in a utter wilderness, but still very beautiful; round it runs a grassy path, and in the middle of the path on each side towards the further extremity of the garden is a funeral urn supported on a pedestal'.[86] Each of the visitors from the *Rattlesnake* acted exactly in the manner described so acutely by

93

Lady Bartram and other writers. Midshipman Packe, who appeared to be very eager to visit the tombs – Lady Bartram thought that young naval men, in their first flush of romance, were particularly prey to this pilgrimage – visited the tombs as soon as he could the day after the *Rattlesnake* anchored in Port Louis' harbour together with George Heath, a fellow naval cadet, and dutifully broke off a piece of Virginia's tomb. Reverend King, who deplored this kind of practice, adding that the wretched state of the tombs was caused by chipping away at them, brought away two rose buds to be placed in albums, one of which belonged to his secret love, a Miss L. Robert Gale sketched the tombs and the surrounding scenery as his memento, and also paused long enough to collect eggs from a green lizard and a twig from a nearby camphor tree. Huxley also sketched the scene and chastised those 'relic-hunters, who are as shameless here as elsewhere', though he, too, managed to pluck a couple of roses for his workspace.[87] MacGillivray, with far less emotion and not wishing to give in to sentimentality, remarked that he only visited the tombs to pick some flowers for his sister's album, and took the opportunity of collecting land shells in an adjoining coffee plantation.[88]

For naval people, especially hydrographic surveyors, Mauritius had an additional but altogether different meaning. It was here that Matthew Flinders, after being the first European to circumnavigate Australia and after sailing for thousands of miles west from Australia on his way to England in a badly leaking ship, arrived in December 1803, and was promptly arrested and held captive by the French governor, General De Caen, for nearly seven years.[89] Stanley must have been acutely aware of the irony of himself, as a naval captain and surveyor instructed to complete the survey of the Torres Strait which Flinders began, visiting the same island more than forty years later but under totally different political and social circumstances. The significance of the historic moment was enhanced by the fact that before he departed on the *Rattlesnake*, Stanley had met Robert Brown, now aged seventy-four, the botanist who accompanied Flinders on his outward voyage to Australia.[90]

On Mauritius, as in other places the ship visited, the officers did most of the sightseeing alone or in small groups. Reverend King's trip to Paul and Virginia's tombs was in company with John Thomson, William Brown, the master, and Josiah Messum, one of the ship's clerks. Huxley appears to have gone on his own, as did MacGillivray. Later during their time on Mauritius, King joined Frederick Brady and Huxley for an excursion of about 35 miles return to the interior of the island to see the Tamarin Falls. The party trudged out of Port Louis, but after 15 miles of hot walking, they failed to make the correct turn in the road (perhaps their French was not up to scratch or the directions were wrong) and ended up walking away from rather than to the falls. Fortunately they stumbled into an auberge with good, cheap wine and where the owner informed them that they should forget Tamarin and instead head for Chamarel Falls, an altogether more beautiful place, but even further away. Both Huxley and Brady were fading fast while King kept up his relentless search for shells. The next day, with the help of a young boy sent as a guide by Baron d'Unienville, on whose property the falls were located and whose father, it turned out, had entertained Flinders, they came upon their goal and it was decided it was well worth the effort. 'I shall never forget them,' Huxley wrote:

> the scene struck me as the most extraordinary I had ever beheld. The Rivière du Cap rises among the high land towards the centre of the island, thence winds its way as a quiet rivulet, till it reaches Chamerelle [sic], when it precip-itates itself over the edge of a huge chasm, sheer down for 350 feet; at the bot-tom it breaks into rainbows of foam against the rocks and then becomes a dark still pool of many acres in extent, ultimately finding its way to the sea by a fis-sure in one side of the rocky basin . . . The sides of the pit are all covered with large trees and the whole aspect of the place conveys to the mind at once the strongest ideas of wildness and of richness.[91]

When, after a three day round trip, they returned to Port Louis and recounted their tales, so impressed were some of the others with the descriptions that a party consisting of five officers plus King (who could-n't resist another look) struck out immediately, partly by sea and partly on foot, to see the Chamarel Falls for themselves.[92] Other, shorter excursions were made to the two mountains behind Port Louis: Pieter Both, named after the first Governor-General of the Dutch East Indies, which looks as though a boulder has been placed on its summit; and Le Pouce, shaped like a thumb (hence the name). King was especially eager to see the tree ferns at the summit of Le Pouce which had impressed MacGillivray. King also intended to collect land shells which MacGillivray had praised as being interesting and plentiful. Attempts to collect marine shells had proved disappointing since little of interest had come up with the dredge.[93]

Apart from one grand ball thrown by Sir William Gomm, the Governor of Mauritius, at Le Réduit, his country residence a few miles to the south of Port Louis, there was little in the way of social entertainment for most of the officers. Mauritius lacked the kind of social networks that had been built up in Madeira among the expatriate and tourist community. Captain Stanley was an exception to the rule. According to his fifteen-year-old aide-de-camp, Philip Ruffle Sharpe, Stanley was constantly being entertained by the governor, by planters and by the island's surveyor-general, Colonel John Augustus Lloyd. He toured the island together with Captain Talavera Vernon Anson of HMS *Eurydice* (the *Eurydice* was in Simon's Town with the *Rattlesnake* and had sailed to Port Louis to be on station there), accompanied by their aide-de-camps, and saw all the sights his officers did and more.[94] The two captains must have had a lot to reminisce about as Anson had been both on the *Rattlesnake* and the *Britomart* (Stanley's ship between 1837 and 1843) in the 1820s. Robert Gale, by contrast, was mostly confined to the ship to cater for the social arrangements Stanley foisted on him with little or no warning. Regular visits to the market and one excursion to the tombs of Paul and Virginia were his only entertainment. Stanley was away from the ship for more time than he was on it while they were in Mauritius, which hardly endeared him to those who weren't so well entertained.

Still, for MacGillivray, it was a visit packed with excitement and fully justified his comment to Edward Forbes that 'it is one of the few places which I have ever left with regret', the opposite of what he had said about Simon's Town.[95] MacGillivray made the most of his time in Mauritius, even though his collections were not enormous. With the first available ship he sent home his first case of specimens – molluscs and birds – and his first letter to Edward Forbes, the beginning of an important and detailed correspondence, some of which was subsequently published.[96]

It was now time to leave Port Louis for Australia and the survey, but just before Stanley was ready to pack up, he received a request from Governor Gomm to convey £8,000 in small British coins to Hobart and Sydney to bolster the size of the military chest in those colonies.[97] Without much hesitation, he agreed to do it and told Beaufort on 17 May 1847, the day of the sailing, of his revised plans stating that he was conveying £4,000 to Hobart but omitting to mention the other £4,000 for Sydney.[98] As Stanley's brother Charlie was now in Hobart (they hadn't seen each other since September of the previous year), and as he would stand to earn a reasonable commission for the assignment, Midshipman Packe was more than justified in calling the order 'a capital excuse for the Captain'.

PART THREE

CHAPTER V

Australia Felix:
Hobart, Sydney and Twofold Bay, 1847

About a week before the *Rattlesnake* anchored in the harbour at Port
Louis, Reverend Robert King began a letter to Sir William Hooker at the
Royal Botanic Gardens. King had corresponded with Hooker before and,
during his time in England, had become acquainted with him, his wife and
their son Joseph Dalton. Though not a botanist himself, King, so energet-
ically enthralled by the natural world around him, was as intrigued by the
wonders of the floral world as he was with the faunal world. While at the
Cape of Good Hope, King had come across a small parasitical plant that
'may possibly have escaped observation'.[1] It was small enough to be
inserted into the letter and he accompanied it with a description of what
he could discover by observing its parts through a microscope and a drawing of the whole plant just in case the specimen did not arrive in a state
good enough to give an idea of its form.

 This letter, written at sea and sent to London from Mauritius, offered
King an excellent excuse for telling Hooker, who was not yet in contact
with anyone on the ship, about the voyage to date. The passage, which was
now into its fifth month, was given short shrift and summed up in a single
phrase, 'tolerably pleasant as regards winds and weather'. It was not the
voyage *per se* that occupied his thoughts. 'In other respects', he wrote, 'it
has been not tolerably but exceedingly pleasant'. He was thinking here of

Sydney Heads

his companions, those who did science and those who enabled it. Of Stanley he could hardly withhold his enthusiasm. 'I like (him) more and more every day. Indeed it could not be otherwise as he has been extremely kind and attentive.' The towing net could only have become King's constant companion because of Stanley's support for his activities. 'Although no naturalist himself, Captain S appears to make it his pleasure to assist the study of these interesting sciences in every possible way.' Huxley, the man with whom King probably spent most time on the ship when it came to scientific pursuits, was next. 'The assistant surgeon . . . is very zealous in the good work . . . of zoology and has made several very accurate and interesting dissections of the various animals we have obtained in the towing net.' MacGillivray, whom King observed shooting birds from the jolly boat and dredging the sea bottom on the occasions he could, came in for high praise: 'indefatigable in his exertions', 'well up to his work', were the phrases used; and to underpin the compliments, King told Hooker that MacGillivray already had a large case stuffed with birds, shells and crustaceans, ready for shipment home. Zoology was, therefore, extremely well served on the voyage but the same could not be said of botany. While King acknowledged that John Thomson had an interest in botany, he did not collect. It was a pity, King concluded, that a voyage which was taking in the almost unknown islands off the coast of New Guinea had no one on board to take advantage of this exceedingly rare event.

As the *Rattlesnake* pulled out of Port Louis on its passage to Hobart, Reverend King, with a fortnight's rich and diverse experiences behind him, could well reflect on the accuracy of his impressions of the ship's scientific men and look forward with eagerness to sampling the marine life that he hoped lay ahead of him. Stanley took the *Rattlesnake* down the western coast of Mauritius, leaving the island at Cape Brabant, and then planned to set the ship on a southeasterly course towards the French islands of Amsterdam and St Paul and eventually to the latitude of 40 degrees south where, with the help of brisk westerlies, he would steer the ship across the Indian Ocean for the southwestern corner of Australia.

Not yet out to sea on the day after leaving Port Louis, Stanley picked up where he had left off on the passage between Simon's Town and Mauritius, and hove the ship to at 1 p.m. as usual for the first of many readings of sea temperatures. King's towing net was already out but the antici-pation of an interesting haul was sadly disappointed. And this pattern, the heaving to and the uninteresting net, continued for the next week as the ship pushed southwards into cooler and more changeable conditions.[2]

On Tuesday 25 May, the pattern broke and disappointment turned to excitement. King and Huxley struck it lucky. In the net was something for both of them. King took away a tiny mollusc with an intriguing shell while Huxley seized on 'some fine *Diphyes*'. This pleased Huxley no end because, as King was aware, this creature had been on his mind since mid-April when he first began working on them while the *Rattlesnake* was making its way to Mauritius.[3] If his experience with the Portuguese man-of-war was anything to go by, *Diphyes* would become the subject of the next scientific paper.

While King and Huxley were reaping the rewards of a bountiful sea, life on board ship was about to take a turn for the worse. On Tuesday 1 June, two weeks out of Port Louis and on the 35th parallel just to the north of Amsterdam Island, and with a long way to go before reaching land, the order was given to extinguish the galley cooking fires after noon.[4] Dinner-time, normally set for 5 p.m., was abruptly altered to noon. The large cop-per vessels which were used to heat liquids and boil stews and the like and which had their own individual fires, however, continued to be kept hot, so that tea could be served later in the day. Candles were rationed to the crew and everyone was on short allowances. 'No hot grog,' Huxley quipped.[5] It turned out that Frederick Brady, the purser, had made a grave error and had ordered less than half the amount of coal that was needed. One can imagine the roasting Brady received from Stanley.

On the deck, as the ship plunged southwards, temperatures were steadily falling, making the crisis in the galley even worse. Lieutenant Dayman, whose job it was to take daily weather observations, recorded the daytime temperature of 60 degrees Fahrenheit on the day that the fires were first put out (it was nearer 80 degrees when they pulled out of Port Louis) and then watched as it fell into the mid-40s on subsequent days.[6] The men, Gale remarked, 'were wrapping up and putting on shoes'.[7]

As the days wore on, as the temperature fell even further, and as they entered the roaring forties, the weather became much worse and the ship began to roll very badly. They 'were scarcely able to keep things on the table'.[8] Despite this, however, and in the odd moments of relative calm, sea temperatures were recorded, King threw and hauled in his towing net, Huxley got some more specimens of *Diphyes* and MacGillivray even managed to take a shot at a small albatross which quickly joined the rest of his collection.[9] But all the rolling was worthwhile for the *Rattlesnake* was making extremely quick time on its way to Australia. On 10 June 1847, they were on the same longitude as Cape Leeuwin in western Australia, though 350 miles to the south of it in the Southern Ocean.[10] For the next two days they were buffeted by squally weather, with a mixture of rain and hail. It was still very cold. Then on Sunday 13 June 1847, the weather became abruptly worse with constant hail storms. It was probably the worst day since they had left the English coast. And then, just as suddenly and wholly unexpectedly, by 9 p.m. the wind died away. The next day, 14 June 1847, it was quite different. 'The wind quite gone from us and left us in a dead calm, sea gone down to a long subsiding swell . . . sails hanging straight.'[11] The *Rattlesnake* was as good as stopped in its tracks.

No time to waste. Stanley had tried twice, and unsuccessfully at that, to take a deep-sea sounding. His first attempt was on 12 January 1847, when the ship, in almost identical conditions, was just north of the equator in the Atlantic; the second time was on 19 April in the Indian Ocean. On the first occasion, Stanley had run out 2,400 fathoms of line (14,400 feet) without touching bottom. This time, still in the Southern Ocean, and with perfect conditions, Stanley prepared to attempt again to find the sea floor. Even though he had been unsuccessful previously, he now set his sights even higher, attempting *to prove* he reached bottom by bringing up a sample of the sea floor.

The problems in retrieving bits of the bottom of the deep sea were substantial. Sending the weighted line down hundreds, even thousands of fathoms, was difficult enough, given the fact that the line had to be strong enough to carry the weight and withstand the pressure on it from sudden erratic movements of the ship. Bringing up sediment from substantial depth posed its own problems, not least of which was the time that it took to wind in the line and the risks this would carry to the precious cargo. According to MacGillivray, what Stanley planned to do had never been attempted before.[12] Stanley must have turned over the issues of deep-sea sounding and bottom sampling in his mind ever since he failed to reach the sea floor in the Atlantic. Now he had come up with, in MacGillivray's words, 'an ingenious apparatus', which would, hopefully, do the trick. Stanley had contrived a device consisting of a line to which was attached a weight of 256 pounds (8x32 pounds of shot) in an iron frame. When the weight reached the bottom, it would detach itself from the line, leaving the frame and a lightly weighted arm covered with tallow. The arm would make contact with the sea floor and whatever was present would attach itself and the line would be hauled back into the ship.[13]

With only the light swell of the sea causing the ship to roll gently, the line was thrown overboard in the late morning at a point in latitude 40 degrees south and on the same longitude as King George Sound in present-day Western Australia. The line went out very smoothly and quickly. Fifteen minutes passed before 1,000 fathoms of line ran out and about the same for the next 1,000 fathoms. After 2,500 fathoms, and still no bottom, the line began to uncoil more slowly. And then, at a length of 3,500 fathoms, the line suddenly became weightless and it was clear that the whole device, weight, frame and arm, had somehow dropped off the end. Two hours had passed and there was nothing to show for it. In reporting the results of the experiment to Beaufort, Stanley could not hide his frustration. He blamed the line for giving way.[14]

Meanwhile, MacGillivray, who until now had had very little to do as far as natural history collecting was concerned, apart from the small albatross and the careful observations he had been making on the occurrence of sea birds which he had begun in early February, took out the jolly boat and his guns and made up for lost time.[15] In the time he was out, he brought down six birds, all specimens of sea petrels. Once skinned, they joined the rest of his collection of albatrosses, puffins, shearwaters and petrels.[16] King was also not idle and found an interesting and unusual type of barnacle in his trove.[17]

The quiet weather did not last. The next day, the sea got up again and the ship began to roll as heavily as before. Though not as piercingly cold as it had been, the weather was foul, wet and windy. The stock of coal continued to fall and reached such a low level that even the galley fires were not lit. 'O for some coals', wrote Robert Gale in his diary on 21 June 1847. The fires in the copper vessels were now extinguished at 4 p.m. and that was the end of the day as far as cooking and heating drinks was concerned.[18] Yet, despite these privations, science continued much as before, especially for King and Huxley. On 18 June, King got his net over and 'obtained several curios, the principal (ones) were some very fine and perfect specimens of Physophora which I surrendered to the tender mercies of Huxley and a small Cephalopod which I kept myself'.[19] Huxley must have been grateful and excited by King's harvest but, as he himself confessed, just a few days later, he was seized by a fit of melancholy; it was not for the first time. From past experience he had learned that the best way of dealing with this kind of mood was to concentrate his mind on work. 'It took me an hour and a half walking on the poop however to accomplish the cure.'[20] He began to sketch out a structure for a paper on *Diphyes*, which, he told himself, he would send to London when the ship arrived in Sydney. He did not lack for material, thanks to King's incredible energy. Their relationship was, at this point, closer than it had been and now, and perhaps for the first time, they began to talk together about the great issues in taxonomy that Huxley found so challenging and on which he decided to make his mark.[21]

It became clear, as they were heading along the southern coast of Australia, that the fuel crisis would soon be over for the wind, instead of buffeting the ship from all directions, suddenly turned to come directly from the west, thus pushing the *Rattlesnake* quickly towards its destination. They were now covering as much as 200 nautical miles in a day.[22] On 23 June, they sighted the South West Cape of Tasmania, the first bit of land in more than five weeks of what MacGillivray dubbed 'a monotonous voyage'.[23] During the night, the ship rounded the South East Cape and early in the morning of 24 June 1847, began to make its way up Storm Bay towards an anchorage at Hobart Town, as it was then called. Around noon, a boat bearing a pilot named William Lawrence (or Laurence) presented the ship with a bunch of flowers and reported the good news that the *Windermere*, which had left England at the beginning of October in the previous year bearing Charlie and Eliza Stanley, and the Governor, Sir William Denison and his family, had arrived safely at the end of January.[24] They were as good as home.

They were not yet, however, at their anchorage. There was no wind to get them up the Derwent River towards Hobart Town. Lawrence, the pilot, 'a man well to do in the world' and blessed with a 'jolly face and [an] English tongue' invited a number of officers (King and MacGillivray volunteered to go as well) to accompany him to his property on nearby Bruny Island, and furnished them (at a price?) with fresh provisions (bread, milk and beef steak) and fuel.[25] Lawrence returned to the *Rattlesnake* with the officers and stayed with the ship to pilot it into Hobart Town when conditions improved.[26] That evening, and for the first time in a month, hot food was served at the appointed hour.

During the night, a light breeze began to blow and slowly the *Rattlesnake* approached its anchorage in Sullivan Cove. Signals were sent to the shore that Captain Charles Denison, the aide-de-camp to and brother of the governor, Sir William Denison, and who had joined the *Rattlesnake* in Plymouth, was on the ship and well. Sir William must have been delighted at the news because he had departed England before his brother and had not expected the *Rattlesnake* to come into Hobart.[27] The news of the *Rattlesnake*'s arrival must have swept through Hobart Town rapidly and to the undoubted great surprise of Charlie Stanley. Not long after that, a government whaleboat appeared bearing him to the *Rattlesnake*. He and Stanley were 'delighted to see each other'.[28] Despite the excitement, the *Rattlesnake*'s progress towards its anchorage was painfully and frustratingly slow. Several of the officers together with Reverend King, MacGillivray and Huxley couldn't wait for the ship to anchor and commandeered the jolly boat to take them to shore. Finally, 'soon after the ship got a start of wind' at 4 p.m. on 25 June 1847, the anchor was dropped into the sediment below the water's surface and the *Rattlesnake* could truly be said to be in Hobart Town.

MacGillivray and Huxley continued a tradition they had initiated in Rio de Janeiro back in January, and retired to the Ship Inn and 'before a huge fire . . . there stuck, imbibing considerable quantities of toddy, until ten or eleven o'clock'. 'We were all invited to a ball that evening', Huxley wrote, 'but it had no charms for me compared with that splendid wood fire.'[29] And so, certainly for the captain and his steward, the ship's officers, the midshipmen, the medical men, and the naturalist, and no less so for the crew, began what Huxley so perceptively referred to as 'a round of lesser and greater debaucheries'.[30] The number of social engagements was overwhelming and the invitations flooded in from throughout the colony of Van Diemen's Land (as Tasmania was still called at the time) and not just Hobart Town, sent to groups of men and individuals alike. For the most part the invitations came from total strangers.

Though it had only been a British settlement for just over forty years, Hobart had grown into a substantial town, and with a population of 20,000 people, it was the third largest city in Australia.[31] Its reputation as the 'gaol of England' certainly lingered, but the early days of single male convict gangs receded in the face of a growing middle-class and family-centred society styling itself as the 'Athens of the Southern Ocean'.[32] Institutions such as libraries, art galleries, the Church, private schools and hospitals, and learned societies abounded for the upbringing of the Hobart Town gentleman.[33] The hinterland of Hobart Town, sparsely populated by both Europeans and indigenous Aborigines, presented opportunities for seeing magnificent nature and extensive cultivation. Between the town and the countryside, there was something for everyone to do.

Stanley spent most of his time in the company of his brother and sister-in-law who had now been in the colony for just more than half a year. Though their early days had been difficult – they did not have their own place and relationships between Charlie and the Governor were fraught – during the last three months life was improving for them.[34] When not with his family, Stanley visited Government House and travelled through Van Diemen's Land to the northern town of Launceston. He sketched nearly everywhere he went. His only scientific activity was to visit the Rossbank Observatory, partly to check the readings of his portable magnetical observatory and partly to re-establish old acquaintances and reminisce.[35] The Observatory, situated on the banks of the Derwent River opposite Hobart Town and under the shadow of Mount Direction, had been started in 1840, one of a string of British colonial observatories.[36] Captain James Clark Ross, during his expedition to the Antarctic with the ships *Erebus* and *Terror*, had brought the personnel and instruments necessary to establish the observatory to the colony. One of the lieutenants on the *Terror*, Joseph Henry Kay, became the Director of the Observatory, and a lieutenant on the *Erebus*, Joseph Dayman, accompanied him as his assistant.[37] Stanley briefly worked at the Observatory in 1840 when he was in command of HMS *Britomart* and it was there that he first met Dayman who was in special charge of magnetical and meteorological readings.

Because the *Rattlesnake* was such an attraction, a magnet for social attentions, invitations came from far and wide. Thomson, along with Lieutenant Simpson and MacGillivray, accepted three invitations from strangers 'to go into the interior and witness life in the bush'.[38] They began their journey by hopping on the Launceston coach which they left at a point some 70 miles to the north of Hobart Town, where they were greeted by 'two small gigs and a riding horse sent us by the gentleman from whom we had received the invitation'. After a short stay there – this man, whose name remains unrecorded, farmed 50,000 acres with as many sheep – the three men from the *Rattlesnake* were shunted to their second and then their third host. After such a whirlwind social experience, the trio returned to Hobart Town wondering, perhaps, what it was all about. MacGillivray had no opportunity for collecting and did none. He vowed, however, should he get the chance to return on this voyage, that he would head off to the west, into the wilderness, which, he was certain, would yield new riches.[39]

Reverend King spent the first few days in Hobart Town strolling around town, visiting the Observatory in the company of Dayman and Thomson, climbing Mount Wellington – it was snow-covered at this time of year – with Brady and Huxley, and, as always, conchologizing wherever and whenever he got the opportunity.[40] King, too, received invitations to visit, one from a man named George Foster, whom he had never met but who, nevertheless, invited him to spend a few days at his house in Brighton, to the north of Hobart Town. From there, other invitations flowed so that at the end King had spent at least four days away from the *Rattlesnake* meeting people whom he had never before met.

Because of Thomson's absence in the interior, Huxley was largely confined to the ship but he had another treat in store. Stanley had introduced him to Dr Edward Bedford, in charge of Hobart Town's first private hospital, St Mary's.[41] It was most likely through Bedford that Huxley was invited to attend an operation in which ether anaesthetic was used. Ether had first been used as an anaesthetic at the Massachusetts General Hospital in Boston in October 1846 and was not used in London until December in the same year, by which time the *Rattlesnake* was at sea.[42] This was, therefore, Huxley's first view of this revolutionary treatment and one of the first operations of its kind in Hobart Town, the very first having taken place on 17 June 1847, a week before the arrival of the *Rattlesnake*.[43] We do not know when Huxley saw this operation but on 7 July, the very last day the ship was in Hobart Town, both King and Thomson also witnessed an ether operation.[44]

Robert Gale also had his share of social engagements, and like others, thanks to invitations from people he knew and from perfect strangers. He, in common with others, found Hobart Town a home away from home. 'The town is so thoroughly English', he wrote in his diary, 'every time I land I feel more at home.'[45] No matter how much he enjoyed and yearned for shore life, Gale's social movements had to be carefully timed so as not to clash with Stanley's own social calendar. Besides entertaining his brother and sister-in-law, Stanley invited parties of men and women onto the ship on various occasions, providing them with lunch and dinner and thrilling them with what Gale called 'his playthings', namely the ship's instruments and, especially, his magic lantern. Stanley was, obviously, very proud of his 'set of dissolving views' but Gale turned his nose up at the whole affair. He thought it ridiculous. 'Captain like a child,' he wrote dismissively on the occasion of a show for six; and, several days later, when sixteen people came on board, Gale recorded his observations and feelings. 'Cabin made dark for magic lantern, but regular mess of it as with every other thing – O dear! How silly and childish – the party dispersed highly gratified at the wonders we did show them.'[46]

Gale's relationship with Stanley had been anything but easy, yet one can only assume that, in some sense, it worked since they had now been together for some time. Gale clearly did not like Stanley showing off, as he might have put it, but this was nothing compared to how he felt about what Gale considered to be Stanley's hypocrisy. Gale was a devout believer. Whenever divine service was, for some reason, not performed on the ship on a Sunday, Gale conducted it in private for himself. He went to Church whenever he had the opportunity on the voyage. On the first Sunday that the *Rattlesnake* was in Hobart Town, Stanley performed divine service, as usual on the ship, but this time in the presence of his brother and sister-in-law. Gale obviously did not like how it was done: 'a very hurried affair,' he recorded. But what really offended him was Stanley's behaviour. 'The same lips', he wrote, 'which curses and swears and demoncers [*sic*] is appointed to minister to us of those things which concern our souls. Captain in a very disagreeable temper for day or two.'[47]

The *Rattlesnake* remained in Hobart Town for exactly a fortnight. The visit was not part of the original plan but a side trip to deliver bullion from Mauritius. The real destination, Sydney, lay ahead, just a few days' sailing away. Stanley was very pleased to be with his family and to see them well established in their new home, and not wanting to part from them so soon, he invited them to sail with him and the *Rattlesnake* to Sydney. On 8 July 1847, having discharged Captain Charles Denison and the bullion, the *Rattlesnake*, now carrying Charlie and Eliza Stanley and another passenger, John Gregson, a friend of Lieutenant Dayman's, weighed anchor and began to run down the Derwent River towards the open sea. Van Diemen's Land pleased everyone. Even Midshipman Packe, who in the past had shown himself not to be the party type, found it impossible to turn down every invitation. True to form, however, he only attended functions at the home of those hosts he knew.[48]

Getting down the Derwent proved to be much faster than getting up. Having weighed anchor at 10 a.m., they were in Storm Bay by the afternoon and were rounding the western side of Tasman Peninsula, the site of the notorious penal colony of Port Arthur, in the evening. Through the night, the wind dropped and their progress was slowed. Early morning on 9 July found the *Rattlesnake* off Cape Pillar and heading in a northeasterly direction.

The day was a quiet one and King lost no time in getting his towing net over the side. When he brought it on board, he immediately noticed that he had 'obtained a splendid and perfect specimen of *Diphyes*. This was the first time we had succeeded in obtaining the two parts united.'[49] It went straight to Huxley for further examination.

For the next several days, the weather turned cold and wet but the wind was favourable. They were progressing steadily up the coast of New South Wales until, on Tuesday 13 July, just off Cape Dromedary, about 150 miles to the south of Sydney, they found themselves in a dead calm. Frustrating for some, perhaps, but for King it was another, and perhaps the last, chance to net some pelagic specimens. This time he struck gold. Amidst the various crustaceans, which invariably littered the net, there were 'three magnificent specimens of a new species of Diphyes. They were quite perfect and between an inch and a half and two inches in length. Of course Huxley has been hard at work at them ever since their capture.'[50] Huxley could now complete the paper he had constructed in his mind in the Indian Ocean a few days before landing in Hobart Town.[51] MacGillivray, too, lost no time; he commandeered the jolly boat and went out shooting. He had noticed that one species of albatross, *Thalassidroma nereis*, was constantly around the ship, so he shot two of them.[52]

Rougher weather returned the next day and continued for several more. Progress was slow again because of the difficult conditions, with high seas and heavy squalls. In the evening of Thursday 15 July they were within sight of Sydney Heads but decided to wait for first light before entering Port Jackson. 'A most beautiful morning,' reported Gale as the *Rattlesnake* slipped through the opening into the wide expanse of the bay.[53] At 11 a.m., on Friday 16 July 1847, they took up their anchorage in Farm Cove, Sydney. Waiting for them was Captain Phillip Parker King who immediately boarded the ship and greeted the son he had not seen for more than five years. Next off was the £4000 from Mauritius, safely dispatched to the commissariat.

Though the ship had stopped in a number of exotic and thrilling locations along the way, the lives of those on board had been, in a very important sense, on hold for more than seven months. Letters, the lifeline of communication between the *Rattlesnake* and family, loved ones and friends at home in Britain and elsewhere, had all been sent to Sydney to await the ship's arrival. Immediately after the anchor was dropped, a boat was sent to the Post Office in Sydney to collect the ship's mail. Everyone waited eagerly for news. Even so, since letters from London to Sydney took three months, there would be no news more recent than March at the latest.

Huxley described how he felt as he anticipated letters from home: '. . . as we neared Sydney and its homes and shipping became gradually more defined my heart throbbed with joy at the near prospect of obtaining news from home after seven long months of absence.'[54] But the pain of not receiving a letter could be drastic, even overwhelming, and there were several on the *Rattlesnake* who were thus affected. Huxley, for one, was beside himself with anger when he learned that there was nothing for him. 'I damned everything and everybody but sat down to dinner in a temper that Satan need not have envied, vowing I would never write home again.'[55] Robert Gale, also without any letters to his name, was less enraged than Huxley, perhaps, but certainly no less disappointed. 'Really quite greivous', he wrote in his diary, 'as I looked forward with confident hope.'[56] Midshipman Packe reacted with a mixture of envy and disenchantment. Everyone else, he observed, was getting four or five letters and he, both surprised and disappointed, received nothing, 'not even a newspaper'.[57] These moods of despair quickly evaporated, however, when more letters arrived. When the *John Fleming* arrived in Sydney at the end of July bearing April's post, everyone got excited again and, this time, Gale was blessed with a letter from his love – which he read and reread – and Huxley heard from his family. 'My disappointment was purely accidental,' Huxley now told himself.[58]

Once the letters that had been awaiting their arrival had been devoured, the anxiety aroused by distance and separation continued to grip their emotions. Every time word got out that a vessel had been seen heading into Sydney harbour, the anticipation that it was from London was overpowering and the disappointment, when it turned out to be from somewhere else, crushing. And then, as John Thomson wrote to his wife, one was not released from powerful emotional forces when a letter arrived. 'Never before when away from home have I ever experienced the hopes and fears that I do now when news are arriving. I feel almost frightened to break the seal and make the revelation to myself and yet how anxious do I look out for the arrival of the packet so anxiously that my avidity could not be satisfied by an arrival every day.'[59] He had good reason to feel this way, as he had just learned by the latest post that he was a father, his son John being born on the last day of May. Trying times lay ahead for both mother and son.

Sydney was the base for the *Rattlesnake*'s operations. From Sydney northwards, it was not until one reached Timor in the Indonesian Archipelago that a ship could be revictualled or repaired. Excursions from Sydney had to bear this in mind. Stanley's instructions from the Admiralty began at this point. To everyone on the ship as well as to Beaufort in London, the *Rattlesnake* was at the beginning of its real work. 'I look forward', wrote Beaufort to Stanley, 'to a quick succession of interesting despatches, new discoveries and singular adventures. You have really a delightful ball at your feet if kicked and rolled dextrously and diligently.'[60] In the meantime, there was much to be done to prepare the *Rattlesnake* for its northward cruises, work that would take a couple of months to complete.

The *Rattlesnake* was not the only ship that needed to be refitted. Stanley was informed in his instructions that upon arriving in Sydney, he was to take charge of two tenders, the *Bramble* and the *Castlereagh*, which would be waiting for him there. As the *Rattlesnake* made its way down Sydney harbour to its anchorage in Farm Cove, the *Castlereagh* appeared in the distance but even from afar it was noticeable what a 'horrible beast she was'.[61] As soon as Stanley saw the ship, he vowed to get rid of it immediately.[62] This tender, according to Stanley, was 'utterly useless as a surveying ship': she was beyond repair, at least at a reasonable cost and, more to the point, would undoubtedly impede his progress.[63] (He had learned that in beating against a prevailing trade wind, the *Castlereagh* took seven weeks to cover the same distance as the *Bramble* did in nineteen days.)[64] He decided to try and sell the *Castlereagh* as he felt that there was a good market in Sydney for a ship of this size. Beaufort already knew of the *Castlereagh*'s defects but thought that Stanley might still be able to use the ship 'as a baggage cart'.[65]

The *Bramble*, however, was nowhere to be seen. The ship, as it turned out, had been in Sydney since the beginning of March waiting for the *Rattlesnake* to appear. At the beginning of July, while the *Rattlesnake* was in Hobart Town, Sir Charles Fitzroy, the Governor of New South Wales, learned that five convicts had escaped from the penal colony of Port Arthur and were holed up on Gabo Island, located some 200 miles south from Sydney and offshore from Cape Howe. Fitzroy ordered Lieutenant Charles Yule, the commander of the *Bramble*, to capture the convicts.[66] When, on 14 July, they arrived at the island, they discovered that 'the birds were flown'.[67] With nothing to show for their efforts, the *Bramble* sailed back to Sydney and entered the harbour on 17 July.

Stanley now saw that the *Bramble* was also in a poor state but not as hopeless as the *Castlereagh*. The ship would need to be extensively repaired and the sails replaced, just enough to enable the ship to do one extensive cruise to the north.[68] Anything more would have been too expensive and time consuming, thought Stanley. Even though he had been instructed to take two tenders, he felt that he could do the job with only one.

The *Bramble* had been a tender to HMS *Fly* on the earlier and incomplete survey of the Torres Strait and the southern shore of New Guinea. When, in December 1845, Captain Francis Blackwood decided he had enough of the survey and was returning to England, he gave instructions to Lieutenant Yule just before his departure to continue the survey himself in company with Lieutenant David Aird who had taken command of the newly commissioned *Castlereagh*. Both ships left Sydney for the Torres Strait in the same month as the *Fly* returned home.

When all three ships met up in Sydney, many of the crew and officers of the *Bramble* and the *Castlereagh* had been away from home for more than five years. They were not happy ships. There were disciplinary problems galore, accusations of drunkenness and dereliction of duty; 'a most blackguard set of officers the Asst Surgeon excepted', in Midshipman Packe's opinion. Stanley, as we know, didn't like the look of either ship but he considered the officers 'the greatest defect of all'.[69] On 31 July, he mustered the crew and officers of the *Bramble* and *Castlereagh* on the *Rattlesnake* and paid them off. He now prepared to send them home, apart from Yule and Archibald McClatchie, the assistant surgeon on the *Bramble*.[70] While they waited for a ship bound for London, Stanley offered the *Castlereagh* as a temporary home.[71] 'We threw off our uniform & donned our shooting coats & snakebelts,' recalled John Sweatman, the clerk in charge of provisions on the *Bramble*. Events moved quickly. Three weeks after they were paid off Stanley arranged a contract for passage home and a dozen men were put on the *Thomas Arbuthnot* bound for London. The others, apart from one who remained in Sydney by choice and another who was detained by creditors, decided to work their way back to England on a merchant ship.[72] Though they were all tired and yearning to return home, their departure was more ignominious than joyful. Their leaving certificates did not sing their praises and one of the midshipmen, George Walsh, was told by Stanley that he should never attempt to join the service again.[73] The return voyage was nothing short of a nightmare: they were confined to tiny dark cabins in steerage, the food was inedible, the skipper was a 'most disagreeable old beast who used to eat himself mad with opium' and the chief mate, 'a great vulgar bully, was almost as bad'.[74]

As a leader, Yule left something to be desired.[75] By the end of the voyage to New Guinea he was on bad terms with everyone except McClatchie. He had confessed to Beaufort that he could not get the men to do what he wanted.[76] There was even a mutiny when the *Bramble* was in Timor. Yule was tired and wished to return home.[77] He was thirty-eight years old and his naval career was anything but impressive, though he did start late. He was twenty-eight years old when he joined the navy and thirty-three years old when first appointed to HMS *Bramble* in January 1842. He was promoted to the rank of lieutenant a few days before the *Fly* left England. Yule's elderly mother, afraid that she would not live to see her son again if he remained in Australia, had been writing to Beaufort and urging him to get her son back and to be promoted for his services. Beaufort tried to assure her that while he understood perfectly how she felt and agreed that her son had been out a very long time, in the Admiralty's eyes, however, he would be jeopardizing his promotion by returning. Whether it was Stanley's persuasion – Yule was a godsend as far as the surveying voyage ahead was concerned since he probably knew more about the Torres Strait and New Guinea than any naval person – or Yule's own reflection on his career possibilities, in the end he decided to stay with Stanley, but only until a replacement could be found.[78] Though Beaufort knew Yule's failings, he did think that he would work 'admirably en second'.[79]

Once the question of command of the *Bramble* was settled, the ship went into the patent slip for repairs and a refit. Besides getting new sails, the timbers in the side of the ship and the copper sheathing needed to be replaced.[80] Stanley sold the *Castlereagh* for the tidy amount of £601, 'a sum nearly equal to her original cost'.[81] Beaufort was happy, Admiral Dundas at the Admiralty was happy and so was Stanley.[82]

Sydney was a very good place to be happy. With a population of nearly 50,000, Sydney had been a British settlement for more than fifty years and had developed into the most important commercial and financial centre in the southern latitudes. There was something for everyone to do and the hospitality was 'unbounded' and at least as generous as it had been in Hobart Town.[83] The *Rattlesnake* was a singular attraction. The last Royal Navy vessel to find its way into Sydney Harbour was HMS *Fly* two years earlier. 'In this corner of the universe where men of war are rather scarce, even the Old *Rattlesnake* is rather a lion, and her officers are esteemed accordingly,' wrote Huxley to his sister Eliza.[84] Thomson agreed, certain in the thought that 'the people are all glad to make too much of us.'[85] They were both right. Less than a week after the *Rattlesnake*'s arrival, the Governor threw a ball at Government House situated on the brow of a hill overlooking Farm Cove and the *Rattlesnake*.

And this was just the start. There were dinner parties, theatre evenings, picnics, walks in the Domain and the Botanic Gardens, more balls and much else beside. 'Nothing that has taken place in this money making and pleasure hunting city has ever given such unmatched pleasure as our entertainments' was how John Thomson summed it up.[86] Huxley bragged that he 'had managed 3 balls and 2 dinners in the course of a week'.[87]

At one of these an event took place that changed Huxley's life.[88] It was here that he met a young woman named Henrietta Heathorn. Only a few months younger than Huxley, Henrietta was living in Newtown, several miles to the south of the centre of Sydney, in 'Holmwood', the house belonging to her youngest half-sister, Oriana, and her husband, William Fanning, a prosperous Sydney merchant.[89] Henrietta had come to Australia shortly before Christmas in 1843 with her mother and older half-sister to join their father in Jamberoo, a village nearly 100 miles from Sydney, where he ran a mill complex.[90] Oriana followed the rest of the family to Australia from England shortly thereafter and soon met and married William Fanning, settling in 'a pretty house at Cook's River'.[91] About a year later, Henrietta paid the newly-weds a visit, which was supposed to last 2 months: in the event she ended up staying more or less permanently while keeping house for them.

At this first meeting, Huxley and Henrietta spent little time in each other's company but several days later on 22 July, at the first of the government balls, they met again and this time they were hardly apart.[92] Several more meetings took place at other parties and dances in Sydney and it became clear to both of them that something quite magical was happening.

And then an odd thing occurred, at least from Henrietta's viewpoint. Huxley seemed to disappear from view. In fact, sometime in early August, Huxley became ill. After a period of three weeks, during which time he remained on the ship, Huxley, now recovered, journeyed to Port

Stephens, to the north of Sydney, to restore his health. Reverend King had invited Huxley to 'Tahlee', which was the home of his father, Captain Phillip Parker King, where he had been living since 1839 when he was appointed as resident commissioner of the Australian Agricultural Company.[93] Huxley went first to 'Tahlee' and then, in the company of Philip Gidley King, Robert King's brother, rode out to Stroud, to the northwest of Port Stephens. This was where the Australian Agricultural Company had its headquarters and Gidley King was responsible for the cattle and horse studs in the locality.[94] Here Huxley endured an attack of gout, which lasted ten days. Gidley King's attendance and kindness made the stay tolerable and no doubt Huxley would have been intrigued by the fact that Gidley King had been a midshipman on HMS *Beagle* with Darwin. The two men had much to discuss but the stay at Stroud turned out to be longer than was intended.[95]

Huxley was away from the *Rattlesnake* for all of August and when he finally did return early in September he missed a picnic hosted by the officers of the ship to which Henrietta and the Fannings had been invited. Henrietta expected him to be there, and when she found out he was absent, she 'began to think all that had gone before was my imagination or that this was just a sailors way'.[96] Some time later, perhaps a week, Huxley heard that he had been asked about by the 'New Town' folk and decided to pay a visit to 'Holmwood'. He spent about an hour at the house, surrounded by Henrietta and her half-sisters. To Huxley's surprise (and delight), there ensued a teasing, flirtatious discussion about his possible acceptance into the family. Ostensibly as a brother, one sister in favour and one against, it was agreed that the final decision should be left to Henrietta.[97] 'My heart leaped,' he remarked. This was their fourth or fifth meeting and though Huxley feared it was all too quick, they saw each other again and this time there was no more teasing, no more talk of brotherly acceptance: they were in love and they wanted to be together. They met again at the end of September at another very grand Government ball where they 'found that taste and habit of thought in each harmonised, and more than all found that the other was loved'.[98] There was no time to waste. The *Rattlesnake* would be leaving any day. They agreed to meet again on Monday 4 October. They became engaged.

Huxley was not the only one to find romance in Sydney. MacGillivray,

Captain Owen Stanley in a contemplative pose on the deck of HMS *Rattlesnake*. Commanding a naval ship was a lonely job, and captains often spent long periods of time on their own in this way.
The *Rattlesnake*, pictured in the centre-right, being fitted out in Portsmouth harbour. The hulk to the left of the *Rattlesnake* served as a temporary home to many of the crew during the time of the ship's refit. About a month later the *Rattlesnake*, ostensibly ready for sea, headed out on its four-year voyage to the tropics.

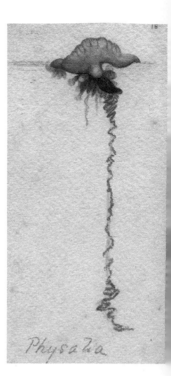

3 This daguerrotype shows Huxley, the *Rattlesnake*'s assistant surgeon, just before he was assigned to the ship.

4 Huxley staked his reputation and his desperate hopes to join the scientific community on his analysis of this superb example of *Physalia*, or Portuguese man-of-war, the first of which was caught and dissected in the South Atlantic in January 1847.

Physalia

5 Surveying, the chief purpose of the voyage, required work from all the ships and boats. This picture shows the flotilla at sunrise, preparing for a long day's toil in the baking sun of the Torres Strait. It is October 1848 and the ships have been surveying between the eastern coast of Australia and the Great Barrier Reef for four months, covering, in minutest detail, an area 600 miles in length

6 Surveying parties often landed on the coast, or on an island, to take the various measurements (especially angles) necessary for the survey. This picture shows the variety of instruments that were used.

7 Taking soundings in order to measure the depth of the ocean floor was a key part of the ship's scientific purpose. This winch, recently invented, was designed to take much of the drudgery out of the work. However, because of the immense forces at work, even this clever device could not guarantee that the rope carrying the heavy weight would not fail.

8 This picture shows two officers from the *Rattlesnake*, surrounded by a number of local Madeirans, using a device (probably the dipping needle invented by Robert Were Fox) to take readings of magnetic inclination on Pico dos Bodes, one of the island's most impressive peaks.

9 Putting one of the sails over the side of the ship and then raising it until it trapped sea water was a frequent, safe and very pleasurable way for crew and officers to have a 'bathe'.

10 The *Rattlesnake* 'crossed the line' on 13 January 1847, just over a month after leaving Portsmouth on a cold winter's day. The initiation rituals lasted all day but it wasn't all fun: one of the crew died from what we would now call exposure. For many on the ship this was their first experience of burial at sea.

Cockroaches were a constant problem on ships. The *Bramble* was sunk in February 1849 and lay the bottom of Sydney harbour for a week to rid the ship of the vermin. This picture shows the reparations to raise the ship. Fifty men were involved in the operation.

Midshipmen's quarters were very cramped. This picture shows a group of midshipmen enjoying emselves on a ship very similar to the *Rattlesnake*.

13 Picnics and balls were a regular feature of the entertainment enjoyed by the *Rattlesnake*'s company during their stay in Sydney in July 1847. On one occasion, as shown in this picture, the main deck of the *Rattlesnake* was transformed into an elegant ballroom for more than a hundred guests. 14 Picnics were held at picturesque spots on the shore lining Sydney harbour on its northern and southern side. The *Rattlesnake*'s boats, as shown in this picture, were used to ferry the invited guests to and from these picnic sites.

Tamarin Falls was, at some 13 miles distant, the closest natural beauty spot to Port Louis, Mauritius. An excursion there was considered a must for any visitor to the island.

The story of Paul and Virginia, the doomed young lovers, was set in Mauritius. Written by Jacques-Henri Bernardin de Saint-Pierre and published in 1788, it was an instant bestseller and was translated into virtually every European language. It literally put Mauritius on the map. No one visiting in the nineteenth century could claim to have seen the island without visiting the garden with the tombs of Paul and Virginia (pictured here). So gripping was the tale that most thought it depicted true events.

17 Oswald Brierly, the marine artist and Captain Stanley's guest during the latter stages of the *Rattlesnake*'s voyage in Australia and New Guinea, pictured in later life.

18 When Oswald Brierly, the artist of this picture, first came to Australia in 1842, he was installed b his boss, Benjamin Boyd, as the manager of a whaling station in Twofold Bay. This picture, showin the southern shore of the bay, was painted in October 1847 when Captain Stanley visited the settle-ment. The masted ship may be HMS *Bramble* (on which Stanley sailed from Sydney to Twofold Bay).

too, appears to have fallen under the city's spell, but much less is known of his romantic life. Once the *Rattlesnake* arrived in Sydney, MacGillivray, who was not subject to naval regulations when not on the ship, left the world of the *Rattlesnake* temporarily behind. He went to live with Frederick Strange, a natural history collector and specimen dealer who had been living in Sydney for several years and who, thanks to his wife, had a boarding house on Princes Street.[99] Strange was very much a nodal point in the world of Australian natural history collectors and, sooner or later, anyone passing through Sydney with such interests would end up at his doorstep. MacGillivray was no exception. He knew Strange as they had already met in 1844, or possibly as early as 1842, when MacGillivray was on HMS *Fly*, and stayed at his home in Sydney on more than one occasion during the ship's voyage.[100] Strange was a busy man, acting as an agent in Australia for John Gould, Lord Derby, the Bishop of Norwich, and other collectors in England.

Perhaps it was when he was in Sydney with the *Fly*, or more likely, sometime between July and October of this year, that MacGillivray met Williamina Paton Gray, who, at the time, was twenty-two years old and had been in Australia for twelve years.[101] We know nothing about their romance but most likely, sometime before he left Sydney for the next part of the *Rattlesnake*'s voyage, MacGillivray and Williamina became engaged.[102]

Huxley was certainly surprised by his romance. He didn't consider himself much of a party goer and though he didn't shun the social demands of Sydney – 'nothing but balls and parties the whole time' – he chose to do the rounds, 'to go into what society was to be had and see if I could pick up a friend or two among the multitude of the empty and frivolous'.[103] To his amazement, he found that his 'grave' demeanour was not only lightened by his finding romance but also that from it he derived an enormous surge of new energy to get his scientific work done.[104] It was probably this renewed vigour that helped Huxley complete his paper on the *Diphyes* that owed so much to Reverend King's untiring work at the towing net. Just like his earlier paper on *Physalia*, this paper, with the grandiose title of 'On the anatomy of the *Diphyes* and on the unity of composition of the *Diphydae* and *Physophoridae*', was sent from Sydney to the Linnean Society in the care of its president, the Bishop of Norwich, arriving 15 May of the following year.

The first part of the paper, ignominiously ascribed once again to 'Will. Huxley', was communicated on 16 January 1849 and then continued, in three further instalments, until the final section was read on 5 February 1850.[105] The complete paper remained unpublished but a brief extract appeared in the Society's proceedings in 1855.[106]

As for MacGillivray, quite how his romantic life fitted in with his natural history programme is unclear, but what is certain is that in Sydney he was back on home turf. He wasted no time in donning his collector's outfit – '"reef boots", flannel trousers, leather belt, checked shirt open in front, a shooting jacket . . . and an old straw hat' – and headed for the bush.[107] Accompanied by Frederick Strange, he ventured in early August to the north of Sydney, in and around Broken Bay and Brisbane Water, where the Hawkesbury River meets the sea. He was attracted to the area because Strange had shown him the skin of a shy and relatively rare species of brush kangaroo, *Halmaturus Thetidus* (actually a wallaby).[108] MacGillivray knew the animal well, for back in December 1842, when he was collecting in the area of the Paterson River (north of present-day Newcastle in New South Wales), he managed, with the help of an Aboriginal guide, to catch several specimens.[109] This time, however, he had no such luck, despite remaining with Strange in the area for more than a fortnight. Yet, MacGillivray was 'pleased with the excursion as a reminder of former bush life and a training for future work on the N.E. coast'.[110] All was not lost, however, for his eye caught sight of enormous mounds of *Arca* shells, 'which at first . . . may be mistaken for raised beaches . . . often twenty feet or more and several hundred yards in length'. The *Arca* was, according to MacGillivray, the principal food of the indigenous people. He was sure that western civilization had been pernicious for them and that they were on the point of extinction.[111] Dredging in the creeks and main channels leading into Broken Bay proved equally unpromising, apart from a few shells and starfish.

Broken Bay turned out to be a bit of a disappointment and the bush experience, while undoubtedly pleasing, returned little in the way of tangible goods. But better luck was on its way. While dredging in Sydney harbour, MacGillivray scooped a real find, a large number of *Trigonia*, a clam-like mollusc also known as a brooch shell, which had been thought extinct and had only recently been rediscovered in the warm waters off the east coast of Australia by two French zoologists on the scientific voyage of the *Astrolabe* in 1826.[112] MacGillivray dredged up more than two-dozen specimens and most of these he sent back to London to Forbes. A few he kept back and gave them to Huxley for further analysis. In his letter to Forbes, describing the occasion of finding *Trigonia*, MacGillivray showered Huxley with praise: 'Huxley has worked out the anatomy of *Trigonia*, and figured the animal in his usual masterly manner. The perseverance and skill which he has shown in his anatomical researches will give a great additional value to the zoological results of the voyage.'[113] Forbes had the results published in 1849.[114] MacGillivray's admiration of Huxley's work was genuine but mixed with envy. As he explained it to Forbes, he would have liked to have done more analytical work himself but the demands of the job simply didn't allow it – 'having been unassisted to make collections in all the departments, my duties too often merge into those of a mere collector and preserver of specimens'.[115] MacGillivray completed his collection of shells by venturing out to Penrith and the Nepean River, to the west of Sydney.[116]

For both Huxley and MacGillivray, Sydney was intoxicating from the beginning. They enjoyed it in so many ways. The city may have affected others romantically at the same time but the details remain unknown. Yet not everyone found it fun. Midshipman Packe was one who didn't. Though he lost some of his flair for social avoidance in Hobart, here in Sydney he deliberately retreated into being on his own as much as possible. A walk in the Botanic Garden, just a couple of days after arriving in Sydney, proved to be a mixed blessing: he enjoyed the walk but found the place suffocating – 'the snobs walk about all day in the Garden'. Governor Fitzroy's invitation to the government ball on 22 July he turned down and with it any such outing – 'not liking the Sydney aristocracy I do not intend to go to any parties or at all mix with the people of New South Wales'.[117]

Robert Gale and James Wilcox didn't find romance, or at least not on this occasion, but like MacGillivray they took the opportunity of this stay in Sydney to continue and enlarge upon the collections they had been making for the Bishop of Norwich. One box of bird skins had already been sent from Rio de Janeiro but now they could concentrate their efforts on Australian natural history, a new pursuit for both of them.[118] To mark the occasion, Gale wandered into town on Wednesday 21 July, bought a gun and got himself measured up for 'shooting clothes'.[119] The next day he had another gun repaired and, while waiting for his outfit to be ready, headed out to the bush with Wilcox to shoot. A few days later Gale's tailor brought him his 'shooting dress' and he was all set to return to the bush with a flurry. And so he did. Whenever there was an occasion, a picnic, a free day, a trip to the market, Gale and Wilcox went shooting. They bagged so much that they were often at work late into the night skinning and preserving.[120]

For Stanley, however, while it felt 'like coming home again', Sydney was more of a bittersweet experience.[121] Stanley knew the city very well, having visited it on several occasions between 1838 and 1841 when he was in command of HMS *Britomart*. Just like Huxley and MacGillivray, Stanley also fell in love the first time he was in Sydney. Her name was Anna Macarthur.[122] The Macarthurs were a formidable and famous New South Wales family with a history stretching back to the early days of settlement. Her uncle was Phillip Parker King, whose family was as renowned in the annals of New South Wales as the Macarthurs. The advantage of becoming part of this powerful double dynasty was not lost on the twenty-seven-year-old, ambitious Owen Stanley. Unfortunately, no sooner had he met and fallen in love with Anna Macarthur, than she met and fell in love with Captain John Wickham, in command of HMS *Beagle* on its third voyage.[123] Their romance put an end to Stanley's budding hopes. Captain Wickham and Anna Macarthur were married in 1842 and the couple went to live in Moreton Bay, where he became a police magistrate.[124]

The Macarthur homestead was a place called Vineyard in Parramatta, to the west of Sydney.[125] Stanley would have been expected to call but, as he told his friend the surveyor Charles Tyers, he was far too busy even to dine there, adding, 'to be sure there is no longer quite the same attraction'. His aide-de-camp, the midshipman, Philip Ruffle Sharpe, who had been introduced to the Macarthurs by Reverend Robert King, appears to have spent much time at Vineyard.[126] Perhaps there was something magical about Vineyard for Sharpe seems to have taken fondly to the two youngest Macarthur daughters, Emmeline, aged nineteen, and Emma, aged fifteen, both of whom were living at home. Sharpe, only sixteen years old, spent as many Sundays as he could at Vineyard and attended as many dances as possible, perfumed in verbena and fitted with white gloves.[127]

In return for the generosity that Sydney showered on the *Rattlesnake* and its officers, Stanley decided to throw a party for the cream of the city's society. The event began at lunchtime on Saturday 4 September with a picnic – there had already been many of these – down the harbour to Camp Cove where a lunch had been prepared for the guests. 'After rambling about and enjoying the scenery for a short time, they returned to the *Rattlesnake*, the deck of which had in the meantime been converted, by a tasty arrangement of the flags, into a ball-room.'[128] When the guests arrived on board in the early evening, they were treated to a tea dance, followed by a sit-down supper, culminating in the grand ball, which lasted until midnight. According to Robert Gale, who was responsible for much of the festivities, more than 100 guests enjoyed the entertainment.[129] Several days later, Stanley invited a large company of people on board to see a magic lantern show.[130] This time Gale made no comment about his commander's toys.

Stanley's treats were, however, not simply a gesture of thanks. They were also a mark of his own historic relationship with New South Wales. This began when he was in command of HMS *Britomart* and played an important role in the establishment of a settlement at Port Essington, in northern Australia, where he would, in time, return. Then he was young and, though a commander of a ship, not yet a captain. Now he was back in Sydney, a captain in command of a major surveying and scientific expedition. The presence of his brother Charlie helped his standing in the corridors of colonial government. Charlie and his wife Eliza stayed at Government House and at Parramatta where they were entertained by Sir Charles Fitzroy and his wife. They were also invited to Port Stephens to stay at Tahlee with Captain and Mrs Phillip Parker King. When not away on social excursions and on board ship, the Stanleys took part in many of the intimate picnics and dinners arranged by Owen Stanley.[131] Unfortunately, the good times had to come to an end since Charlie was in Sydney for a vacation rather than official business. Nearly six weeks after arriving in Sydney on the *Rattlesnake*, Charlie and Eliza boarded the brig *Emma* for the short passage back to Hobart Town. The parting could not have been easy for despite the fact that Stanley was quite prepared to interpret Admiralty orders for his own benefit, they could not be sure when and whether they would meet again in Australia. As it turned out, they did meet once again – for a very short time.

*

Not long after Stanley reached Sydney, the colonial government asked him to help them on a matter that was causing some concern. Some 400 miles to the south of Sydney, a small but prosperous commercial centre was developing in and around Twofold Bay. Based partly on shore whaling and partly on sheep and cattle production inland, the commercial activity in the area was lively enough for the colonial government in 1846 to install two custom officers in the township of Eden to collect the necessary dues. At the time of their appointment to these posts, the two men, Hamon Massie and Edmund Gibbes, were the Branch of the Customs Depart-ment of New South Wales, but without a building, though plans for such a permanent establishment were in place.[132] Now, in September 1847, the government maintained that the roving nature of the customs officer's work was inefficient and that the Branch needed a customs house and a safe anchorage as soon as possible. But deciding where to locate the building was proving to be extremely controversial. There were, in fact, two possible sites, one on the northern shore of the bay, in the tiny government settlement of Eden, and the other on the opposite side, in Boydtown, a much larger but privately owned and run settlement. The Legislative Council of New South Wales had already been receiving petitions from experienced commanders of merchant vessels offering their opinions on the most appropriate site.[133] A decision had to be made swiftly and Stanley was the man who could speed the process. His brief was to survey the bay and give his candid and independent opinion on which side of the bay offered the better anchorage and, therefore, the site of a permanent customs house.

The excursion to Twofold Bay would certainly give Stanley a foothold in the colonial government as an adviser, and eventually his name would be heard in the corridors of the Treasury in London, the ultimate source of decisions regarding the administration of the customs in the colony. That was on a high political plane but the Twofold Bay voyage also provided Stanley with more immediate and local opportunities. He could try out his newly refitted tender, HMS *Bramble*, and see how he got on with Charles Yule, its commander. So on 13 September 1847, Stanley and Yule, in company with his newly reassigned subordinate officers and some thirty petty officers and seamen, sailed HMS *Bramble* through Sydney Heads south to Twofold Bay.[134]

The voyage took four days to complete. They arrived at Eden, on the north side of the bay, on Wednesday 17 September. Midshipman Packe thought that it was 'a very pretty place . . . but it smells most horrible of decayed whales'.[135] The *Bramble* remained on this side for almost a week during which time the boats were sent out daily to survey this part of the bay. On Tuesday 23 September, with this part of the job completed, Stanley and his men went over to the south side to finish the survey.

Greeting them as they arrived was the customs officer, Hamon Massie, and a man named Oswald Brierly. Stanley must have felt in destiny's hands when he met Brierly for here, in a backwater of New South Wales, tens of thousands of miles from home, was a man whose background and interests were so similar to and at the same time so complementary to those of Stanley as to be uncanny. What was even more amazing was that Stanley's brother Charlie had a very similar experience in Hobart when he fell in with Francis Simpkinson, a naval officer and artist (incidentally Sir John Franklin's nephew by marriage), who was working at the observatory.[136] They immediately became best friends – 'besides him I have scarcely anybody who can join me in any of my pursuits' – and spent much time in each other's company, sketching and painting.[137] Stanley had now met his own kindred spirit and Brierly recounted how he came to be in this remote corner of the world.

Brierly was born in Chester in 1817 and showed an early interest in drawing ships. His father, a doctor and amateur painter, encouraged him to be a marine artist and to go to sea.[138] Brierly learned his artistic craft at Henry Sass's Academy, a private drawing-school in Bloomsbury – 'a preparatory school' for the Royal Academy and the British Institution, where the likes of Rossetti, Millais, William Frith and Edward Lear studied – and his nautical skills in Plymouth. Having honed his marine talents, he set off for Cowes to paint the ships of the wealthy members of the exclusive Royal Yacht Squadron Club. In 1839, at the age of twenty-two, Brierly exhibited two drawings of naval ships at the Royal Academy, and in the same year, in Cowes, fell in with Benjamin Boyd, one of the most adventurous, flamboyant and crooked speculators of the time.[139]

In his early forties, Boyd, the second son of a substantial southwestern Scottish land-owning family, was a man with connections in all parts of the economy and in many parts of the world. His centre was the London financial world. He was shrewd and he had style. Baron Rothschild knew him well. '[He] is a tight hand at a bargain,' he remarked about Boyd, 'for when I deal with him in French Rentes I always lose money by him; he is such a screw.'[140] Around 1839, Boyd set his sights on New South Wales as a natural extension of his wheelings and dealings in the City. Boyd's love of travel and risk-taking shaped him as a colonial adventurer rather than just a businessman looking for new outlets. His model may have been James Brooke, the self-styled White Rajah of Sarawak, whom he had probably met at Cowes and who had sailed for Borneo in this same year to establish his claim to a private kingdom in the East.[141]

Boyd took his first step to Australia by setting up a bank, the Royal Bank of Australia, and an export business, the Australian Wool Company, in London in 1840. They were both created hastily and built on shaky foundations. Boyd did not remain long in London to nurture his creations. He had already bought an ocean-going schooner yacht of 140 tons, the *Wanderer*, in the previous year and with it membership of the Royal Yacht Squadron in Cowes.[142] A trip around the world was what he was planning and he began to fit out the yacht and hire crew and invite friends to accompany him. One of his companions was Oswald Brierly whom he had asked to become the voyage's artist-in-residence. Brierly accepted without hesitation and the jolly party set sail from Plymouth in November 1841. A flotilla of other Boyd vessels – impressive steamships – were already on their way to Australia bringing the new bank's employees as well as money.

After a long and at times dangerous voyage, the *Wanderer* arrived in Port Phillip (Melbourne) in June 1842. Boyd wasted no time in constructing his private colonial empire. Within a fortnight he had purchased a prime sheep station to the southwest of Melbourne and, in what would become a typical strategy, made its former owner his manager.[143] Two weeks later, the *Wanderer* put into Sydney Harbour and Boyd began his real work, but New South Wales was not the boom world Boyd had imagined. It was in economic turmoil. Boyd's vision enabled him to take advantage of the situation.

He decided that it was too dangerous for his creation, the Royal Bank of Australia, to engage in the banking activities he had planned. Instead of issuing notes as originally intended, the bank restricted its operations to transferring bills of exchange between London and Sydney and to discounting the bills of settlers, holding their property as collateral. As settler upon settler failed to meet their payments, Boyd accumulated mortgages, property, livestock and sheep by the score. What he didn't get this way, he bought using money borrowed from his own bank and became its chief customer. Within a couple of years, Boyd was one of the largest landowners and stockowners in the colony.[144]

Boyd singled out the Maneroo District of New South Wales as a special area for his pastoral activities. Situated nearly 300 miles south of Sydney, the Maneroo District had fabulous pasturage, the land being fed by run-offs of water from the Snowy Mountains to the north. Within two years of his arrival in Sydney, Boyd owned a quarter of a million acres of this fertile land. As luck would have it, this whole area funnelled into Twofold Bay, having a natural harbour on the south Pacific, which was also the site of an important whaling industry. Boyd knew exactly what to do.

Boyd paid a visit to the bay late in 1842 and liked what he saw. Whaling was in full swing, organized by members of the Imlay family, who had been in the area for a decade, and worked almost entirely by highly skilled Aboriginal labour.[145] The New South Wales government had already decided to establish a settlement on the northern shore of the bay, and a land survey had been completed. When Boyd and Brierly visited the area at the end of 1842, the only evidence of the settlement plans was 'one or two posts and rails indicating the lay of the principal streets'.[146] Within a short time, however, the New South Wales government's plans for the area were put into operation and a sale of land on both its northern and southern shore was announced in March 1843. Boyd purchased the whole of the southern section and three lots in the northern section, the township of Eden.[147] As the sole landowner on the southern shore, Boyd appropriately named the site after himself: 'founders of a new City we hoisted a blanket, nailed to a pole as our standard and with all the proper forms named the town Boyd Town.'[148]

With extensive plans for a village of 400 houses, a church, an inn and a lighthouse, Boyd Town was to be the capital of Boyd's southern enterprises: a port for his pastoral activities up country, a harbour for his ships and a station for processing the products of the shore whaling activities. It was an integrated enterprise. 'The settlers of the back country will be able to ship their wool and cattle within a distance of fifty miles instead of having as formerly to send it nearly three hundred to Sydney. Twofold Bay will also be the port where whalers may get their supplies instead of being obliged to go up to Port Jackson.'[149]

Boyd appointed Brierly as his representative in the area giving him responsibility for managing the whaling operations. Boyd Town was a tied company town, having its own store and issuing its own currency. Brierly was the only permanent fixture in the town. Others drifted in and out as they felt. Brierly built himself a nice cottage to the east of the whaling works overlooking the bay below. Twofold Bay may have lacked the social glitter of Sydney, but it held particular attractions for Brierly. It was precisely here on the Australian coast of the south Pacific that he could get the kind of practical experience he needed in order to call himself a marine artist. Not only did he have the sea at his doorstep, but he also had a real maritime operation, with ships, jetties, warehouses and whales, at his disposal. As if this wasn't enough to work with, Brierly also had the good fortune to be surrounded by Aborigines, an exotic and, for him, an endlessly fascinating group of people who were an integral part of the maritime world of the area. For the budding marine artist and sensitive observer, all seemed well in Twofold Bay.

Stanley remained for five days on the southern shore, surveying the bay and spending as much time as possible in Brierly's company, riding through the area and sketching the local sights and people.[150] He also witnessed an extraordinary and unique sight.[151] Whaling in the Twofold Bay area consisted primarily of ship-based whaling using sailing ships and shore-based whaling using whaleboats, but it was the latter which was unique to the area.[152] In their seasonal migration, right whales swam by Twofold Bay providing the local industry with its catch. But the bay also attracted a pod of killer whales who worked in concert with the whalers to harass and round up the catch. Surrounded by the whaleboats and the killer whales, the right whales were harpooned and the killer whales dragged their prey to the bottom where they feasted on those parts they most enjoyed. Some twenty-four hours later, the bloated body of the right whale would rise to the surface and the whalers could now easily tow the carcasses into shore.[153] The Aborigines, who generally manned the whaleboats, believed that the killer whales were reincarnations of their ancestors and gave them appropriate personal names.[154]

Undoubtedly, Stanley would have liked to have remained longer with Brierly, but it was the survey and not the social pastimes that mattered. The survey having been completed, the two men parted on 27 September. What they said to each other and what plans they made can only be guessed at but this would not be the last time they would meet. After a side trip to nearby Gabo Island to inspect a proposed site for a lighthouse, the *Bramble* headed north back to Sydney where the ship arrived on 1 October to anchor again in Farm Cove.

When Stanley was first asked to survey Twofold Bay, he may not have known about the history of the area nor how difficult it would be to arrive at a clear, unambiguous decision as to where to site the Customs House. His report to the Colonial Secretary, Edward Deas Thomson, while not alluding to the history of the area, certainly reflected the difficulty in choosing between the two sites. The report made it clear that from the viewpoint of anchorage there were disadvantages and advantages on both sides of the bay and that the decision as to where to put the Customs House, as far as he was concerned, 'will depend more upon the facility afforded by Eden or East Boyd for communication with the interior'.[155] Although Stanley slightly favoured Eden, he thought the Surveyor General should be called in to add his voice. In the end, the colonial government chose Eden and work began on the new Customs House in the following year. To what extent the decision was made on political rather than surveying grounds is unclear, but it would have seemed odd to site a government department in what was a private settlement unless the practical considerations were overwhelmingly in its favour. Whatever the reason, the decision turned out to be fortuitous because no sooner had the building foundations been laid in Eden than Boyd's empire began to unravel.

In Sydney, Stanley could not have been more pleased with the results of his trip to Twofold Bay. The *Bramble* was in good shape and Yule had proved himself an able commander. Stanley had been away for more than a fortnight and the gaieties had not abated in his absence. He even missed another government ball held the day before his return to Sydney. There were some outstanding social debts to pay. A French corvette of twenty-four guns, *La Brilliante*, commanded by Count du Bouzet, had arrived in

Robert Gale's sketch of 'the Rattlesnake family'

Sydney just before Stanley set sail in the *Bramble* and was still there on his return. During Stanley's absence, the first lieutenant, together with Robert Gale, had done their best to entertain the French officers but now, with Stanley's return, it was time for him to invite the Count du Bouzet to dine on the *Rattlesnake*. This took place on Sunday 3 October. Two days later, the *Brilliante* set sail. The same day, Yule gave his thanks to Sydney's well-to-do by throwing a party of his own consisting of a trip on the spruced-up

Bramble to Rose Bay and a picnic on shore.[156] The guests were then ferried to the *Rattlesnake* where Stanley provided tea followed by a lavish dinner and a dance. Midshipman Packe, as usual, turned up his nose at the whole business.[157]

There were a few more, smaller social events in the coming days but this part of the Sydney experience was coming to an end as the time for heading north rapidly approached. Farewells were said for the time being. Huxley was no sooner engaged than he was on his way again. It was probably the same for MacGillivray. The Great Barrier Reef awaited the *Rattlesnake* and *Bramble* but the survey was not the only task that lay ahead for Stanley had meanwhile accepted another request from the colonial government.

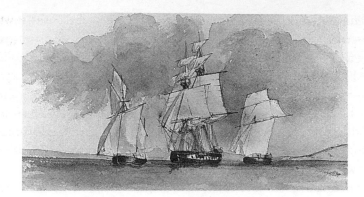

CHAPTER VI

Not Waltzes and Polkas:
The Great Barrier Reef, 1847 & 1848

Stanley had come halfway around the world to do what he knew best: surveying and its productions – maps, charts, tables, views, and sailing directions. He was now in his element and, by virtue of his experience and training, one of a very small band of experts on Australia and its surrounding waters. Stanley's duties and responsibilities were contained in the two sets of instructions he received, one from the Admiralty, and the other from Beaufort. And now, as he sailed out of Sydney, he could look upon them with a clearer sense of their relevance and immediacy than at any time on the voyage out to Australia.

Surprisingly, the Admiralty instructions did not exactly correspond to those issued by Beaufort.[1] Their Lordships instructed Stanley to continue the work of his predecessor, Francis Blackwood, commander of HMS *Fly*. Ships plying between Sydney, the Far East and Europe had to travel up the east coast of Australia until in the vicinity of Cape York, the northeastern-most point of land, they turned to the west and proceeded through the Torres Strait until they found themselves in open sea. From Breaksea Spit just off Fraser Island about 200 miles north of Brisbane, the eastern coast of Australia is fenced in by the Great Barrier Reef, which winds its way north-wards following the coast until, nearly 1,500 miles later, it comes to an end near the southern coast of New Guinea. James Cook called a substantial

HMS *Rattlesnake, Bramble* and *Asp*

part of the waters on the inside of the reef the Labyrinth, because the whole space seemed to be strewn with rocks, shoals and all kinds of submerged, lurking dangers. Sailing up Australia's east coast in 1770, his voyage almost came to grief when his ship, HMS *Endeavour*, hit a reef, which he appropriately named Endeavour Reef. He couldn't wait to leave it.

The longest reef system in the world, the Great Barrier Reef was in the late eighteenth and nineteenth century a major challenge to European shipping. Ships travelling up the east coast could choose to sail either in what was called the inner passage, between the reef and the coast, or the outer passage, that is on the open sea to the east of the reef. Both passages had their own advantages and problems. The inner passage was relatively smooth but dangerous. Even with charts, ships had to proceed cautiously always looking out for hidden dangers. They could travel only during the day. The outer passage, by contrast, provided unimpeded sailing, but was frequently rough and exposed to the full force of the Pacific Ocean. At some point, though, a ship choosing the outer passage had to enter through an opening in the reef barrier in order to proceed around Cape York and into the Torres Strait. There were few openings in the reef system which would allow a ship to pass into the inner passage safely. Some were not wide enough and others, while in theory navigable, were in practice dangerous given the force of the seas crashing onto the reefs – the wreck of the *Charles Eaton* was a salutary reminder. Phillip Parker King had produced a detailed chart of the inner passage in 1819, but because of its length and the intricacies of its formation, he left plenty of work to be done by later surveyors.[2] Nevertheless, thanks to his survey, the inner passage became a viable alternative to the outer passage, fuelling a debate that raged in the pages of the *Nautical Magazine*, the source of the most up-to-date information on maritime matters, for more than two decades.

Francis Blackwood set to work on the Great Barrier Reef more than twenty years after King. His job was to survey the outer passage and, in particular, to find and survey a safe entrance into the inner passage and to erect a beacon to assist shipping in getting through the Great Barrier Reef. Though there were many openings – most mariners had their own favourites some of which they publicized, in the pages of the *Nautical Magazine* for example, and some of which they kept to themselves – Blackwood's job was to find an opening that could be permanently etched

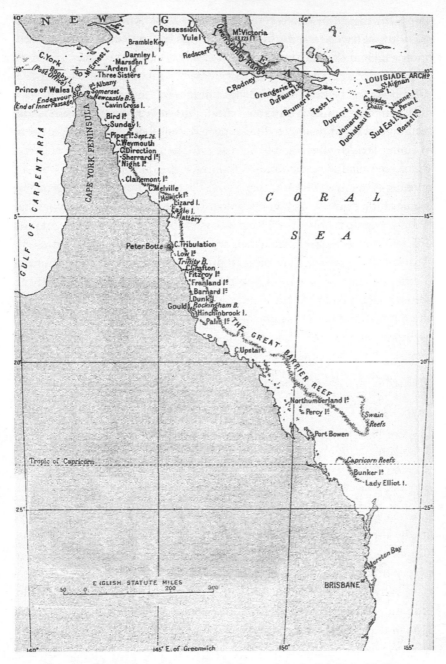

East coast of Australia, south-east New Guinea and the Louisiade Archipelago,
places visited by HMS *Rattlesnake*, 1848 and 1849

onto a hydrographic chart. He found a convenient one in the reefs just to the north of Raine Island, about 150 miles to the southeast of Cape York, upon which in 1844 he duly erected a beacon – just a few miles, in fact, to the north of Great Detached Reef where the *Charles Eaton* came to grief.[3]

Though the beacon was visible in fine weather at a distance of thirteen miles, in other, less favourable, conditions it was easy to miss. The Admiralty wanted Stanley to find and survey another opening to the north of Raine Island, which could be used as an alternative for those ships which, because of unfavourable conditions, had overshot Blackwood's opening.[4] There's no doubt that Stanley was up to the task and, equally, there is little doubt that it was very worthwhile. However, it was not what Beaufort wanted him to do. Indeed, Beaufort's instructions were not only different from but also explicitly critical of those of their Lordships.

Beaufort was absolutely clear about this. No mention was made of Blackwood. Instead, Beaufort linked Stanley's work to Phillip Parker King who, though producing an excellent survey, 'had not time or means to effect it with the same accuracy that will be in your power'.[5] 'By carrying on this system of correction and improvement in our present charts', he continued,

> along the narrow navigation which is generally known by the name of the In-shore Passage between the coast and the Barrier Reefs, great benefit will be conferred on those Masters of vessels who would be more readily inclined to adopt that channel if certain parts of it were so clearly delineated, and the soundings so spread on either side of the track, that they could sometimes continue under sail during the night.[6]

Beaufort paid lip service, and no more, to the need to 'contribute as much as possible to the safety of those vessels who choose the outer voyage by the Barrier Reefs', thus sidestepping the Admiralty instructions. Beaufort's choice of language when describing the inner and outer passage is very striking. The former was tranquil and secure while the latter was a risk. Why Beaufort's instructions to Stanley differed from those of the Admiralty is not clear. He was certainly not enamoured of their Lordships. Late in 1846, in his 17th year as Hydrographer, he was promoted to the (in this case derisory) post of 'Yellow Admiral'– that is, he was promoted to rear-admiral on the retired rather than the active list, while still staying in the job.[7] This may have been enough to make him bitter towards their

Lordships, who, it was well known, handed out honours to men much less esteemed than Beaufort. But, from what we know of Beaufort, he wouldn't have acted spitefully.[8] More probably he instructed Stanley differently because he was much more knowledgeable than their Lordships about the relationship between the navy in peacetime and the economic and political development of the British Empire. A clue as to why Beaufort was not interested in furthering the survey of the outer passage lies in a comment he appended to the end of the instructions for surveying the Great Barrier Reef. 'The accomplishment of this object', he told Stanley, 'will prove to be of peculiar importance when steam communication between Singapore and Sydney shall be established.'[9]

The subject of steam communication between Australia and Singapore, and, by implication, India, China and Britain, had been discussed ever since the first steamship arrived in Sydney in 1831, but it was not until 1846 that agitation in both London and Sydney raised the temperature of the debate.[10] That year saw the first of a number of meetings in Sydney of the Select Committee on Steam Navigation with England under the chairmanship of Edward Deas Thomson, the Colonial Secretary. The Committee solicited evidence from a number of people, not least of whom were Phillip Parker King and Francis Beaufort.[11] Both of these influential men, together with a number of prominent merchants, argued an impressive case for favouring a route between Sydney and Singapore whose Australian branch involved the inner passage of the Great Barrier Reef to the Torres Strait and beyond. The arguments centred on the advantages of smooth water in the inner passage, much more suited to the design and technology of steam ships. They maintained that despite having to anchor each night, the inner passage effected a shorter journey time to Singapore. The Sydney merchants, while being fully aware of Blackwood's discovery of the opening in the reef, thought it made no difference to their argument.[12] Beaufort's hand is everywhere visible in the debate. It is not surprising, therefore, that both Stanley and Yule appeared before the committee in April 1848 to give evidence, both of them maintaining the superiority of the inner passage.

Stanley's survey work was as much political as it was practical. It played into the politics that Beaufort pursued with his masters at the Admiralty as much as it did in Australia with the colonial authorities. And it was even more complicated than that. There was also the political relationship between the Admiralty and the colonial government of New South Wales, apparently a very sensitive issue. Stanley was probably unaware of this to begin with but Beaufort made sure he understood it in future communications.

Stanley had already carried out the survey of Twofold Bay on behalf of the colonial government and now, in October, he was on his way northwards to fulfil two other colonial requests, as well as the survey of the inner passage, which was his main priority. Stanley must have thought to himself that there could not be any possible objection to these requests since they were not taking him out of his way. From a merely personal point of view, Stanley could only benefit from this undertaking, as he would endear himself to the New South Wales authorities and, especially, Edward Deas Thomson.

One of the requests concerned selecting a site for the Customs House at Moreton Bay, pretty much the same sort of work he had already done at Twofold Bay. The *Rattlesnake* arrived in Moreton Bay on 16 October 1847, five days after departing Sydney. The Moreton Bay area, in common with other parts of Australia, had been settled as a penal colony. The main and first significant settlement, at Brisbane, was a fair distance up the Brisbane River, but by the time of the *Rattlesnake*'s arrival, there were other small urban communities both close by and further upriver that were competing for Brisbane's commercial and administrative position.[13] This, together with the difficulties of large ships navigating the Brisbane River, and the opening of the Darling Downs to the west for sheep pasture, led to an increasing chorus for the establishment of a port on Moreton Bay itself, rather than upriver at Brisbane.[14] The place suggested by those seeking an alternative to Brisbane for the site of the port and, therefore, the Customs House, was Cleveland Point, to the south of the mouth of the Brisbane River. Though Sir George Gipps, the then Governor of New South Wales, declared Cleveland Point unsuitable when he visited the site in 1842, agitation for an alternative to Brisbane refused to die away.[15] An unbiased hydrographic survey of the area would decide the matter one way or the other and that is where Stanley came into the picture.

Stanley began to assess the Cleveland Point site soon after arriving in Moreton Bay. It did not seem to take him long to come to the conclusion that Cleveland Point was unsuitable for the purposes intended and that Brisbane, which he also visited, was, by far, the better site for a Customs House.[16] This he communicated to Edward Deas Thomson on 1 November 1847, less than a fortnight after arriving in Moreton Bay.

While at Moreton Bay, Stanley met and entertained Captain John Wickham, the ex-commander of HMS *Beagle* and now police magistrate in Brisbane. Stanley had been in love with Anna Macarthur before she became Wickham's wife and despite the awkwardness of the situation, he invited her, and Wickham and their two daughters, to be his guests on the *Rattlesnake*. They remained on board for several days. The two men did some surveying work together on the north side of Moreton Bay and Stanley entertained the family with a showing of his magic lantern.[17] Robert Gale, Stanley's tetchy steward, accepted them on board grudgingly – 'females are awkward things in a ship,' he remarked.[18]

On 2 November 1847, the Wickham family left the *Rattlesnake* and, two days later, Stanley took the *Rattlesnake* out of Moreton Bay heading towards Port Curtis where the Colonial Government had invited him to look into another matter. This time though, he was being asked to pass judgement as to whether this northern spot on the Australian coast, just south of the Tropic of Capricorn, 'would be available in the event of an idea being again entertained of forming an establishment here'.[19] By 'an idea being again entertained', Stanley was referring to the aborted penal settlement, planned and put into action by the New South Wales government in 1846 in response to an order from William Gladstone, the Secretary of State for the Colonies, that transportation was going to be extended to a vast area to the north of Brisbane, the new colony of 'North Australia', with Port Curtis as its capital.[20] In accordance with that demand, an expedition of eighty-eight would-be settlers and soldiers, headed by the fifty-four-year-old Lieutenant Colonel George Barney of the Royal Engineers, who had been commissioned by Gladstone to be the colony's superintendent, left Sydney early in January 1847 and arrived at its destination in tropical Australia at the end of the month. Nothing, however, seemed to go right for the fledgling settlement from the start. Plagued by mosquitoes, unwelcoming Aborigines, torrential rains, followed by drought and unbearable heat, the colony clung on as best it could. Given the name Gladstone, the settlement was no sooner begun than Barney received orders in April 1847 to abandon the site and return without delay to Sydney. Earl Grey, who had succeeded Gladstone in July 1846, appeared to side with many in New South Wales who did not want a convict society growing up on their doorstep and ordered Port Curtis to be abandoned in November 1846. Not longer after, Grey announced that transportation would be suspended for two years.

Lieutenant Colonel Barney arrived back in Sydney on 9 July 1847, just a week before the *Rattlesnake*. Barney was clearly disappointed to be ordered back so suddenly and, though his final report to Governor Charles Fitzroy doesn't say it in so many words, it was clear that this was a personal setback for him.[21]

Barney was convinced that Port Curtis would be settled in no time as settlers, with large stocks of sheep, were already in the area looking for suitable pasture. As the only decent harbour in this part of Australia – Barney thought it was inferior only to Sydney and Hobart – Port Curtis was the obvious place for commerce. He urged the government to act before the area became settled by private enterprise rather than under state control.[22] Barney's arguments found favour with Governor Fitzroy who, on 2 August 1847, sent a despatch to Earl Grey in London in which he maintained that, subject to a satisfactory survey of the harbour by Stanley, 'it would be desirable to proclaim an extent of country in the vicinity of Port Curtis as a county; and thus bring it . . . within the settled districts of the colony of New South Wales'.[23]

The *Rattlesnake* arrived at Port Curtis on 7 November 1847 and took up a safe anchorage several days later. Stanley now began his survey of the harbour, a task that took him three weeks to complete. He concluded that the harbour was good but that during the dry season it would be difficult, though not impossible, to find fresh water. Stanley didn't come across any settlers. He was aware that they were close by and, so as not to waste any time, he ordered Yule back to Moreton Bay in the *Bramble* to ensure that Governor Fitzroy received his opinion and chart of Port Curtis as soon as possible.[24]

The evidence of Barney's hastily abandoned settlement was scanty. 'A pile or two of bricks, some posts stuck in the ground as a provisional "Government House", the ruts of wheels in the hardened mud, and numbers of broken bottles (the last an unfailing mark of Australian colonization) were nearly all that we found remaining of Gladstone', was how MacGillivray described the scene when he first came across it.[25] Two horses and a foal, 'in too wild a state to be caught' completed the pathetic picture of this, the first attempt by Europeans to settle the tropical east coast of Australia. For the time being, 'the gum trees . . . their existence unmolested by the axe and the kangaroos and opossums have it all their own way again'.[26] The numerous Aboriginal inhabitants kept their distance, though their fires were clearly visible at night. Midshipman Packe probably got as close to them as anyone but reckoned that they feared to meet the newcomers because Lieutenant Colonel Barney's soldiers had killed several of them.[27]

The survey completed and the *Bramble* on its way south to Moreton Bay, Stanley and the *Rattlesnake* left Port Curtis. There were few regrets. 'You cannot imagine a more dreary and utterly barren spot,' MacGillivray confided in his friend Edward Forbes.[28] The ship set sail on 29 November heading to Goold Island, more than 500 miles further up the coast, offshore from the present-day town of Cardwell, Queensland. Stanley's plan was to water the ship at Goold Island and then work his way southwards back to Sydney, surveying a track in this inner part of the Great Barrier Reef. He estimated that he would be back in Sydney anytime between late-February and mid-March, depending on weather.[29]

Back in London, Beaufort reacted to the news that Stanley had arrived safely in Sydney with joy. One of his top surveyors and a personal friend was about to start the most exciting part of the voyage and Beaufort looked forward to hearing about it. However, his reaction to Stanley's work for the colonial government was not so supportive. Thousands of miles away from the action and not privy to all the facts, Beaufort wasn't certain whether Stanley should have accepted the spate of requests from the government of New South Wales. But he was certain of the Admiralty's stance. 'There are few things of which the Admiralty are more jealous – no matter under what administration –', he warned Stanley, 'than the intervention of Colonial Authorities with the orders under which H M Ships are employed.'[30] In future, Beaufort suggested, he should write to the Admiralty when asked to do anything not in the original instructions.[31] However, Stanley continued to ignore the Admiralty and to do whatever he could to help the colonial government. Finding favour in Australia clearly outweighed the Admiralty's possible displeasure.

Like Stanley, MacGillivray flourished in Australia. He had been waiting for this moment. He was back in the field, his own field. He had spent most of the time from 1842 to 1845 on the east coast of Australia on HMS *Fly*, working up and down the Great Barrier Reef. The aspiring twenty-five-year-old naturalist probably knew Australian fauna first-hand better than any other living European. He belonged to the world of the travelling naturalist, men who roamed the world, typically in someone's employ, who collected flora and fauna for European and American museums of natural history, botany and geology. 'An old straw hat' shielding him from the fierce, hot tropical sun, MacGillivray, sunburnt and unshaven, presented quite a spectacle as he roamed the bush for specimens, with only a compass to guide him. 'With reef boots, flannel trousers, leather belt, checked shirt open in front, a shooting jacket which sadly wanted mending and washing . . . I had to carry water, ammunition, skinning materials, a double barrelled gun, insect net, collecting boxes, a quantity of Botanical papers and boards, besides . . . provisions.'[32] He was happiest in the field, intrepid but careful, inquisitive but selective. He knew what was rare and what was common, though he did not have ready access to reference works.

Specimens of *Articulata*, namely insects and crustacea, went directly to Adam White, the assistant keeper of zoology at the British Museum, and his bird specimens to John Gould. Other specimens went to Edward Forbes before they were sent on to their final destination. While he couldn't imagine himself doing natural history other than at the coalface, he knew that collectors like himself were treated as mere providers for the armchair naturalists back home. In a letter to Forbes, he said as much. 'Some friends of ours at home who have always found abundance of occupation in describing and amassing the productions of other countries are little aware of the physical labour required to supply them with the requisite materials.'[33] And all that physical effort could not guarantee a worthwhile quarry. There was as much luck as hard work involved. And as for his appearance, he continued, if he'd shown up at the doors of the British Museum dressed as he now was in tropical

Australia, the functionary 'might be inclined to do a charitable act by directing my steps towards Bedlam'.[34]

MacGillivray was very pleased with the treatment and assistance he received from Stanley and, in his letters to Forbes and Gould and others, he frequently referred to his commander with approbation. Stanley often praised MacGillivray's work when writing to Beaufort, thereby underlining the fact that he was the right choice for the job and implying that the good relations enjoyed by both may not have obtained had someone else been the naturalist. Stanley's support for MacGillivray and, by extension, natural history as a scientific pursuit was given a further boost once the *Rattlesnake* left Sydney for the voyage north when MacGillivray was given an additional cabin in which to store his collection.[35] Given the shortage of space on the ship, this was extremely generous of Stanley.

MacGillivray wasted no time in filling his cabin with specimens. Barely out of Sydney harbour, MacGillivray showed he meant business when 'a rare bird of the noddy kind perched on the rigging towards evening, and was added to the collection; for even the beauty and innocence of a tired wanderer like it was insufficient to save it from the scalpel.'[36] On the same day MacGillivray scooped a good quarry of molluscs in the towing net, one species of which, he was certain, was new to science. And indeed it was. When Forbes received the sketch of the animal, plus 50 specimens of its shell, he declared it a new species and promptly named it in honour of its discoverer – *Macgillivrayia pelagica*.[37]

Next up for MacGillivray and much more his line of work than the towing net was Moreton Island, one of two large islands that protect Moreton Bay from the Pacific Ocean. Nineteen miles long and four and a half miles wide, Moreton Island consisted of sand-hills and appeared wind-swept, its trees stunted and its grasses coarse. Both the eucalyptus and *Banksiae* abounded, unsurprisingly, but MacGillivray also noticed the presence of the Pandanus pine, a tropical species, and concluded that this must be its southernmost habitat.[38] With these observations, MacGillivray embarked on a task that he must have accepted with a certain amount of trepidation. He had begun a herbarium, and his first haul only amounted to 220 species, which he thought was paltry. He was not a botanist but, in his own estimation, he was doing his best trying to collect plants he had never met with before.[39] But not being a botanist, as he told Adam White at the

British Museum, 'I thought it better to lay hold of as much as I could leaving to others to sift the chaff from the wheat.'[40] The parcels of plants he sent back to London were destined, in the first instance, for Forbes, but it was Sir William Hooker at the Royal Botanic Gardens who was entrusted with the job of making a complete set of specimens for the British Museum.[41] However hard he tried, MacGillivray felt far less confident in this department than he did in other branches of natural history. He was very apologetic when he wrote to Hooker, stressing the difficulties of drying plant specimens in hot and humid conditions and the demands placed upon him in other areas of collecting – he did not collect any seeds, for example, because, as he put it to Hooker, he was 'unassisted' and had to 'sacrifice some department or other'.[42] He didn't even offer an account of his voyage, as he had done for Forbes and Gould, because he felt that Hooker would not be interested – in his words, 'I could not write as a Botanist.'[43]

While the *Rattlesnake* was at anchor in Moreton Bay, MacGillivray spent almost all his time, two weeks, on the island, collecting natural history specimens. But he also began compiling a vocabulary of the languages of the Aboriginal inhabitants of Moreton Island, being struck, particularly, by the fact that members of the group he was observing were speaking two different dialects. He was also impressed by their fishing techniques, relying on porpoises to round up a catch of fish for them. When the fish headed towards the beach in an attempt to escape from the porpoises, the Aborigines caught them with spears and scoop nets.[44] MacGillivray's stance with regard to the Aborigines was detached observation peppered with a good degree of respect. Though he had seen a species of porpoise that he believed was new to science, for example, he resisted the temptation to make a specimen of one of them because the mammal was held in special regard and its destruction would lead to 'direful consequences'. As he explained, 'I considered the advantages resulting to science from the addition of a new species of *Phocæna*, would not have justified me in outraging their strongly expressed superstitious feelings on the subject.'[45]

Moreton Island was the *Rattlesnake*'s first contact with Aborigines. MacGillivray had little to say, apart from commenting on their nakedness and referring to them as 'specimens' as though he were describing flora or fauna. Of course, MacGillivray had seen Aborigines before and the novelty of the encounter had worn off. For John Thomson, however, this was his first encounter and he shared his impressions with his wife, in a letter from Moreton Bay. Like MacGillivray, it was the nakedness of the Aborigines that struck him most: they 'delight in the dress that nature gave them still apparently without the slightest ideas or feelings of shame'.[46] Thomson was, of course, clothed and he made a point of describing himself, possibly to make the cultural point. 'I wear a striped cotton shirt and a pair of flannel trousers and white straw hat,' he wrote to Mary. Thinking of Aborigines as children was quite normal for Europeans at this time, as it was to refer to them as 'creatures', and to place them in the pecking order well below civilized Europeans – in Thomson's words 'but one remove from the lower animals'. To stress the physical differences from Europeans was also fairly typical: 'their figure is good being rather tall,' he told Mary, 'the trunk of the body is very well formed but the limbs, both arms and legs, too slender to suit European ideas of good proportion ... the eyes are good but the nose is large and flat and the mouth too capacious'. In addition to remarking on their dress, or lack of it, it was also usual to stress what was perceived as primitive technology, habitat and a no-care-for-tomorrow pattern of existence, and Thomson was no exception here. However he described the inhabitants and however far he felt removed from them, he, nevertheless, depended on them when it came to hunting. He frequently went out into the bush accompanied by an Aboriginal youth whom he recompensed with ship's biscuits and tobacco. The Aborigines of Moreton Island had long been in contact with white people from whom they had learned the art and craft of smoking: Thomson thought it was 'universal amongst them'.

No one on the *Rattlesnake* at this time tried to get to know any of the Aborigines on Moreton Island as individuals, although both MacGillivray and Thomson spent some time with them. For now, the perception of Aborigines remained stereotypical, as summed up by Huxley: 'They were miserable poor devils enough but very sociable and to all appearances happy as sandboys.'[47]

Less than a week later, the *Rattlesnake* was at anchor in Port Curtis, between the mainland and Facing Island. It was not as prolific in natural history as Moreton Bay – fewer plants and animals were collected, and there were no rare birds. Encounters with wild life took the form, primarily, of shooting them for the pot: MacGillivray probably scored a record with the killing of a 22.5-pound bustard – 'the goodness of its flesh was duly appreciated by my messmates,' he commented.[48] As for the Aborigines of Facing Island, they remained entirely aloof from the men of the *Rattlesnake*. MacGillivray and Huxley returned to their habit of pursuing natural history together – Huxley had taken a side-trip to the Darling Downs while the ship was in Moreton Bay – by spending a number of days exploring Facing Island and dredging. One haul of the sea floor brought up interesting molluscs, which Huxley quickly dissected and pronounced upon – MacGillivray was becoming quite used to Huxley's resolve to make a name for himself. Nothing passed him by. MacGillivray proudly told Forbes that when he had been stung by a kind of red algae, Huxley, after getting some amusement from seeing the naturalist reduced by the occasion, also 'had a theory on that subject'.[49]

The *Rattlesnake* remained in Port Curtis for three weeks. On 29 November 1847, Stanley took the ship northwards, leaving his colonial work completed and his survey work about to begin. While he reported both to Beaufort and Edward Deas Thomson that he would be away from Sydney for three months or more, in truth there were already signs that this was, at best, optimistic and, at worst, impossible.

New South Wales was experiencing one of its worst droughts. This was already known when the *Rattlesnake* left Sydney. Fresh water was available in Moreton Bay, but once the ship began its northward voyage, every search for fresh water proved fruitless. Facing Island presented creeks with brackish water and, on the mainland, one of the wells dug by Barney's settlers was entirely dry and the other no more than a puddle of brackish water.[50] There was some water inland but too far away to be conveyed to the ship.[51] Even the quantity of fresh provisions was disappearing fast, compelling the officers to shoot and fish for their supper. Obviously the Aborigines had water but that avenue was not explored.[52]

Stanley knew he could get water on Goold Island. Named by Phillip Parker King on his voyage in HMS *Mermaid* in 1819, Goold Island, just to the north of the much larger Hinchinbrook Island in Rockingham Bay, was well populated and, thanks to its elevation, had plenty of water flowing to the sea near a good anchorage – it had become well known as a good watering spot for passing ships.[53] But, as the *Rattlesnake* made its way through the Labyrinth, anchoring first at the Percy Islands, then at one of the smaller islands in the Cumberland Group, and finally, through Whitsunday Passage, at Port Molle, no fresh water could be found anywhere, though all of these places had yielded some on previous occasions. The drought had taken its toll. All of the freshwater lagoons MacGillivray had previously seen and the Aboriginal wells they came across at Port Molle were dried up.

Port Molle was reached on 8 December 1847, ten days after leaving Port Curtis. For the first time, the monotony of the coastal view, dominated by gum trees, gave way to luxuriant growth, 'in which one might observe every shade of colour from the sombre hue of the pine to the pale green of the cabbage palm'.[54] It was a naturalist's dream come true. There were rare birds to be seen, hordes of butterflies and a magnificent example of *Megapodius*, sometimes called a jungle fowl, scrubfowl or mound bird, which lays its eggs in huge mounds (upwards of 50 feet in circumference) of its own making – the heat generated by the decaying moist organic material incubates the eggs.[55]

The ship remained for two days. Then Stanley decided to run for Cape Upstart, about ninety miles further north up the coast, to look for water. HMS *Fly*, three years earlier, had found water there. Arriving on 10 December 1847, the 'great desideratum', water, was nowhere to be found: 'we found the deep bed of a river and extensive water holes capable of affording a large quantity of water in ordinary seasons, but all were dried up and the ground was quite parched,' Stanley informed Beaufort.[56] The very next day, 11 December, a year to the day that the ship had left England on its survey voyage, Stanley decided that, under the present weather conditions, he could not risk travelling further away from his only certain source of water, Moreton Bay, and ordered the *Rattlesnake* to retrace its steps. At the same time, he cut the water allowance to about a quart per man per day.[57]

Sailing southwards at this time of the year was difficult and frustrating: gales and strong currents and then sudden dead calms frequently impeded their progress. It took them five days to get from Cape Upstart to Port

Molle: the other way had taken them just one day. They continued south-wards. During a period of calm, MacGillivray hauled out the dredge reaching down 150 feet into coarse sand and pulled up a goodly number of crustacea and molluscs. Preserving them, for want of water, was out of the question. MacGillivray was relieved to have Huxley as his naturalist partner, for his drawing of one of the more interesting crustacea was all that survived after 'the specimens were accidentally thrown away'.[58] December 21 found them at anchor, fighting a strong gale, at one of the Great Keppel Islands, within a reasonable distance of Port Curtis. MacGillivray took the opportunity of exploring as much of the island as he could but, as he confided in Forbes, 'found little of interest having spent most of my time in extricating myself from the mazes of a mangrove swamp into which I had forced my way after some birds'.[59]

On Christmas Eve they were within sight of Facing Island but, aside from the consolation that they were heading towards water, there was little to gladden their hearts on this day. 'No joviality of any sort going on', wrote Charles Card in his diary, 'in fact we are not half as jolly as we are of any other night and I think I can safely say it is the most miserable one I have ever spent in my life . . . miserable fellows on the barren coast of Australia, no friends or relations to talk to or any thing else.'[60] The misery was only broken by the excitement of a near disaster when the ship was heading straight for rocks 'a couple of ship's lengths ahead', a catastrophe averted, at the last minute, by a sharp look out officer.[61] Christmas Day was equally dull, enlivened, this time, by a few men getting very drunk.[62] Huxley thought it pathetic: 'It is a cruel mockery to call a drinking bout among a parcel of people thrown together by the Admiralty "spending a merry Christmas".'[63]

Two days later, the ship was within 30 miles of Breaksea Spit, the beginning of the Great Barrier Reef. Water allowances were cut again. Soon, however, they were in the open sea and able to take full advantage of the winds without fear of shoals, rocks and reefs. Their progress was quick. On New Years Eve day, they sighted Cape Moreton and soon thereafter, the '1st cutter and jolly went on shore and brought off some beautiful water so that we can now have as much as we want'.[64] On 2 January they were reunited with the *Bramble* and, several days later, the two ships set sail for Sydney whose harbour they entered on 14 January 1848.

The lack of water had shortened the cruise but it was, nevertheless, a success. Stanley had managed to survey the inner passage both northwards and southwards, and, by staying away from the well-trodden track laid down by Phillip Parker King, had added substantially to the safety of this route.[65] Beaufort was very pleased when he learned of Stanley's work. 'I am glad to see . . . that you wisely eschew the beaten tracks on the chart', he told Stanley, 'and thus ransack the channels for dangers – the true vocation of a surveying vessel not being to save herself (only) but to save others.'[66] John Thomson was also pleased with the voyage, having enlarged his knowledge of botany and collected a large number of shells.[67] And MacGillivray, though he felt he had to apologize to Sir William Hooker for the paucity of his botanical specimens, concluded that this first voyage had gone well. He even showered praise on his friend Huxley – 'actively employed with his microscope and pencil and with the most important results' – and on his commander – 'Captain Stanley who has throughout taken a great interest in our pursuits, affords us every facility for zoological investigation.'[68]

Had they found water, then the *Rattlesnake* would have returned to Sydney much later than mid-January and history would have told a different tale of the ship and its men. As it was, some on board, such as Stanley, were disappointed by the shortness of the voyage, but others, such as Huxley, were delighted. Love had struck him deeply and bewilderingly. 'I had been with Netta the two preceding days', he told himself as the *Rattlesnake* left Sydney for the aborted northern cruise, 'and the pain of parting from her was the feeling uppermost in my mind.'[69] While she would be in his mind as 'an ark of promise in the wilderness of life', he continued, 'I conceive it my duty to set her aside, as it were, lest too frequent regretful thought should deprive me of the energy and temper required for the proper prosecution of my studies.'[70] In a show of surgical precision, he told himself he would ration thoughts of her to one hour just before bedtime.

No matter what he told himself, he was far too much in love to be able to control his thoughts. Many of these he committed in extended letters to his beloved. When, on 12 December, it became clear that the ship would have to retrace its steps for want of water, Huxley was delighted. 'Sydney in five weeks! Bravo.' he wrote in his diary, as the ship worked its way through Whitsunday Passage. An unexpected letter from Henrietta, received at Moreton Bay on 7 January 1848, only served to quicken his resolve to see her: 'Good night, darling, within a week if the gods be not very unpropitious, I will answer that orally.'[71] And the gods were on his side. 'We anchored in Sydney harbour on the afternoon of the 14th Jany. and as soon as etiquette would permit, I was on the back of a horse and off to New Town – where a happy meeting made up for long separation. Would it were the last or the longest.'[72]

Unfortunately for Huxley and others aboard the *Rattlesnake*, the stay in Sydney turned out to be short. No sooner had they anchored in Farm Cove and taken part in the festivities, especially the regatta on 26 January 1848, celebrating the sixtieth anniversary of the founding of Sydney in 1788, than they up-anchored for another spot of colonial business. This time Stanley had been asked to inspect a number of lighthouses in and around Bass Strait, the stretch of water that separates mainland Australia from the island of Tasmania. These lighthouses, located at Cape Otway, on the south coast of the present-day state of Victoria to the southwest of Melbourne, and on a number of small rocky outposts dotted between Wilson's Promontory on the Victoria coast to the southeast of Melbourne and Cape Portland in Tasmania, were crucial to the safety of intercolonial shipping. Stanley's task was to report on their effectiveness, in this, one of the most dangerous channels in Australian waters.

This request, agreed to by Stanley partly to keep in with the colonial authorities and partly to rate his chronometers and take more magnetical readings, took five weeks to complete. During this time, the ship spent several days anchored in Port Phillip Bay, giving the *Rattlesnake*'s men an opportunity to visit Melbourne, Australia's second city, a place with around 15,000 inhabitants and clearly on the way up. With its industries and its rich pastoral land inland, Melbourne, founded only twelve years earlier, had grown prodigiously during the decade, giving its movement for political independence from New South Wales and, therefore, Sydney, powerful support.[73] No one from the *Rattlesnake* who took the trip up the Yarra River by steamer or on foot could help but be impressed both by the city and its desire for separation.[74] Another, shorter stop was made at Port

Dalrymple, at the mouth of the Tamar River in northern Tasmania, some 40 miles from the town of Launceston, the colony's second town.

The *Rattlesnake* returned to Sydney on 9 March 1848. Stanley found the lighthouses working to his satisfaction.[75] MacGillivray, for his part, found a treasure trove on the beach, in rock pools, on accessible reefs, in the towing net and in the dredge. He kept very busy in all the places the ship stopped, accumulating specimen after specimen of molluscs but his most important find was another new species of *Trigonia*, dredged up from 45 fathoms, in the ocean not far from the opening into Port Phillip Bay.[76] Stanley was very impressed by MacGillivray and his 'indefatigable' pursuit of natural history and told Beaufort so.[77] Thomson, too, kept up his naturalist's interests and added substantially to his shell collection by scouring the beach at Port Dalrymple.

Huxley was busy too, finding things that interested him in MacGillivray's haul. With a bunch of new invertebrates from Port Phillip Bay to examine in the microscope, he 'had plenty to do'. It was all part of a larger project and in the intervening periods, when not enjoying himself on shore with his friend and fellow assistant surgeon, Archibald McClatchie, or thinking about Henrietta, he was working on a paper focusing on the anatomy of the *Medusae*, jellyfish.[78] This was a big paper, a 'turning point', ambitious enough for him to try and get it read at the Royal Society, which was at the apex of Britain's learned societies.[79] As he neared its completion while the *Rattlesnake* was anchored in Port Dalrymple, Huxley thought he would send it to Sir William Burnett, Physician General of the Navy, who first accepted him into the service: not out of 'sycophancy', he told himself, but because 'I feel that I owe the old man much, and I would do this simply as a matter of respect.'[80]

But it was not to be. Just after completing the inspection of the last two lighthouses at Goose Island and Swan Island in Bass Strait, Stanley came into the chart room where Huxley was putting the finishing touches on his drawings to accompany the paper. Huxley told him what he was planning to do with the paper but Stanley advised that it would be better to entrust it to his father, the Bishop of Norwich, whose influence in the world of gentlemanly science would ensure its reception.[81] And so it was settled. The paper was ready by 21 March. Before parting with it, Huxley handed it over to William MacLeay, the famous naturalist who had come to live in

Sydney in 1839 and whose authority Huxley respected and whose ideas he shared.[82] MacLeay approved of what he read and the paper was now ready to go. Stanley enclosed it with a letter he wrote to Beaufort on 28 April 1848, adding that 'I am not Naturalist enough myself to judge of its merits and demerits, but the drawings are beautifully correct and neither time or labour has been spared in making them.'[83] And Stanley, as an accomplished artist himself, knew what he was talking about and MacGillivray frequently echoed the same sentiments. The paper reached Stanley's father near the end of September and had its reading at the Royal Society, as Huxley hoped, in June 1849 and was subsequently published in the Society's *Transactions*.[84]

The paper proposed a radical reclassification of invertebrates, arguing that the jellyfish, stinging nettles, man-of-war and other creatures were 'members of one great group, organized upon one simple and uniform plan, and even in their complex and aberrant forms, reducible to the same type' and not, as Cuvier and his followers maintained, distinct and different animals.[85] With this simple but powerful conclusion, the paper criticized naturalists who were content to state, as he put it, 'matters of detail concerning particular genera and species, instead of giving broad and general views of the whole class, considered as organized upon a given type, and inquiring into its relations with other families'.[86] Huxley implied that these other naturalists pursued their research in this way, by implication erroneously, because they did not have the opportunities he had now to see a whole range of creatures in the same environment. Fieldwork, as we would now call it, was the key to understanding nature. The difficulties in examining the *Medusae* were, Huxley argued, greatly exaggerated. With a steady ship, 'a good microscope and a good light' and 'a good *successive* supply of specimens, as the more delicate oceanic species are usually unfit for examination within a few hours after they are taken', he 'never failed in procuring all the information [he] required', on the east coast of Australia and Bass Strait.[87]

Things were definitely improving for Huxley. He was feeling confident about himself. 'All this goes to the comforting side of the question, and gives me hope of being able to follow out my favourite pursuits in course of time, without hindrance to what is now the main object of my life. I tell Netty to look to being "Frau Professorin" one of these odd days,' he told his sister.[88] On board ship, he was in fine shape as well: 'I am on good terms with everybody.' And as for Stanley, he could not have been more complimentary or grateful. 'I must say this for the skipper – oddity as he is, he has never failed to offer me and give me the utmost assistance in his power, in all my undertakings, and that in the readiest manner. Indeed, I often fancy that if I took the trouble to court him a little we should be great friends.'[89]

March 1848 in Sydney was also a highlight of MacGillivray's life. On the 23rd of the month he married his fiancée, Williamina Gray, at St Andrews, the Scots Church, in Sydney, in the presence of the bride's brothers and Huxley, Joseph Dayman and John James Brown, the *Rattlesnake*'s master, who gave the bride away.[90] The ships were festooned with garlands to celebrate the event. Charles Card, recently promoted to the rank of clerk, commented that 'great joking [was] going on as to who is to be next'.[91]

PART FOUR

CHAPTER VII

Edmund Kennedy and Cape York
1848

While the *Rattlesnake* was making its way to Port Phillip, the 29-year-old Edmund Besley Court Kennedy arrived in Sydney, exhausted but in good health and spirits, after an extremely arduous and near calamitous exploration of inland Australia. He had set out in March of the previous year from Sydney with a party of eight men, an Aboriginal guide and a team of pack horses and carts, to follow the course of the 'Victoria' River, believed to flow northwards into the Gulf of Carpentaria.

Kennedy had only been in Australia for seven years and had done very well for himself. Arriving in 1840, the then twenty-one-year-old was taken under the wing of Charles James Tyers, a close family friend and a surveyor in the colony's Survey Department. At the time, Tyers himself had only recently arrived in Australia, having being commissioned to make the first survey for the proposed settlement of Port Essington in northern Australia. It was through this that Tyers had first met Owen Stanley, then a lieutenant in command of HMS *Britomart*.

After rapidly qualifying as an assistant-surveyor, Kennedy cut his teeth in his new career – he had followed some instruction in surveying and engineering in London just before embarking for Australia – in company with Tyers as they set out for Portland Bay from which they were to survey the rich hinterland behind the new settlement.[1] He remained in the area for a few years and then was recalled to Sydney, back to the Survey Department, where he languished because of the absence of surveying work.[2] But all this was about to change.

In 1845, Thomas Livingstone Mitchell, the Surveyor-General, and, therefore, Kennedy's ultimate boss, received orders to proceed on an expedition to find an overland route from Sydney to Port Essington. This was in direct response to a report of the Legislative Council in 1843 recommending such an expedition, on the grounds that it would secure a route through a huge part of Australia to the northernmost settlement, and, therefore, beyond to Singapore and the Far East.[3] Mitchell chose Thomas Townsend as his assistant but, at the last moment, he was reassigned to another survey and Kennedy, somewhat surprisingly given his junior position in the department and his relative lack of experience in Australia, took his place.[4]

Mitchell believed in the existence of a great river that flowed northwards into the Gulf of Carpentaria and he was certain that on this overland expedition he would encounter it.[5] The thirty-man party, together with a substantial number of horses, bullocks, sheep and carts, left Sydney in November 1845 heading in a northwest direction towards modern-day Bourke in the western part of New South Wales before planning to turn north.[6] Over the next nine months the party moved steadily northwards, into what is now western Queensland, Mitchell constantly on the lookout for the great northern-flowing river. By September 1846, Mitchell, leading a small advance party and leaving Kennedy with most of the men behind at a base camp, had reached a point near the present-day Queensland town of Isisford where he was certain that the river he was following – named the Victoria by him – would flow northwards into the Gulf: 'leading from temperate into tropical regions, a river leading to India'.[7] At this same point, however, Mitchell, facing dangerously low levels of provisions, extreme weariness and hostility from the indigenous people, reluctantly decided to call it a day and retrace his steps back to Sydney, confident that he had found the great river. Mitchell took a month to return to base camp and he and Kennedy were reunited in October 1846. The party headed back to Sydney, Mitchell arriving on 29 December 1846 and Kennedy, with most of the men, on 20 January 1847.

On the return trip to Sydney, Kennedy volunteered to take an expedition, as soon as it was possible, back to the place on the 'Victoria' River where Mitchell had stopped. Mitchell agreed.[8] Events had to move fast because Mitchell, upon his return to Sydney, had applied for a twelve-month leave of absence to allow him to go to England on urgent private business. A quick round of introductions to the new Governor, Sir Charles Fitzroy, was followed by Kennedy calling in person and a set of instructions laid out by Mitchell. On 25 February 1847, Kennedy received formal authority to proceed and several weeks later, on 13 March 1847, the party, consisting of Kennedy, seven men, a young Aboriginal guide and carts and pack horses, set off from Sydney following Mitchell's detailed route and instructions, 'the principal object of the journey being the determination of the course of the Victoria, and the discovery of a convenient route to the head of the Gulph of Carpentaria'.[9] A fortnight later, Mitchell sailed for England.[10]

Kennedy, not yet twenty-nine years old and having only been in the surveying service for seven years, was now in charge of his own expedition, focused on completing the previous year's expedition and determining whether the Victoria was the great northern river. Kennedy seemed convinced of his boss's assertion though he was more open-minded. 'Sir Thomas has pledged his character as an Explorer', he wrote to his sister, 'that the River empties itself into the Gulf, and I am inclined to think so too, but please Providence I shall see.'[11]

For several months the party toiled its way along Mitchell's route until 12 August 1847 when they reached a point on the 'Victoria' River that they were convinced was Mitchell's furthest. Kennedy was now into his own exploration. They began following the river but, each time they thought it was about to flow north, instead, it flowed southwest. Day after day Kennedy found himself pushing further to the southwest, but all the time being torn between not losing hope that Mitchell was right and realizing that he was wrong. A side excursion up a tributary of the 'Victoria', which seemed to flow northward and which Kennedy named the Thomson River after Edward Deas Thomson, the Colonial Secretary, only added to the growing sense of disappointment when it turned to the northeast.[12] As for the 'Victoria', no matter how much further they followed it, it doggedly stuck to its south-south-western course while at the same time it wormed its way into more and more inhospitable, exceedingly hot, dry and barren country. The 'Victoria', Kennedy concluded, did not flow into the Gulf; it was nothing more than the upper reaches of Cooper Creek, an insignificant flow of water followed by the explorer Charles Sturt in 1845 from the west into the same kind of wasteland that now threatened to engulf Kennedy and his party. Short of water and food and under a relentless sun, on 9 September 1847 Kennedy ordered a retreat.[13] He renamed Mitchell's 'Victoria' the Barcoo, the native name for the river, signalling the end of a dream. The return trip almost ended in tragedy for want of fresh water but the party, alive but exhausted, returned to Sydney in February 1848.[14]

Kennedy filed his report with the Colonial Government. He was disappointed with the negative results of his expedition. This was not simply a matter of geography for geography's sake. Kennedy understood implicitly that what really mattered was finding a convenient route to the Gulf of Carpentaria, and, on the way, traversing and mapping land that might be useful to the colony. Unable to do that, he had, in desperation, and after realizing the futility of following the 'Victoria' any further, tried to head straight for the Gulf.[15] Though he succeeded in determining the course of the 'Victoria' he had failed, he said, 'to render my journey of any practical use to the Colonists'.[16] Sydney, contrary to Kennedy's expectations, welcomed him as a hero and showered him with praise, so much so that the Colonial Government seemed already to have made up its mind to send Kennedy on another expedition.[17]

The Colonial Government, that is, not the Survey Department. Mitchell was away in England. Edward Deas Thomson, who had little time for Mitchell, took charge of the new expedition.[18] No doubt he was pleased that while Mitchell's 'Victoria' River was erased from maps and minds, the Thomson River was enshrined on these same documents. As early as late February, Kennedy knew that he was going to lead an expedition whose objective was to complete the last expedition, find a convenient route to the Gulf, plus explore 'the Country forming the Promontory terminating in its Northernmost extremity at Cape York'.[19] Port Essington, the destination of previous expeditions and most spectacularly that undertaken by Ludwig Leichhardt in 1844 and 1845, was now dropped from the itinerary. It had struggled to become a permanent settlement since 1838 but very little seemed to go its way. As damning reports of its unsuitability as a permanent settlement began to circulate widely, from the pens of Francis Blackwood and Joseph Bette Jukes, commander and naturalist, respectively, of HMS *Fly*, and John MacGillivray;[20] as its most ardent supporters were retiring from office, and as little return was being seen for the amounts invested by the government, thoughts of abandoning Port Essington started to emerge.[21]

By contrast, Cape York was beginning to impress the Colonial Government and the Admiralty as a place of some importance, though very little was known about it. Blackwood, Jukes and MacGillivray, in their various communications in 1845, praised its location and climate, and its future role as a coaling station for the steamer traffic expected to increase between Sydney and Singapore. Aided and spurred on by the volume of admiration for this far outpost of the colony of New South Wales, Governor Gipps, in December 1845, pleaded with Lord Stanley, the Colonial Secretary in London, not to delay any longer in settling a corp of marines at Cape York.[22] Beaufort got in on the action fairly swiftly instructing Yule on HMS *Bramble* in September 1846 to 'minutely examine all the coast immediately contiguous to Cape York, either east or west of it, for it would be very gratifying to my Lords to find out a safe and secure little harbour or cove about there, where a vessel might be certain of refuge, safety, and water, and where a small settlement and depot might be formed.'[23]

Kennedy probably had little inkling of the shift in importance from Port Essington to Cape York. Early in March 1848, less than a month after his return from the Barcoo, Kennedy called at Deas Thomson's office and submitted a draft he had been asked to draw up outlining how he was going to conduct his new expedition to the Gulf and Cape York.[24] Kennedy planned to head up to the Gulf from the point at which the Barcoo began to flow southwest by whichever river he could find: he would then push on to Port Essington, if he found himself in the southwestern corner of the Gulf, or Cape York if in the southeastern corner. But Kennedy seemed to be missing the point: Port Essington was no longer an option. Thomson impressed upon him the changed circumstances and sent him away to redraft his plans with that in mind. By 18 March 1848, the draft plan had progressed enough for Governor Fitzroy to inform Earl Grey at the Colonial Office in London that he was going to send Kennedy to explore the area up to the Gulf and then the peninsula ending at Cape York.[25]

But then something happened to alter Kennedy's plans. Before the end of March, Governor Fitzroy invited Stanley to discuss Kennedy's plans with him. Stanley had already decided to commence his survey at Goold Island and work northwards once his ships had been refitted and supplies taken aboard.[26] At that meeting, Stanley suggested to Fitzroy that it would make sense to tie Kennedy's expedition in with his survey of the inner passage – '[he] has taken my advice implicitly,' he told his family proudly.[27] Having a Royal Navy man-of-war involved in a major land expedition would have sounded very impressive, for all the advantages it would confer, and though it had never been done before – Mitchell, for example, would not have countenanced it – the idea had been around for some time, having been expounded most recently by no less an authority than Roderick Murchison, President of the Royal Geographical Society.[28] If Stanley's ideas were to be adopted then Kennedy would need to reverse his plans, beginning with an exploration of the Cape York Peninsula and then pro- ceeding to the Gulf and southwards to the Barcoo before returning to Sydney. Fitzroy liked what he heard and agreed to the plan Stanley put for- ward. Kennedy would be landed at Rockingham Bay, on which Goold Island was located, with his men, animals, carts and supplies, from where he would proceed northwards to Cape York. Stanley would meet him there, together with provisions for his onward journey to the Gulf and beyond, in October.[29] Once Fitzroy approved the idea, no time was wast- ed. He arranged for Stanley and Phillip Parker King, who had just come down to Sydney from his home in Port Stephens, to meet with Deas Thomson and Kennedy on 8 April to discuss the details.[30]

Though Stanley had not met Kennedy before, he knew Charles Tyers, Kennedy's superior and friend in the Surveyor-General's Office, very well. Tyers no doubt spoke of his young protégé in glowing terms and Sydney society had already been greatly impressed by the reception of his last expedition. Stanley, for his part, contributed to the outpouring of compli- ments in informing Beaufort of the proposed expedition and assessing

Kennedy, the man, for him, as an explorer and surveyor. 'I am happy to say that the Colonial Government are going to send another expedition to explore the interior . . . under the command of Mr Kennedy a young man of great talent and energy . . . It will be an arduous undertaking,' Stanley explained, 'but Mr Kennedy is quite the person to carry it out and in addition to great experience in the Bush he is a good Observer and a fair Lunarian, so that we may hope to have pretty accurate Longitudes of the different places visited.'[31] Though Stanley didn't mention it to Beaufort, he also believed that Kennedy would be able to hold his party together much better than the Leichhardt and Mitchell expeditions which were marred by dissension.[32]

The meeting went well. Three days later, a set of instructions was drafted by Phillip Parker King, which detailed Kennedy's route from Rockingham Bay, northward first to Princess Charlotte Bay and then to Cape York, continuing down the eastern shore of the Gulf of Carpentaria (the western side of the Cape York Peninsula), and tracing the route of a number of rivers to their source in the southeast until reaching the northernmost point of Mitchell's 1846 expedition.[33] On the following day, 12 April 1848, Stanley wrote to Deas Thomson formally agreeing to give Kennedy all the assistance possible. The idea was for Kennedy, together with twelve men, horses, sheep, bullocks and carts, to be taken to Rockingham Bay on a suitable vessel in the company of the *Rattlesnake*. Once the party was landed, the vessel would continue on its way and the *Rattlesnake* would begin its survey.

Kennedy was to be furnished with rockets – 'They can never be mistaken for native fires and they are also of great use in driving natives away from the camp' – in order for him to be able to communicate with the *Rattlesnake* or any of the other vessels, such as the *Bramble*, employed in the survey.[34] Stanley had arranged for a ship to meet him at Cape York in October with supplies to allow him to continue his survey of the Torres Strait. Consequently he suggested that Kennedy only take supplies sufficient to get him to Cape York and that the supplies for his trek south from Cape York should be sent on the same ship as Stanley's.[35] The instructions were formally approved on 16 April.[36]

A suitable vessel, the *Tam O'Shanter*, a barque of 270 tons and recently arrived from London, was in Sydney harbour and though originally destined for Adelaide, its owners changed its routing to Rockingham Bay, Port Essington and Batavia (present-day Djakarta).[37] Refitting took a fortnight.

Kennedy had twelve men with him; five of them, William Costigan, John Douglas, James Luff, Charles Niblett and Thomas Wall, had been with him on his 1847 expedition. All of them, apart from Wall who was a natural history collector, were ex-convicts and on conditional pardon because of their good work on the expedition.[38] Volunteering to spend months in the bush again is, perhaps, a measure of Kennedy's force of personality. Four more of the party, Edward Taylor, William Goddard, Dennis Dunn and Edward Carpenter, were convicts, serving sentences ranging from ten years to life and all but Taylor had already committed crimes in New South Wales. This was their last chance. The remaining men in the party consisted of James Mitchell, a servant, and acquaintance of Kennedy's, William Carron, a botanist and official naturalist to the expedition and, at the eleventh hour, an Aborigine named Jackey Jackey, taking the place of Harry, the Aboriginal guide on the previous expedition.[39] There were also 27 horses, 250 sheep and three carts, supplies for several months, surveying instruments and guns.[40]

Kennedy's expedition was unusual and bound to invite the wrath of Thomas Mitchell, the Surveyor-General and all those who were in sympathy with him. Mitchell was still in England. Organized and mounted by Deas Thomson behind Mitchell's back, the expedition had the full consent of the Governor. Governor Fitzroy was convincing in explaining to Earl Grey, the Secretary of State for the Colonies, why he was sending Kennedy on the expedition, why his instructions had been reversed, and why he was asking for further financial assistance because of the sea passage to Rockingham Bay. He maintained that the expedition could only benefit from having Stanley 'on a parallel with the line of march of the Expedition', and, because the surveying duties meant that the *Rattlesnake* would be working its way slowly up the coast, Kennedy would be 'able in case of necessity to fall back upon the point of the Coast where the '*Rattlesnake*' would probably be found'.[41] Timing was also on their side for Stanley, Fitzroy continued, expected to be at Cape York about the same time as Kennedy. And then with both of them there, the marine and the land surveyor, a proper and early report could be made on Cape York in regard to its suitability as a site for a settlement, a coal depot for steam communication and as a place of refuge.

Not only did Deas Thomson act as if he were the Surveyor-General, but he also gave some of the planning to a number of people who had nothing to do with the Surveyor's Office but who, instead, were eminent scientific people. Stanley was the key to the enterprise, but his role was more accidental than it may seem, for had he not been forced to retreat from the north by the drought, he'd probably never have encountered Kennedy. He reflected the changed thinking about Cape York versus Port Essington, manifested in his giving compelling evidence on this issue to a Select Committee hearing on 16 April, it is true, but it was the fact that he was on the spot that made it possible for Kennedy's expedition to dove-tail with Stanley's survey. Stanley enjoyed the prospect of making himself available to the colonial authorities yet again and they, for their part, appreciated his generosity and his scientific abilities.[42] Without Stanley's presence, it would not have been possible to organize the expedition in this way. Phillip Parker King's presence at the first meeting with Stanley, Kennedy and Deas Thomson gave authority to the change in route for he knew more about the inner passage and the eastern coast of Australia than probably any man alive, and also knew Stanley well. A few days before the expedition left Sydney, Stanley invited Colonel George Barney, of the abandoned Port Curtis settlement, and Reverend William Clarke, the eminent geologist and friend of the others, to the *Rattlesnake*, together with Kennedy and King, to discuss some of the details of the expedition.[43]

Stanley's confidence in participating in Kennedy's expedition rang through his correspondence. He boasted that the 'Governor . . . has taken my advice implicitly and Captn. King who is just come down also thinks highly of it.'[44] In response to Beaufort's warning that the Admiralty didn't like their men and ships to be loaned to the colonial authorities, Stanley simply explained that he was not losing Admiralty time in assisting Kennedy: at Rockingham Bay, 'we must have remained at anchor there to hoist the large boats and rate the chronometers', and at Cape York, 'we must wait in the ship till the provisions arrive from Sydney.'[45] Besides which, he continued, rather cleverly, while the *Rattlesnake* is at anchor, apparently doing nothing, 'the *Bramble*, Decked Boat and all my surveying force will be employed in searching for rocks in Endeavour Strait and surveying the Channel north of Prince of Wales Islands. The nature of the country round Cape York shall be carefully ascertained so that in the event of Government wishing to form a settlement there they will be in possession of all the necessary information.'[46] Unlike his other colonial undertakings where his role was passive and where he was being asked to help in making decisions in which, as he himself understood, his expert input was minimal, here in the Kennedy expedition he was central. He was also the talk of the town. The *Sydney Morning Herald* ran a feature on the expedition on 26 April and praised Stanley no end.[47] Speaking of Kennedy's proposed route, the article emphasized that

> He will go out with considerable advantages – not the least, that he will be conveyed, without waste of valuable time and unnecessary and destructive fatigue, at once to the borders of the territory, and on arriving at the limit of his journey – the *Ultima Thule* of exploration, that he will meet with a supply of provisions to refresh and recruit his party, when most needed.[48]

'Three times three congratulating and farewell cheers', the article concluded with a fanfare fit for a royal visit,

> for KENNEDY and STANLEY – and for Torres Strait and York Cape – the one destined before many years to be the highway of navies, and the other the home of a thriving and prolific swarm from the great Australian hive. May prosperity and happiness attend the explorers by sea and land, and success crown the traveller and his convoy of *Rattlesnakers*![49]

As the *Rattlesnake* prepared to leave Sydney, Stanley, buoyed by his new-found fame, penned his final message to Deas Thomson with some more information about his intended whereabouts. Confirming what he had previously said, he would be in Cape York in October, but now added that he expected to be in Princess Charlotte Bay, a point Kennedy was to head towards, in July.[50]

Before the *Rattlesnake* left Sydney, Stanley welcomed a guest on board who would remain with the ship for two years. Oswald Brierly, whom Stanley had met and befriended in Twofold Bay, had shown up in Sydney on 22 April 1848, having quit his position in the Boyd business empire.[51] Since he and Stanley last met in Boyd Town, things had not gone well for him, despite the fact that he had been made a magistrate in Eden, across the bay. In late 1847, Boyd began to face tremendous financial difficulties and lost interest in Twofold Bay. Brierly found it hard to manage his work under these circumstances when he had to follow the orders of one of Boyd's associates in Boyd Town, with whom he was soon in conflict.[52] On top of that, Eden had been chosen as the site of the Customs House, with the attendant diversion of trade away from Boyd Town.[53] Brierly decided to leave.[54]

Brierly had invested much of his spirit and life in Twofold Bay and left it with a heavy heart: 'so blue and still was this cloudless morning in the corner where I made my home,' he wrote in his journal on the day of his departure.[55] Stanley was pleased to have Brierly with him, but, officially, he was not the ship's 'artist', but a guest of the captain's, 'an amateur', he told Beaufort, 'who goes . . . to study sea effects and seamanship'.[56]

And so, on a wave of optimism and with a sense of great adventure, the *Rattlesnake* got under way from Farm Cove around 9 a.m. on 29 April 1848. With some hearts torn apart by separation and others, such as Midshipman Packe, desperate to be rid of Sydney ('we sailed . . . from this stinking hole from amongst Jews, Rogues and Vagabonds . . .'), leaving Sydney was a mixed experience.[57] Just before clearing the heads, Stanley received Deas Thomson and the Treasurer to the Colony on board for a 'repast with Champagne', another sign that this was an extremely important occasion.[58] Several hours later, and out to sea, the *Tam O'Shanter*, bearing Kennedy and company, came up under the *Rattlesnake*'s stern and then went ahead of the heavier and slower ship, heading northwards for a point at which both ships could enter the inner passage of the Great Barrier Reef. 'Had a look at the Sydney light this evening', wrote Charles Card, 'and wished it good bye for a twelvemonth. At 11 Tam showed a blue light and at 12 we did the same, she being a long way ahead.'[59]

Sailing northwards from Sydney proved, at first, to be painfully slow. For more than a week, alternating bouts of calm and rough winds on top of relentless adverse currents hampered the progress of the *Rattlesnake* and the *Tam O'Shanter*. An average of 30 miles a day was recorded. But then on 8 May, they caught the southeast trades and the ships pulled ahead cutting through the sea at a brisk pace. The *Rattlesnake* was racing along at more than 9 knots leaving the *Tam O'Shanter* behind. Several days later, Great Sandy Island (Fraser Island now) came into view and soon thereafter Breaksea Spit and the beginning of the Great Barrier Reef. Next in sight was Lady Elliot Island to the south of which the *Rattlesnake* on its previous cruise, and other ships normally, entered the inner passage. This time, however, Stanley decided to push forward to enter at a point to the north that had been surveyed by HMS *Fly* several years earlier. This point, between Swain Reef and the Capricorn Group of islands was, according to Stanley, preferable to the southern entrance and he recommended that steam ships should seriously consider taking this route. Stanley took a certain pride in this recommendation and reported it to Beaufort as a major improvement in shipping. He explained tersely that he hadn't taken the usual opening at Lady Elliot because 'light winds and strong currents rendered the passage . . . rather tedious'.[60] Though this became the official story, some observers on board the *Rattlesnake* recounted the event rather differently. Thomson, the surgeon, talked about plans for entering the inner passage at Lady Elliot Island being abandoned and presents a more complicated set of circumstances and choices than Stanley reported to Beaufort.[61] Card thought that a navigational mistake had been made and that the Lady Elliot Island opening was missed rather than not attempted by choice.[62] Huxley did not proffer an opinion. Navigational issues bored him. 'We have this time taken a peculiar route', he wrote in his diary, '[it] is considered to be more convenient by the "cognoscenti".'[63] The *Tam O'Shanter* was nowhere to be seen.

Upon entering the inner passage, on 14 May 1848, the *Rattlesnake* made steady progress heading, in the first instance, for High Peak Island in the Northumberland Group. Islands and capes went by in rapid succession: Cumberland Group, Percy Group, Pentecost Island and Holborne Island; Cape Townshend, Cape Gloucester and, finally on 19 May, Cape Upstart, and their first anchorage since leaving Sydney. Brierly, who had never been this far north, and so had never seen the serene beauty, nor heard the exquisite peacefulness of the inner part of the barrier reef, was beside himself with almost child-like excitement. 'Oh such a beautiful day' was how Brierly, with the precise and penetrating eyes of an artist, described his first day in these waters, '– a cloudless sky overhead, and being in soundings the water had changed from the heavy deep blue of deep water to a beautiful Emerald tint – the ship with studding sails set going before a light Breeze and every sail full and motionless – and, from the absence of all swell, not flapping in the manner they do when running before it with a swell . . . the sunshine striking down on the main deck – glittering and glancing from the Polished Brass-work, white hammocks neatly stowed along the railings, ropes coiled down, the officers in their uniforms . . . the men walking the deck forward in their clean white trousers and blue shirts . . .'[64] The next day was even better and the evening a delight almost too lovely to describe in words. 'The tint on these islands towards sunset became peculiarly rich and beautiful,' he wrote, '– deep shadows of a purply tone with points jutting out and catching warm lights – while one side received a general breadth of warm glowing light – the ship with her cloud of sail stealing along silently and rising up against the evening sky.'[65] The play of light fascinated him, as did the illusory effects of objects seen from a distance. Brierly tried to make sense of the latter receiving instruction from Stanley on how to use a sextant to measure heights. When it came to colour and form, Brierly didn't rely on science but simply noted what he saw: '– a very beautiful effect', he wrote,

> is when the larger Islands of the Group are seen opening over the smaller and nearer ones – which from their local colour being lighted up by the sun – and tracing strong shadows, give the most beautiful aerial effect to the Islands beyond them – these distant Islands do not become mere Blue masses under these circumstances but the most tender white Grey . . . in the lights with very lightly defined shadows – and when the water is calm . . . the sea at the Horizon . . . is of so delicate and light a Grey that these Islands seem to float in air . . . [66]

And so it continued. No opportunity was lost to sketch in pencil while noting the colour effects in words.

At Cape Upstart, there wasn't much time set aside for going on shore but that didn't stop the collectors from raking over the beach and ground close by. And this, despite the ravaging bites of thousands of flies emerging from the long grass that spread inland from the beach. MacGillivray, stoically enduring the bites – '[they] added a finishing touch, as if to test the powers of human endurance' – was glad to get on land.[67] His only stab at natural history since leaving Sydney was dredging down to 30 fathoms off one of the Cumberland Islands during which time he got a new species of mollusc.[68] And aside from seeing, but not shooting, a few passing birds and the rare visit of a butterfly to the ship, there was little material available. Though he had only a short time, MacGillivray got into his stride immediately. He grabbed a few shells and a number of plants, though his chief interest was a species of wallaby, which he failed to find. Thomson found some shells and plants as well. Brierly, covering his face with his handkerchief in a vain attempt to protect himself from the insects, sat down and began to make his first sketch of Australia north of Sydney looking seaward from the coast, the result being much admired by Charles Card.[69] Stanley took a few measurements and, after spending an evening at anchor, the *Rattlesnake* set sail again in the afternoon of 20 May, to take up its intended position near Goold Island.

Cape Bowling Green passed on the port side, followed by Cape Cleveland, the Palm Islands, Hinchinbrook Island and then Goold Island at 4 p.m. on 21 May. The *Tam O'Shanter*, not seen since the *Rattlesnake* entered the inner passage, was waiting for the ships, having arrived the day before. The next day, the *Bramble* joined them, having been sent ahead from Sydney to complete the survey of Port Macquarie and Port Curtis.

After some difficulty they found a convenient landing place at the very northern end of Rockingham Bay, a good distance away from where the ships were berthed.[70] Stanley gave the order to weigh anchor and moved all the ships to an anchorage at one of the Family Islands, probably Timana, just to the southeast of the proposed landing place.[71] For the next two days, most of Kennedy's stores, horses, sheep, dogs, carts, instruments and provisions, were removed from the *Tam O'Shanter* and, with the help of the *Rattlesnake*'s boats and about sixty men, hoisting and slinging beasts into the sea, and shouting contradictory orders accompanied by the tunes of the pipe and fiddle, landed on the shore. As luck would have it, instead of enjoying the usual fine, relatively calm weather of the area, on the days of landing the operation had to withstand substantial swells that crashed onto the beach. It was, by all accounts, a hair-raising affair. 'While you were all busily engaged at Sydney with the preparations for the Supper and Ball on the Queens Birthday, we were not less so in landing Kennedys horses and sheep in half a gale of wind on a dead lee shore, and I can assure you it was no joke,' Stanley told Deas Thomson.[72] Fortunately, there was only one casualty – one of the horses drowned in the swell. Stanley was overjoyed at the success of the operation and of Kennedy's prospects. 'Nothing I assure you can be more satisfactory than the way in which Kennedy and all his party are going on – they every one of them seem up to their work and eager to commence and all Kennedy's arrangements are very good indeed.'[73] To commemorate the event, Stanley named the spot where Kennedy landed as Kennedy Bay and the anchorage of the *Tam O'Shanter* as Tam O'Shanter Point.[74] The next day, the *Asp*, the *Rattlesnake*'s covered boat, reported that the fresh water stream known to exist on nearby Dunk Island was in full flow, and the following day, 26 May, the *Rattlesnake* was moved over to an anchorage at the southern end of Dunk Island to fill the tanks with the precious liquid.[75] Farewell dinners were given on board and the horses acclimatized before the expedition could get under way.

Though the landing place was convenient for discharging the stores and setting up the first camp, it was not chosen as a spot from which the expedition could begin moving inland. Indeed, finding a way through the bush behind the beach was a much more difficult task than finding a site for the camp, and took several days. 'I have visited the Bay at 3 different points', Kennedy confided to an unknown correspondent, 'and confess a viler looking country never looked me in the face before. Ranges of 4800 feet (at the highest) encircle the Bay. They are very abrupt and densely wooded . . . I must get inland as soon as possible, as the Coast Range will not permit of travelling with Horse carts.'[76]

Kennedy decided that he needed to get a better idea of the lie of the land than he could make out from the beach. He formed a light party of five men to reconnoitre a wider area and planned to be away for between four and six days. He chose John Douglas, his faithful servant, and James Luff, both of whom had been with him on his last expedition, and Jackey Jackey to accompany him while leaving the other nine men at the camp. He also took Huxley who, restless and low in spirits, sick of being cooped up in the ship, 'intensely miserable, hot, wet and stinking', with little to do but sleep, convinced Kennedy to take him along.

The party first tried to go westward but immediately met a ridge through which there was no passage. Then they tried to go south to the Hull River and to follow its course inland, but that proved to be useless as they soon found themselves in dense wood that seemed impenetrable, try as they might to hack their way through. They returned to the beach, went further south before trying to go west again and though at first hopes rose when they saw open forest land in the distance, soon marsh and dense woods stopped them again. Several days had gone by and they were no nearer a way into the interior. On 2 June, Kennedy and company tried to go northwards but met conditions similar to those they'd encountered in the other directions. The only option left to him was to cross the Hull River and go south to find a route west. It worked. He could see a way out. As pre-arranged, he signalled to the *Rattlesnake* his intention to pack up and head out by firing a rocket into the evening sky.

The next day, 3 June, Stanley and Lieutenant Henry Simpson, taking the pinnace and a galley with them, met Kennedy at camp to help transport his entourage across the mouth of the Hull. The operation took more than a day to complete. Huxley, Simpson and Kennedy spent the evening when everything had been accomplished 'in sweet discourse variously interrupted by eating and drinking under the tent'.[77] Next morning, with breakfast completed, farewells were said and Kennedy was on his way.

The *Rattlesnake* people, Huxley included, returned to the ship. Everyone went about their business as usual, Stanley taking sights and magnetical measurements on Dunk Island and nearby Mound Island, Brierly sketching madly, MacGillivray filling his bags with shells and plants, Thomson doing the same. But Huxley began to sink into despair. He had enjoyed the experience of exploring and wanted more of it. He wanted to get off the ship and go with Kennedy to Cape York. Kennedy, short of a medical man and liking Huxley, had asked him to join the expedition. 'He was very desirous that I should accompany him as far as Cape York', he wrote to Nettie, 'and if the requirements of the service would have permitted it I certainly should have done so – two or three months in the bush would have set me up in strength for the next three years . . . '[78] Huxley also liked Kennedy a great deal and felt an emotion for him that he hadn't felt for anyone else on the ship. 'Wholly without pretension' is how he described Kennedy in his diary, and to his darling Nettie, 'He is evidently a man of great determination (a quality of which as you know I am rather enamoured) and he clearly understands everything necessary to his present office – I believe that he will accomplish all that can be accomplished in his undertaking –'.[79] Stanley, too, was very upbeat about Kennedy's prospects. Writing to Deas Thomson, Stanley expressed enormous faith in the expedition, but understating the difficulty of the terrain. 'Kennedy and his party went away in high spirits and I hope under favourable auspices – they had a little swampy province to encounter at first but after that the country seemed clear enough . . .'[80] To his father, Stanley was even more forthcoming, especially in regard to his role in the expedition. 'I cannot tell how very pleased I am', he wrote, 'to find all has, as yet, gone on so right, as I consider the whole arrangements of the route of the expedition to be my own.'[81]

Huxley probably felt it more personally than others on the *Rattlesnake*; there was some excitement missing now that Kennedy had gone. The *Tam O'Shanter* had set sail on 31 May, continuing to Port Essington before going to Batavia and Singapore. In the minutes leading up to the ship's departure, everyone who had letters to write took advantage of this last opportunity of communicating with the rest of the world, to tell families and loved ones that they were well and at anchor in Rockingham Bay, at latitude 18 degrees south, well inside tropical Australia, and unlikely to see another ship for months. The *Bramble* had also left, gone south to Palm Island to examine a shoal. The excitement of the Kennedy expedition was over for now, but they had the rendezvous in Princess Charlotte Bay at the end of July to look forward to and, if that didn't happen, there was Cape York in October.[82]

Now, free of other obligations, the *Rattlesnake*'s main task lay ahead: to survey and produce charts and sailing directions for an absolutely safe track in this inner part of the barrier reef, stretching up to the very tip of Australia at Cape York, a distance of about 600 miles, covering 7.5 degrees of latitude and 4.5 degrees of longitude. Stanley was full of confidence. There was not going to be any repetition of last year's aborted mission. The east coast had had substantial rain between January and April. Water would be found in all the usual places. 'I have now as you say a delightful Ball at my feet', wrote Stanley, echoing and expanding upon Beaufort's metaphor, 'and you may depend upon its being rolled and kicked to its utmost extent.'[83]

But there was no getting away from the fact that no matter how confident the commander nor exciting the prospect of having one's name permanently etched on to an Admiralty chart, the process of surveying was tedious and time-consuming, and required the full resources of both the *Rattlesnake* and the *Bramble* and all of their boats. The work was divided between taking astronomical observations and measuring angles from fixed points, usually islands and soundings. A section of coast, between twenty or thirty miles in length, would be chosen, and the latitude and longitude of a fixed point would be taken. Then, the contours of the coast would be recorded until the next fixed point, and so on, until the coast ran out. One of the draughtsmen on board would then commit the bearings to paper giving as precise a view of the line of the coast as possible. Meanwhile, soundings from the edge of the reef to the coast would be taken to determine the depth of the seabed, the frequency depending on the scale of the chart.

Sounding took a heavy toll of patience and interest. It was very repetitive but required great concentration. Errors could lead to disaster. Philip Sharpe, the sixteen-year-old naval cadet, was detailed for sounding duties on the *Asp*, the 42-foot decked launch, which went away from the *Rattlesnake* for several days at a time for surveying. He provides a very vivid account of an activity that is normally unrecorded:

> The 2nd Lieut. Dayman, was in command, Smith and Earle, both midshipmen and myself, were the cabin party, and seven men and a boy, formed the crew ... The routine used to be; – turn out about 5.30, stow bedding, wash and dress; Breakfast at 6 o'clock, clean, then weigh and commence work shortly before 7. Directly we were underweigh, my duty was, to sit down, right aft ... and watch the dial of the patent log (which registered our distance run) and noting all the soundings at every tenth or half tenth, or oftener according to the scale of the survey, and *here I sat* the whole forenoon until dinner time, when we usually anchored, and I got a respite during the dinner hour. If we did not anchor, but continued right through, I had to stick to my post till Smith or Earle had their meal and came and relieved me whilst I got mine; then back again. In the afternoon (usually from 1.15 to 5.30 or 6 o'clock) I had to repeat my morning's work, so that I had generally 9 to 9½ hours sitting continuously in a cramped position, with plenty of writing all the time, as I had also to record all the observations of the surveyors in the sounding book ... We dined a little before 7 o'clock, again after a short rest after which I turned to and wrote in ink in the fair sounding book, all that had been done in the day, and *then* I was pretty well ready for bed.[84]

As long as the weather was generally favourable, soundings could be taken continuously but bearings required a degree of visibility. The result of all this work was a chart showing the coast line, prominent land features, the depths of the seabed, dangers and obstructions – such as reefs, shoals and rocks – and a central track for safe shipping.

Mound Island (present-day Purtaboi Island just off the northwest corner of Dunk Island), whose bearings and observations were taken by Stanley and Kennedy on 29 May, formed the first station. By the time the ships reached Cape York, MacGillivray reckoned that they had stopped at thirty-seven separate islands, not to mention the many detached reefs that were strewn here and there.[85] The *Rattlesnake* weighed anchor on 6 June, heading for the Barnard Island Group and the Frankland Island Group, and after a fortnight it reached Fitzroy Island, near Cairns, the rendezvous point for the *Bramble*, which had been working its way to the northward from Palm Island.

Those who did the actual surveying were, in an important sense, well catered for. The work was monotonous but at least it was work. For many others, not directly involved in surveying, or only involved from time to time, the difficulty was to find something to do. Charles Card, newly promoted to the position of clerk, was certainly expressing a shared emotion on the occasion when the *Rattlesnake* fell in with a brig, the *Gazelle*, off one of the Frankland Islands. As the ship was coming up, 'some of us', Card noted, 'began to hope it might be a vessel sent up to send us to China but we were deceived.'[86] To pass the time, many on the ship simply amused themselves, swimming, shooting game for the pot, walking around islands and, above all, scouring the beaches for shells. MacGillivray thought that about half of the ship's company went searching for shells whenever they were given the chance.[87] They would collect in the hundredweight and knowledgeable they were too. MacGillivray, one imagines with a wry smile, recounts the story that when he spotted one of the men rustling among the top branches of a tree and asked him if he'd found a nest, the man replied: 'Oh no, Sir, its these *geotrochuses* that I am after.' Shell collecting not only helped pass the time, but shells provided important mementos of far-away places and, occasionally, a rare item could be sold for a tidy sum.[88]

John Thomson even built a cabinet for himself to house his growing collection of shells.[89] When he wasn't collecting shells, he pursued his passion for plants, collecting on every occasion he could. There was little illness on the ship and, as he told his wife, 'as far as the mere survey went I never felt in the least degree interested ... collecting shells and plants was my only amusement and employment.'[90] But collecting was not all child's play:

> Whenever the weather permits I am on shore with my gun and haversack and keep toiling through scrub and over hill in quest of whatever appears rare with a perpendicular sun the perspiration pours down off me and my clothes are as wet as if I had walked through a pond – and roasting with thirst how delightful to come across any little water – at other times I am for half a day up to the neck in water looking after shells with many of which I have already replenished my cabinet.[91]

He crammed his journal with the name of each plant he bagged. For MacGillivray, however, collecting was not a pastime but a duty. As he told Gould, the relentlessly slow progress of the *Rattlesnake* as it moved from island to island, landing for sights and discharging the boats for the finer work, was a godsend for him: 'I had capital opportunities of landing.'[92] And the results were impressive. Not being very big, the islands did not yield large animals but there were plenty of smaller ones to interest him, including a new species of fly-catcher, the 'bandicoot of India', 'doubtless introduced by some wrecked vessel', a new species of flying-fox (large fruit-eating bats), kingfishers, fishing-eagles and, perhaps the most impressive of all, 'a new and splendid rifle-bird, which Mr. Gould . . . named *Ptiloris Victoriæ*, as a mark of respect and gratitude for the patronage bestowed on his great work on the Birds of Australia'.[93] As the ship got closer to Cape York they encountered the Torres Strait pigeon in profusion: on one occasion, MacGillivray recounted, seven shooters killed 159 birds in one hour.[94] There were also many kinds of fishes and water-snakes and endless shells to delight him. MacGillivray collected over 900 specimens of 230 or more species of molluscs alone. Botany was not neglected, though, as he explained to Sir William Hooker's son, Joseph Dalton Hooker, 'at present I am so busily employed all day and half the night with my own peculiar province that I am unable to attend to more'.[95] Not every island was quarried and, in most cases, the haul of specimens was small.

That same frustration, which MacGillivray had expressed to Sir William Hooker, he echoed in his letter to Joseph: 'You must not expect much that is new,' he wrote, 'for I am not botanist enough to avoid sending a quantity of rubbish so I beg you will take the will for the power.'[96] To sweeten the communication, however, MacGillivray told Hooker that at Rockingham Bay he had managed to get several specimens of *Balanphoraceae*, a parasitic plant of great interest to Hooker and known to inhabit the Indonesian Archipelago. The plant had not previously been recorded in Australia and this was probably its southernmost habitat. MacGillivray put the specimens, preserved in brandy, in jars and accompanied them with a coloured drawing made by Huxley, which showed its colours in the wild, in case they did not survive the long immersion in spirits.[97]

Though like-minded and sympathetic individuals surrounded him – Huxley, Thomson, Wilcox and Stanley were the closest – MacGillivray, nevertheless, felt isolated pursuing natural history. The problem was that he was not receiving any acknowledgement from Edward Forbes, his chief correspondent and recipient of his collections, and he had no idea whether he was doing anything worthwhile. It made him anxious. '. . . You must know how cheering it is to me so far from home as I am to hear of any novelties that may have been transmitted by me,' he wrote in a short letter to Forbes.[98] MacGillivray was, however, grateful to Forbes, for, while he hadn't replied to them, he had published a number of MacGillivray's letters in the *Annals and Magazine of Natural History*. Interested parties, therefore, could learn of MacGillivray's exploits before seeing the fruits of his labours. MacGillivray was walking a delicate line between, on the one hand, being in Forbes's debt and, on the other hand, chiding him for being silent.

Huxley shared MacGillivray's anxiety and frustration at being so far from where his career was, or was not, being made. He knew nothing of the progress of the various papers that Stanley had forwarded on to London, 'the success or failure of whose results must determine my prospects'.[99] A modicum of self-doubt had already accompanied him to Rockingham Bay – 'Have I the capabilities for a scientific life or only the desire and wish for it springing from a flattered vanity and self-deceiving blindness? . . . if his silver talent be nothing but lead after all, no Bedlam fool can be more worthy of contempt.'[100] With the experience of exploring with Kennedy behind him, a kind of dark despair and self-questioning began to overtake him on the cool blue and emerald waters of the Great Barrier Reef. Hardly any entries were made in his diary after the ship departed from Rockingham Bay. The zeal for examining the weird invertebrate world seemed to have evaporated, to be replaced by reading Dante's *Inferno*. He was, as he said, 'getting very apathetic of late, and I think I never was so mortally sick of anything as of this monotonous cruise. I care for little else but sleep, and I have a great mind to coil myself up and hibernate until we get letters at Cape York.'[101] He harboured a demon, he told Nettie, that made him irritable and gave him 'unfortunate fits of mental and bodily instability'.[102] A vortex of uncertainty was beginning to consume him and he was unable to disentangle his yearning for her from all that was around him. He was desperate for contact, for a letter, at least. 'Oh Nettie darling do not leave me – without you my world would be but a weary circle of duties – with you what may it not be.'[103]

Thursday 22 June started like any other day: boats preparing to take rounds of angles, sounding between islands, looking for shoals, landing for water, and observing the flora and fauna. The land was low and the sea a constant smooth bluish green. It was a scene that everyone on the ship had become accustomed to, and some increasingly bored by. And then, literally out of the blue, in the mid-afternoon, 'we were astonished [when] a strange boat came round the point with an English Ensign hoisted. Some fancied it was a shipwrecked crew, others a coaster.'[104] 'An infinity of speculations' rippled through the *Rattlesnake*, as the boat's identity excited the imagination. 'Some thought she was a cruiser bringing us dispatches with immediate orders to move on to China,' wrote Huxley, perhaps secretly hoping it was, clutching at anything that would let him escape from his awful boredom. As the boat got closer, its identity became less of a mystery than why it was there.

It was the *Will o' the Wisp*, a yacht, known to many of those on the *Rattlesnake* who had encountered it in the races held in the Sydney Regatta back in January. But what was a pleasure boat, more suited to the confines of Port Jackson than the open ocean, doing so far from home? The second galley was sent out to find out, and what they learned both shocked and perplexed them.

There were six men aboard, a master, a mate, and four others. The master and one of the crew, a native of New Caledonia, were in a desperate condition. Both had had severe blows to the head. The master was worst off: his scalp had been horribly beaten for several inches and his skull was fractured – he was lucky to be alive.[105] Both Thomson and Huxley rushed to the aid of the unfortunate, 'laden with lint and bandages, with thoughts of amputations and fractures . . .'[106] Neither medical officer had experienced anything like this on the voyage so far.

Once the master and Sam, the New Caledonian, were stitched up and made comfortable, the story began to emerge. The *Will o' the Wisp* had left Sydney on 5 May, almost a week after the *Rattlesnake* had departed. It was no coincidence. The *Will o' the Wisp* was a small boat and had been sent by Robert Towns, a wealthy and powerful Sydney merchant, to search the islands north of Moreton Bay for sandalwood, an extremely precious commodity, which fetched a good price in China and was thought to be growing off the eastern coast of Australia. Sam was on board because New Caledonia was a major source of sandalwood and he knew all about it.[107] Towns, not wishing to draw any attention to himself – sandalwood brought out the rush in people like gold – decided to send this inconsequential vessel instead of a larger one to scout the area, but just to be on the safe side, in case something went wrong, he decided to send it out in the wake of the *Rattlesnake*. Thanks to the publicity surrounding the Kennedy expedition, Roach, the master of the *Will o' the Wisp*, knew the *Rattlesnake*'s intended route.

All went well for the boat as it worked its way up the eastern coast of Australia by the inner route. By mid-June it had reached Cape Upstart and, on 18 June, took an anchorage near one of the Palm Islands, to the south of Rockingham Bay. The local inhabitants appeared friendly and bartered for goods. They were invited to the boat. But then, at around 4 a.m. on 20 June, according to the mate, two or three dozen – no one seemed exactly sure of the number – boarded the boat, took positions around the hatchways, and began throwing lighted bark into the boat. Sam, the New Caledonian, whose watch it was, rushed up from below, where he was storing firewood, and was met by a club to the head. Roach, awakened by the commotion and the smoke, attempted to get out, but he too was clubbed. The others now awoke from their sleep and the mate,

177

grabbing a cutlass, began to fight his way out of the situation, first by killing one of the attackers and then, as he got on to the deck, running his weapon through others. It was a scene of carnage. How many of the invaders were killed outright and how many drowned as they attempted to get back into their canoes, no one could tell, but everyone on the *Will o' the Wisp* was alive, though both Sam and Roach barely so.

The mate patched up both men as best he could and set sail northwards for Goold Island for water and, incredibly, given what had happened, to search for sandalwood. The peace did not last, however, and near Goold Island, another battle ensued between the locals and the *Will o' the Wisp*, pistols set against spears. Another two dozen or so Aborigines were killed, and the boat, leaving a scene of devastation behind, pulled up anchor in search of the *Rattlesnake*. On 21 June they fell in with some of the *Rattlesnake*'s boats away on surveying duty and were told where to find the ship.[108]

Everyone was deeply moved and frightened by the events. Midshipman Packe simply recorded, 'now we know what Blackguards they are'. Thomson, whose job it was to attend to Sam and especially Roach, was astonished by the calculated nature of the attack on the *Will O' the Wisp*, hiding, as it was, behind a veil of friendship and reciprocity. Stanley, whose responsibility it was to report the incident to the colonial authorities, shared these thoughts – 'I have been induced to send this statement', he wrote to Deas Thomson, 'in order to show how often the natives are tempted to make an attack and stand the consequences.'[109] He blamed the owners of small vessels such as these who, he thought, were easy prey for attack and gave the attackers confidence to move on to larger vessels.

Thomson attended to Roach until he improved enough to skipper the boat back to Sydney. On 2 July Thomson gave Roach the all clear and the next day, the small vessel set sail. Before they left, Stanley took depositions from the *Will O' the Wisp* men and forwarded these, together with his comments, to Deas Thomson. What happened to the *Will O' the Wisp* was a salutary lesson for Stanley. He immediately ordered that shore leave would only be granted in uninhabited places.[110]

The *Bramble* rejoined the *Rattlesnake* at Fitzroy Island on 27 June 1848. Two days later, the ships once again parted, the *Rattlesnake* heading for its next fixed point in Trinity Bay. About a month later, and after a substantial bout of surveying by all the boats and ships, the *Rattlesnake* and the *Bramble* met again and anchored at Endeavour Reef, a place steeped in history and so-called because this was the spot where Captain James Cook ran his ship the *Endeavour* onto the coral and almost ended his voyage in June 1770. The *Bramble*'s stay was very short, for the very next day, Stanley ordered Yule to sail directly to Princess Charlotte Bay, to meet Kennedy and to survey the area between the shore and the reef.[111]

Stanley had arranged with Kennedy that he would signal by means of lighting three fires, equally distant from each other, the middle being the largest, and firing a rocket at 8 o'clock into the evening sky.[112] The *Bramble* anchored in Princess Charlotte Bay near Flinders Island. That evening, three fires were seen on the mainland but no rocket. The next day, they saw the same fires smoking and assumed they were from an Aboriginal camp. The survey of the bay began on 31 July when Yule went on shore to get his first round of angles to fix the points. Still no sign of Kennedy. They sounded and charted for the next few days and, on 7 August, the *Bramble* was moved into a new position closer to the shore. They were now giving up on Kennedy. Midshipman Packe thought 'he perhaps has found a river or something in his way and had to trace it inland, as he would have no means of getting his carts across it if it was of any size. This part to the Gulf of Carpentia [sic] has never been travelled over before and there is no knowing what sort of a country it may turn out to be.'[113] The next few days turned out to be extremely unfavourable to sounding as the winds were strong and the sea was up. On 13 August, 'we were disturbed at 9 pm by 3 of the men who said they had seen a rocket go off over the land. We fired one in answer but only a ½ one.'[114] Three days later, in the evening, they thought they saw a rocket and learned from one of the boats that had been sounding near Cape Melville to the east that a gunshot had been heard. This was extremely promising and George Inskip, the second master, went across the next day, 17 August, to where they thought the rocket had been fired. 'It will be very curious if he does not find Kennedy as ever since Sunday [13 August] we have seen Rockets or something very much like them at about 8 pm.' Inskip returned in the gig, 'having seen nothing of Kennedy'.[115] For almost a month, the *Bramble* remained in and around Princess Charlotte Bay surveying but no fires or rockets were seen again.

On 15 September the ship was anchored at Pelican Island, to the north of Princess Charlotte Bay, and then headed for a rendezvous with the *Rattlesnake* near Sunday Island, off Cape Grenville, at Latitude 12 degrees south, within reasonable sailing distance of Cape York and which the *Bramble* reached on 29 September 1848.

For the next few days the two ships threaded their way near the coast until, on 6 October, they reached and anchored at their destination in Port Albany, between the mainland and Albany Island, which Yule had surveyed and named when he was there in the *Bramble* exactly two years previously.[116] They had reached their final anchorage on this very long voyage. They had all had enough. MacGillivray, normally cheerful when scurrying around after flora and fauna, was buckling under the strain of tedium. 'The monotony to everyone on board but myself was very great,' he wrote to Gould, 'latterly I too got rather tired, no adventure of any kind having occurred, no meeting with vessels, scarcely any intercourse with the natives – every day, in fact, pretty much like its predecessor.'[117]

At least they had made it. The exciting prospect of the arrival of the provision ship with letters and news and fresh supplies was buoyed up by the relief that the survey was as good as over. The closer the *Rattlesnake* and *Bramble* approached to Cape York, the greater was the anticipation of meeting the ship. 'Every one begins to be rather anxious now about the provision ship which is to be here the first week in October,' wrote Charles Card in his diary on 30 September.[118] Stanley had arranged for the ship to be stuffed with provisions, including more than a thousand pounds of lemon juice: several cases of scurvy had already appeared on the *Bramble*.[119] And he stipulated that it should arrive at Cape York by the beginning of October:[120]

> But no provision ship here to cheer us up, which we have been looking forward to so long.[121]

And there was no sign of Kennedy.

CHAPTER VIII

The Cape, the Furnace and Cockroaches
1848 & 1849

While they waited for supplies and for Kennedy, the *Rattlesnake* and the *Bramble* anchored in Evans Bay, just to the south of Cape York. There were natural wells under the surface of the beach, which provided a convenient source of water for the ships. The bay was a traditional meeting place for the Gudang – the inhabitants of the northeastern part of Cape York – and the people from the nearby Torres Strait Islands, particularly the Kaurareg from Prince of Wales Island, but there were also visitors from Darnley Island and others from further afield. MacGillivray estimated that more than 150 locals and visitors – not counting the ship's company – flocked to the bay every day.[1]

For the locals white people were an unusual sight but not a new one. European ships had been passing and stopping for water for decades. But for most of the company of the *Rattlesnake* and the *Bramble*, the indigenous people were a new experience and they were very curious about them and eager to meet them. Stanley, however, probably anxious about what happened on the *Will o' The Wisp*, ordered that only officers would be allowed on shore.

Disappointment flooded through the ship – 'after all our wishing to get up to Cape York so as to have some view of the manners and customs of the natives on the main land', most of the men would have to make do with second-hand information.[2] That, however, was freely available. Charles Card learned on the first day that the local people were 'very friendly and well disposed'; that they freely offered the turtle eggs that they had just successfully procured; that they were also keen to share their store of dates, 'which were very good'; and that they smoked tobacco from 'a long pipe made of bamboo' which made them 'quite drunk for two or three minutes'. By the end of the following 48 hours, he had also learned that the local people helped in using the seine net to catch fish but not digging for water and that some of them used bows and arrows, though no one was 'quite certain whether they belong solely to the Darnley Islanders or whether the natives here use them themselves'.[3]

It was not long, however, before even those who were confined to the ships got a first-hand experience of the local people. The *Bramble* was the first ship to be boarded, by two boys, Kaiow and Maipei. They were known to the *Bramble*'s last cruise and appeared delighted to get on board.[4] Several days later it was the *Rattlesnake*'s turn when two or three natives came on board in one of the watering boats. The men managed to get one of them below decks and 'set about rigging him out'. Card gave 'him an old broad brimmed hat . . . and the rim of an old tin dish for a gold band, and an old oil-skin cape: sent him off in high spirits'.[5] Not much later, the entertainment became more exciting, apparently for both parties. 'A canoe load of them came alongside', Card recorded in his diary, 'and were soon seated among the lower deck eating biscuit and drinking tea in immense quantities. They did not seem to care much about music as in the middle of it they would hold out their hands and sing out for "bitchcuit"; one of them got an old pair of drawers and went up to the top mast crosstrees.'[6]

Once the first tentative steps had been taken, relationships between the visitors and the locals began to warm. The day after the tea party, just a week into the anchorage in Evans Bay, a large canoe holding ten men visited the *Rattlesnake*. Though they were not allowed on the ship at first, they eventually climbed up the side and got on board. They all spent the night on the ship, sleeping in the hammocks that were slung below decks. Having already learned that they did not have huts but slept wherever they happened to be and that the men went naked while the women wore only 'a long fringe of grass', Card and his friends went after the only actually collectable item and 'got as many native words as we could, all of which we put down on paper'.[7]

Attitudes to the local people varied enormously and unpredictably. Midshipman Packe, for example, whose water collecting duties took him ashore although he wasn't an officer, found he enjoyed being surrounded by them, accepting their gifts of fruit and shooting parrots for them, in spite of his previous intensely critical attitudes to everyone not British.[8] On the other hand, John Thomson, usually restrained and fair in his judgements, expressed his contempt in a letter to his wife – 'so many black savages men and women, roaming about in a state of nudity, and approaching, as near as may be approached where such a distinctive difference has been instituted between man and the brute, the lower animals in all their feelings and instincts. They appear to know nothing more and to care for nothing more than the gratification of their animal appetites . . .'[9] Thomson's only personal interaction with the local people came when he 'chose one to be my servant to accompany me in my wanderings and the first law I taught him was the power of the fowling piece'.[10]

By contrast, Brierly, now thirty-one, had already spent six years in Australia, five of them among the Kudingal people on Twofold Bay. He worked with them, whaling, made friends with them and even fell in love with a young and 'beautiful Aboriginal' woman.[11] As the captain's guest he was free to go ashore when he wished, and he went daily and interacted freely with the Aboriginal people. A young man, Billadi, became his 'self-appointed protector'.[12]

Brierly began sketching some canoes that had been hauled up on the beach. 'My proceedings in this way soon attracted the attention of the older men', he noted in his journal:

> At first they watched the preparations – cutting pencils, arranging paper, etc. – with silent curiosity, but as the sketch proceeded, they began to take great interest in it and seemed [to be] recognising each part of the canoe and seeming highly delighted, pointing first to the canoe and then to the sketch, repeating the names of the different parts to each other.[13]

Soon the sight of a white man drawing one of their canoes attracted the attention of other locals, and a large number of women, who had been shelling further along the beach, surrounded Brierly, offering him oysters galore. Next to join in was

> an old man with three little children . . . bringing a basket of pretty white shells – nuts, olives, etc., some of them beautiful specimens. The children took them out of the basket and held them up to me in tiny handfuls, saying *Cotaiga?* [friend] and appearing quite delighted as I took them. Then they ran behind one another and took hold of the old man's legs and indulged in such small hearty laughs that I laughed too . . .[14]

Next day Brierly was taken to the encampment in the bush, where he observed the women busily occupied making matting for sails (for the out-rigger canoes) and baskets, and crushing the fruit of the Pandanus palm. Many of the children, Brierly observed, appeared 'in a dreadful state covered with raw sores on which flies settled', and 'looked prematurely old – big pendulous bellies with frightfully thin arms and legs'. The women were very proud of their children and showed them off eagerly. Brierly also observed (as did others from the ships), that women did most of the work, while the men, they felt, did little except socialize with their colleagues and enter into barter exchanges with the visitors.[15] Not too far from where the fruit was being crushed, Brierly was invited – 'they cleared a space removing the leaves and grass aside, and made signs that I should sit down with them' – to sit down with a group of men who were smoking a bamboo pipe. It was made of a large piece of bamboo, two or three feet in length and four inches in diameter. A small bowl containing the lighted tobacco was fitted at one end and the other end remained open. One of the smokers sucked the smoke into the space within the bamboo, and then the bowl was removed and, keeping that end shut, the pipe was handed round so that each person could have a draught.[16]

Brierly was also befriended by an older woman, Baki, and another young man, Dowatha, who showed him an amazing brush turkey mound, 190 feet in circumference at the base, 12 feet in height and 48 feet in circumference at the top.[17] In return, Brierly invited both Billadi and Dowatha on board the *Rattlesnake* and Stanley welcomed them – his 'kind manner reassured them and they appeared to be perfectly at home.'[18]

The next day he encountered 'another and more beautiful canoe'. This, much larger, canoe was more extravagant than the craft he had seen until now: it was 'painted red at the sides and carved and ornamented with a string of cowries which hung down in a graceful festoon in front of the bow. In the stern three rods were stuck up. On these were attached long streamers of some kind of leaves which hung down in the water in a very beautiful manner.' They came to barter with a bow and arrows and shells and ended up staying on board through the night. Brierly learned that these people were from another island to the north of Cape York, Prince of Wales Island, and that the canoe, named Kie Marina, belonged to a man called Manu.[19] They left the ship very early in the morning and when Brierly turned up on the beach later, these islanders invited him on to their canoe for a session of barter. Tobacco, a silk handkerchief and other unrecorded items were exchanged for a mask, a mother of pearl and a wig. Brierly was impressed. His artistic eye captured the moment. 'These men', he wrote,

> were in every respect superior to any other natives we had seen. The beautiful workmanship of the canoe, the taste shown in the different modes of orna-menting it, was something so much beyond the mere utility of the other canoes . . . I had long admired but I had never till now seen anything that realised so much the idea of beauty.[20]

As the tide was beginning to rise, the islanders took advantage of the change to set sail for their home. Before setting off, however, the crew helped Brierly out of the canoe in such a gentle and warm manner that he was amazed:

> one of the tallest stepping out into the water stooped down that I might kneel on his shoulders while another walked by my side and gave me the assistance of his shoulder that I might the more steady go on shore. In this way I was car-ried for some distance until they came to the dry sand where I was put down with as much care as though I had been a basket of eggs.[21]

While Stanley searched for a bay suited to being a harbour and coal station for steamers using the inner passage on their way to Singapore, and Brierly got to know the local inhabitants and their visitors, the company of the *Rattlesnake* and the *Bramble* became increasingly desperate for the supply ship to arrive. Scurvy was beginning to appear.[22] On Friday 13 October, they ate the last of the peas.[23] The level of anxiety was so high that the sails of the boats attached to the survey were frequently mistaken for the hoped-for provision ship. 'Everybody is in a state of irritability, suspense and dis-content', Huxley confided in Nettie, and he was not immune from it: 'I myself feel very much inclined to have a row with some person or persons unknown.'[24] To help defuse the atmosphere, Stanley ordered the pinnace to sail to Booby Island for news.

Booby Island, located on the edge of the Arafura Sea and on the west-ernmost edge of the Torres Strait Islands, had been an unofficial place of refuge for British and Australian shipping since its discovery by Cook. Nothing had been done to fix the place up as an official refuge, providing provisions and the like, until 1837 when Captain William Hobson, then in command of the very same HMS *Rattlesnake*, erected a post office on the lone, uninhabited island. A flagpole signalled the location, in a cave, of a strong box, containing printed forms, pens and ink, for passing ships to record their safe arrival and useful hints for other ships. In addition, a pro-vision of preserved meats and ship's biscuit was laid down.[25] By the time of this voyage of HMS *Rattlesnake*, it had become customary for passing ships to leave post for ships they knew were in the area, as well as newspa-pers and other kinds of useful information.

The pinnace's journey to Booby Island took three days. When it returned to Evans Bay, the news was encouraging. The provision ship hadn't left Sydney until the middle of September, and, as a voyage from Sydney to Cape York took an average of three weeks, it could be expected any day, as long as it hadn't foundered on the way.

And so they waited, growing daily more anxious and hungry. As John Thomson remarked to his wife in a letter, 'you will remember the old proverb, a hungry man is an angry man – each one on board exhibited himself quite in a new light showing exultations of temper and disposition for which he previously had not received credit.' Even Thomson himself – whom Huxley described as having a 'hard-headed soul' and adhering to 'the most undeviating uprightness of principle' – was not immune from the prevailing atmosphere, and was known to 'vomit forth a whole belly full of bile'.[26]

Thankfully, the seemingly interminable wait did eventually end. On Saturday, 21 October, a fortnight after the *Rattlesnake* and the *Bramble* took up their anchorage in Evans Bay, 'some one sung "Ship in sight".'[27] A few hours later, the *John and Charlotte*, a 93 ton schooner, stuffed with provisions, letters and newspapers, anchored between the *Rattlesnake* and the *Bramble*. Despite their hunger, it was not their stomachs that most needed satisfying but their desperation for news, from family, loved ones and friends. The bags of letters were hauled on board the *Rattlesnake* and, in Stanley's cabin, they were sorted while everyone else held their breath on the other side of the door in painful anticipation. When a lucky recipient's name was shouted, he grabbed his precious pile and disappeared into a corner of the ship, racing through the letters for news and, then, once satisfied, reading and re-reading, over and over again, the words etched on the thin paper.[28] The newspapers were also pored over for the smallest detail and told them of the alarming revolutionary events in France. But that was half the world away. It was the personal news, especially good news, of course, that cheered them up: 'This being Trafalgar Day, too,' Charles Card noted, 'we have all been very jolly.'[29]

The *John and Charlotte*, as they discovered, had left Sydney on 19 September, pretty much when it was supposed to, in company with another, smaller schooner, the *Ariel*, which was carrying supplies and a surgeon, Dr Adoniah Vallack, and a stockman, for Kennedy. The two ships became separated in a gale off Port Stephens, not long after leaving Sydney. The *John and Charlotte* came up the east coast by taking the outer passage, that is, sailing on the outside of the Great Barrier Reef.

Over the next few days, the provisions were cleared from the *John and Charlotte* and the holds refilled on the *Rattlesnake* and *Bramble*. It took five days to unload the supplies and Evans Bay sand was substituted for food and drink in the holds of the provision ship. Then, on 27 October, just as this was completed, another ship's sails were spotted on the horizon. This time it was the *Ariel*. As became clear, the *Ariel* had suffered very badly in the gale off Port Stephens but the damage was not so much to the ship as to the live provisions. The ship lost 70 sheep, 2 horses and a bullock during the gale and the commander, Captain Dobson, had returned to Sydney to replenish the stock. Eventually, the *Ariel* left Sydney again on 3 October, taking the inner passage for the voyage up the coast.[30]

The *Bramble* took the occasion of the arrival of both the *John and Charlotte* and the *Ariel* to return to the survey of Endeavour Strait, the preferred passage out of the Torres Strait, located to the west of Cape York and running in a southwesterly direction between Possession Island and Entrance Island off the southeastern corner of Prince of Wales Island. As for the *Ariel*, the stock was removed to a stockade on Albany Island, to be tended by the stockman, a Crown Prisoner, who was already beginning to show signs of insubordination and being neglectful of his duties.[31] The *John and Charlotte*, its loading of ballast completed, and now also carrying quickly written letters from the *Rattlesnake* and the *Bramble*, set off on the rest of its voyage, first to Port Essington and then on to Manila.

The arrival of the *Ariel* reminded everyone, if they needed reminding, that Kennedy should have arrived long ago. Once again, there was nothing to do but wait but, given that the ships lived mainly off the provisions they brought with them, the *Ariel* included, the wait could not be indefinite. Neither the *Rattlesnake* nor the *Bramble* could remain in the area much longer as both ships had surveying work to do in the Torres Strait. Stanley conferred with Dr Vallack, who had also been given responsibility for Kennedy's stores, as to the best plan. It was agreed that the *Ariel* would remain at the anchorage for as long as possible, given the state of the provisions and the costs to the Colonial Government, and that Vallack would ultimately be responsible for deciding when to leave.[32] It seemed possible for the *Ariel* to remain at Cape York until the end of January. The last thing the *Ariel* was to do before leaving the anchorage, assuming that Kennedy had still not arrived, was 'to bury the beef, flour, and other articles that will keep under ground', in a convenient and well-marked spot and then return to Sydney.

The *Bramble* arrived back from Endeavour Strait on 1 November, just as the orders for the *Ariel* were being completed. The next day the survey ships took their leave of Cape York, the *Rattlesnake* heading westward for Port Essington and the *Bramble* back to Endeavour Strait to put the final touches on the survey. Before the ships left, it was also agreed that the *Rattlesnake* would make its way through the Torres Strait using the Prince of Wales Channel, the passage to the north of Hammond Island, and, once its business at Port Essington had been completed, would head back to Sydney by going around Australia counter clockwise. The *Bramble* would return to Evans Bay once its work in Endeavour Strait was completed and then beat its way back to Sydney by the inner passage, something that had only been done by a handful of sailing ships. No other ship had done it twice. This was the *Bramble*'s second time, the first being in April 1845. 'It is a great question as to who will be the first in Sydney', Charles Card remarked, 'and has produced many bets.'[33] Betting was a major pastime on the ships.

The *Ariel* remained waiting and watching for Kennedy's appearance. The *Bramble*, meanwhile, in its continuing survey of Endeavour Strait, made its first anchorage near Possession Island and was immediately met by two canoes, 'bringing tortoise shell and spears etc. to barter; we had several on board, their canoes are far larger and of a superior build to the Cape York ones and they speak a different language'.[34] For the next few days the ship moved around Endeavour Strait looking for shoals, reefs, and any impediment to clear sailing.

On 9 November, the *Bramble* anchored off Cape Cornwall, on the southern side of Prince of Wales Island. This was the first time the ship had anchored off an island that was clearly inhabited.[35] Two days later, several canoes approached the ship from the island bringing tortoise shell and spears but the *Bramble*'s men seemed to have had their fill of these souvenirs. While the artefacts did not attract their attention, the men in the canoe did. One of them, called Tomagugu, was instantly recognized as Baki's son and there were also two more that the *Bramble*'s men recognized from Cape York.[36] The next day was even more exciting. Midshipman Packe took up the story:

> Two canoes came alongside the first thing this morning bringing two or three women or girls I may say with them; these are a far superior race of niggers to the main land and the women are good looking for blacks. They wanted us very much to go on shore with them and some made signs that they would remain behind as hostages. I really think they would have treated us well but it would be madness to ask the old man as he would fancy it was running to certain death.[37]

The visitors managed to get on to the vessel and were evicted with some difficulty. Yule had earned a reputation for being nervous about Aboriginal people and characteristically ordered the anchor to be weighed and made for Wallis Island, about as far away as one could get from Prince of Wales Island and still be in Endeavour Strait.

What the *Bramble*'s men did not realize was that there was much more to the invitation than they imagined, as they would discover in the following year.

For the next few days, the *Bramble* continued surveying around Wallis Island and making its way slowly back through Endeavour Strait to Cape York, which it reached on 20 November. The *Ariel* was still there, at its anchorage. But there was no sign of Kennedy. Yule, fearing that Kennedy was seriously delayed, urged Dr Vallack to try to hang on at Cape York for as long as possible, indeed, longer than Stanley had thought was possible. If Vallack used up some of the sheep that had been stockaded for Kennedy, thought Yule, then he could delay his return to Sydney until the beginning of March. Then he should bury the provisions, as directed by Stanley, together with sundry letters giving Kennedy an update on what had happened in his absence. Yule even painted a white cross on the rocks at Cape York itself, pointing Kennedy to the spot on the ground where the provisions were to be buried.[38]

With that done, Yule set sail, on 24 November, down the east coast of Australia using the inner passage with the northwest monsoons blowing behind him. Several days later, on 27 November, in Temple Bay, Yule encountered the local inhabitants whom he had 'strong reason to suspect . . . to be treacherously inclined'. A canoe approached the ship in order to barter tortoiseshell and spears for ships biscuit: Packe observed that they 'do not appear to care a bit for tobacco and are marked on the chest like the Cape York natives but not on the breast and shoulders'.[39] The next day, and still at the same anchorage, Packe noted that George Inskip, one of the *Bramble*'s surveyors, fired a volley at a canoe: Packe agreed with Yule's assessment of the locals – 'They are a braver set here than on most places on the coast, they had the impudence to attack the *Bramble*'s men when they were wooding on one of the Holme [sic] (Home) Islands but had a good volley fired at them when they retreated . . . [They are] all well armed with no good intentions.'[40] The *Bramble* continued to work its way down the coast and, on 2 December, anchored under the lee of the famous landmark of Restoration Island – within sight of Cape Weymouth – where Captain William Bligh first made landfall, just under sixty years earlier, on 29 May 1789, after entering the inner passage in his open boat from the Friendly Islands in the South Pacific. Just under a fortnight later they passed Dunk Island; on 20 December, they passed Cape Upstart and, on the 23rd, they took their leave of the inner passage and proceeded to Brisbane, to get fresh provisions, where they arrived on New Years Eve. After a short stay, the *Bramble* arrived in Sydney on 15 January 1849 and anchored off Fort Maquarie.[41] The voyage was a tremendous achievement. Not only had Yule done something that very few sailing ships had accomplished, but, more importantly, he had demonstrated beyond a shadow of a doubt that the key to sailing the inner passage was precise, up-to-date charts and sailing directions. His proof? Once he cleared the Claremont Isles, roughly the first 20 per cent of the sailing distance of the inner passage from Cape York to Breaksea Spit, he sailed day and night, without a break.[42]

When he left Cape York, Stanley was justly proud of the work that had been accomplished by both ships and was looking forward to Yule completing the survey of Endeavour Strait and the return journey through the length of the inner passage. He was also pleased, as he explained to Beaufort, 'that during the course of the Survey no accident has happened to either of the vessels or their Boats; we have not had a man seriously ill during the whole time; we have been equally fortunate in avoiding collision with the natives.'[43] However there was still no sign of Kennedy, and now as the *Rattlesnake* headed across the vast space of the Gulf of Carpentaria towards Cape Wessel, its northwesternmost point, the prospect of Port Essington loomed.

Port Essington, the largest bay on the Cobourg Peninsula in what is now the Northern Territory, was Britain's third attempt to settle northern Australia, the other two attempts having failed miserably.[44] The threat of Dutch and French territorial expansion dominated the decision to settle the area, though commercial and maritime concerns were never far behind.

Phillip Parker King had surveyed the bay in 1818 and recommended it as a site for settlement, but the plan to settle this area did not materialize until 1837. By then it had attracted a number of powerful backers, including Francis Beaufort.[45] Two ships were commissioned, HMS *Alligator*, commanded by Captain Sir Gordon Bremer, and HMS *Britomart*, commanded by the young (twenty-seven years old) Owen Stanley, to lay the

Port Essington and
South-East Asia in 1837

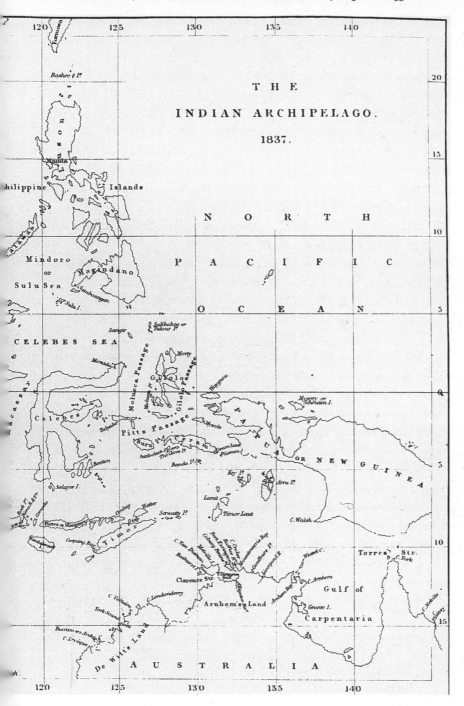

THE

INDIAN ARCHIPELAGO.

1837.

foundations for the settlement. Both ships left Plymouth in February 1838 and arrived in Sydney in July of the same year. It was an exciting moment. All of the necessities of a new settlement, including provisions for eighteen months, a prefabricated church and some prefabricated public buildings, were put together over the next few months, and an expeditionary force was launched for the north.[46] On 7 September, a flotilla consisting of the *Alligator*, the *Britomart*, and the *Orontes*, a transport ship, departed Sydney for Port Essington.[47] Just over seven weeks later, on 27 October 1838, the *Alligator* anchored near Point Record followed by the *Britomart*. Two days later, a site for the future settlement was decided upon, on a point of land called Minto Head, about 16 miles from the open sea, and work began to build a new town, what everyone hoped would become a second Singapore.[48]

Everything seemed to be going well for the fledgling settlement. Buildings were raised, a garden was started by a botanist sent out from Kew, buffaloes and other fresh provisions from the nearby islands to the north arrived, and a theatre was built – its first production, 'Cheap Living', was performed on 24 August 1839, produced, directed and stage-set by Stanley. But the honeymoon period was very short. On the night of 25 November 1839, winds began to lash Minto Head. HMS *Pelorus*, moored in front of the settlement, took the full brunt of the force. The winds took hold of the ship and drove it relentlessly towards the shore. Just after midnight, the winds increased to hurricane force and totally devastated the ship, driving it into the soft mud that lined the floor of the bay. None of this was witnessed by the settlement in the pitch-blackness for it, too, was being ripped apart. It was not until the morning, with the weather moderating, that the full extent of the devastation was seen. Eight men had been killed on the *Pelorus*. Their bodies were washed up over the succeeding days and, as for the settlement, there was hardly anything left standing. The burial ground, hardly laid out, now received its first victims.[49] The settlement was in ruins.

It was not a good start. By the time Stanley took his leave of the settlement in September 1841, it was still reeling from the devastation. And in the intervening years, a number of factors – including the climate, the poverty of the soil, disease, a lack of investment in land and in trade, and the unrelenting appetite of the termites – undermined Port Essington. As

Stanley returned in 1849, he already knew that the settlement was sick and dying.

The settlement had been launched with a publicity campaign, which extolled the virtues of life in this remote part of Australia. It sounded like paradise. The claims continued to be made during the first few years of the settlement's history and the public were, according to some, being duped into believing that everything was going well in Port Essington.[50] John McArthur, the settlement's commandant and ardent supporter, was beginning to concede that the place was unhealthy and maybe not right for a settlement, but he kept his opinions hidden from the public.[51]

John MacGillivray, however, saw Port Essington for what it was and refused to keep silent. He had first visited the settlement in August 1843 when he was aboard HMS *Fly* but remained there for just a few days. In September of the following year, the *Fly* returned to Port Essington, and this time MacGillivray took up residence in the settlement so that he could spend more time collecting for Lord Derby, his patron. While he lived in the settlement, MacGillivray became very friendly with an indigenous inhabitant called Neinmal, who accompanied and helped him in collecting. When the *Fly* returned for MacGillivray in January 1845, Neinmal 'begged so hard to continue with me that I could not refuse him'.[52] Consequently Neinmal joined the *Fly* when it continued its survey work, visiting the Torres Strait, the coast of New Guinea, Singapore, Java and Sydney, and returning to Port Essington in HMS *Bramble* under Yule's command, in June 1846.

While in Sydney, MacGillivray wrote a devastating assessment of Port Essington for publication in the *Sydney Morning Herald*. The article appeared on Wednesday 15 October 1845. In it, he attacked those who had promoted settlement, both in London and in the colony – 'parties interested in buoying up the delusive hopes entertained at home of its capabilities for growing various valuable articles of tropical production, and of its becoming an emporium'. He exposed the truth about its climate: it was not temperate, as its supporters had maintained, but tropical, hot and stifling, whether in the dry or wet season, and 'decidedly unhealthy' – 'the burying ground tells this tale in language not to be misunderstood'. Fever, ophthalmia, ulcers were common complaints but there was a general unhealthiness throughout, the lie of the land and the excessive rainfall during the wet season conspiring to produce boggy conditions – 'The noxious exhaltations from any of these swamps are at times so powerful as to produce a feeling of nausea in any one walking over them.' The land was incapable of supporting more than a small number of cattle and sheep, it couldn't grow vegetables – although fruit was less of a problem – while the supplies of fish and shellfish were precarious. In short, as MacGillivray put it in very stark terms, 'There is not a ship in the British navy the men of which are not better victualled than the residents of Port Essington.' He concluded with his view of the future:

> It has been the grave of a fearful amount of European life; and, after a fair trial, has entirely failed in promoting the objects of its founder and supporters, with the solitary exception of having afforded assistance to a few shipwrecked crews. When the Home Government shall at length have arrived at a true knowledge of the merits of the case, it is hoped that the place will be given up; and, if we must have a settlement on these coasts, that a more advantageous spot will be selected.[53]

And that spot, he suggested, should be somewhere on Cape York.

As the *Rattlesnake* crossed the Gulf of Carpentaria towards Cape Wessel the temperature began to rise. Charles Card and Robert Gale both commented that the ship was becoming intolerably hot: 'our decks are like ovens . . . this weather makes one feel rather languid and indolent,' remarked Gale.[54] On 9 November, the ship rounded Point Smith, at the eastern corner of the opening to Port Essington, and at 4 p.m. anchored just below Minto Head. 'Very hot indeed,' Gale wrote in his diary, 'I fear we shall suffer from it.'[55]

It was clear that the place was a disaster. 'Much the same as 1841' was how Stanley described Port Essington to Beaufort.[56] The gardens were a failure, the climate, he thought, had worsened on the grounds that there was more illness, invalidity and death in the settlement than previously, and, to make matters worse, all the buildings, constructed from wood, were infested with white ants [termites], and 'injured to such an extent that at the period of our visit none could have held against a moderate gale of wind and no house in the place at the approach of the rainy season was even water tight overhead'.[57]

No one wanted to stay. MacGillivray called it a 'pestilential furnace' and rushed around getting some natural history specimens that eluded him on his last visit, including some finches for Gould, a few land shells and the bower of a bird. Cleverly, he spent most of his time at Coral Bay, not far from the opening to the sea, where a kind of a sanatorium had been erected, and where there was a refreshing sea breeze.[58] To his deep regret, he also heard from 'a very intelligent native who had it from an eye-witness', of the murder of his friend Neinmal by members of another local tribe in September 1847.[59] The other news, that of the death from fever of Father Angelo Confalonieri in June 1848, a Catholic missionary who had been in the settlement for just under two years, shook him less but reinforced his impression of the morbidity of the site.[60] John Thomson couldn't find a good word to say about Port Essington. 'We called at Port Essington', he told Mary in a letter, 'and remained there for five days only to give our ship's company a little more sickness and if possible to make what was sufficiently unpleasant already still more so. To speak of this place as a settlement is a mere abuse of words. The country in the neighbourhood is the most wretched, the climate the most unhealthy, the human beings the most uncomfortable and the houses in a condition the most decayed and rotten.'[61] He blamed Stanley for taking the ship there and increasing his workload.

Huxley agreed with these sentiments and found nothing to contradict the impressions he had already received. 'It is fit for neither man nor beast' is how he summed it up; the only exception being that the pineapples were excellent.[62] Unlike other observers, Huxley didn't think that there was any evidence of endemic disease, no predominant fevers and no dysentery. He felt that at least half the mortality was down to poor management of men and resources – overwork and bad food.[63] And the blame, he maintained, fell squarely on the commandant's shoulders, whom he thought 'a litigious old fool' (he was fifty-seven years old at the time).[64] The officers, five in total, were constantly at each other's throats – 'there is as much petty intrigue, caballing and mutual hatred as if it were the court of the Great Khan' – 'and the only thing in which they were united was in the most unqualified abuse of the whole settlement'.[65]

While Huxley's attitude to Port Essington was, in essence, no different from others on the *Rattlesnake*, there was a bitterness, a caustic, unforgiving attitude that, he himself recognized, was taking over – 'the last two months of our survey were very miserable to me – a sort of "hope deferred" sensation was creeping over me and I was falling into a kind of dogged apathy.'[66] He had already made up his mind, for example, before casting his eyes on the settlement, that he could only detest it: 'the only break [in the voyage]', he told Nettie, 'will be our week's visit to this odious Port Essington, a place I heartily wish blotted out of the maps.'[67] His vitriol, when in Port Essington, was not confined to the settlement and its commandant. In the firing line were the Aborigines, Father Confalonieri (whom he had never met) and Stanley, whom he ridiculed as having 'an especial vocation for prying into all concerns, whether his own or other people's'.[68] He wasn't pleased with himself either. He had let opportunities for work pass through his fingers like sand on a beach, allowing himself to be occupied, instead, by 'foolish discontent at the present and still more foolish anticipation of the future'.[69]

Only Brierly seemed to visit with an open mind. Each day he went on shore as soon as he could, visiting the settlement in the way a tourist might, taking in the major sites – the hospital, Victoria Square, the Officers' Quarters, and the burial ground – talking to the officers and rank-and-file marines and accepting their hospitality, learning about the history of the settlement and its personalities, taking notes to help him in his sketching and painting, and spending time with the local indigenous people. While he observed the same things as the others did – the ravages of the termites and the intense heat and light that made it impossible for him to work after ten in the morning – he seemed to get some pleasure from it. John McArthur, to whom he was introduced by Stanley, he described in genial terms, very unlike Huxley's: 'a tall thin old man who appeared to warm up at the sight of new strangers'.[70] His only disappointment was in the Aborigines whom he found indifferent – '[they] did not, as we have generally found they do, make any signs or call or attract our attention – they seem to partake of the same spirit of apathy which appeared to rest upon and pervade everything around' – and even the animals were similarly struck: 'a sulky dog came out of another hut but after looking at us for a few minutes he went in again; the execution of barking would evidently have been too much for him.'[71] A list of questions that he had carefully prepared for himself as an aide-memoire, covering topics such as marriage, death, beliefs, weaponry, and relationships with the white population, was dispensed with.

Brierly was unusual. Everyone else, it seems, couldn't wait to leave. The weather, they thought, played on their nerves. Robert Gale had an almighty row with Stanley while they were in Port Essington. Stanley, according to Gale, constantly treated him 'shamefully'. He felt abused by that 'little-minded tyrant' and feared 'the utter extinction of that feeling of pleasure and respect I would rather bear towards my employer'. Gale thought their differences were resolved at the time but didn't expect harmony to last: '[it] ended in his promising better treatment for the future. I hope it will hold good but I almost doubt it.' He was right, as it turned out.

On 16 November the *Rattlesnake* pulled up its anchor and set sail for Sydney. Such was the lack of breeze in this reach of the bay, it took more than a day to sail out of Port Essington to the open sea. No one on board would ever see the settlement again, though some would re-encounter its inhabitants in a different place and time. Stanley took the ship towards Timor then turned to the southwest towards the northwestern corner of Australia before heading due south towards Cape Leeuwin. Hopes for a stop at the Swan River settlement were dashed when Stanley decided to plough on. Expectations of a visit to Adelaide were also disappointed. 'At length on January 24th, a long and monotonous passage of sixty-eight days brought us to Sydney, from which we had been absent for nine months.'[72] The *Rattlesnake* pulled up alongside the *Bramble*, which had been at anchor since 15 January.

Sydney was just preparing for the regatta performed annually on 26 January to celebrate the founding of the colony of New South Wales. It was a relief to be back, to return to family, friends and loved ones. There were surprises in store for many. MacGillivray, for example, learned that he now had a daughter, Isabella, born just over a month earlier. The atmosphere was not as frenetic as it had been on their first arrival in Sydney in 1847; no more balls, fewer dinners and picnics. Some of this social slowdown was to be expected: the *Rattlesnake* was no longer a novelty. But, thought Thomson, there was something else going on, something more troubling and undermining, which did not augur well for the future. 'A great difference of feeling now exists in the ship from what did this time last year,' he wrote to his wife. 'The Captain has treated some on board very badly constantly snarling at them from an ungovernable temper which he has and scarcely treating them with ordinary civility and this has tended to raise up their animosity to him.' 'The gaieties which were so frequent on board when we were last in Sydney,' he continued, 'are a good deal thrown aside. I suppose that it arises from the cordiality of feeling between the Captain and officers not being so great as formerly.'[73]

Social outings also tended to be more subdued and individual. Besides which, there was a lot of work to do, preparing the charts and sailing directions to be forwarded to Beaufort in London, and planning for the next, and potentially very exciting, voyage to New Guinea. One of Stanley's first outings was a farewell dinner for Phillip Parker King who was sailing for London within a few days to attend to the business of the Australian Agricultural Company. King was extremely fond of Stanley. They had remained close friends ever since Stanley served on HMS *Adventure* under King's command. When King arrived in England, he told Beaufort how highly he thought of Stanley's work – 'he seems not a little proud of his pupil' – 'the more especially as you have he says expunged all the impertinent rocks that others had intruded into his Inner Route'.[74]

King sailed on 5 February. On the very same day, the *Bramble* crossed over to Mosman Bay to undergo a desperate treatment. The ship was infested with cockroaches, and not for the first time. In December 1845, Yule had tried to smoke them out, and when that failed, he attempted a more daring plan. John Sweatman, who, at the time, was acting as Clerk of Provisions, recorded the process. 'The fires were lighted, sulphur thrown on, and the latches battened down, but when they were opened again [two days later] we found to our chagrin that the smoking had no effect beyond slightly stupefying the cockroaches, which were congregated about the lower deck in regular masses. Mr Yule accordingly resolved to try another plan . . . he got the commissariat fire-engine on board and thoroughly washed out every hole & corner, lower deck, hold and every place where a hose could be led. Millions were destroyed this way . . . but it was impossible to extirpate them entirely as many of them took refuge in the bulwarks . . .'[75] Not a total success, but the ship was more comfortable for a while. Six months later, the cockroaches were back. By now the ship was in Port Essington without any of the resources of Sydney. Yule 'resolved to take the most vigorous measures to exterminate them, by sinking the vessel altogether . . .'[76] Everything was taken out, and a deep cut was made in the ship's side to let in water, and, at high water, the ship was completely covered. The cockroaches, according to Sweatman, poured out in their millions: 'Their old place of refuge inside the bulwarks, availed them nothing now, and by night the vessel was completely cleared of them.'[77] Or so he thought. But they, or their replacements, were back again, and Yule, now in his third battle with the vermin, could think of nothing but sinking the *Bramble* for a second time. The ship was cleared of everything that wasn't permanently fixed, and was sunk in Mosman Bay on 10 February, and remained on the bottom for a week. Fifty men were enlisted to raise the *Bramble* from the muddy floor, and on 17 February, the ship was once again riding on the sea cockroach free, for the time being.

CHAPTER IX

The Tragedy of Kennedy
1849

The two ships had now been in Sydney a few weeks and questions about Kennedy were still being asked. The *Ariel* was either heading back to Sydney, or was about to do so, with or without Kennedy. Since there was no way of knowing which, the Colonial Government decided to send a relief ship, the *Coquette*, to Cape York. On 16 February 1849, the 72-ton schooner, Captain Elliott in command, set sail.[1] Five days later, it was back in Sydney, having sustained serious damage to the fore topmast in a gale, and, after some quick repairs, was back at sea on 23 February.[2]

More than a week went by and, with no sign of the *Coquette*'s return, everything seemed to be going according to plan. But then, on 4 March, 'a beautiful day, lots of people sailing about', a small schooner, the *Clarissa*, pulled into Sydney harbour and snippets of the shocking news began to come out.[3] While in Trial Bay, about halfway between Brisbane and Sydney, sitting out a storm, the *Clarissa*, on its way to Sydney from Moreton Island, was joined by the *Ariel* from Cape York. Once the storm abated, the two ships resumed their voyage back to Sydney. The *Ariel* hadn't yet arrived but the news had: Kennedy was dead.[4] Only two of the original party of thirteen had survived.[5] They were both on the *Ariel*. The full story and the identity of the survivors would have to await the arrival of the ship, expected any day.

Graves of Wall and Niblett, Albany Island

Next day, 5 March, the *Sydney Morning Herald* carried the news from the *Clarissa*. The entire party, apart from the two survivors, it reported, had all been 'destroyed by the blacks'. The people on the *Ariel*, the report continued, had spotted a 'native who had a belt which had evidently belonged to a white man: this induced the persons in the *Ariel* to suspect some of the party must be in the neighbourhood, and detaining the black as a hostage, they commenced a search, which ended in their finding two of KENNEDY'S men in great distress . . . The black referred to is a prisoner on board the *Ariel*.'⁶

Before the Herald readers could put down their papers and contemplate the bare facts they were offered, the *Ariel* arrived in port. Stanley went over immediately to find out what had happened. The *Herald* report was misleading. There were, in fact, three survivors, William Carron, the botanist to the expedition, William Goddard, one of the convicts, and Jackey Jackey.

The tragic story began to unfold. The expedition, it turned out, had had a terrible start. Looking for a way through the thick bush took the expedition in a southwesterly direction for more than six weeks before they were able to turn to the north. The party was so weakened that by the time they got to Weymouth Bay, Kennedy decided to split it in two, leaving eight behind at the camp, while the others pushed on to Port Albany. It was early November 1848. The smaller party worked its way north but owing to a combination of unfortunate accidents – one of the party had damaged his knee and another accidentally shot himself, but not fatally – and rapidly diminishing supplies (they were now eating their horses), Kennedy again decided to split the party into two, leaving the two injured men and another at a camp overlooking Shelburne Bay, while Kennedy and Jackey Jackey made a dash for Cape York hoping to send the doctor back.

They were about 100 miles from their destination and it was the end of November. Kennedy and Jackey Jackey, carrying minimal supplies, headed north. They got to Escape River, with Albany Island in sight in the far distance, when they were surrounded, followed and finally attacked by local people. Kennedy was speared and died. Jackey Jackey managed to escape and, after thirteen days, reached the mainland, opposite Albany Island, where the *Ariel* was anchored.

Dr Vallack now took up the story. It was 23 December:

The first part of the 24 hours commenced with a light breeze and cloudy. 7 am heard a strange cooey in the main land abreast the vessel, Master took the spy glass and saw a color'd man with blue short and drawers on, and a black hand-kerchief on a stick waving. He took a hand in the dingy and pulled over to him; and found it to be one of Mr. Kennedy's men who gave Mr. K's memorandum book and compass to recognize himself, and after having some refreshment and sleep, etc., and gave the following account . . .[7]

Vallack began to take down what Jackey Jackey told him as a kind of state-ment and also immediately instructed the Captain to get the *Ariel* ready to set sail as quickly as possible to pick up the other parties. The next day, 24 December, the *Ariel* weighed anchor and proceeded to Shelburne Bay, to the spot where the party of three had been left. The *Ariel* anchored in the bay on 26 December, near to where Jackey Jackey remembered the last camp to be. The next day, 'the master, Doctor, Jackey & 5 hands left the ship all arm'd to look for the men, landed before daybreak . . . examined a canoe on the beach and found part of a blue cloak belonging to the men, said to be left there sick, Jackey recognising it immediately, got into the Boat to go down and examine the camp for the remainder of the men's clothes.' The party scoured the mangrove swamps that covered the shore looking for the hill where the camp was made. They climbed a hill to get a better look at the surrounding countryside. Jackey Jackey

climbed the highest tree to see if he knew the country, when he came down he told us we could not search today, saying that he could see a hill not far off where men sit down. We asked him how long it would take us to go there and back, he answered 3 days. We then agreed that there was no possibility of the men being alive and only two hands . . . on board the vessel, and no provisions with us, it would be madness to proceed.[8]

With that, the party returned to the ship and at 5 a.m. the next day, they set sail to the south, heading to Weymouth Bay to search for the party of eight. They reached their destination several days later, on 30 December, and this time they were luckier. They found the camp without any problem but, instead of eight, there were only two – Carron and Goddard. The other six had died from starvation.[9] The next day, the last day of 1848, they made a dash for Sydney.

The news was very distressing, but there was one thing that Carron and

Goddard reported that caused great unease on the *Rattlesnake*, and espe-cially on the *Bramble*. The survivors claimed that they had seen the *Bramble* when it sailed into Weymouth Bay in early December on the way down the inner passage, at a time when five of them were still alive. '[They] had made signals to her by means of fires and rockets but had not been seen; they had actually seen the *Bramble* lower a boat and pull towards the shore and were so elated at the thought that she was coming for them that when they saw her go back again it was the death of three or four.'[10]

Next day, a hearing was held to consider Jackey Jackey's statement and other relevant evidence as to the unfortunate outcome of the expedition. Giving evidence at the Water Police Office were Carron, Goddard, Vallack, and William Dobson, the Captain of the *Ariel*. MacGillivray attended the hearing. He was deeply moved by the experience. 'I shall never forget the appearance which the survivors presented on this occa-sion,' he wrote, 'pale and emaciated, with haggard looks attesting the mis-ery and privations they had undergone, and with low trembling voices, they gave their evidence.'[11] Carron produced a written statement, which in simple, stark detail, spoke of the terrible time they had getting through the scrub during the early phase of the expedition, the dreadful tale of the deaths of his colleagues, and the heart-breaking sighting of and attempt to signal to the *Bramble*. Goddard filled in a few details of what had hap-pened before they were rescued, but his statement corroborated Carron's. Vallack and Dobson provided information about the search for the two parties.[12]

The minutes of the hearing were passed on to the Government. The *Herald* published the evidence for all to read but it also took the opportu-nity, not only of praising Kennedy – 'as far as earnestness of purpose, unshrinking endurance of pain and fatigue, and most disinterested self-sacrifice, go, the gallant leader of the party exhibited a model for his sub-ordinates' – but also of suggesting that the result might not have been so tragic had they not been so exhausted by their first few weeks. This was probably as far as anyone went, at this time, in apportioning blame for the disaster, at least officially. It seems John Thomson had doubted the wis-dom of the plan:

> Very early I had my misgivings of the prudence of landing the party at the spot
> where they commenced their exploration and the details given in the newspa-

pers shew clearly that all their difficulties arose from this first false step the country being so impracticable that their course lay for 5 weeks to the s-w instead of to the Northward which was the direction in which they wished to move. The expedition as far as I could judge was planned in ignorance and carried out without a sufficiency of means having been provided.[13]

When Stanley's father learned of the Kennedy disaster, he wrote to his son with his condolences, and reminded him of his part in the planning of the expedition. Speaking of Kennedy, Bishop Stanley wrote, 'If I, who knew him not, save through your report, feel it so acutely, how much more you. I do indeed condole and sympathise with you on such a fine and promising expedition, planned as it was and escorted by you, should have so mournfully terminated.'[14]

Stanley did not attend the hearing. Instead he went on a sketching excursion. He invited Jackey Jackey to the *Rattlesnake* on the following day to hear for himself about the last days of Kennedy. Robert Gale observed that Jackey Jackey had a spear wound over one eye and in his side. Stanley did comment on William Carron's insistence that he had seen the *Bramble*, in a communiqué to Beaufort. He wrote:

> I think the *Bramble* not having seen the flag hoisted by the party at Weymouth Bay may be easily accounted for as she was at least 6 miles distant from the coast at the time the boat was lowered – The signal I had arranged with Mr Kennedy in the event of his wanting to communicate was that three fires should be made in a line of which the central one was to be the largest in order to distinguish his signal from those of the natives who are very numerous on that part of the coast and generally light fires to attract the attention of vessels as they pass along the coast. In the evening the *Bramble* anchored 8 or 9 miles from the camp at which distance it would be difficult to see rockets unless the exact place from which they were to be fired was previously known.[15]

And with that, the matter, but perhaps not the impact on Stanley, came to an end, at least for the time being. On 9 March, as if to signal the end of the sad and sorry affair, Edward Deas Thomson published a short statement about the expedition. In it, he praised Kennedy's courage, specifically, and, one must conclude, intentionally, towards the latter part of the expedition – no mention was made of the difficulties in the first part. He paid tribute to Thomas Wall, the expedition's naturalist, who died at the Weymouth Bay camp, and to William Carron, who kept the party together as best he could. The greatest tribute, however, was paid to Jackey Jackey, whose courage in the last few weeks of the expedition and his narrative of those events, showed 'him to be possessed, in a high degree, of some of the best qualities of our common nature'.[16]

But the story still wasn't quite ended.

Stanley was a busy man. The *Rattlesnake* and the *Bramble* had been away from Sydney for nearly 10 months. The fruits of their voyage, the seemingly endless stream of observations on angles and depths, and the location and extent of rocks, shoals, reefs and every other kind of nautical impediment, threatened to swamp him. All of those numbers had to be made meaningful by placing them on charts and sailing directions. 'To give some small idea of the work we had to do and most of which I had to do myself,' Stanley commented in a letter to his cousin Louisa, 'our fair charts of Torres Straits took ten of the largest sheets of drawing paper and when put together measured 30 feet in length and contained more than 40,000 soundings to say nothing of the calculations necessary for constructing these said charts.'[17] To his old friend, the surveyor Charles Tyers, he complained that his workload was so great that he had had no time for 'a single Holyday'.[18] Good Friday passed without any notice, as Charles Card recorded, 'as the Captain has been busy at work in the chart room all day and says he has got nothing in his orders which tells him to have church on Fridays and therefore he cannot afford the time'.[19]

On top of the chartroom work, Stanley had to write a report to Deas Thomson giving his opinion on the future of Port Essington and any other possible settlement in northern Australia. In it, he maintained that the Port Essington settlement had not satisfied the objectives for which it was established and, if these were still relevant to British policy in the area, 'they would be much better attained by removing the Establishment to Cape York or its vicinity'.[20] He received similar requests from the Governor, Sir Charles Fitzroy, and from the Admiralty, and replied in the same way. Besides attending to paperwork, Stanley also superintended the refitting of the ships, caulking and painting them and replacing their sails. And all this had to be done under the pressure of time, for the ships had to leave Sydney as soon as the southeast monsoon began, in April or May. They were heading to a part of the world where European vessels did not venture and, without a passing ship to act as a mail staging post, therefore, all of the chart work had to be completed in Sydney and sent off to England before they could sail.

It wasn't all work, however. Stanley found time to enjoy himself at dinner parties, a ball or two and a few picnics. He even managed to take some art lessons from the renowned artist, Conrad Martens, who had been on the second voyage of the *Beagle* with Charles Darwin and had been living in Sydney since 1835.[21]

While Stanley finished his precious charts, there were murmurings within the Colonial Government that the Kennedy affair was not yet satisfactorily wound up. Not that there was any need to go over the details of the tragedy. That had been done to the satisfaction of the authorities, and no further action was taken once the Colonial Secretary and Governor had received the papers from the enquiry into the deaths of the ten men. Given the way in which the expedition had been organized, it is no surprise that the matter rested with the men at the very top of the colonial administration. But there were, however, a few loose ends to tie up – were there any survivors at Shelburne Bay, where a thorough search had not been made? Did Kennedy's papers survive? Would it be possible to locate Kennedy's body, or what remained of it, and give it a proper burial?

In late March, about a fortnight after the enquiry, the Colonial Government charted a brig, the *Freak*, under the experienced sea captain and trader, Thomas Beckford Simpson, to answer these questions.[22] It was intended at this time for Simpson to take with him William Wall, the brother of Thomas Wall, the expedition's late naturalist, and William Goddard, one of the survivors, in addition to Jackey Jackey and his brother, who would act as guides.[23] When, however, the ship was ready to sail on 6 April, both Wall and Goddard had disappeared, for unknown reasons, from the passenger list and, instead, Simpson sailed with Jackey Jackey and two of his brothers.[24] The plan was for Jackey Jackey and his brothers to remain on board the *Freak* until the search was completed, at which point they would transfer on to the *Coquette*, which was at Cape York still waiting for Kennedy's appearance, while Simpson went about his own business.

Stanley was involved in this expedition as he had been in Kennedy's. On 22 March, Stanley hosted a dinner party on the *Rattlesnake*, at which the invited guests included Edward Deas Thomson, Colonel Barney and Captain Hutchinson Browne, one of the two Justices of the Peace presiding over the enquiry (all close friends by now).[25] He had also arranged for Captain Simpson to write to him at the earliest convenience with the latest news of the search.

The *Freak* cleared Sydney Heads on 6 April 1849 heading for Weymouth Bay, their first stop and the location of the camp where Carron and Goddard were the only survivors. This they reached on 3 May. Jackey Jackey had no trouble finding the place where the men had camped. A thorough search of the area initially yielded little of value. Strewn around what had been the campsite were portions of books, parts of harnesses and belts, tins for carrying water, and bones, skulls and feathers. No manuscripts and no parts of a natural history collection, both of which they hoped might have survived, came to light. Following Carron's advice on where to look, Captain Simpson believed he had recovered the bones and skulls of Thomas Wall and Charles Niblett, the two men who died last and were not buried.[26] He collected the bones for later burial on Albany Island, which had been selected as the spot for the last remains of the expedition's dead.[27] The next day, the *Freak* weighed anchor and headed for Shelburne Bay, the site of the last camp, where three men had been left behind. Jackey Jackey thought it was pointless going inland to search for survivors as Dennis Dunn, one of those left behind at Shelburne Bay, told him that he would make his way down to the beach whatever happened. Consequently, Captain Simpson launched the whaleboat to scour the coast for signs of the men but nothing was seen of any survivors.[28]

With Shelburne Bay yielding no further information, the *Freak* got under way for Escape River and the search for Kennedy's body and his papers. As the ship approached its destination, the sails of another ship were observed and this turned out to be the *Coquette*, which had been at Cape York since 17 March. It was making its way down the coast, back to Sydney, because it had already heard about Kennedy's death from the *Sea Nymph*, a passing ship.

The *Freak* and *Coquette* now joined company. Captain Simpson and Jackey Jackey and his two brothers continued their search in the Escape River area. The place where Jackey Jackey had buried the saddlebags containing Kennedy's journal and other papers was located, but they had disappeared. There was also no sign of Kennedy's body at the place where Jackey Jackey had buried him. The only consolation to this unsuccessful and, for Jackey Jackey, emotional return, was that they found a roll of charts and some small memorandum books, but these had been badly water damaged.[29] Seeing that nothing further could be accomplished there, the two ships set sail for Albany Island, which they reached on 10 May. Three days later,

> having put the remains of Messrs. Wall and Niblet [sic] in a coffin . . . [we] landed and went up to the highest hill on that part of the island, and on the top, a clear open place, we dug a grave and interred the remains of the unfortunate individuals, Thomas Wall and Charles Niblet, reading the funeral service over them; about ten or twelve natives were present, and we fully explained to them what we were doing, they conducted themselves with propriety while the funeral service was being read. Poor Jackey was much affected, and could not refrain from tears.[30]

Simpson now fulfilled his final instructions. He wrote the letter to Stanley giving him a brief report on what had happened, and he moved his passengers on to the *Coquette*.[31] The two ships sailed to Port Essington and then on 26 May, they parted company, the *Coquette* to Sydney and the *Freak* to Shanghai to unload a cargo of sandalwood. The *Coquette* arrived in Sydney on 6 July 1849 with very little to show of the relief expedition.

Though the search revealed little, at least it drew a line under the expedition. Everything had been done to recover what they could. Because the saddlebags were never found, Kennedy's version of events would never be known. Jackey Jackey withdrew from the scene. William Carron became the expedition's official spokesman with the publication, in August of the same year, of his narrative.[32] In order to flesh out the events at which he was not present, and to bring the story to its final conclusion, Carron appended to his narrative the statements of the survivors given at the enquiry in Sydney together with an extract from the log of the *Freak*.

As far as the public was concerned the Kennedy tragedy was over. There were other, more pressing matters, such as the possibility of the resumption of transportation to New South Wales.

But for one man, the Kennedy affair was not over, and could not, in a sense, ever be closed. Thomas Mitchell, the Surveyor-General, was still fuming. He had arrived back from his trip to England in late July 1848 only to discover that Deas Thomson had interfered in his affairs and department and sent one of his most promising surveyors on an exploring route, which he had not only not authorized, but was contrary to his intended continuation of the master plan to find a river that flowed northwards into the Gulf of Carpentaria.

The anger Mitchell felt at Deas Thomson was nothing to what he felt when he learned of Kennedy's death. Colonel Thomas Kennedy, Kennedy's father and a close friend, was one of the first to be made aware of his fury. The first letter, sent to London, was written on 8 March, two days after the judicial enquiry. He told Colonel Kennedy how his son 'had been taken from under my control and that of my Deputy' and made to travel the full length of Cape York, on both sides, instead of exploring the interior of the continent; and that the real danger lay 'in the known character of the savage natives' and that they were at their most savage precisely where Kennedy met his death. 'I never entertained any hope of your son's return', he told Kennedy, 'or his party from the hour I arrived here, and heard where he had been sent – I could not write to you any tidings to inspire hope and awaited the result in hopeless despair.'[33] The finger of blame, he suggested, should be pointed at 'irresponsible' persons, 'who know nothing of the interior and exploring' and who advise the Governor. Two days letter he fired off another letter, repeating many of the same points and adding that the 'idea of making such a party to depend on ships to await them on unknown shores', an idea that he had strenuously opposed during his tenure, was absurd. The plan, he concluded, 'was to doom them to inevitable destruction'.[34]

Mitchell didn't take his complaint about the Colonial government's meddling in his department directly to Deas Thomson until more than a year later. On that occasion, he repeated his assertion, which he had already communicated privately, that the workings and plans of his department had been ignored and one of his top surveyors had been 'detached' for Government service; and outlined the reasons why he thought the expedition failed – namely, that they were overwhelmed by 'the pestilential climate and the difficulties presented by the features of the country'.[35] Placing Kennedy and his party in Rockingham Bay was foolhardy, Mitchell commented, as the range of mountains came right down to the coast at this point. In what was a deliberate attack on the group of advisers he alluded to in his letter to Colonel Kennedy, Mitchell singled out Phillip Parker King, who, he suggested, should have known better. 'Yet the near vicinity of these high ranges to that shore and the deep indent of the coast were both facts known to navigators, and recorded in the charts and works of Captain King and others.'[36] Thomson replied to Mitchell that he would send a copy of his submission together with the Governor's reply to the Secretary of State for the Colonies in London, knowing full well that since the Secretary of State approved Kennedy's instructions, Mitchell's complaints would fall on deaf ears.

And so it was. Earl Grey, the Secretary of State, responded to Mitchell in April 1851, through Governor Fitzroy, that in daring to question the acts of his superiors he should be prepared 'for immediate dismissal from his office'.[37] That threat was enough to stop the matter in its tracks and the Kennedy episode was truly laid to rest.

PART FIVE

CHAPTER X

Tristes Tropiques:
The Louisiade Archipelago and New Guinea, 1849

The wedding of Charles Yule, commander of the *Bramble*, to his sweet-heart, Jane Priddle, on 17 March, at a ceremony in Sydney, first broke the gloom spread by Kennedy's fate. And then, just over a month later, Stanley received a wonderful gift, a totally unexpected visit from his brother Charlie, who boarded HMS *Havannah* at its unscheduled stop in Hobart Town. The two brothers had not seen each other for almost two years and, given Stanley's workload, they had to make the most of every opportunity in their short reunion – Charlie was not in Sydney on official business and the *Rattlesnake* was nearing its date of departure. On 4 May, Charlie left for Hobart Town. Stanley told his cousin Louisa in a letter that he 'was fortunate . . . in having a flying visit from Charlie', but was sorry that he had left Eliza, his wife, behind.[1] Charlie returned to Hobart Town safe and sound but the brothers would never see each other again, and Eliza's memories of her brother-in-law would remain those of his visit to Hobart Town in late June and early July 1847.

The expedition to the Louisiade Archipelago and the coast of New Guinea was getting closer by the day. Both the *Rattlesnake* and the *Bramble* were nearly ready to go to sea in early April, but a last minute problem with the new sails – they were not the right size – delayed their

Coral Haven canoe, Louisiade Archipelago

departure, luckily for Stanley and his brother.[2]

While Stanley's instructions from both the Admiralty and Beaufort expressly asked him to examine the Louisiade Archipelago and the southern coast of New Guinea, Beaufort added that he wished to know more about the channels to the north of Prince of Wales Island in the Torres Strait. Here he was acting to safeguard British interests in the area as well as to aid navigation. What he would do with the information would depend on Stanley's discoveries. 'Supposing a good safe passage be there,' he mused, 'there can be selected clear good land marks among the islands for running for it. This is partly necessary for the benefit of our own navigators – and partly to see what mischief can be done to us by either friends or foes by taking up their quarters there – and therefore when I receive it I shall make it known or cushion it *selon les circonstances*.'[3] The idea behind placing a settlement at Cape York was to be able to observe ships going into and out of the Torres Strait but this depended on the only navigable route being visible from the Cape.[4]

The voyage promised to be exciting. John MacGillivray saw that this was the highlight of his commission. Being 'previously unexplored ground', the Louisiade Archipelago and the southern New Guinea coast promised to be bountiful in flora and fauna, particularly, he hoped, Birds of Paradise, only seen once before in the wild by a European naturalist.[5] Stanley was optimistic about the forthcoming trip, remarking to his cousin Louisa that it promised to be of far greater interest than the last one. He promised to keep her informed, as best he could, of their 'adventures', but added, half-jokingly and half-seriously, that this depended on the 'New Guinea people' not making a meal of him.[6] 'From all I can learn,' Stanley remarked, 'they are rather partial to human flesh [and] look upon a white man as a dainty morsel and prize his head above all things as an ornament for the doors of their houses. I hope however to teach them better manners and to instil a better taste with regard to their household ornaments and their cuisine . . .'. He continued exploiting the cannibalistic motif, be it to thrill his cousin or to relieve his own fears. 'If they try me they will have a tough morsel enough but we have some fine fat boys in the ship who would roast well and amongst others your protégé Hogan would not go amiss . . .'[7]

On 8 May 1849, they were ready to leave. Brierly, after leaving the

Rattlesnake immediately on its arrival in Sydney, showed up at the last minute. MacGillivray, who had also left the ship to be with his wife and baby daughter – 'in the course of time [I] became duly initiated into the mysteries of nursing' – also turned up just in the nick of time.[8] He had been summoned by an officer, bearing a letter from Stanley to 'repair on board immediately on the receipt of this order, and report yourself to the Commanding Officer'.[9] MacGillivray followed orders, presuming that Stanley had misunderstood his absence as an intention to abandon ship. He found the episode 'as unnecessary as unpleasant'.[10]

Stanley had provisioned the ships for six months and arranged for a supply ship to meet them in Cape York in early October. In the morning, Stanley took a set of sights as a reference point, and three hours later the *Rattlesnake* and the *Bramble* cleared Sydney Heads. They were on their way. Stanley was about to embark on a new chapter in his professional life, with expectations of rewards galore. Beaufort, ever the turner of phrases, put it best. 'You are now at the summit of your ambition – turned Discoverer – and bringing to light the latent riches and beauties of the Papuan Islands – and you can do nothing more useful to Geography in that part of the world or more agreeable to me; I would only beg of you to go on *lentement* – make sure of what you do – do not leave interesting questions to be answered at the next visit – give names to Capes and Islands, rational names – and bring yourself and your people back without quarrels, scars, or fevers.'[11]

However, their high expectations soon flagged. The breeze that took the ships clear of the Heads soon abated. For several days, it was a dead calm. At one point, five days out of Sydney, the ships found themselves going backwards as the speed of the current exceeded that of the wind. A precious week of sailing was lost in this way.[12] They decided to put in to Moreton Bay, which they reached on 17 May. After watering the *Rattlesnake* and the *Bramble* – 'I filled up every hole and corner with water not knowing how or where we might get the next supply' was how Stanley described it – loading fresh provisions and a flurry of letter-writing, the ships left Moreton Bay on 26 May, heading in a northeasterly direction for the extreme eastern point of the Louisiade Archipelago, Cape Deliverance.[13]

This time they reached the open sea, where they were greeted not with calm but the opposite – fierce winds and a very heavy sea. Church was cancelled on Sunday, their first day at sea. The wind became even stronger – 'it came on to blow from the eastward and increased so much that at last we were obliged to lay to with our head to the southward.'[14] Then the tiller ropes 'gave way strand by strand' so that the *Rattlesnake* had to be steered by its sails.[15] As if this wasn't bad enough, in spite of the caulking done in Sydney, the ship began to take in water, 'the after gun-room, gun-room and cabins thereto adjoining were all flooded.' It was more than irritating. Huxley knew whom to blame – 'If them — had been 'tending to the ship, 'stead o' givin' picnics in Sydney harbour, we shouldn't 'a had this piece o' work.'[16] 'Everybody felt qualmish and headachy and there was no sleep for any but the lucky possessors of hammocks.'[17] The rain fell in torrents and remaining down below became dangerous. 'We were therefore all standing under the poop looking very miserable and wishing we were any where else.'[18] Life on the *Bramble*, was, if anything, worse. The ship was constantly washed over by the sea and several of the livestock drowned. George Inskip, the *Bramble*'s second master, recorded, in exasperation, the feelings he had at this moment in his journal: 'So much for my zeal. I think any zeal is pretty well evaporated – God send this will soon be over.'[19] In the midst of the mayhem, the two ships parted company and lost sight of each other on Monday 28 May. Stanley thought they were going through a 'young hurricane – or as hard words are all the go now – a "Cyclone"'.[20]

And then, as if by magic, the wind slackened and the seas started falling. They were out of the worst. 'We [let] the vortex go past, and we then followed or rather crossed its track with fine weather.'[21] The 2nd June brought a most beautiful day. 'Nothing can be more beautiful than this smooth sea, just sufficiently broken into waves to give an appearance of life to the deep blue waters; this deep infinite blue sky, with here and there a summer cloud floating dreamily along, or hanging like a hovering bird . . . Even the old ship looks well with her pile of canvas just distended by the soft gentle breeze.'[22] 'The evenings are now very beautiful,' added Charles Card:

> every [one] seems happy as you see on the poop a lot of wardroom officers playing singlesticks, then come ourselves on the quarter deck at the same fun, and the men forward on the forecastle being amused by our band which is very

strong amounting to no less than 3 instruments, viz. 1 Fiddle, 1 Fife, and 1 Triangle; some dancing and some at singlestick; this is just at sunset which this evening was remarkably beautiful and the ship laying on the water as though she was in harbour.[23]

On the *Bramble*, they celebrated the change in the weather by drinking a toast to sweethearts and wives.[24]

The next day the *Rattlesnake* picked up the southeast trades, and off they went. But, as they got closer to their destination, they entered a new kind of weather: 'hot, wet, rainy, muggy'. They weren't entirely surprised because the last person to come this way at this time of the year and who wrote up his adventures, the French explorer Captain Dumont D'Urville, experienced precisely the same kind of weather. Huxley, who had become philosophical when the bad weather broke – 'a thousand thousand thoughts chase one another through my brain' – now started to turn reflection into depression: 'I am becoming a very morose animal,' he wrote, 'worse than I was last cruise I think. I feel inclined to avoid everybody, and to shut myself up in my own pursuits.' Remarking that D'Urville had incessant rain on his voyage, Huxley's gloomy mood was reinforced by the climatic prison he imagined: 'Are we to have the same pleasant weather during the whole of our three months hereabouts?' he asked sarcastically. 'I fear yes' was his answer.[25]

In the early morning of Sunday 10 June, after streaming across the Coral Sea, they spotted high land about 25 miles distant, reported to be Rossel and Sudest Islands. The next day, the *Rattlesnake* fell in with the *Bramble* in the neighbourhood of Cape Deliverance on Rossel Island, the intended rendezvous point in case of separation. The *Bramble* had reached Adèle Island, to the southeast of Rossel Island, several days earlier and had already done some reconnoitring.[26]

It wasn't just that this was the first landfall since leaving Moreton Bay a fortnight before. No, there was something quite magical about the view in front of them that brought on lyrical descriptions from people who, judging from their journals and diaries, were not normally moved by the landscape. Charles Card was one of these. This is how he described Rossel Island as the *Rattlesnake* made its way along the reef protecting it from the open sea:

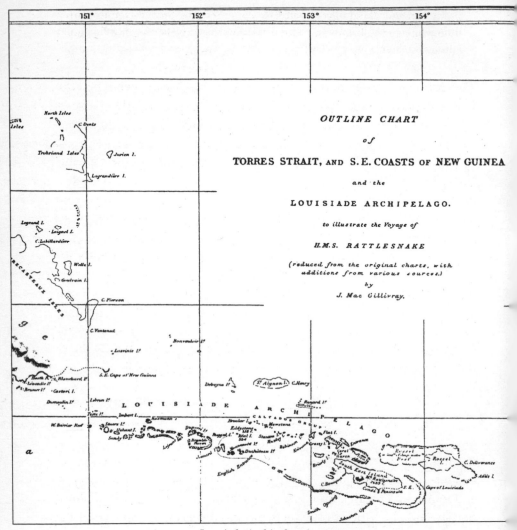

Lousiade Archipelago in 1849

Rossel is the most beautiful island we have ever yet seen, high and well wooded, cocoa nut trees, banana trees all over the island and [there] a patch of
green grass looking like a meadow . . . Several of their huts or rather houses
were seen, they were much larger and looked more compactly built that any
we had seen before. How we did envy the niggers their cocoa nuts and
bananas and beautiful shady places to lay down under the heat of the day,
some of them too had gone higher up the mountain as though to get more of
the cool sea breeze . . . The beautiful color of the water inside the reef was very

pretty being of a kind of very pale blue color here and there mixed up with a little white spray, forming a beautiful white fringe and setting it off to great advantage.[27]

The instructions given to Stanley by the Admiralty hardly mentioned the Louisiade Archipelago and the coast of New Guinea, remarking simply that he should 'explore the safety of the sea' between there and the Great Barrier Reef. They were more concerned, in these instructions at least, that he should not fall foul of 'the treacherous disposition of their inhabitants'. They implored him that 'all barter for refreshments should be conducted under the eye of an officer – and every pains taken to avoid giving any just cause of offence to their prejudices – especially with respect to their women.'[28]

Beaufort's instructions, by contrast, were much more specific and provided a justification for why this area needed a marine survey. The survey of the Louisiade Archipelago and the coast of New Guinea was part of a much larger survey of the entire Coral Sea, bounded by New Caledonia on the east, the coast of Australia on the west and New Guinea on the north, designed to provide a safe passage for ships voyaging from the Pacific to the Indian Ocean through the Torres Strait.[29] To complete the job, Beaufort also asked Stanley to examine Bligh's Entrance, an opening in the easternmost reefs in the Torres Strait, which Bligh had discovered in 1792. The *Rattlesnake*'s surveys were, therefore, not simply a matter of attending to desiderata, but were part of defining and constructing a political space connecting the Pacific to the Indian Ocean by the Torres Strait and integrating the commerce of the South Sea Islands, Australia, China and India. Sir Roderick Murchison, President of the Royal Geographical Society and close friend of Francis Beaufort, had already spoken of the importance of this largely unknown (to European states) maritime world in his presidential address a year before the *Rattlesnake*'s departure from England.[30]

The French were the first to chart this part of the world. The Spanish navigator, Luis Vaez de Torres, was probably the first European to see this part of New Guinea in 1606 but he didn't chart this part of his voyage. Louis Antoine de Bougainville was the next European explorer to arrive, after an interval of more than a century and a half, in 1768, after sailing westwards from New Hebrides towards the eastern coast of Australia. As he was approaching the Australian coast, he almost came to grief on a detached reef some 100 nautical miles from the coast. It was enough to convince him not to proceed in this direction any further and instead he headed northwards until he reached a bay off the coast of an 'undiscovered' land. This bay he named Cul de Sac de l'Orangerie and though he wanted to head westward at this point to look for a possible way to the Moluccas (he did not know of the existence of the Torres Strait), he headed eastward instead, sailing along the southern fringe of an archipelago, which he named Louisiade, until he reached its end at Cape Deliverance, which he also named. He then sailed away from the area. Twenty-five years passed before another French navigator, Antoine-Raymond-Joseph Bruny d'Entrecasteaux, turned up in 1793, not so much looking for the Louisiade and New Guinea, as for his fellow navigator, La Pérouse, who was last seen in the area in 1788. D'Entrecasteaux sailed along the northern edge of the Louisiade Archipelago as best as he could, looking for his colleague, naming islands, such as Rossel, after one of his lieutenants, Joannet after his surgeon, and charting the seas as he went along. D'Entrecasteaux couldn't spend too long on charting, since this was not his main reason for being in this part of the world, and very soon after arriving in the Louisiade, he headed northwards searching the islands lying off the northeastern coast of New Guinea.[31]

D'Entrecasteaux was the last European explorer to come this way for a long time. Though Matthew Flinders and Phillip Parker King rounded Cape York and went through the Torres Strait, neither of them ventured towards the New Guinea coast. It was not until 1840 that an interest in the area was sparked and, once again, it was the French who were on the spot. Approaching from the southeast after leaving New Zealand, Captain Jules Dumont D'Urville and his two ships met the Louisiade Archipelago at the same point, Cape Deliverance, as Bougainville more than seventy years earlier. D'Urville and his men were not in good physical shape – D'Urville, in particular, was in dreadful pain – and they spent as little time in the area as possible, heading westward along the southern shore of the Louisiade until they reached Cul de Sac de l'Orangerie, doing Bougainville's voyage in reverse. This took no more than four days and, incredibly, D'Urville and his draughtsman, who was also ill, managed to carry out a running survey of the area, the first of its kind. By the time Stanley arrived in 1849, D'Urville's was the best chart available for the Louisiade and the southeastern coast of New Guinea. This guided their survey.

Beaufort was meticulous, even obsessional, about surveying. Rocks, according to him, were impertinent and interrogative, visible at times and not at others, 'like the track of a mole it pays its frequent visits to the surface'; shoals were a nuisance but reefs he hated the most, obviously because of the damage they caused to ships, but more significantly in that they were living, growing organisms.[32] He reserved his choicest language for these formations. 'Monstrous' was how he described the Great Barrier Reef. Reefs, in general, were 'hidden dangers which lurk and even grow in that part of the world'. And the best way of ensuring safety from the monsters of the deep was a proper and accurate chart. 'Hydrography', Beaufort stated, 'is best served by one accurate chart than by ten approximate sketches'; and, continuing in a similar vein, 'the true vocation of a surveying vessel not being to save herself (only) but to save others'.[33] And when he talked about surveys, he meant proper surveys, using methods of triangulation, employing boats and involving the shore. Running surveys, done from the main ship, he had little time for. Do 'not waste your time and means in what are called running surveys in which much work is apparently executed but no accurate knowledge obtained useful either to mariner or geographer whatever you do is to be done effectually.'[34]

The Louisiade Archipelago, as Stanley discovered, consists of a number of island groups, stretching for more than 250 miles to the east of the island of New Guinea, each of them encircled by reef. Stanley's surveying problem throughout this part of the voyage was that of finding an anchorage for the *Rattlesnake*. What he discovered very quickly was that anchorages outside the reefs were extremely difficult, the depth varying enormously over a very small distance, and that anchorages within the reefs were more secure, provided he could find a way in. On the 13 June, the first day of exploring this *terra incognita*, as they called it, Stanley, who was, incidentally, celebrating his thirty-eighth birthday, encountered these very difficulties. Once they turned around westward from Cape Deliverance, the two ships proceeded slowly along the outside of Rossel Island's reef looking for an opening to get closer to the island.

Rossel Island is about 20 miles in length and as they ran about two miles from the shore, the views were, as Card had already noted, stunning. Stanley gave his family an idea of what he was seeing, in a long letter written in the form of a journal. 'Nothing could be more splendid', he wrote, 'than the scenery about Rossel Island . . . High towering peaks clothed with the most luxuriant vegetation up to their very summits – and from the sides of these hills every now and then would come out a stream of smoke like the jet of steam from a high pressure engine, apparently intended to attract our attenton.'[35] The contrast with the flat, 'green-brown Australian' landscape of the previous voyage, could not have been greater.[36]

But, as the ships ran on, the frustration of not getting through to the island was beginning to grow. 'On we went in perfectly smooth water', Stanley continued,

> and skirted the Coral Reef which surrounds the Island without finding a single gap by which we could get inside it, and the soundings had shown no bottom at 80 fathoms outside. This was the more tantalising because as we advanced, the Island became, if possible, more beautiful. The natives were seen fishing on the edge of the reef, gazing in wonder at the large 'Canoes' that were passing. In shore we could see their houses beautifully situated under groves of cocoa nut trees with well laid out gardens around them in which plants were placed with as much regularity as any farmer in England would sow a field of corn.[37]

Charles Card spoke of his mortification in finding Rossel Island surrounded by a reef: 'What a pity it is', he recorded in his journal, 'that so beautiful an island should be rendered so unapproachable'.[38] As they were just about to leave the westernmost point of the Rossel reefs, which stretched for about 30 miles from Rossel Island, they spotted what appeared to be an opening but, as the sun was setting, the glare off the sea made it impossible to see ahead from the mast head and further sailing was ruled out. The first day in the Louisiade Archipelago ended with the ships being hove to on the outside of Rossel Island's reef.

The next day found the ships, thanks to a strong current, farther to the west than they had expected. They had, in fact, drifted well beyond the reef. Instead of returning to the eastward to explore the opening they had spotted through the Rossel reefs, Stanley decided to press on to the westward. Very soon they found themselves staring at another reef system, this one protecting Peron Island (named after D'Entrecasteaux's draughtsman). The reef continued to the westward with no break, as the ships gingerly sailed along the outside fringe; 'at last,' remarked Stanley, 'just as I was beginning to fear that we should see as little of the Louisiade as our predecessors, the French officers, the *Bramble* made the signal, "The Channel is clear but though narrow is practicable."' This was enough and 'following her we stood for the edge of the reef on which in all points save our very little opening the sea was breaking very heavily.'[39] With the roar of the surf behind him, Brierly caught the excitement and strain of the moment as the ships passed through what he called 'a regular case of Scylla and Charybdes' – 'as we neared the order was given "keep perfect silence on deck", given in a tone that in an instant stilled the hum of voices to a whisper, the silence only broken by the Quarter Masters as they "spoke" the soundings quickly and distinctly, the ordinary method of singing them too slow at a critical moment like this.'[40]

The opening was just 200 yards wide. The ships swept through. 'We were gliding on into a broad expanse of smooth water surrounded by the most beautiful islands, on the nearest of which was a native village the houses being raised from the ground upon light poles, magnificent cocoa nut trees shooting up in all directions.'[41] They were now truly inside the Louisiade Archipelago. They named the enclosure Coral Haven. But could they find an anchorage? 'The water remained deep for some little time,' continued Stanley, 'leading us to fear that we should not find anchorage inside. But after a few minutes of the most intense anxiety I had the pleasure of hearing Matthews sing out: "Eleven fathoms" from one of the chains, and directly afterwards the same from Coleman on the other side.'[42]

Stanley was certain that no European had ever been here before. Only surveying ships, he thought, could have come in through the opening in the reefs. The inhabitants of the surrounding points of land were clearly visible but, at first, they kept a safe distance from the visitor. They had not 'as yet experienced any injury from Europeans who, though they carry trade and plunder wherever they can, have not yet reached these people whom Robert [Robert Gale] calls "men in an unsophisticated state"'. Stanley's experience and acquaintance with the islands of the South Seas, however, told him that the inhabitants would soon come out to trade, despite their present reticence.[43]

Sure enough, the next day, 15 June, as the *Rattlesnake* moved closer into Coral Haven, the first tentative steps to bartering goods took place, as a coconut was exchanged for a handkerchief. The visitors offered tobacco, as they had done on Cape York, but the local people did not appear to know what it was, even though they took it and placed it with the articles they had acquired.[44] Bartering was a process of discovery. Both sides tried different articles to barter until a successful exchange could be made. The visitors wanted coconuts and yams, and souvenirs such as spears and articles of jewellery; while the local people were particularly interested in iron, red cloth and paper.[45] They approached the ships in single outrigger canoes, which were propelled by paddles, shaped 'like the ace of spades with a long handle' and a single large sail. While the bartering took place, one of the canoes slipped behind the *Bramble* and a crutch (a forked metal support for an oar), which happened to be lying loose in one of the boats tied at the stern, was taken by one of the paddlers. 'Like any dextrous London thieves', commented Huxley,' they passed it from hand to hand and concealed it at the far end of their canoe, and when charged with the theft looked as innocent and impassive as M. de Talleyrand himself could have looked under similar circumstances.'[46] After some yelling and screaming, the item was handed back and the canoes returned to whence they came.

Stanley wanted to get closer to the people with whom they were bartering. They seemed to be coming from an island close to the anchorage. The following day, 16 June, a party of officers from the *Rattlesnake*, including Huxley, MacGillivray and Brierly, landed on the largest island close to the anchorage, to look for water and to 'establish a communication with the natives'.[47] Though water was found, it wasn't in sufficient quantity to fill the ships. Human contact was somewhat more successful. The first islander the visitors met was a 'bright copper-coloured gentleman who appeared like Paul to be the "chief speaker" bearing a green branch in his hand which he frequently waved'. He preferred to remain at a distance from the intruders. MacGillivray thought he detected a Malay dialect but when he tried to respond to the spokesman with a number of key words, such as those for fire and water, and found that he was not being understood, he gave up this idea. Making real contact was proving very difficult. The green branch of the spokesman gave the visitors an idea. 'We too gathered branches and waving for the dear life and making all sorts of unearthly noises, supposed to express our pacific disposition, went towards them.' The visitors were desperate for contact and their attempts to get closer to the inhabitants took on farcical proportions. Each forward step of the visitors was met by a backward step of the inhabitants. 'At last,' wrote Huxley, 'MacGillivray, leaving his gun with us and taking a branch in each hand, went jumping and dancing with all sorts of antics towards them. They allowed him to come up but still seemed disinclined for our society. Brierly then took upon himself to do the agreeable and advanced in the same way but with such wonderful antics that the niggers seemed irresistibly attracted and committed themselves to several acts of barter. After a while, laying my gun aside I went to them, and had a very interesting and polite interview with friend coppery and two other gentlemen who were quite black and had large fuzzy heads of hair with combs a foot long, narrow and very long-pronged, stuck into the front of their very remarkable coiffure.'[48] Huxley began sketching one of the locals but, whether he just got bored sitting there or something else took his fancy, the man went off before Huxley could finish his piece.

This being the first landing in *terra incognita*, MacGillivray set to work, observing, recording and collecting what he could, but the pickings weren't great: a few land shells, but nothing new to science, and a range of flora that appeared to be similar to vegetation found in tropical Australia and the islands of the South Seas.[49] The people, by contrast, provided much richer material. MacGillivray's observations included descriptions of their appearance and physiognomy, emphasizing differences and similarities to Australians, 'with whom I naturally compared them as the only dark savage race which I had seen much of'.[50] Hair and skin were the most important markers of race typing for the white observers, but they were also interested in body markings, such as scarification and tattooing, as well as body piercing. These islanders were 'dark copper coloured' and 'fuzzy-headed'.[51] 'Many wore circular ear-rings apparently made of the operculum of a Turbo [sea shell, often green in colour] and cut to the centre so as to allow of the pierced lobe of the ear being passed in. And the septum of the nose was ornamented – save the mark! – with a long white bone or some such thing stuck through it.'[52] MacGillivray noted that 'nearly all the men carried in their hair a comb projecting in front or on one side ... [it] is usually made of wood, but occasionally of tortoise-shell, a foot in length, thin, flat, and narrow, with about six very long, slightly diverging, needle-shaped teeth . . .'[53] They were not scarified, nor were they missing any front teeth, as was the case with some aboriginal Australians. They appeared to chew some kind of substance, which MacGillivray and others thought was betel nut, partly because of the stain it produced and partly because of the implements they carried to keep the substance and the lime that accompanied it.[54] Their homes were built on piles, with a roof covered with a thatch-like material. Inskip was impressed. 'They are', he remarked, 'to all appearances better than many a hovel you will see at home.'[55]

The next day, the same party returned to the as yet unnamed island, to look for water and to barter. Once again the search for water was unsuccessful in the quantities needed but the bartering was, as on the previous day, successful. In exchange for a handkerchief and a knife, Brierly and Huxley managed to get themselves a live pig, which came tied to a pole. But while the exchange was friendly, an atmosphere was building up which the men from the *Rattlesnake* found very uncomfortable. The visitors found themselves being surrounded by men with spears and someone stole Huxley's pistol. Gingerly, the visitors made their way back to the boat while MacGillivray, brandishing a double-barrelled shotgun, covered the rear until they reached the beach. No one could understand why this day was so different from the previous one.[56] It seemed appropriate enough to name the place Pig Island.

All the excitement was one thing, but not finding sufficient water on Pig Island was troubling. They had run out of water before and the length of their stay in the Louisiade depended entirely on finding an adequate supply – the closest certain source was Cape York, 800 miles away to the west. Thankfully, an exploring party led by Yule returned to the *Rattlesnake* with news that they had found a suitable watering place on nearby Sudest Island.[57]

Over the next few days, the ships carried on sending surveying parties to take soundings and to look for other passages from Coral Haven and bartering with the canoes that approached. Iron, or 'kalooma' as they called it, was always the most desired item. In return the visitors got plantains and cooked yams and sundry ornaments. One of these, Stanley observed, was a 'human lower jaw bone with all its teeth . . . which we obtained at a very cheap rate'. Seeing an ornament made of human parts gave Stanley an opportunity to remark about barter. 'I have no doubt,' he wrote, 'that a white man's skull would be the most precious thing they could possess.' 'And', he continued in a very surprising twist to an old theme, 'I am not quite sure that some of the Naturalists on board would not be quite as glad to get hold of one of theirs. I can easily see Dr Huxley superintending the boiling down and subsequent steps required to prepare a skull, should we by misfortune become possessed of one.'[58] Stanley didn't think much of the trinkets the inhabitants were offering. He called the objects 'trash' and only found an intellectual value in them as they showed 'the change that takes place in the customs and manners of the natives of the Islands as they approach the Eastern coast of Australia'. Besides not thinking much of their wares, Stanley also didn't think much of them. He was very much on his guard, the incident with the pig adding to his caution. 'They are not to be trusted', he reflected, adding a surveyor's in-joke, 'one inch or one bit (or whatever scale you may apply to distrust).'[59]

MacGillivray and Brown, the *Rattlesnake*'s master, and a few others went to search the watering place but found that as they proceeded further up the creek, the water turned brackish and the water course narrowed, but fortunately for them, upon exploring another opening in the mangrove, they found excellent drinking water.[60] The anxiety of running short of water was put to rest. On the 25 June, the *Bramble*, having taken water from the *Rattlesnake*, proceeded to explore the south side of Sudest Island, the largest island in the Louisiade, and then to venture southwards towards the reef encircling the island to see if there were any passages through to the open sea. Meanwhile the *Rattlesnake* moved its anchorage closer to the north side of Sudest Island near the place where Brown and MacGillivray had reported a source of sufficient water. The next day, Stanley took charge of the watering expedition. 'Went away at sunrise to examine a watering place and had to pull about a mile up a narrow winding creek with the most luxuriant vegetation on each side till we reached a rocky barrier extending from one side of the creek to the other over which a most beautiful cascade of good water was falling so as to ensure an abundant supply . . . I cannot tell you the relief to my mind when we found such a supply which will render us nearly independent till we reach Cape York.' For the following week, 'every cask, bucket – and in short everything that would hold water was put into requisition', and by its end they had managed to collect a mighty weight of 78 tons of water.[61]

MacGillivray took the opportunity to explore the flora and fauna of this part of Sudest Island but found again that the specimens here were known elsewhere, particularly in the Indonesian Archipelago and in Australia. Some of the plants, such as tree ferns and mangroves, appeared much larger here than they did elsewhere. Though there was nothing new to science, the observations and collections were useful in enlarging the knowledge about the biogeography of the region.[62]

The watering was completed on 2 July and the *Rattlesnake* was moved westward about 18 miles and took up an anchorage near a small island to the southwest of the tip of Sudest Island. Over the next few days, various parties, including Stanley, MacGillivray, Thomson and Huxley, landed on the nearby island to barter and explore. On 3 July, the pinnace and a galley, led by Lieutenants Simpson and Dayman, and accompanied by Brierly, were sent to explore Joannet Island, a few miles to the north.

The small island where the *Rattlesnake* was now at anchor was only about one and a half miles in circumference, yet well wooded with a central ridge just under 350 feet. The island was intensively cultivated and supported about thirty to forty people in two villages.[63] Partly because it was so small, the visitors were able to peep into every corner. Between Huxley and Stanley sketching away and MacGillivray interrogating his hosts for their vocabulary, there was no rest for the inhabitants, but they didn't seem to mind these strange white people examining their village. MacGillivray and the others managed to get very close to their huts: '[we] had thus an opportunity of examining one of them minutely, besides verifying what we had before seen only from a distance, and with the aid of the telescope.'[64]

The first three days of visiting went well for all concerned. Bartering consisted of the now familiar exchange of cloth and iron for food. On the fourth day of visiting, a great deal was struck for both sides: seventeen axes

19 The naturalist John MacGillivray, sketched in later life when he was living in Australia.
20 When a lieutenant and in command of HMS *Britomart*, Owen Stanley participated in the establishment of the northernmost British settlement in Australia, Port Essington. All the buildings, including the theatre pictured here, were prefabricated in Sydney and assembled in this lonely spot. This production of *Cheap Living* in August 1839 was produced and directed by Stanley, who also designed and painted the sets.

1 Port Essington's burial ground accepted its first residents not long after the settlement was established. The bright colours that the artist – John McArthur, Port Essington's commandant – used in this picture deliberately mask the fact that the cemetery was one of the busiest places in this very sick settlement.

22 Edmund Kennedy, the highly respected and brave surveyor who would meet his untimely death on this exploration of the interior of Australia's eastern coast, is here depicted at his first camp in Rockingham Bay in late May 1848. Kennedy is at the entrance to the tent while Stanley is to his right, using a sextant to measure angles.

23 Landing Kennedy's stores and animals from the *Tam O'Shanter* (the ship that brought him to this place in company with the *Rattlesnake*) proved to be very difficult and dangerous in the rough seas. Despite the atrocious conditions, it was successful: only one horse was lost.

24 This picture shows Huxley's face being painted by a local inhabitant with the same markings as his own. The scene is probably in the vicinity of Rockingham Bay in May or June 1848.

25 Within a few days of setting up his first camp, Kennedy came face to face with the realization that finding a way out of the area to begin his northward journey was proving difficult, if not impossible. A sense of the impenetrability of the surrounding forest is immediately conveyed in this sketch. Kennedy is at the front of the picture (with a pointed hat); Huxley is in front of him, hacking a way through the scrub.

26 Coral Haven, named by Stanley, is a lagoon sheltered by reefs and small islands to the northwest of Sudest Island in the eastern end of the Louisiade Archipelago. It was here, in June 1849, that the *Rattlesnake* had its first encounter with the local people. Stanley cautiously allowed barter to take place, but forbade anyone to leave the ship.

27 An inhabitant of Dufaure Island in the Cul de Sac de l'Orangerie, on the south coast of New Guinea, in early September 1849. This is possibly the first picture of a local islander by a European artist. Brierly was very sensitive to aboriginal people and depicted them exactly as he saw them – without, as he would say, prejudice.

28 A sketch of a man from one of the Duchateau islands, in the middle of the Louisiade Archipelago. The *Rattlesnake* anchored near one of these islands in late July 1849.

Everyone on board the *Rattlesnake* and the *Bramble* was certain that they were the first Europeans to anchor in this part of the world. To celebrate the occasion of this anchorage in Coral Haven in June 1849, Brierly produced this elaborate watercolour, showing the *Rattlesnake* in ghost-like appearance (in the background) with the local inhabitants in their canoes (in the foreground).

Stanley invited the inhabitants of Brumer Island to the ship on 25 August 1849. The women, dressed in petticoats, struck up a dance, as shown here. This was a moment of great excitement for the whole ship's company for they were no more than two miles from the as yet unexplored coast of New Guinea. Excitement, however, soon gave way to desperation and anger as Stanley resolutely refused to let anyone land.

31 Queen Baki of Evans Bay, Cape York. Baki paved the way for the dramatic meeting between Barbara Thompson (who was shipwrecked and had been living with a group of islanders from the Torres Strait for five years) and the men of the *Rattlesnake*.

32 A panoramic view centred on Evans Bay, Cape York, where the *Rattlesnake* anchored in both 1848 and 1849. The scene, showing the *Rattlesnake*, the *Bramble* and their boats, together with a number of mainland and island canoes, faithfully reflects the fact that this was a crossroads for commerce and culture.

Europeans had been visiting Darnley
Island, in the eastern part of the Torres Strait,
for many decades. This picture shows officers
and crew bartering with the local inhabitants. It
was here, during the second week of December
1849, that the *Rattlesnake*'s purser was offered –
and purchased – the mummy of a deceased
boy.

An islander paying respects to his ancestors
on Mount Ernest Island in the Torres Strait. It
was here that Oswald Brierly discovered why
had been given the name Tarrka.

March 13th At an early hour Captain Owen Stanley of the Rattlesnake departed this life, having retired to rest in the previous evening he is supposed to have fallen from his cot in a fit – Deeply and Universally regretted – Hoisted the colors half mast.

15th The remains of Captain Stanley were interred with Military Honors in the Burial Ground of St Leonards on the North side of the river, he having expressed a wish to that effect – Minute guns were fired from the Ships.

35 Captain Owen Stanley's funeral on 15 March 1850 was a major event attracting thousands of onlookers and participants. This drawing has never been reproduced before. It was made to accompany the journal entry by Henry Keppel of Stanley's sudden death on HMS *Rattlesnake* two days earlier, also reproduced here for the first time.

and a few knives yielded 368 pounds of yams. MacGillivray collected 130 words of the islanders' language, proudly proclaiming that this was the first ever obtained by Europeans in the Louisiade Archipelago. Though the visitors never seemed to tire of poking about, driven by a rampant curiosity – Huxley was extremely desirous of sketching one of the island's women, trying to barter his way to a sitting and nearly giving offence – the islanders were by now becoming weary of the intruders and were 'anxious to get rid of us'.[65] Reluctantly, the visitors piled into their boats and headed back to their big canoe.

So ended the most prolonged and friendly meeting between the European visitors and the Louisiade inhabitants to date. The island in question appeared to have the name Chaumont Island and this is the way the *Rattlesnake* people spoke of it. But looking at D'Urville's chart, on which the island appears, the positions of Chaumont Island and the island where the visitors spent three days are not identical. Whether this was the excuse Stanley needed is not clear, but in any case he named, or renamed, the island Brierly Island, honouring his friend Oswald Brierly by enshrining his name on an Admiralty chart. At the same time, he gave the name Chaumont to another island, described as 'a mass of dead coral with a few stunted bushes upon it', well to the south.[66]

The *Bramble* had now returned from its voyage south, exploring the coastline of Sudest Island until Presqu'ile Condé and the fringe of reef that protected the island on this side. To Stanley's relief, Yule found two passages through that reef into the open sea, wide enough to take the *Rattlesnake* and ships like it. The passages were carefully surveyed and given the names Johnston and Smith Passage, after one of the master's assistants and a midshipman respectively.[67]

Everything was now ready for resuming the survey westward, apart from the return of the pinnace and galley from their exploration of Joannet Island. Next day, 6 July, the two boats returned but with bad news. While they were away surveying, they were attacked, they reported, by a group of inhabitants of Joannet Island, in a bay, thereafter named Treacherous Bay. The inhabitants had, it appears, approached the boats to barter and all went well. But then one of them attempted to grab the anchor of the galley while others began dragging it towards the shore. A fight ensued. Two of the boat's men were injured, one by a club and the other by a spear. Shots were fired back from pistols, muskets and a brass Howitzer. The inhabitants jumped overboard and rushed back to the shore, leaving at least one of their canoes floating in the water. The visitors sustained only slight injuries. Of the inhabitants, there seemed to be little doubt that some of them must have been killed.[68]

Stanley was shocked but not surprised. 'I hope our friends have had a lesson which they will not forget in a hurry,' he commented, and continued with a warning of what the future would hold:

> and our people too [who] in spite of all I could tell them of my experience to the contrary were beginning to think that implicit confidence might be placed in these natives, as they seemed to be so much more civilised than those of Australia, have also received a lesson they will not very easily forget, and which will, I hope, have the effect of preventing anything like such an attempt on the part of the natives in future. But it will also lessen our chance of friendly communication with them, which I am very sorry for on the natives account as they might have obtained so many valuable things from us.[69]

Charles Card immediately felt a distinct change in atmosphere. 'I have now given up all thoughts of landing,' he wrote in his journal, 'at least till we get to Cape York, as the Captain would no more think of allowing us to land for pleasure than he would of landing himself, which I am pretty sure he will be careful about after this.'[70] They had been in the Louisiade Archipelago for twenty-three days and had landed on sixteen of them. Card feared that this was over and he was right.

Very little happened over the next few days, and then, on 10 July, Stanley gave the order to move the *Rattlesnake* in a south-southwesterly direction. He had intended to trace the inner edge of the reef westward but as he got closer to it he found himself amidst numerous detached masses of reef. Stanley decided to anchor rather than go any further.[71] The *Bramble*, the pinnace and a cutter, meanwhile, were dispatched to survey the islands to the west, the Calvados Group, and to find, if possible, a passage westward for the *Rattlesnake*. Several days passed, and then in the evening of 14 July, the pinnace was spotted hove to at some distance from the *Rattlesnake*. Stanley, possibly on his own, jumped into one of the galleys and rowed towards the pinnace into the fading light. He returned several hours later.

Card thought it was 'a mad trick of his, going away all that time of night'. As to the reason for this rash move, Card could only think of one: '. . . it was just after dinner to which cause we must attribute it.'[72]

The news from the pinnace was good. The *Bramble* was some thirty miles to the west and had surveyed and named a large number of the islands of the Calvados Group – Huxley got an island, as did the *Bramble*'s new assistant surgeon and virtually all of the midshipmen and master's assistants. (Beaufort advocated naming places after the men on the ship, rather than after absent friends and patrons – 'The officers and crews have a better claim to such a distinction, which slight as it is might help to excite an interest in the voyage.')[73] More immediately important, however, Simpson reported that he had found a passage to the westward but it required the *Rattlesnake* retracing its steps back to Brierly Island before heading in the desired direction. Navigating and finding safe anchorages in this part of the Louisiade Archipelago proved to be very nerve-racking, as Stanley told his family. He helped them imagine how difficult it was:

> Being anxious to anchor and for some time obtained regular soundings with from 20 to 25 fathoms, the sail was taken in and all was ready to let the anchor go. But before giving the final order, one more cast of the deep sea lead was got, shewing that in less than a 10th of a mile the depth had increased from 20 to 40 fms which was rather too deep to anchor in so we had to make sail again.

Progress was grindingly slow and the weather, which turned very misty and rainy, didn't help. Finally, late on Sunday 23 July, after a week of plodding along, the *Rattlesnake* anchored near three, low islands, which D'Urville had previously named Isles du Château.

The three Duchateau Islands (as they were called), small, low and woody, were uninhabited but frequently visited by canoes from islands in the Calvados Group to the north, principally for the purpose of hunting turtle.[74] This was the first anchorage near land for almost a fortnight. Some on the ship, such as Charles Card, had not been off the ship since it left Moreton Bay. Stanley, sensing little danger here, let his people out on the island to stretch their legs, bathe and have a bash at shooting game for the pot. The weather turned very bad, the visibility being so poor that surveying was out of the question. There was nothing to do but wait it out.

*

Though the islands were uninhabited, Stanley took no chances since the Joannet Island incident. All shore parties were armed to the teeth, but clearly Stanley was always on the lookout for the first sign of trouble. On one occasion, on 27 July, while Lieutenant Dayman and Master's Assistant Brooker were taking magnetic readings on the middle island, two canoes landed. Upon seeing this from the ship, Stanley immediately dispatched a cutter to provide backup cover. Not long after the cutter appeared, the canoes set off heading to another destination.

Huxley was on the island at the time and he appeared surprised at Stanley's reaction, since one of the canoes had two little girls in them. 'They had no evil intention,' he wrote. But what irritated Huxley the most was the aftermath. As he described it, 'To hear the Captain talking in the evening you would have thought that a bloody battle had taken place at the least, or at any rate must have taken place had it not been for his extreme care and providence in sending the cutter. What a Sir Joshua Windbag the little man is!'[75]

This was quite an attack on Stanley. But it was not the first time that Huxley was critical of his captain. The first rant, in written form, at least, took place on 13 June. Stanley's dog had died that day, and this is how Huxley wrote about it. 'The skipper's black dog, "Native", weary I suppose of leading a dog's life and among the middies, committed suicide last night, by walking into the sea out of the main chains. The skipper and his dog', he continues, 'had this in common, that they liked one another, and were disliked by every one else.'[76] A fortnight later, Huxley was again sniping at Stanley's heels. This time he viciously attacked Stanley's artistic abilities, after having a swipe at his lack of discernment in other departments. 'That little skipper of ours is a greater ass than I thought,' he began. 'That he had neither smell nor hearing nor taste sufficiently refined to enable him to distinguish one sensation from another, sulphuretted hydrogen from Millefleurs, "God Save the Queen" from "Old Dan Tucker", strawberries from mulberries – I knew long ago, but I now find that his eye is equally defective.' The cause of this rage was that he thought that Stanley's coloured sketch of the watering place on Sudest Island was ridiculous – 'Last night the little man sent for me. I went and lo! the sketch, which with a look as much as to say "you don't see anything like that every day" he submitted to my inspection. I nearly burst out laughing. Words won't describe the absurdity of the thing.'[77] Stanley, certainly unaware of Huxley's feelings towards him, thought that Huxley was a pretty good artist and esteemed his superior skill in depicting human faces.[78]

A few days later, Stanley was again under attack for the manner in which he approached the inhabitants of Brierly Island: '. . . the skipper with his usual want of savoir-faire looking as stupid as a stockfish'. Huxley did not state what Stanley was doing that annoyed him so much, but Stanley's version is worth recounting. As he told his family,

> In order not to alarm the natives, I beached the Galley well clear of the canoes, and having seen that all the arms were ready for service, I landed alone and unarmed (except a small double-barrelled pistol in my pocket) and went towards the natives who came forward in considerable numbers all armed with spears and evidently much inclined to doubt the nature of our visit. The Galley's crew had orders to fire in case of any attack being attempted on me, but I must confess it was rather nervous work advancing alone as the natives did not seem to wish to have any communication with us. But at last having got within 20 yards of them I tied a piece of coloured handkerchief to a stump on the beach and retired making signs for them to come and take it. After some little hesitation one man came forward and took it – the rest soon followed and in less than 5 minutes I had the whole tribe round me eagerly asking for iron hoops which they prize beyond anything we can give them.[79]

In Huxley's version of the day's events, it is Huxley who manages to get the islanders interested in the visitors. 'After a while it occurred to me in my presumption that this was not the way to do any good, so I said "I don't know that there are any orders about staying in the boats" and holding up my coat tails waded ashore. I began to dance and the niggers began to dance, and then we sat down and began to draw some of them, and then some more of the officers came ashore and we were very good friends.'[80] Not only was Stanley stupid, but worse, he was arrogant, thought Huxley – 'He seems to be much of Louis XIV's opinion – La France, c'est moi.'[81]

Up to this point Stanley merely seemed to irritate Huxley. In spite of Stanley's efforts to be helpful by sending Huxley's paper to London to try and have it read at a meeting of the Royal Society, Huxley's irritation grew. Now, towards the end of July, at anchor off the Duchateau Islands, Huxley's tone became much more accusatory, directly questioning Stanley's assess-

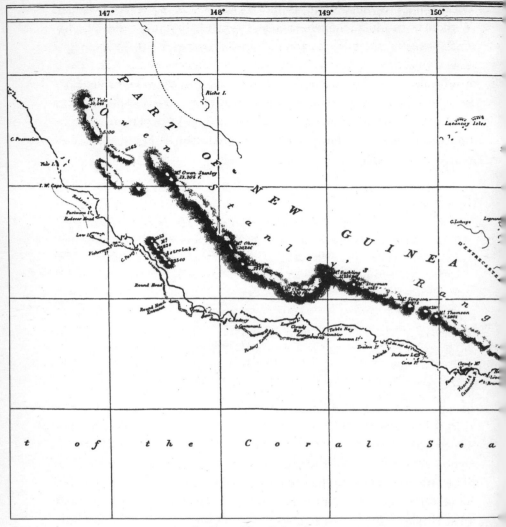

Southeast New Guinea in 1849

ment of the encounters between the officers and crew and the local inhabitants. Huxley's accusations over the next couple of months became even more damning as he looked out for anything in Stanley's behaviour, which he, Huxley, could construe as evidence of incompetence.

On 4 August, with the weather moderating, the ships weighed anchor and continued their passage to the west. The problem of finding an anchorage once again presented itself, as the sea floor was extremely irregular. Without a handy anchorage, Stanley decided that he would take the *Rattlesnake* to the open sea and survey the outer edge of the reef while Yule would take the *Bramble* and survey the inner edge and the islands nearby. As soon as he passed out of the reef, Stanley immediately felt a great weight lifted from him. 'Very glad we all were to feel the long ocean swell once more, after having been six weeks out of it,' he wrote. He continued to explain why the open sea was so preferable:

> Those only who have known the intense anxiety attendant upon a 48 hours cruise amongst a mass of shoals and reefs, can at all understand the delight with which I went to sleep when we were fairly clear for the nature of the reefs among these Islands is such that the lead gives no warning whatever ... isolated patches [of reef], many not larger than the ship, rise suddenly from comparatively deep water, so that if you hit them hard enough to cause a serious leak, you have every prospect of going down in deep water with some little chance of saving the lives of the crew, but none whatever of saving anything for them to eat.[82]

Not everyone, however, was glad to be out to sea. Charles Card, perhaps speaking for many, recorded in his journal that 'we are now anxious to come to an anchor again as we have been out a week tomorrow and have had quite enough sea for once'.[83] Huxley's opinion was that Stanley was being overly cautious, preferring 'discomfort to avoid a little – very little risk!'[84] The occasion of Huxley's latest criticism was that Stanley had chosen to heave to in the open sea instead of following the *Bramble* into a lagoon enclosed by a reef where there was a perfectly good anchorage. 'The little man's heart (if he had such a thing) failed him,' Huxley stated bluntly. 'I am sick of the brute,' he continued, now turning on Stanley and what Huxley thought was an abuse of authority, 'he has been like a little fiend all day, snubbing poor old Suckling [Senior Lieutenant] in the most disgusting manner, and behaving like a perfect cub to all about him.'[85]

For the next week the *Rattlesnake* traversed the open sea, alternating between tracking towards the reef and sailing away from it. Though progress was slow, Stanley was proud of this work because, as he explained it, he was proving that there was a safe sailing channel on the southern side of the reef.[86] As day broke on 12 August, they were within sight of the Dumoulin Islands (named after D'Urville's hydrographer), the rendezvous point for the two ships. They were now out of the Louisiade Archipelago, two months to the day since first entering it. They could just make out the coast of New Guinea to the north, 'a blue mountainous mass'.[87] Yule was ordered to find an anchorage here and indeed found one under the westernmost island in 25 fathoms. But Stanley refused to follow the *Bramble* and instead took the *Rattlesnake* to the open sea in a south-westerly direction. 'We are standing off – why, God knows,' exclaimed Huxley, totally exasperated with Stanley's behaviour.[88]

The *Rattlesnake* continued traversing the sea until, finally, several days later, on 16 August, 'a miracle has happened, we are at anchor but where they got the courage to come in here I cannot understand – however, here we are.'[89] The *Bramble* had preceded the *Rattlesnake* to find the anchorage. They were now at the westernmost and largest of the Brumer Islands, just over two miles from the New Guinea coast. 'After a fortnight of about the most anxious cruising I have ever had . . . now all was forgotten and the ship fairly anchored off the main land of New Guinea where no ship that we know of ever anchored before.'[90]

They had arrived, not just in the sense of place, but, more importantly, in the sense of a great adventure. Huxley's anticipation of the great discoveries, as he stated it to his sister before embarking on the *Rattlesnake*, was undoubtedly shared by many others:

> New Guinea, as you may be aware, is a place almost unknown, and our object is to bring back a full account of its Geography, Geology, and Natural History. In the latter department with which I shall have (in addition to my medical functions) somewhat to do, we shall form one grand collection of specimens and deposit it in the British Museum, or some such public place, and this main object being always kept in view, we are at liberty to collect and work for ourselves as we please.[91]

It looked as though all the anticipation was going to be satisfied. The *Bramble* had already had contact with some of the islanders and had established that there was profusion of coconuts and yams to be had, in exchange for iron hoop and red cloth. The island was beautiful, rocky and high. 'It is absolutely covered with cocoa nut trees from the summit to the water's edge and is in many places laid out into fields regularly fenced in with a kind of wicker work very much like hurdles . . . there is a village round on the east side of the island.'[92] In the afternoon on 17 August, the day after they anchored, several canoes and catamarans came alongside the *Rattlesnake* and the first contact took place, yams and coconuts being bartered for cloth and iron, as predicted. One of the islanders began beating an old tin pot he had received in exchange for some yams and very soon, Stanley ordered the drum, fife and fiddle to join in. 'They jumped and danced with the most frantic gestures on the frail boat they came off in, keeping fair time to the music, and it was not till the sun was getting low in the horizon that they left us, and I have no doubt that tomorrow we shall get some of them to come on board, and that we shall be able to land amongst them without much chance of being eaten.'[93]

Sure enough, the next day, canoes and catamarans from the island and the mainland arrived at the *Rattlesnake* and some of their occupants accepted the invitation to come on board and, as the day before, music was struck up and dancing commenced. Coconuts and yams were exchanged for iron and cloth and the day ended on a warm note. This was evidence enough that the 'natives were friendly' and the following day, after another visit from the islanders, Stanley ordered the cutter to visit the village to find out if there was any water they could get. The party consisted of Lieutenant Simpson, Thomson, MacGillivray, Brierly, Huxley and several midshipmen and cadets. Stanley remained behind. The landing was difficult, almost everyone getting wet, but once on the beach, they were met by a number of islanders who proposed they should visit their village, called Tassai. The village covered about half an acre and consisted of 27 huts, raised as much as six feet from the ground and about 30 feet long. Prying was kept to a minimum. The search for water proved fruitless: no streams and wells were discovered and it was assumed that the coconuts provided the liquid the villagers needed. Simpson ordered everyone back to the *Rattlesnake*. The visit lasted no more than fifteen minutes.[94] Nevertheless, between this visit and the contact the day before, the visitors were able to describe the local people. The most striking feature of the Brumer Islanders was that the women were excessively and stunningly tattooed. 'The tatooing [sic] extends over the face, fore part of the arms, and the whole front of the body continued backwards a little way over the shoulders, usually, but not always, leaving the back untouched. The pattern for the body consists of series of vertical stripes less than an inch apart, connected by zigzag and other markings – that over the face more complicated, and on the fore arm and wrist it is frequently so elaborate as to assume the appearance of beautiful lace-work.'[95] The men, by contrast, were simply tattooed, 'confined to a few blue lines or stars upon the right breast'.[96]

The next day, 19 August, Stanley ordered the cutter to return to the village to barter for coconuts and yams, as a substitute for water, and to get a pig. Brierly, Huxley and MacGillivray accompanied the party. Landing was easier this time but on arriving at the beach, there was hardly anyone there, in sharp contrast to the day before. The party worked their way down the path towards the village. Upon entering the village, they were surprised at the silence. There were no men present and the one person they encountered, who had been very friendly to them on the day before, appeared agitated at their visit. The visitors got the message and retreated back to the beach and the cutter. This time, they had spent no more than five minutes in the village. When the cutter returned to the *Rattlesnake*, they found that all the men from the village were at the ship bartering their yams, coconuts, breadfruit, bananas and sugarcane for iron hoop, 'the current coin'. They then understood why their visit to the village was unwelcome.[97]

Visits from canoes and catamarans continued over the next few days, including one very large canoe, about 40 feet in length, carrying almost thirty people, and commanded by an elderly man with a headdress of cassowary feathers who, everyone agreed, was the spitting image of the Bishop of Norwich, Captain Stanley's father. Huxley managed to get a drawing made of him. Bartering, which, until now, had been somewhat of a free-for-all, now came under strict control when it came to Stanley's attention that some of the petty officers and crew had been cheating the local people, 'giving them copper and useless pieces of metal instead of Iron'.[98] Stanley stopped the men bartering, 'excepting one man from each mess and he has to send in his name to the 1st Lieut. and officer of the watch and what he has to barter with'.[99]

On 23 August, the ship got its first visit from a woman. Two days later, a crowd of them poured on to the ship and proceeded to demonstrate their dancing routine, which was quite different from those of the men, 'much quieter and steadier . . . they merely joined hands and paced up and down the quarter deck keeping time with their feet . . . they remained on board nearly two hours . . .' Some of the women had 'been rigged out in white petticoats and old shirts made into petticoats and several bead dresses . . .'[100] One of the islanders remained behind to be entertained by Stanley's magic lantern show. Stanley had brought the device with him at great expense halfway around the world for this very purpose. The old man, Stanley said disappointedly, 'did not show half the surprise as the children in Brook Street [Stanley's London home]'.[101] As some sort of compensation, he appeared very amused by the scene of a man in bed catching a rat.

Stanley had stayed longer at the anchorage than he wanted. He found himself on the morning of 26 August being buffeted by strong winds, which not only delayed his departure but also meant that the island canoes would not be able to come to the ship to get their colleague. [102] After waiting in vain for a canoe, Stanley ordered that a boat be lowered to take him back to his island. For the next few days, the weather worsened, delaying further the continuation of the survey. One day it rained so heavily that they were able to get as much as 7 tons of water from the awnings. Finally, on 30 August, after a stay of a fortnight, the *Rattlesnake* weighed anchor from Brumer Island heading westward along the New Guinea coast for Cul de Sac de l'Orangerie, Bougainville's great bay. Stanley wanted to get there badly, champing at the bit of exploration and discovery. 'For many years', he explained to his family, '[it has] been a place of Interest and Mystery to me. The French surveyors failed in getting near it, according to their own accounts and survey, but so they did at the Louisiade; but we have been nearly all over every part of it without any very great trouble or risk.'[103] The *Bramble* had been sent ahead to find a good anchorage.

The ships had been at Brumer Island for a fortnight. During that time, there was a great deal of contact between the white visitors and their island and mainland hosts but almost all of it, apart from a couple of hours, took place on board the *Rattlesnake*. The 'explorers and buffon collectors', as Card called the surveyors and naturalists, hardly got a look in and came away empty-handed. MacGillivray, on this natural history *terra incognita*, came away with a solitary land-shell, a few feathers and nothing else. 'As shooting could not be practised without running the risk of involving ourselves with the natives', MacGillivray told John Gould, he got no birds.[104]

MacGillivray was obviously disappointed but it was Huxley, already suspicious about Stanley's behaviour and accusing him of cowardice, who expressed the outrage in being kept away from the rich quarry so close by. He recorded his feelings in his diary as the *Rattlesnake* departed the island. 'We left Brumer Id. On the 29th,' he began:

> We had plenty of visitors from the island on the 28th and I fancy must have left a very good reputation behind us, unless indeed our non-acceptance of their numerous and hospitable invitations has given them the idea that we are not very sociable. We spent a fortnight at Brumer Island, and have been allowed to touch the shore twice, and our visit on each occasion did not exceed a couple of hours. Although the natives have shown us the friendliest possible disposition, those who would gladly have done so have not been permitted to take the slightest advantage of the opportunities afforded them . . . we knew as much of its botany, similarly zoology, when we anchored, as we do now. The domestic life and habits of the natives, so interesting from their near relation to the unknown New Guinea men, after the fairest opportunities remain only known to us through their behaviour as visitors – when probably so much is constrained and artificial. The mainland was not half a dozen miles off and there appeared to be some promise of a large river. Not a boat was sent to explore the coast . . . If this is surveying, if this is the process of English Discovery, God defend me from any such elaborate waste of time and opportunity.[105]

Stanley, perhaps sensing a feeling of disappointment from the scientists, or perhaps anticipating some future recrimination, attempted to explain to his family why there was so little shore time. 'It may seem odd', he began:

> that with all the confidence the natives have shewn towards the ship, that we should have seen so little of them on shore, but the answer is easily given. In the first place, the landing place is very bad for boats at all times as a heavy surf breaks on coral reef some distance from the land; and in the second place, the village being on the other side of the hill is perfectly out of sight of the ship, so that a party going there could not trust to her guns for protection; and thirdly, though I am quite sure we might trust the Island people to a great extent, yet so many of the natives from the main land who would have nothing to lose in case of a row, remain at the Island after disposing of their barter alongside . . . I do not conceive that the chance of risking a human life is at all equal to the result obtained by landing to obtain a few yams or cocoa nuts.[106]

So there it was. In his eyes he was simply acting prudently to keep his men alive.

From Brumer Island, the *Rattlesnake* coasted along in a westerly direction, taking soundings off and on the coast while the *Bramble* did the inshore work. On 4 September the ship anchored near Dufaure Island, on the eastern side of the Cul de Sac de l'Orangerie, where they also met the *Bramble*. Yule reported that he had had an affray with a number of canoes on his way to this anchorage. As he told the story, on 30 August, while the *Bramble* was at anchor in Farm Bay, to the west of Tissot Island, about 40 canoes, carrying upwards of 300 people, surrounded the ship. Some of the men in the canoes had spears and Yule ordered that the muskets be loaded, but before anything could happen, a breeze sprang up and the *Bramble* sailed out of possible trouble. The ship continued working and surveying its way westward towards Dufaure Island. The next day, 3 canoes approached the *Bramble*, bringing nothing to barter but wishing to board. Recognizing one of them as being from Brumer Island, Yule gave him and a friend permission to board. After showing them around the vessel, Yule 'made signs to them to be off', but they didn't budge. At the same time, some 17 canoes had amassed at the stern of the ship. Yule again, and more desperately, 'made signs for them to be off' but nothing happened. He now loaded his gun with shot and fired over the nearest canoe and then ordered the marines to load their muskets with ball. After a few rounds, the canoes dispersed and returned to wherever they had come from.[107]

This was Yule's version of the events, but, as Card remarked, 'there are about a dozen different yarns about it . . . and consequently none of them to be believed.' There was no corroboration in the accounts Card heard from two of the middies on the *Bramble*, about the amassing of seventeen canoes at the stern of the ship. In the story Card was told, Yule became jittery after he saw the 40 canoes the day before and exaggerated the threat from the three canoes that actually visited the ship that day. The musket ball 'passed between the outrigger and canoe – had it hit the canoe it must have killed three at least'. Card also related that 'Yule thinks he has done something brave and says that he thinks they have got a pretty good lesson, while it is the opinion of nearly every body on board that it [was a] great piece of treachery on the part of old Yule and that he deserves to have a couple of spears through him the first time he lands.'[108] George Inskip, who was aboard the *Bramble*, thought there was 'scarcely . . . any real cause' for the action taken.[109] Huxley's take on these events was little different from that of Card, but added the following provocative thought: 'Suppose we landed at a village, the natives received us with every appearance of friendship, took one or two of our numbers up to their houses, and then as we were shoving off treated us to a shower of spears? What should we say? When should we have held forth sufficiently about their treachery?'[110] Stanley supported Yule's actions. It was further proof, if it were needed, that the 'natives' could not be trusted. In chilling language, he made the case to his family. 'One native was distinguished amongst them who came alongside the *Bramble* as the same who had been most kindly treated on board both vessels at Brumer Island, shewing how very little dependence can at any time be placed in them. And I am quite sure that any party landing and straying out of sight of the ship would at once be cut off and murdered for the sake of their skulls only.'[111]

The ships remained in the area until 10 September. It rained heavily most of the time, enough to collect 15 tons of the precious liquid. Canoes came to the ships to barter the usual coconuts and yams for iron. The *Bramble* tried to get to the head of the bay but was forced back by a rush of water: Yule thought he saw the mouth of a river at that point. No one landed, however. It was not looking good. As Card commented, 'What good have we done here I can't make out as old D'Urville thought there was a river and can only think so as no one has been anywhere near it.'[112]

The weather during the *Rattlesnake* and the *Bramble* voyage was pretty much as it had been for D'Urville, wet and hot. D'Urville sped through the area and the weather acted as a cloak obscuring the land behind the coastline. It seemed that Stanley and his men would be equally unlucky, but on one occasion, about an hour before sunset, they got a glimpse of the shape of the interior. 'A change came over the scenery', Stanley recalled,

> far more magical, far more sudden than anything ever attempted on the stage when the dark green curtain is drawn up to shew the opening scene of a new Pantomime. All at once the clouds began to lift, the mist dispersed and in the course of an hour, the coast of New Guinea stood before us, clearly defined against the sky, tinged with the rays of the setting sun. The mountains seemed

piled one above the other to an enormous height and were of a deeper blue than I have ever seen before, even in the Strait of Magellan. They were intersected by tremendous gorges . . . [113]

The mountains were at least 40 miles behind the beach. Stanley concluded that the mountain range followed the coast like a backbone, eastward and northward. 'If from so great a distance the effect is so grand,' he continued,

> what must it be amongst those mountains, what splendid passes and valleys there must be, but I fear that . . . the natives are warlike, very numerous, well armed and very treacherous; and as the bow and arrow is used in this neighbourhood, we may well suppose that many a sheaf of them will be used to repel the Invaders, for such they will certainly consider the first party who attempt to advance towards the interior, whether by land or water.[114]

(A pity he didn't know that later they were named the Owen Stanley Range.)

With Stanley so fearful of the native people there was no chance he would allow the eager would-be explorers ashore. They shared the frustration of Joseph Jukes, the naturalist on HMS *Fly*, who'd also failed to land in 1845. 'New Guinea!', he wrote in his narrative of the voyage, 'the very mention of being taken into the interior of New Guinea sounds like being allowed to visit some of the enchanted regions of the 'Arabian Nights', so dim an atmosphere of obscurity rests at present on the wonders it probably conceals.'[115] The islands had been interesting and they'd collected some specimens, but everyone knew it was the mainland that promised new discoveries and Stanley was preventing them from fulfilling their dreams of glory.

Both the *Rattlesnake* and the *Bramble* weighed anchor on 10 September and continued the survey westward. On most days, the weather was very heavy and with only a light breeze. At best they could get an occasional glimpse of the shore and the high land behind it. The ships, following D'Urville's track, passed Table Bay, Cape Rodney, Round Head and a number of islands, most of which appeared inhabited. No landings took place. On 19 September, they spotted Mount Astrolabe, which D'Urville had named after one of his ships. They were now off Cape Passy, where

D'Urville's running survey ended. From here on, they were voyaging where no other European ship, to their knowledge, had ever been. The very next day, the weather broke momentarily and they were able to spot another peak, even higher, in the distance. Stanley honoured his late predecessor and surveyor by naming the peak Mt D'Urville (he had perished in 1842 in one of France's first and most catastrophic railway accidents).

September 21 found the *Rattlesnake* off a point of land Stanley named Redscar Point, after a place he knew near Preston, in northern England, which he visited after attending Charlie's wedding. A short excursion to three neighbouring islands, the Pariwara Islands, to look for water and get some angles for the survey, proved largely uninteresting. The islands were uninhabited and there was no water. MacGillivray, who accompanied Lieutenant Simpson, still managed to collect a few plants, but there were no surprises – all of them were well known to science.[116]

The ships continued over the next few days through calm and exceedingly hot days. On 26 September, off South West Cape, three canoes approached the *Rattlesnake* to barter. Though they had brought little with them, they parted with their bows and arrows in exchange for pieces of clothing and glass bottles. This was the first time the visitors had encountered bows and arrows on their westward voyage: at the eastern edge of the Louisiade Archipelago no arms were visible and, as they voyaged westward, they passed through a zone where spears were common.[117] The local people had no interest in iron whatsoever, not even having a name for it. What struck the visitors most about these people's appearance was the manner in which they dressed their hair: 'it is usually shaved off the temples and occasionally a little way up the forehead, then combed out at length, and tied midway with a string, leaving one part straight, and the remainder frizzled out into a mop projecting horizontally backwards.'[118] That evening, as the breeze picked up, the *Rattlesnake* anchored off a large island, which was subsequently named Yule Island, in honour of the *Bramble*'s commander. They were now within sight of Cape Possession, the point at which Yule's earlier survey had ended.

As far as the survey was concerned, they had reached the end of the line, and just in the nick of time. All those failures to find water were beginning to be felt. Water on board was now very scarce and Stanley decided that the time had come to leave the shores of New Guinea and head for

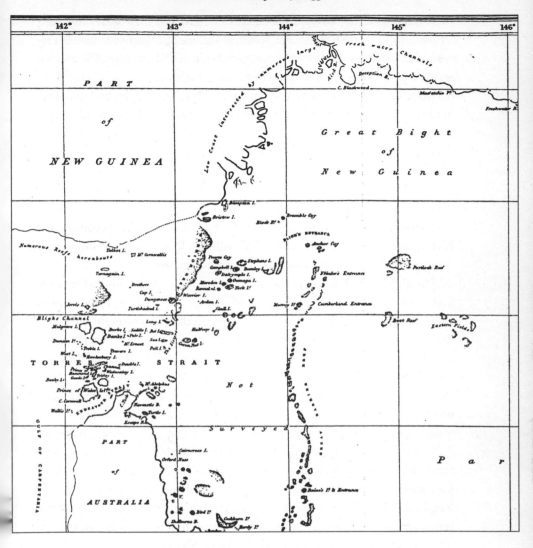

Cape York, Torres Strait and the south coast of New Guinea in 1849

Cape York, for water, for provisions and for news – 'after being so many
months out of the civilized world to hear what has been going on in it'.[119]
On Thursday, 27 September, the *Rattlesnake* and the *Bramble* began
heading to the southwest for Cape York. Entering the Torres Strait by
Bligh's Passage, they passed Bramble Cay and Darnley Island, Stephens
Island and Marsden Island. On 30 September the *Bramble* went its own

247

way to Booby Island hoping to find a letter from Thomas Beckford Simpson of the *Freak* about the result of the search for Kennedy's body and his papers. A day later the *Rattlesnake* pulled into its old berth in Evans Bay.[120]

CHAPTER XI

A White Woman and Darnley Island
1849 & 1850

Stanley was relieved to be back on familiar shores, full of excitement at what he had accomplished, though tinged by a little bit of disappointment. 'What my feelings were on dropping the anchor here in safety I can hardly tell you. Mentally, intense gratitude prevailed; bodily, intense fatigue, which I had not felt at all before, came on at once, and I must have slept twelve hours without turning round, or even dreaming.'[1] He hadn't lost a single man, either through illness or through confrontation with the local inhabitants in the Louisiade Archipelago and New Guinea. (He later admitted that he thought his chances of getting back in one piece were only 50/50.)[2] His accomplishments, he felt, were notable. Along the coast of New Guinea, as he told Beaufort, he had 'sounded out a clear channel at least 30 miles wide leading directly to Bligh's entrance' for the benefit of vessels passing from the Pacific to the Indian Ocean. As for the Louisiade, he had surveyed in and around most islands, found passages through the reefs from the open sea, visited a number of islands and bartered with their inhabitants, establishing that iron was the most demanded item. Despite that he didn't think that there was much opportunity for trade, as opposed to barter, as no 'article fit for commercial purposes was brought off to the ship'.[3] As for science, he stated that MacGillivray 'procured many valuable additions to our collection of Natural History', and collected words from

Canoes, Evans Bay, Cape York

the islands visited. Stanley had also managed to collect arms, implements and ornaments from the people of both the Louisiade and New Guinea. Had it been safe to go into the interior even for a short distance, he added, 'much more might have been done, but . . . although the natives were very well behaved in the presence of a superior force, they were much inclined to be troublesome when they met a small party.'[4] To his family and friends, however, he spoke of the 'natives' with far less restraint. They were war-like, well armed and very treacherous, and it was this that prevented them from 'landing with any confidence on the thickly inhabited islands'.[5]

Stanley's disappointment was muted, yet what he had accomplished, in terms of human contact, was far short of what he, himself, had hoped for, namely to surpass the discoveries of his French predecessors. By keeping on the inside of the reef systems, in other words by producing a 'proper' survey, as Beaufort put it, he concluded that he 'had a better chance of learning something of the natives than the French expeditions under D'Entrecasteaux and D'Urville who merely contented themselves with a distant view of the land from the outer edge of the Barrier Reef, which they took care not to approach too closely'.[6]

If Stanley didn't notice or care to admit the shortcomings of this part of the voyage, there were others who did. Huxley was certainly one of them, as his frequent criticisms of Stanley's actions make clear. Charles Card, in his own way, also felt that it was a bit of a useless exercise, having done lit-tle more than D'Urville did. But it was John Thomson who was particu-larly enraged by what had, or perhaps more correctly, had not happened. He told his wife confidentially that Stanley was already on edge, afraid to explore, even before the ships got into their first anchorage in Coral Haven, in the Louisiade Archipelago. 'At this time', he wrote, 'I never saw greater fear exhibited than was done by Captain Stanley, although I must confess after consulting my own judgement I could not discover the small-est cause for such. Indeed I began to augur that all my anticipations of interest and pleasure that I formed had been false and that the realization would be more tedious, monotonous and irksome than what were experi-enced during our last cruise.' And he continued, charging Stanley with actively blocking and denying the opportunities for discovery. 'The pru-dence – did it not absolutely amount to fear and cowardice? – of the Captain would not allow us to enjoy the advantages that were held out to us. And now we have left this great *terra incognita* . . . without knowing anything more or being able to communicate to the world anything more than was known before our visit . . . I cannot now conceal my chagrin and disappointment at the course which was adopted of restraining us from going on shore among the natives . . .' The mood on the ship, fuelled as it was by disappointment and tension caused by being confined to the wooden world and watching unique opportunities evaporate, must have been unbearable. But there was more to it than that. Thomson also criticized Stanley's performance as a surveyor, at least as damning as his fear of venturing on shore. D'Urville, Thomson pointed out, drew up his charts in just three days and 'so accurately', he added in a sharp accusatory tone, 'that after our prolonged survey of four months we have not been able to find fault with it'. 'But,' he went on,

> at the commencement of our operations it was currently reported that this chart of the Frenchman would not be of the slightest assistance to us, nor could it be relied upon as being at all accurate, and these surmises were thrown out that those on board might be blinded to imagine that our voyage was really one of discovery and would be attended with unheard of dangers . . . The survey was begun with an attention to minuteness and accuracy that was scarcely expended on our former survey [i.e. the Inner Passage] where it was so much demanded . . . .[7]

There was a deep rift between Stanley and the scientists. The scientific part of the voyage was now complete and there were no more possibilities of discovery. 'I can scarcely convey to you my feelings of deep disappointment, at being for so long employed upon a coast where so few opportunities of landing occurred' is how MacGillivray summed up four months to Gould.[8] This was the second time that he had been frustrated in venturing into the interior of New Guinea – when he had expressed an eagerness to do this while on HMS *Fly*, his friend and correspondent was horrified: 'Should he venture to leave the neighbourhood of the forests in Papua I fear his fate is sealed, the savage anthropophagi will never distinguish between a Briton and a Dutchman.'[9] From now on little would be seen that hadn't been seen before, in some cases, many times.

Although contact with the people of the Louisiade Archipelago and New Guinea was fleeting, they made a strong impression. Brierly recognized that they should be approached with as little prejudice as possible.

They needed to be understood entirely on their own terms. What he said was remarkable for the time:

> The difficulty in communication with [them] is to divest the mind of the ideas and opinions gathered from Books – to look at them for yourself and not thru the eyes of those who may have preceded you – to record what actually passes under your own observation – any characteristics traits or circumstances which transpire under your own eyes should be written down while the impression is fresh and as quickly after their occurrences as opportunity may allow – in doing this you will constantly be surprised to find the savage something so utterly different from what your preconceived ideas would make him.[10]

Other visitors, such as Huxley and Inskip, who have left us their impressions, expressed a not unusual (Brierly might have called it biased) view that they were in a state of blissful innocence. Huxley wrote: 'The people seem happy, the means of subsistence are abundant, the air warm and balmy, they are untroubled with the 'malady of thought', and so far as I see civilization as we call it would be rather a curse than a blessing to them.'[11] Inskip's reflections were very similar. 'The more I see of native life,' he noted in his journal, 'the less I think civilisation improves them, for it is the vices of the white man only they acquire, whilst the virtues are seldom if ever followed.'[12] Charles Card voiced a not unfamiliar European viewpoint, saying that the local people didn't deserve their landscape – 'it really seems a pity that such a beautiful country should be inhabited by a savage set of people.'[13]

As soon as the *Rattlesnake* had anchored in Evans Bay, the first cutter was dispatched to the shore to see if the wells were full of water. Fortunately, they were. There were several locals on the beach, some of whom were known to the *Rattlesnake*, and they immediately enquired about the friends they had made here, a year ago. It all seemed so homely, and a far cry from New Guinea. What's more, the next day, the provision ship, the *Sir John Byng*, showed up and the men of the *Rattlesnake* began to devour the letters and papers, even though the latest news was from 20 April, 'six months behind the rest of the world'.[14]

MacGillivray and Brierly wasted no time in contacting their old chums, Brierly especially anxious to 'indulge [his] fancy for talking to the natives and gain if possible some ideas of their peculiarities and appearances, etc., an employment which on board had received the name "niggerizing'".[15] Huxley poured over his love's every word, and also found out from the postbag that part of his *Diphyes* paper had been read at the Linnean Society, that Forbes was scheduled to read his *Trigonia* paper at the Zoological Society, and that the Royal Society *Medusa* paper was in the pipeline.[16] The message from Forbes, apart from giving the good news about his papers – 'it . . . shows', he wrote to Nettie, 'that I do not altogether labour in vain' – also praised the work, claiming that Huxley would make for himself 'a high name as a naturalist'.[17] It looked as though his dreams of using scientific investigation as a means of either getting promoted in the service or of opening 'many chances unconnected with the service' were going to be realized.[18] With that secured, he could plan to marry Nettie. He was a happy man.

Stanley, like everyone else on the ship, had been reading through his correspondence, several letters of which were from his family. One of them was from Hobart Town: its news was devastating. Charlie, his brother, had died suddenly, on 13 August, aged thirty, from a stomach ailment.[19]

Stanley wrote to his father that he was 'distressed by the melancholy news from Hobarton received so suddenly and unexpectedly', and added that he felt comforted by the thought that God's will will be done. Catherine, his sister, he felt, would be very disturbed by this loss, as she and Charlie were so close. His main concern now was for Eliza, Charlie's widow, who would have to return to England. If he received orders to return home, he would, of course, give Eliza a passage back.[20]

Stanley remained on the *Rattlesnake* for a week before finally venturing on shore on 8 October to take measurements. His days were taken up by preparing the rough tracings he hoped to send to Beaufort with the provision ship, which was heading to Manila very soon. Several days later, on 12 October, Stanley led a large party to Albany Island to visit the grave of Thomas Wall and Charles Niblett, whose remains had been interred on this site several months earlier by Thomas Beckford Simpson. There they planted two coconut trees and placed a wooden slab with an inscription at the head of the graves.[21]

Watering continued on shore; Stanley devoted himself to his charts, taking a little time out to visit the beach; Brierly spent each day with his local friends; MacGillivray looked to improve his collections and Thomson went botanizing.

October 16 began very much like any other day. The shore was full of *Rattlesnake* and *Bramble* men washing their clothes in the plentiful streams and spreading them out on the beach to dry in the sun. Brierly told the story:

> 1 p.m. Lieut. Simpson, Dr Thomson and Mr Brady and self went on shore. Simpson and self having a match at rifle shooting crossed over to a small sandy beach behind the rocky point abreast of our anchorage and continued our shooting until about 3:30. A boat was to be sent for us at four . . . we proceeded down to the beach where the jolly boat was now waiting for us. Then we saw three people coming up the beach . . . Captain Levien, master of the *Byng*, who was in advance of the others but at some distance, began to call out and walk quickly towards us, waving his hand for us to go to him. When we were within hearing he told us the Blacks had brought a white woman down to the beach. I did not stop to hear anything more and Simpson and self set off and began to run down to the other end of the beach where some of the men of the *Rattlesnake* had been washing clothes all day and where the Blacks were always to be found when anywhere in the bay. As we neared the party, saw a mixed group of Blacks and marines and sailors from the ship all together. Before we reached them Scott, the Captain's coxswain, met us and said he had given the white woman one of my shirts and they had made her all comfortable. When we got up close to the party we saw a young woman very much browned by the sun. The men had given her two shirts; one white she wore in the same manner as a man, and the other, a blue one, hung tied round her waist so as to form an under petticoat. She sat on a bank with her head hanging down and had a tin plate with some meat and a knife and fork, which the men had given her, on her knees before her. One Black sat close to her with his arm passed behind her, others were standing close to her. Her manner was very curious and she replied to our questions something in the manner of a person just waking up from a deep sleep and had not had time to collect her ideas.[22]

The white woman answered their questions partly in English and partly in a native language. From the English words they were able to work out what she meant to say. They discovered her maiden name was Barbara Crawford and she had lived in Sydney with her parents. Her father was a tinsmith. She had married a seaman named William Thompson four or five years ago. She and a few crew members had joined him on his small vessel, the *America*, on a voyage from Moreton Bay to Port Essington. The boat had struck a reef and sunk near an island to the north of Evans Bay. Everyone, apart from herself, had drowned. She had been saved by a number of natives from a nearby island who were out in a canoe that day. Allika, the middle-aged man with what appeared to be a burnt face, one of the native men – her 'brothers' – surrounding her now, had lifted her out of the water. Another of the men who were with her had also been in the canoe. He was Tomagugu (well known to the *Rattlesnake* people from last year's visit), a Gudang man, a native of Cape York, but married to an islander. They took her to their island, a large one that they called Morolaga [Muralag]. They gave her a native name, Giom. At first they made her fetch water and do other hard work but later she just looked after the children while the other women were busy. They treated her very kindly, but they didn't want her to leave them. She promised them knives, and other implements, which she said she could get from the ship if they would take her there. They agreed and said they wanted to go with her.[23]

She volunteered other, fascinating information. She knew about Kennedy and about his murderers, a tribe to the south; and it was Queen Baki (another well-known figure from the previous year's visit), 'a very good woman, good friend', who told her about the arrival of the ship. But there was little time, or inclination at this point, to go into details. The priority was to get Barbara Thompson off the beach and on to the ship.

It had been pre-arranged that a boat would come for the *Rattlesnake* shooting party at about 3 or 4 p.m. When it arrived Richard Mew, the Sergeant of Marines, put Barbara Thompson on board. Tomagugu and the middle-aged man, Allika, accompanied her to the ship. On the way the questioning continued. 'Did they give you plenty to eat?' they asked. 'Some days good living, some days hungry,' she answered. 'When not questioned she would talk by starts, with pauses between, during which she passed her hand over her forehead as she tried to recollect. "Give them some old tin cans – this man Kupankilligo, my brother, brought me a pipe and some tobacco and that is my mother – my mother dead." There was a pause in which she stooped down her head – her eyes had a dim look and the right one appeared as if it was going, giving a dreaming vacant expression.'[24] She continued. 'I sat on the island all day looking at the ship. I said tomorrow *kusto kalloo* and with your people. And I told them lies to make them take me in the vessel. I saw my country people in their little boats – *arawai gool*.'[25]

An hour later, the boat came alongside the *Rattlesnake*. The stranger presented a curious sight, wrapped up in two men's shirts. Sergeant Mew had apparently taken Mrs Thompson into the bush and 'washed and parted her hair'(it was quite short), but though he tried to make her more presentable as a white woman, her whiteness had become obscured by living out in the sun.[26] Robert Gale recoiled somewhat at her appearance: 'very dirty and hair smeared with turtle fat' was his first impression.[27] 'Disfigured by dirt and the effect of the sun on her almost uncovered body' was Huxley's description, though he suspected that through the dirt and sunburn he detected the makings of a young woman, who, 'when . . . appropriately dressed, and . . . rid of her inflamed eyes . . . will be not bad-looking'.[28]

Lieutenant Simpson ran to Stanley with the news. By the time he arrived to greet his unexpected guest, everyone on board knew of the remarkable meeting on the beach and who this stranger was. Stanley immediately took her to his cabin and gave her some tea and apple pie. 'I never thought of tasting the likes of this again,' she remarked as she became more comfortable speaking English. (She had told the *Rattlesnake* men on the beach that she used to sing songs to herself before falling asleep in order to remember English.) 'When I first met her on deck', Stanley recalled, 'she was very much frightened and could hardly speak three words of English together, but when I got her down to my cabin and gave her some food and tea, she became more composed but still very shy.'[29] He asked her whether she wanted to stay on the *Rattlesnake* and go with them to Sydney or to return to the island with the men who had accompanied her. Her answer was blunt and to the point. 'I am a Christian,' she said. With that Stanley began to disburse the items that Barbara Thompson had promised her brothers: a knife, an axe, some tobacco and plenty of ship's biscuit – 'their baskets . . . were so crammed that they could scarcely hold any more.'[30] Allika and Tomagugu spent the night on board ship.[31]

As he described it to his sister Mary in a letter, Stanley now had a dilemma on his hands. The difficulty wasn't that his guest was a woman. He had had several women as passengers on the *Rattlesnake*, including Mary herself, on the ship's first leg to Madeira. He could accommodate Barbara Thompson in Mary's old cabin. The problem was: 'To admit a person of whom I knew nothing to mess with me seemed a dangerous experiment, and at the same time to send her to mess with Robert, the only other alternative, seemed rather worse.' Stanley considered the matter very carefully, weighing the pros and cons, and finally decided that she should mess with him and Brierly (they usually dined together). 'Honi soit qui mal y pense,' he quipped.[32]

When the men from the *Rattlesnake* first saw her, Barbara Thompson was, as George Inskip described her, 'perfectly naked having only a small bit of sea weed, which very barely covered her modesty'.[33] Her first words, he believed in recognition of her state of undress in European eyes, were 'I am a white woman – I am ashamed.'[34] That was why she was hurriedly draped in the men's shirts. At first during her stay with the islanders she continued to wear the dress she had on when the *America* went down, but over time, as she told Stanley, 'piece after piece was gradually torn away by the bushes until she became in the same state of undress as the native women themselves.'[35] Stanley now set about turning her back into a Victorian woman. 'The morning after her arrival, we looked out for all we had that could in any way furnish her with the materials for making clothes. The blue and white curtain I got for the Courtneys served to make two gowns; Yule had another curtain given by his mother when he left England, which made another gown . . . Of her it is enough to say that tho' badly educated, she has, since her arrival on board the ship, conducted herself with the most perfect propriety, and the moment we supplied her with the means, she began and worked very hard until she had completed a very decent dress.'[36] The transformation was complete by the following day. 'She is now rigged out in shoes and stockings and a kind of gown,' Charles Card noted, 'a silk handkerchief round her neck and her hair parted amidships and fastened down with a piece of ribbon.'[37] The doctors, Thomson and Huxley, also contributed to the make-over. 'Her eyes are much better and her nose is quite well and she looks quite different to what she did when she first came on board.'[38]

*

The *Sir John Byng*, the ship that had brought provisions and news to Cape York and remained there since 2 October, was scheduled to leave on 17 October, the day after Barbara Thompson's sudden arrival into this highly enclosed, male world. The ship's next destination was Port Essington, delivering provisions to that sick settlement, and then Manila, to disembark the 'immense quantity of letters to go overland besides the regular mail bags' and take in a cargo of sugar for Sydney. This was the last chance for some time for the men of the *Rattlesnake* and the *Bramble* to tell their friends, colleagues and loved ones about this remarkable event. There was a flurry of writing. Stanley had just sealed his letter to Beaufort, giving him news of the surveying voyage to the Louisiade and New Guinea, but he started another, more exciting one. 'I have had great pleasure of rescuing a white woman from the natives,' he began, and then told Beaufort about the incident that led to her living among the natives, how they treated her, and what she did amongst them. He added that because she was 'perfectly conversant with the native language we shall be able to gain much valuable information with regard to the manners and customs of the different tribes in the neighborhood [*sic*]'.[39] He was going to take her back to her parents in Sydney. To his father, to whom he had already written about the sad news of his brother Charlie's sudden death (Stanley did not know at the time that his father was also dead), he started a new letter repeating what he had told Beaufort.[40] MacGillivray also wrote hastily, addressing his letter to Joseph Jukes, his naturalist companion on HMS *Fly*. MacGillivray was much more expressive than Stanley about the drama of coming across a white woman in this part of the Australian continent. It was, as MacGillivray, put it, a real shock. 'News came that a white woman was alongside, brought from the shore,' he wrote to Jukes. 'Had I been told', he continued, 'that the blacks had opened fire on us from a mortar battery on Albany Island, or that one of them had brought off a correct solution of the quadrature of the circle made out in the native language, I would have as soon believed it – yet it is true.'[41]

Over the next few days, Barbara Thompson, now returned to her people and reclaimed by her culture, entertained the men on the ship with stories of the natives, both of those she had met and those she had lived among. Over time, some of the details of her experiences, which, at first, were obscured by the difficulty of interpreting what she was saying, became much clearer.

She had been born in Aberdeen and migrated to Sydney with her parents when she was about eight years old. When fifteen or sixteen, she ran away from home with William Thompson to Moreton Bay where they were married. Thompson was friendly with Captain John Wickham, the ex-commander of HMS *Beagle* and now police magistrate in Brisbane. She lived with her husband in Moreton Bay for about eighteen months. They were doing quite well in the settlement, but the stay was cut short when her husband heard about the wreck of a ship in the Torres Strait laden with whale oil that could be salvaged. He was determined to make his fortune and, in September of 1844, the *America*, a ten-ton cutter, set sail with the couple and a small number of crew for Torres Strait and Port Essington. Disaster struck them first in the Torres Strait, when two of the crew were lost when a boat they were using to collect firewood was swamped; and, almost immediately after, the *America* itself foundered in a sudden squall. Everyone on board, apart from herself, was drowned. She was saved by Tomagugu, who jumped into the water, at risk to himself, to save her. Allika had lifted her into the canoe. They took her to an island, which they called Muralag and the inhabitants Kaurareg.[42] Everyone in the canoe, apart from Tomagugu, was Kaurareg. She couldn't say exactly how long she had been with them, but certainly four or five years. This would make her twenty or twenty-one years old. She was unable to be more precise.

When she first arrived on the island, an old man, Peaqui, welcomed her as the *marki* (ghost) or white reincarnation of his dead daughter Giom. She immediately became related to him and his family but she lived most of the time with an old woman called Urdzanna. She said she did not have a Kaurareg husband or any children.[43]

The Kaurareg didn't want her to leave them and never let her off the island, but she wanted to go. She taught some of the islanders an English sentence – 'Mary was on the island' – which, she said, they should repeat to any ship they might encounter, hoping that this would bring white people to the island. The previous year when the *Rattlesnake* was anchored in Evans Bay, Brierly recalled a native trying to make them understand something but no one could make out what he was saying. She also said that

259

Tomagugu would have taken her to the ship then but she was ill with fever.[44]

This year, when she found out from Baki that the *Rattlesnake*, or ghosts' ship as the native people called it, had returned to Evans Bay, she decided she must make contact. Tomagugu, Baki and Peaqui agreed she should go. She told Urdzanna that she needed medicine from the ship for her bad knee and nose and that she would not stay. In return for Urdzanna's help she would get her a knife. After some discussion with other Kaurareg, it was decided that Giom's needs should be met and, on 13 October, four canoes with at least thirty people headed for Cape York. They reached the passage between the Cape and Wamalug (York Island) early in the evening. There they met a number of Gudang men who told them all about the *Rattlesnake*, that they had received biscuit, knives and shirts from the ship and that the men from it were often on the beach washing. They said that the Kaurareg people should stay on Wamalug (York Island). Tomagugu and a number of Gudang people took a canoe and joined the flotilla for Wamalug. For the next two days, the island party went turtling while Giom, too excited to sleep or eat, remained on Wamalug looking at the *Rattlesnake*.

And then, on 16 October, while some of the canoes were away turtling, the Kaurareg decided the time had come to make contact with the white men. The canoes moved off for the short passage to the mainland. The Kaurareg group arrived on shore at a small beach, just around a spit of land to the north of Evans Bay. Soon thereafter, they were met by a group of men, some of whom were Gudang and others white. The two groups exchanged words, few of which were understood, but, in the mêlée, it became clear to one of the white men, a sailor or marine, that one of the women in the Kaurareg group was white and Scottish. He yelled back to the rest of the men from the *Rattlesnake* who were washing clothes on the beach at Evans Bay, 'Scott, Scott, come here. Here's a Scotch girl.' Hearing his name being called out, George Scott, Stanley's coxswain, was seen running over and when he got to the little beach, he took hold of Giom's hand and asked her if she could come over to the larger beach to the washing party. Tomagugu said she could. 'Scott kept hold of my hand and led me along to where the men were washing. He was like a guard to me . . . When we reached the washing place, he took me into the bush and with another man washed me and combed my hair and dressed me in two shirts, one below as a petticoat, the other over my shoulders.'[45] Brierly took down the whole of the account verbatim, reading it back to Barbara Thompson to ensure its accuracy. As for Kennedy, whose murder she mentioned when on the beach at Evans Bay, she remarked that he had been killed for nothing more than the clothes on his back.[46]

Barbara Thompson remained on the *Rattlesnake*, never venturing on shore. Stanley offered to take her across to the mainland but she declined. Instead, she received a stream of visitors on board, no doubt entertaining them with stories of her hosts. Peaqui and his wife, Barbara Thompson's native father and mother, came on board one day not long after she had made her home on the ship. Stanley recorded the touching scene. '[They] came off and spent the afternoon, much amused with all they saw. The meeting with Mrs. T. and the two old natives were very affecting. They kissed her, embraced her and cried over her for a considerable time, and seemed to be very sorry at the prospect of losing her.'[47]

Baki also visited Barbara Thompson, and on more than one occasion. Stanley treated her with huge respect. 'The Queen', he wrote, 'seemed to rule her husband and all the other natives far more than any man I have seen among the natives – indeed she is the only person I have yet seen who possesses undoubted authority with them, but both last year and this, we have found her influence is very great indeed. Tho' no longer young, her Sable Majesty had still a fine commanding figure and an expression of countenance that carries with it the stamp of very superior ability.' He invited her to dine with him and some of the officers. 'She enjoyed dining with us very much and what she could not eat was stowed away in her basket to be divided between the rest of the tribe when she returned to them.'[48] Charles Card, who was also impressed by her presence, thought she was about 40 years old, and at 5 feet 9 inches, was indeed a commanding figure.[49]

Besides telling the *Rattlesnake* men stories about her adopted people, and teaching them words of her acquired language, Barbara Thompson also acquainted them with what the native people thought of the white visitors. They were, as some already knew, considered the ghostly reincarnation of their dead, who returned on ships. Inskip recorded the details as he heard them:

They pity our unfortunate case as they imagine we are obliged to roam about for provisions, that we live on shark and whales and that the pork and beef are those fish preserved in a peculiar way, that the bottles and preserved meat tins etc. that we use and give them are the shells of fish that we catch on the beaches of the places we go to, at low water – that we have gins or women down below and that we don't let them up when they are on board.[50]

Some of the visitors were not as resigned to losing Giom as Baki, Peaqui and his wife. Boroto, one the Kaurareg who was in the canoe when they saved her, tried to persuade her to return and he was not the only one. Kaurareg people would often approach the *Rattlesnake* and shout at her to change her mind – 'only look at these poor ghosts they have scarcely room to move in their overgrown canoe, they hardly know where to sit down; come on shore with us and there you have all the woods to roam in and we will get you provisions; here you will have to wander about to get your daily food, you had much better come back.'[51]

The excitement of Barbara Thompson's arrival on board began to abate after a week or so. There was work to be done. The *Bramble* and two boats were sent away on 21 October to continue the survey to the north of Prince of Wales Island, where Beaufort had asked Stanley to search for the possibility of channels which would act as an alternative passage through the Torres Strait. Meanwhile, there was the Cape to explore, as a possibility for a future settlement. There was watering to be done. Natural history still needed attention. MacGillivray, now armed with new words he had learned from Barbara Thompson, headed out into the bush with his native friends looking for specimens, which he could now describe more clearly than ever before.[52] His newly acquired skill paid off and he came away with a fine collection of new birds.

Not everyone, however, lost interest in Barbara Thompson. Brierly, who had been one of the first to meet her, realized he had been offered a unique opportunity. Here was someone who had lived with native people, learned their language, and witnessed their day-to-day activities, their customs, beliefs, thoughts and feelings. Not having any official duties on board, he devoted himself entirely to her, asked her about the Kaurareg and more, always recording her answers. Hardly a day went by when he was not at her side for some, if not the whole of the day. They talked about everything imaginable: kinship and its vocabulary, food, modes of its preparation and preservation, canoe construction and practices (each canoe had a name like European ships and boats), friends and enemies, courting, love and marriage, death and funerary rites, war, turtling, music, corroborees, power, childbirth, infanticide, cannibalism, trade, language, weapons, cultivation, medicine, magic, hair fashions, clothing, taboos, flora and fauna, houses, beliefs and myths, the heavens, men and women, youth, christening, inheritance, weather and climate, games, singing and dancing. In short, a whole inventory of how another people live their lives, and every word recorded. Strangely, Brierly never published a word about this unique experience.[53]

On 18 November, the *Bramble* and the boats returned from their successful survey. It was time to leave Cape York. There was some filling-in work to be done on the coast of New Guinea and the Louisiade Archipelago before returning to Sydney. Shore excursions and watering the *Bramble* took up most of the remaining days. On 2 December the anchors were lifted and the ships made their way to Mount Ernest Island, about 30 miles to the north of Cape York, where Stanley intended to make some more observations for his chart of the area. Barbara Thompson would never see her native 'family' and friends again.

When the *Rattlesnake* had been at Cape York in October of the previous year, the Gudang people had greeted Brierly by calling him Antarrka, or Tarrka. At the time, Brierly had no idea why he was being hailed in this way, and dismissed it as being without significance. This year, however, with an understanding of local languages, he was able to make sense of the name. Tarrka, it turned out, was a deceased old man and Brierly, it was believed, was his *marki*, his reincarnation. Moreover, Tarrka was a Kulkalaig man from Nagir, Mount Ernest Island. When Brierly landed on Mount Ernest Island on 4 December, an old man on the beach told him that his wife, Domanie, was Tarrka's daughter. Brierly could not leave the island without taking the opportunity to meet his 'daughter' and though, at first, the old man hesitated, eventually he led Brierly and Huxley, who accompanied him, into the scrub. There, Brierly saw three young women. One, who was clearly the oldest of the group, had a child at her breast; the second woman, he thought, was about 16 years old and the third was a few years younger. The older woman looked at Brierly and, in Kowra, the local language, akin to Kaurareg, said, 'I am Domanie, your child, these are your grand-children.' Brierly understood every word. She introduced all her children by name – Dowarr, the oldest, Wyware, the younger one, and Cheedooie, the infant – and Brierly returned the courtesy by introducing Huxley. Domanie told Brierly, whom she called 'Father', all about his 'wife' Ootsarrie, who happened to be away from home visiting another island where she was ill with fever. Huxley was so enchanted by Dowarr that he sketched her. She was as interested in the sketching as he was in his subject. The touching meeting lasted no more than a half hour. Brierly gave his 'family' presents, consisting of biscuit, a new shirt and a few pennies in which he had made holes so that they could be made into ornaments. The women invited Brierly and Huxley to return the next day, but their goodbyes turned out to be permanent: next day they sailed away.[54]

The *Rattlesnake* left Mount Ernest Island and began to thread its way through a number of Torres Strait Islands – the Three Sisters (Poll, Bet and Sue), Coconut Island and Arden Island – heading for Darnley Island. Along the route canoes frequently approached them. Their occupants all knew Barbara Thompson because of their frequent visits to Muralag. On 7 December, when the ship was at anchor, a canoe carrying people from Mount Ernest Island came alongside wishing to barter tobacco and axes, but not biscuit, for tortoiseshell. Stanley managed to get a tortoiseshell mask, which they used in a ritual dance.[55] They too knew Barbara Thompson and had heard of Tarrka, whom they greeted as a long lost friend.[56] After all the exchanges and greetings, the *Rattlesnake* resumed its voyage later that morning.

Stanley had hoped to get water and some fresh vegetables at Darnley Island. Not that 'evil symptoms had shewn themselves', as he told his sister Mary, but, he thought, 'prevention better than cure'. Besides which, he had heard a great deal of the Darnley Islanders and wanted to see them for himself, particularly as to how they compared to the people of New Guinea.[57]

The *Rattlesnake*, now in company with the *Bramble*, came within sight of Darnley Island on 10 December. A canoe from nearby Stephens Island drew alongside and in it were two Darnley Islanders, one of whom, Dzum, recognized MacGillivray from his earlier visit to the island in HMS *Fly*. The next day, the ships anchored in Treacherous Bay. A party from the ship landed at Kiriam, one of the villages, where MacGillivray had a moving reunion with Sewai, a man, now prematurely aged, whom he had first met and 'exchanged names' with almost five years earlier. No water was found. Another village, Bikar, was suggested, but Sewai urged them to visit his village, Mogor, where he said there was plenty. Mogor, it turned out, had water but not in the quantities required. Sewai and his sons asked to visit the ship and slept 'among the folds of a sail upon the poop'.[58]

The next day, a watering party headed for Bikar but for some reason the landing was aborted at the last minute – 'I could see from the boat various things I did not like', Stanley was recorded as saying – the party ending up standing around in the surf awhile and returning, somewhat sheepishly, back to the boats. Huxley, for one, found the whole scene pathetic and lashed out yet again, in his head, at his commander. 'I suppose nothing would satisfy him of the security of his little body but seeing all the bows and arrows in the boat and all the men bound on the beach.' The landscape, tantalizingly within reach but unattainable because of Stanley's prohibition, inspired Huxley. 'Gently sloping hills, bare of trees but covered with verdure, deep dark green vallies thickly wooded, groups of the delicate looking shimmering bamboos, formed the background, a thick belt of trees, mostly cocoa-nuts, skirted the bright white beach, and among them were scattered the whimsical-looking beehive-shaped and palisaded native huts.'[59]

Another attempt to find water and vegetables was made the next day, 13 December. This time Stanley was more adventurous and a party was allowed to land at Kiriam, the village they had first visited a couple of days before. This day turned out to be very active. Barter was rife. Coconuts, yams, bananas and human skulls were exchanged for axes, knives, bottles, cloth and tobacco. MacGillivray got a live opossum in a cage and more words for his comparative vocabulary. Huxley convinced several people to let him sketch them. But the most remarkable 'purchase' was made by Frederick Brady, paymaster and purser, who got a mummy of a 'small child, about a foot long, embalmed and quite perfect and is supposed to have been still born; it was daubed over with a red kind of earth which appeared to be the principal thing that preserved the body'.[60]

The hold was now full of island produce, both vegetable and material, but water was still elusive. Stanley decided that it was time to push off and head for the coast of New Guinea. They got underway on 14 December and headed in a northeasterly direction. Foul weather, however, hampered their plans and they were forced to spend three days at anchor in Bramble Cay. Though not planned, this stay proved to be very useful. They got some water, thanks to the downpour, and a substantial weight of fresh turtle, it being the right season. With these provisions secured, Stanley ordered the ships to cross over to the coast of New Guinea.

He had instructed Yule to take the *Bramble* to Cape Possession, where Yule's previous work had finished, and continue the detailed survey of the coast eastward until they reached Redscar Point, the spit of land where the *Rattlesnake* was now heading. The two ships would meet there and discuss the next and final stage of the remaining desiderata of the survey.

The *Rattlesnake* arrived at Redscar Point on 21 December and the *Bramble* on 28 December. Stanley decided to take his ship directly to the Duchateau Islands for some more readings to establish a meridian distance, and return to Sydney. The *Bramble*, not without a protest, was given yet more work to do.[61] Stanley ordered Yule to take the ship to the eastern end of the Louisiade Archipelago to look for a passage between Rossel and Sudest Island (this hadn't been done the last time they were there), and get sights at Adèle Island before sailing for Sydney. The ships separated on 29 December and each went their own way.

The *Rattlesnake* sailed along the New Guinea coast, catching a view of Mount D'Urville and Mount Victoria looming large in the distance, passing by but not stopping at Brumer Island, and arriving at an anchorage in the middle of the three Duchateau Islands on 6 January 1850. The next day, the readings were taken, while MacGillivray and a few others headed to the westernmost island to do some shooting. A number of canoes from the Calvados Group of islands came to the ship but they had little to offer for the iron hoops they wanted. The work completed, the anchor was raised on 8 January, and the ship began to make its way back to Sydney.

PART SIX

CHAPTER XII

CHAPTER XII

Death of a Captain:
Sydney, 1850

It was a tediously long and fraught voyage. The southeast trade, which they hoped would whisk them down to Sydney, proved elusive. Their progress was painfully slow, averaging no more than 45 miles per day. Many days were spent in a dead calm.

And then something dreadful happened. In the midst of a serene spell, the sea smooth and the sky cloudless, Stanley had a breakdown. John Thomson described it to his wife in a letter. 'The Captain's health began to break down, said to be from the great responsibility of his duties. From whatever cause his illness arose, whether from his peculiar habit or from extreme anxiety, it was of a formidable character and gave me great alarm. There was a complete prostration of strength and of his nervous constitution, and his mind wandered for a few days. During his convalescence ... his temper, which is always waspish, became unbearable and of the most irritable character. He treated everyone, except your humble servant, with a petulance and discourtesy . . .'[1]

Stanley, by his own admission, was taken aback by the suddenness of his illness. 'The excitement being over, I got sick,' he wrote to his family. 'The attack, whatever it was, did not last long but left me very weak.'[2] He had had an epileptic fit – 'so great was the immediate prostration of strength that the Doctors were almost doubtful of his getting over it.'[3] He

Grave of Owen Stanley, Sydney

was on the sick list on 20 January. Thomson '[dissuaded] him from the performance of his duties' feeling that 'unless he relieved himself from the anxiety of office', his life would be in danger.[4] Stanley took the advice and remained confined to his cabin for almost two weeks. Somewhere around the latitude of 20 degrees south, the ship caught the trade winds and the voyage got back on track.

It was only on 5 February, as the *Rattlesnake* was arriving at the entrance to Sydney harbour, that Stanley managed to get himself on deck to take the ship in.[5] But then, he spotted a steam-boat speedily heading for the ship. As it came closer he saw that it was carrying Reverend Robert King, who had been on the ship (as a passenger and naturalist-companion of Huxley's) on its outward voyage from England. Stanley knew instinctively that he was bringing bad news.

King came on board. He saw immediately that Stanley was very ill: 'he was looking very pale, thin and haggard and I was much shocked at his appearance.'[6] This made his task even more difficult, for he had come to break the news to Stanley of his father's death. Edward Stanley, the Bishop of Norwich, had died on 6 September 1849. Surprisingly, given that he had been told less than four months ago of the sudden death of his brother, Stanley, according to King, 'bore it very calmly– more so than I expected'.[7] Although he did not show it to King, Stanley was deeply affected, as he admitted to his family. 'I carried on the duty I believe, much as usual,' he wrote, 'except that as my orders were given in a very low, quiet tone I always come to in the hour of danger, everyone seemed to feel something had gone wrong. At last, to my great relief, the second anchor was let go, and getting down to the cabin and leaving word not to be disturbed unless in case of absolute necessity, I felt I could give vent to my feelings.'[8] In his letter to his family, Stanley did not dwell on his sadness, which he felt pro-foundly, but on the fact that his father, when he died, did not know of Charlie's death, and had lived long enough to 'receive such good accounts from here and V.D.L. [Van Diemen's Land]'.[9]

The ship anchored in its old position in Farm Cove. A boat was immediately sent away for the letters and soon returned with them. Some friends of Barbara Thompson came to the *Rattlesnake* in the afternoon and took her with them to be reunited with her family. Aside from a notice about her story that appeared in the *Sydney Morning Herald* the next day, nothing more was heard from or about her again. Captain Phillip Parker King, who had himself just arrived back from London, came on board and helped console Stanley with good news of his mother and his sisters.[10] Other letters gave him much needed comfort, especially one from Ama, his love in Norwich – it was the first letter he had received from her since leaving England.[11] King's news of the Stanleys and those letters – 'I read and re-read them till my aching head warned me to stop' – helped ease the pain of his father's death, but John Thomson advised him that, in his own best interest, he should leave the ship immediately and recover elsewhere.[12] Stanley accepted his surgeon's advice and removed himself to the care of his friends, Captain and Mrs Browne, in Brenchley, their north shore home.[13]

Sydney harbour, never a quiet place, was particularly busy at this time, as ships were loading hundreds of gold-seekers and their worldly goods hoping to make their fortune in California. Gold had been discovered in January 1848, but the news of it had not reached Sydney until December. The first ships to cross the Pacific in search of the precious metal began to leave Sydney soon thereafter. Only a few ships had made the voyage by the time that the *Rattlesnake* departed Sydney for its surveying voyage to the north. By the time of the ship's return, gold fever was rampant, not only in Sydney but throughout New South Wales and New Zealand. Ships of every type, from the smallest cutter to the largest barque, were heading to San Francisco every few days, carrying thousands of people from one underdeveloped place to another.[14] Even 'reports of sickness, murders, and all sorts of bad things' could not deter the fortune chasers.[15] Ships were still pouring out of Sydney, though soon the flow would begin to fall off and finally reverse.

In the midst of all the excitement, another piece of dramatic news reached the *Rattlesnake*. HMS *Meander*, commanded by Henry Keppel, was due in port any day. The ship had arrived in Port Essington on 13 November 1849 and delivered the news to Captain McArthur, the commandant, that the Government had decided to abandon the settlement in all haste. Taken aback, but without time to think about the consequences of the order, the residents began transferring all their goods, provisions and stores to the ship to return to Sydney, and from there to make their way back to London. The mammoth task of dismantling the settlement was completed in just over a fortnight and HMS *Meander* sailed out of Port Essington on 30 November. The settlement had hung on for just over 10 years, making it the longest-surviving British settlement in northern Australia to date, but like its two predecessors, a failure.[16] Ten weeks later, on 7 February, HMS *Meander* arrived in Sydney with its unexpected cargo and anchored alongside the *Rattlesnake*.

Meanwhile the care of Mrs Browne worked wonders for Stanley. Reverend King confessed that when the ship came into Sydney, 'the medical men had not much hope of his ultimate recovery', but, after a fortnight at Brenchley, 'he certainly looked much better, and was very cheerful'.[17] The only outward sign that the recovery was not complete was that his wrist, which had been badly hurt during his attack, had still not healed and his ability to write was still impaired. His normally smooth, rounded and controlled handwriting had given way to a scraggly, pointed and dishevelled style. Once on the *Rattlesnake*, Stanley was able to write to his sister on 19 February that it was only now that he could 'put pen to paper'.[18] Brave words, indeed, but his wrist seemed to be no better a fortnight later.[19]

Stanley now had to catch up with a number of necessary duties, mostly but not all pleasant. Letters went off to Deas Thomson at the Colonial Office, telling him of his recent surveying voyage and about the lack of commercial possibilities in New Guinea. He also mentioned that he had placed a headstone at the burial site of Wall and Niblett on Albany Island.[20]

Stanley also arranged to send Robert Suckling, his senior lieutenant, back to England because of poor health. He left Sydney on 20 February, bound for London. The unpleasant job was to dismiss his steward, Robert Gale, because of misconduct, as he stated it to Henry Keppel, the senior officer present in Sydney. That word 'misconduct' hid more than it revealed.[21] He gave more away, but without going into details – what they were we can only imagine but must have been particularly heinous – to his sister Mary: 'Robert has been behaving so ill that I have been obliged to dismiss him and get another steward. Robert's insolence was greater than any thing that I have ever met since I have been at sea.'[22]

Much more pleasant was the news that Eliza, his sister-in-law, upon hearing of her father-in-law's death, had decided to cancel her plans to return to London directly and instead had decided to wait in Hobart Town until the *Rattlesnake* arrived in Sydney. When he was in Cape York and first learned of Charlie's death, Stanley feared that Eliza might have already been planning to return to England at the first opportunity and, therefore, they would miss each other in Sydney.[23] Now, Stanley wrote to Eliza, asking her to come and join him 'as soon as she can and to consider the ship her home'. She was not well. As he told Mary, he wasn't certain what the ship's movements might be, but they would, he maintained, 'be in a homeward direction ere long – and I am sure', he continued, 'we can make her comfortable on board here where she knows every one.'[24] Stanley wanted to help her and felt he could, because he would be able 'perfectly [to] sympathize with all her distress and enter into all her feelings – I shall be very glad to have her with me, as I feel sure that I can do much towards making her happy, and I almost begin to consider myself a married man, and am fitting up Eliza's cabin with all due regard to a lady's wants, so far as in my ignorance, I yet know.'[25]

The *Rattlesnake* had now been away from England for almost four years. Many hoped that they would be ordered back home soon – surveying ships, typically, stayed away for between four and five years. But there were no orders waiting when the ship arrived in port. Both John Thomson and Thomas Huxley thought the passage home was imminent, expecting to leave sometime in May, and work their way back to England by the Indonesian islands, Singapore, Mauritius and the Cape.[26] Though ships carrying post from England arrived in Sydney, still there were no orders. Even by the time the *Bramble* had arrived in Sydney, on 2 March, from the, as it turned out, unsuccessful survey of the waters between Rossel and Sudest Island, no one was any the wiser.

What was unknown in Sydney at the time was that, in London, Beaufort had just finalized the *Rattlesnake*'s future movements. On 31 January 1850, Beaufort wrote to Stanley informing him that he should sell HMS *Bramble* – 'too much decayed to be worth bringing home' – and return to England, as soon as he could manage it, and by way of New Zealand and the Falkland Islands.[27] Colonel Edward Sabine, England's leading authority on the earth's magnetic field, wanted to have a daily series of magnetic readings taken across the Pacific, and Stanley was his man – 'knowing not only your never flagging zeal but your scrupulous accuracy'.[28]

Stanley's health had improved. For the next few weeks, though he continued to stay with the Brownes rather than on the ship, he attended picnics, a ball, went up country, and generally got back into the swing of the Sydney society in which he felt at ease. A letter from Ama rekindled his feelings for her and thoughts of marriage became more real. He thought of London, of his future in the navy. Beaufort, he was certain, would be able to arrange a 'shore-going appointment'. 'In 26 years, I have been 22 at sea, which is quite enough.'[29]

But none of this happened. Stanley never received Beaufort's instructions to return home, never saw Eliza or Ama again. Reverend Robert King provided the details:

> On Monday evening [11 March 1850], he had arranged to start for Port Stephens to spend some time with my father, but he felt not so well, and deemed it prudent to stay in Sydney – he had been staying at Capt Browne's, but on that evening he went on board, and slept there. I believe his motive was a kind of presentment of what was coming, a feeling that he might require medical aid. On Tuesday he did not appear worse, and when the surgeon Mr Huxley took leave of him on Tuesday night, he said that he was feeling very comfortable. At 6 the next morning, Dr Thomson saw him asleep in his cot, but at ½ past 7, the cabin boy going into the cabin, found him in a fit. Both Doctors were immediately on the spot, but it was too late, and at 8 am Wednesday 13th March, he breathed his last without a groan, without pain.[30]

Stanley was dead at the age of thirty-eight, comparatively young even for his time. Although the official cause of death was sudden epilepsy, it is likely that what actually killed him was a severe head injury, which he sustained during the fit he had that Wednesday morning.[31] The story that did the rounds, however, was more complicated.

The *Shipping Gazette and Sydney General Trade List*, a weekly paper covering movements in and out of the port, and one of the first to report Stanley's death, commented that his 'health had been gradually giving way under the fatigues and anxieties attendant upon the arduous duty of surveying in a tropical climate. [The] bereavements preyed upon his mind, and acting upon a system already much debilitated, ended fatally, the gallant officer having been seized with an epileptic fit on Wednesday morning, and died about eight o'clock.'[32] This story was repeated in the obituaries that subsequently appeared in Brisbane, Hobart Town and Melbourne, as well as in publications in England. Both MacGillivray and Huxley, in their respective accounts of the voyage of the *Rattlesnake*, agreed with this version.[33]

Stanley had confided in his friend, Reverend William Clarke, vicar of St Thomas's Church, on Sydney's north shore, that should he die in Australia, he wished to be laid to rest in the church's burial ground.[34] Stanley's funeral was a grand event. It took place on Friday 15 March and began with a procession of ships and boats. 'About half-past two o'clock the coffin passed over the side of H.M.S. *Rattlesnake* into the pinnace of that vessel, and was taken in tow by the gig pulled by the late captain's crew and by another boat.'[35] Midshipman Packe produced the following, showing the formation of the procession.[36]

Meander's Pinnace	*Meander*'s Launch
Meander's 1st Cutter	
towing	
Rattlesnake's 2nd Cutter	
towing	
Rattlesnake's Pinnace	
with guard and body	
Rattlesnake's 1st Cutter	*Meander*'s Barge
Rattlesnake's Jolly Boat	*Meander*'s 2nd Cutter
Bramble's Cutter	*Meander*'s 1st Gig
Rattlesnake's 1st Galley	*Rattlesnake*'s 2nd Galley
Bramble's 1st Gig	*Bramble*'s 2nd Gig
Collector of Customs' Boat	Port Officer's Boat
Water Police Boat	Health Officer's Boat
Water Police Boat	Water Police Boat
Followed by line of Merchant Ships	
Boats 4 Abreast	

At Blue's Point a guard of 250 men with the staff colours and band of the eleventh regiment awaited to receive the cortège. The procession to the Church of St. Thomas then commenced. First came the troop, composing the guard of honour, with arms and colours reversed. These were followed by the regimental band, and the brass band of the *Meander*. Next came the hearse, with the pall-bearers: – The Hon. E.D. Thomson, Colonial Secretary; Colonel Barney, R.E.; Colonel Gibbes, Collector of Customs; Captain Scott; H.H. Browne Esq., W.P.M.; Lieutenant Yule (Commander of the *Bramble*); Lieutenant Dayman; and Lieutenant Simpson. The officers, crew, and marines of H.M.S. *Meander*, *Rattlesnake* and *Bramble*, (four hundred in number), followed next in order, precedence being given to those who had served under the deceased officer. The procession was brought up by General Wynyard and staff, all the members of the Military, Civil and Commissariat departments, and by a large number of private gentlemen who attended to pay a last tribute of respect to the memory of the deceased. In this order they proceeded to St. Thomas' Church, the band playing funeral music. On their arrival, the coffin was carried into the church by the crew of the late Captain's gig, and the service was then read by the Rev. R. L. King.[37]

Once King had finished reading, the coffin was removed to a vault where Reverend Clarke read the remaining part of the service. Three volleys were fired over the grave by the guard of honour and the funeral was completed. There must have been upwards of one thousand people attending the funeral and thousands of onlookers. Sydney had never witnessed such a spectacle for a naval captain.

In many ways, Stanley's death ended the story of the *Rattlesnake*. Without Stanley, the adventure was over.

Stanley's mission, as he had interpreted it from the instructions he received from both the Lords Commissioners of the Admiralty and Beaufort, was to complete the survey of the Great Barrier Reef, a task that had been progressing for more than three-quarters of a century, ever since James Cook first sailed between the reef and the coast in 1770; and, for the first time in history, to undertake a detailed survey, and produce an exact chart of the southern coast of New Guinea and the islands of the Louisiade Archipelago. Both of these tasks he and his men accomplished with the quality and accuracy that the perfectionist Beaufort expected of his band of surveyors.

The voyage had been an enormous success. With accurate charts, the inner passage of the Great Barrier Reef could now be used more safely than ever before – the likelihood of another *Charles Eaton* was greatly reduced – and this route could attract steam shipping, the technology of the future. The Indian Ocean, the Coral Sea and the rest of the Pacific Ocean were now connected; trade and imperial ambitions could flow freely from the one ocean to the other.

CHAPTER XIII

Getting Home
1850

The voyage of the *Rattlesnake* may have been over in the sense that its task was over and its captain dead, but the ship, its officers, crew and passengers still had to get home.

On 14 March 1850, the day before Stanley's funeral, Henry Keppel, who happened to be the most senior naval officer in Sydney, appointed Yule as commander of the ship with orders to return back to England. A few days later, Yule received instructions from Beaufort, which proposed a route back to England via Cape Horn and the Falkland Islands. He planned to have everything arranged – disposing of the *Bramble*, tidying up some readings for the charts, provisioning and loading the ship – for a departure on 1 May.[1]

Eliza Stanley, of course, had no idea of what was happening in Sydney. She left Hobart Town on 20 March, before anyone there knew of Stanley's sudden death. When she arrived in Sydney on 28 March even the funeral was over. Both Reverend Robert King and Reverend Clarke rallied round to comfort her, while Captain Phillip Parker King arranged for her to return to England in the *Rattlesnake*. Thomson and Huxley looked after her on board so well that they continued to correspond for several years and Eliza had a brooch of the *Rattlesnake* made for Thomson's wife as a memento.[2]

HMS *Rattlesnake* at sea, Louisiade Archipelago

Not everyone who had been with the ship since Plymouth wanted to return. James Wilcox, Edward Stanley's private natural history collector, remained in Australia. Oswald Brierly transferred to HMS *Meander* as Captain Keppel's artist-in-residence. Room had to be found for many more passengers, including Mrs Yule, Mrs MacGillivray and daughter, and Eliza Stanley and her maid, in addition to the Port Essington people – the officers and a majority of the marines. The *Rattlesnake* had gone out with a company of 180 men and was now preparing to return with some 230 people on board.[3]

The proposed date of departure was rapidly approaching but there was a last minute snag. When news of Stanley's death reached Port Nicholson (Wellington, New Zealand), Captain Erskine, who happened to be the senior officer in the Australian division of the East Indies and China Station, sailed his ship HMS *Havannah* immediately to Sydney to sort matters out. When, on 26 April, the *Havannah* arrived, Erskine was furious to learn that Keppel had already taken matters into his own hand. Erskine considered Keppel to be 'a bird of passage' – the *Meander* was on a world cruise and was simply on its way from one station to another – who had no right to interfere in the appointment. Erskine told Yule that he would be superseded and that the *Rattlesnake* would remain in Sydney until the end of the year as part of the station. Now Keppel asserted his right as the senior officer and ordered the *Rattlesnake* to leave port. The two captains went at each other 'hammer and tongs'. Erskine even threatened to follow the *Rattlesnake* out of port. In the end, Keppel ordered the *Havannah* to stay put and the *Rattlesnake* went on its way unhindered.[4] On 2 May, the anchors were raised and the *Rattlesnake* headed for the Pacific Ocean, amidst 'great waving and interchange of signals', but with 'many sore hearts'.[5]

The voyage home was long and boring. They were supposed to sail to the north of New Zealand, but defects, especially a leak in the after gunroom, which could not be repaired at sea, forced them into the next port. On 16 May, the *Rattlesnake* anchored in the Bay of Islands, near the top end of the North Island. The repairs were completed in just under a week, and the ship set sail for the Falkland Islands on 22 May. It took one and a half months to traverse the southern part of the Pacific, a distance of some

5,000 miles, before anchoring at the relatively new settlement of Stanley on 9 July. The *Rattlesnake* remained here, buffeted by terrible winter weather, for a fortnight while the chronometers were rated. The homeward voyage resumed on 25 July. After a difficult sail in a northeasterly direction, and with the supply of water nearly exhausted, the ship made its way to Fayal, one of the islands of the Azores, and anchored there on 29 September. After being cooped up on board for such a long time, the stop in Fayal was extremely welcome. The sick list, swelled by the effects of seasickness, began to shrink. The land 'was flowing with milk and honey, presenting every necessary and luxury requisite to recruit constitutions debilitated by a continuance of innutritious food'.[6]

On 5 October, Yule ordered the anchors to be raised, and the *Rattlesnake* began the final leg of its long journey. The ship sighted the Lizard on 21 October and anchored in Plymouth Sound the next day. The supernumeraries were discharged. On 24 October, the *Rattlesnake* once more put to sea, this time heading for Chatham, which was reached on 1 November, and the final rite of passage, the paying-off, the settling of accounts – what was owed to whom – began, a process that took more than a week to complete. Finally, on 9 November 1850, after four years in this wooden world, the *Rattlesnake* officers and crew were allowed to leave the ship for ever.[7]

AFTERWORD

The Narrative and Its Review

John MacGillivray wrote the narrative of the voyage of HMS *Rattlesnake* as Stanley had requested.[1] He settled in London near the publishers T & W Boone, with three months' pay from the Admiralty, and the other officers' journals and logs from Beaufort.[2] Huxley was providing the illustrations as Brierly had yet to return. However it didn't go smoothly. The expected completion date, March 1851, passed without the book being finished.[3] Huxley was furious. 'Boone complains bitterly to me about him – and with great justice,' he told John Thomson. 'Boone has advanced him £50 on the book, and can neither get that repaid nor can get the conclusion of the book out of him. I have done all I can, but MacGillivray has lied to me so thoroughly, that I am altogether disgusted.'[4]

In spite of his problems with debt, drink and a growing family (he had two daughters as well as a wife to support), MacGillivray managed to complete the work by November 1851. The narrative of the voyage of the *Rattlesnake* became available in December 1851, though it was not published officially until the beginning of the following year. Dedicated to Owen Stanley's mother, it had two volumes, and a total length of just under 800 pages. Besides the narrative of the voyage and the account of Kennedy's expedition drawn from original sources, which took up the bulk of the publication, the book also had several scientific appendices. The shortest presented hydrographic and magnetic information. The longest and most important appendices were devoted to the various branches of the natural history collections, and were reviewed in the publication by Britain's most eminent experts: George Busk on zoophytes, Edward Forbes on molluscs, Adam White of the British Museum on insects and crustacea, and Robert Latham on linguistics. The publication provided extensive and valuable ethnographic material, including illustrations, as well as vocabularies of Cape York, the Louisiade Archipelago and southeast New Guinea.

The book was well-received in the *Literary Gazette* and *The Examiner* – in the words of the latter's anonymous reviewer, '[it is] one of the best books of travels of its class . . . indeed second only to one to which all books of maritime travels are likely to be second for a long time to come, we mean that portion of the "Narrative of the Voyage of the *Adventure* and *Beagle*" which is Mr Charles Darwin's.'[5] Sir WilliamHooker found it very creditable, 'and better than could be expected from a man of restless uncouth appearance and manners'.[6]

Even Huxley, who in July 1851 had referred to MacGillivray as a 'disreputable scamp', wrote to Eliza Stanley, 'I think the book an exceedingly good one. It is very well and clearly written – concise and very truthful – and what is more it is all in good taste –impressing me in that respect, I must confess, more than in any other. The attention to our lamented chief is I think particularly graceful and proper.'[7]

Eliza Stanley, however, felt the book lacked something. Huxley agreed 'that the book might have been made more graphic. It does not depict the real inner life of such a voyage as ours – but what book of travels does? It is just these wanting points that a judicious review might supply. Unlike a book, an article is allowed to "descend beneath the dignity of history" and to paint facts even as they are.'[8]

Huxley prepared such a review for the publisher John Murray but he didn't publish it.[9]

Instead he was able to offer it to John Chapman, who was remaking the *Westminster Review* into a radical review for advanced thinkers.[10] Huxley's article, 'Science at Sea', appeared in the first issue of the *Westminster Review* of 1854, along with his first review of scientific literature.

Although Huxley nowhere in the article admits explicitly his own participation in the voyage, one inevitably reads his selection of quotations as a reflection of his own experience. When he writes, 'to each there has been a time when the idea of a voyage of discovery filled us with inexpressible longing', we assume he shared these longings.[11] When he maintains, 'Sea-life is as different from shore-life as it always has been. The practical shiftiness required by the sailor, in his constant battle with the elements, is as far apart from the speculative acuteness and abstraction necessary to the man of science as ever'[12]; and adds at another point, 'the captain's good will in a man-of-war is only half the battle; and unless those who act immediately under him, and stand, as it were, between him and the rest of the ship's company, are equally imbued with a sense of the value of scientific researches, your science comes badly off', it is obvious he knows what he's talking about.[13] When he quotes from an officer's journal on hot rain off the coast of New Guinea – 'Rain! rain! *encore et toujours* – I wonder if it is possible for the mind of man to conceive anything more degradingly offensive than the condition of us 150 men, shut up in this wooden box, and being watered with hot water, as we are now'– the scene has the vivid presence of personal experience.[14] As does another quotation, on cockroaches:

> It's too hot to sleep, and my sole amusement consists in watching the cock-roaches, which are in a state of intense excitement and happiness. They manifest these feelings in a very remarkable manner – a sudden unanimous impulse seems to seize the obscene thousands which usually lurk hidden in the corners of my cabin. Out they rush, helter-skelter, and run over me, my table, and my desk[15] ... It is these outbreaks alone which rouse us from our lassitude ... each inhabitant of a cabin, armed with a slipper, is seen taking ample revenge upon the disturbers of his rest, and the destroyers of his books and clothes.[16]

When he quotes from earlier voyages, it is because his experience echoes theirs; whether it's of isolation, 'the ship is the home of the sailor; in voyages of discovery, more than two-thirds of one's time is spent in perfect isolation, between the blue of the sea and the blue of the sky';[17] of monotony, 'the life without you is monotonous and empty, like the mirror of the sea and the blue of heaven which rests over it; no occurrences; no news. Eating-time divides the day by returning twice – though rather to one's annoyance than for enjoyment';[18] or of boredom, 'any adventures ashore were mere oases, separated by whole deserts of the most wearisome *ennui*.'[19]

Worst of all, perhaps, for Huxley himself 'there is no being alone on a ship. Sailors are essentially gregarious animals, and don't at all understand the necessity under which many people labour – I among the rest – of having a little solitary converse with oneself occasionally'[20] – reminding us that Huxley shared sleeping and eating space with 16 boys (the midshipmen).

As well as the irritations that were part and parcel of any long voyage, there were the additional difficulties made by the Navy. About discipline, Huxley says, 'You not only feel the bit, but you see it; and your bridle is hung with bells to tell you of its presence.'[21] As for doing science on board,

> It is a curious fact, that if you want a boat for dredging, ten chances to one they
> are always actually or potentially otherwise disposed of; if you leave your
> towing-net trailing astern, in search of new creatures, in some promising patch
> of discoloured water, it is, in all probability, found to have a wonderful effect in
> stopping the ship's way, and is hauled in as soon as your back is turned; or a
> careful dissection waiting to be drawn may find its way overboard as a 'mess'.
> The singular disrespect with which the majority of naval officers regard every-
> thing that lies beyond the sphere of routine, tends to produce a tone of feeling
> very unfavourable to scientific exertions. How can it be otherwise, in fact, with
> men who, from the age of thirteen, meet with no influence but that which
> teaches them that the 'Queen's regulations and instructions' are the law and
> the prophets, and something more?[22]

Not only the regulations of the Queen's service but the conduct of the
Admiralty in particular enraged him. Their selection of ships:

> exploring vessels will be invariably found to be the slowest, clumsiest, and in
> every respect the most inconvenient ships which wear the pennant. In accor-
> dance with the rule, such was the *Rattlesnake*, and to carry out the spirit of the
> authorities more completely, she was turned out of Portsmouth dockyard in
> such a disgraceful state of unfitness, that her lower deck was continually under
> water during the voyage;[23]

Their meanness:

> works of reference, which are ruinously expensive to a private individual,
> though a mere dewdrop in the general cost of fitting-out a ship . . . a hundred
> pounds would have well supplied the *Rattlesnake*, but she sailed without a vol-
> ume – an application made by her captain not having been attended to;[24]

Their hypocrisy:

> It is of the opinion of the Lords Commissioners of the Admiralty that it would
> be to the honour and advantage of the Navy, and conduce to the general inter-
> ests of science, if new facilities and encouragement were given to the collection
> of information upon scientific subjects by the officers, and more particularly
> by the medical officers, of her Majesty's Navy when upon foreign service: and
> their lordships are desirous that for the purpose a 'Manual' be compiled, giv-
> ing general instructions for observation and for record in various branches of
> science . . . And it will be for their lordships to consider whether some pecu-

niary reward or promotion may not be given to those who succeed in producing eminently useful results.[25]

In publishing a 'Scientific Manual', encouraging scientific research in the Navy while refusing to finance and publish or reward it,

their lordships' minute is little better than an attempt to look well with the public upon false pretences. The *Rattlesnake* was one of the first scientific vessels which returned home after the publication of that minute, and, had it been penned in good faith, we cannot conceive that their lordships should have refused, as they did, to keep the Naturalist upon full pay for a sufficient time adequately to work up his materials; that they should, up to this time, have neglected to promote any scientific officer connected with the expedition, save one, whose seniority already entitled him to it.[26]

He cites his own case, where the Admiralty

refused point blank to assist in the publication of a large mass of investigations whose value has been certified by the highest authorities, made by one of their officers, who was sufficiently unacquainted with Admiralty morality to put faith in official promises.[27]

Huxley's anger with Stanley, however, seems to have dissipated because of his death, the intercourse with his family, and most probably his reading of Stanley's journal. He now recognized Stanley's isolation, 'the social isolation of the captain of a man-of-war must be nearly as complete. All the great responsibilities rest irremovably upon his shoulders . . . he knows that he alone will have to bear the brunt of all consequences';[28] and his sense of being the engine of the survey,

when we first commenced, all sorts of difficulties arose, – this could not be done – that was out of the question; a month's experience, however, soon convinced them all, that all I directed to be done within a given time, could be, and since then, with a little driving, it *has* been done. And the satisfaction of reaching this point – having more than done all I intended to do at starting, within a day or two of the time I named at Sydney – I must leave you to fancy.[29]

Huxley points out that 'care and anxiety, from the mobility of his temperament, sat not so lightly upon him as they must have done, and this, joined to the physical debility produced by the enervating climate of New Guinea fairly wore him out, making him prematurely old . . . he died in harness, the end attained, the work that lay before him honourably done.'[30] Stanley's hydrographical contributions remained the basis for Admiralty charts for at least a century.

He even quotes from Stanley's journal an excerpt that presents in a sympathetic light that caution he denounced at the time as cowardice:

> hostility prevented me from sending parties, as I otherwise should have done, to explore the interior of the islands under which we anchored; ... all the specimens that we could have procured, however rare, would have been dearly purchased by the sacrifice of one human life; and, had any collision taken place on shore, many more lives must have been lost, not most likely on our side, but on theirs, for they seemed to have no idea whatever of the use and effect of firearms.[31]

Huxley's review not only added the human interest to MacGillivray's narrative, and reconciled him to MacGillivray and Stanley, it also began Huxley's association with John Chapman, which provided him with an added opportunity of supporting himself by writing. It also allowed Huxley to embark on a career of interpreting contemporary scientific research for the educated public, which actually brought him fame and fortune.

Dramatis Personae

JOHN MACGILLIVRAY, when he had completed the narrative of the voyage, desperately needed a job. He wanted to go back to sea.[1] Hearing of an expedition Beaufort was planning for the South Pacific, including the Coral Sea, the Great Barrier Reef and Torres Strait, MacGillivray wrote offering his service as naturalist. On 12 January 1852, he presented Beaufort with testimonials from some of Britain's most eminent scientists: Sir William Hooker, who vouched for him as a botanist; Edward Forbes, who did the same for invertebrate zoology; John Gould, who spoke about MacGillivray's expertise in ornithology; and Robert Latham, who praised his work in ethnology and linguistics.[2] The testimonials were impeccable.[3]

As the first choice, Berthold Seemann, was fully occupied writing up the narrative and botanical researches of a previous voyage, Beaufort appointed MacGillivray as the naturalist to HMS *Herald*. Huxley commented, 'it might be difficult to find a better man – and I only trust he will have the good sense not again to blight his own prospects.'[4] Prophetic words.

MacGillivray was delighted with his position and conditions of work. They were, he told Hooker, much better than on the *Rattlesnake*. That voyage, he remarked, was successful but he never got to do what he really wanted and that, he argued, was for lack of space. 'Now in the Rattlesnake', he pointed out to Hooker, 'I had no place of my own . . . – I merely, bit by bit, *annexed* first a small table in the chart room, then a part of a locker, then the remainder & so on – but this took years to accomplish – and I never got the spare cabin for my specimens which had been promised me. The result was that from want of room I did not collect half of what otherwise would have been the case.'[5]

On his new ship it was all going to be different. He would have his own cabin and a workshop, with plenty of light and room, where he would be able to use his microscope and stow his specimens. With this lavish space and opportunities to analyse the specimens he would collect, he would be able to contribute the scientific sections on mammals, birds and fishes to the expected narrative of the voyage. The frustration he had felt during the voyage of the *Rattlesnake*, being the only collector on board, with no assistance and space – 'my duties before were too frequently those of a mere collector' – would not be duplicated on this expedition. He was looking forward to becoming a proper naturalist, as he defined it.[6] He drew up an extensive list of materials, instruments, books, guns, powder, shot and bullets that he needed, most of which he received.[7]

On 22 May 1852, when MacGillivray stepped aboard HMS *Herald*, he was a man at the top of his profession with powerful scientific backers. He was at the height of his career. The *Herald* arrived in Sydney in February 1853 and, almost immediately, MacGillivray headed for the bush to collect. In early September, the ship set sail for its first cruise and MacGillivray had his first experience of the South Seas islands, taking in Lord Howe Island, the Isle of Pines, directly to the south of New Caledonia, and finally Aneityum, the southernmost island of New Hebrides. The *Herald* returned to Sydney on 1 January 1854.[8]

1854 saw the *Herald* continue its survey work, this time heading for New Zealand and then Fiji, which the ship reached in September of the year. The survey continued but then in November, by a strange coincidence, Henry Denham, the *Herald*'s captain, abruptly decided to break off his work in Fiji and sail to Gaudalcanal in the Solomon Islands. He had heard that Benjamin Boyd, who was supposed to have been murdered in Guadalcanal in 1851, might still be alive.

Everyone connected with the *Rattlesnake* voyage had heard of Boyd and some had known him personally. Brierly was his closest contact but MacGillivray counted him as one of his friends. While the *Rattlesnake* was in Cape York, in October 1849, not long after the encounter with Barbara Thompson, Boyd had turned up in Sydney and headed, in his old racing yacht the *Wanderer*, for San Francisco and gold. By the time he got there, in late March 1850, however, gold fever had died away and the human flow was reversing. After trying unsuccessfully to find his fortune in California, he joined the stream of returnees to Sydney in June 1851.

But Boyd, being the man he was, did not simply sail westward. Rather, sailing south from Hawaii in July 1851, he was on the look out for a convenient island, which he could run as his own little empire, along the lines of

Brooke in Sarawak. He tried various localities in the South Pacific and, after a few unsuccessful attempts in the Gilbert and Ellice Islands, continued to sail westward until he arrived, at the end of August 1851, at Stewart Island, to the east of the main Solomon Islands, where he convinced the local chief to sell him his territory. He continued west towards the Solomon Islands where he purchased some more territory. On 11 October he reached Guadalcanal Island, the largest of the Solomon Islands.

A few days later, Boyd left the yacht on a shooting excursion for game and was never seen again. Searches for him proved unsuccessful. His body was never discovered but indirect evidence pointed to him having been murdered. His comrades sought revenge and embarked on a frenzied attack on the villages, burning what they could find, before a tropical storm forced them to leave. The *Wanderer* was set on a course for Sydney, but was wrecked on the east coast of Australia.[9] The yacht's company managed to get themselves to Sydney.[10]

Far too many people had had business relations with Boyd, many of them getting their fingers burnt, to let the matter rest. The Royal Bank of Australia, the Sydney merchants, even the French Government, wanted to know the truth of what happened. It would be like Boyd, they thought, to evade his just deserts by faking death. They demanded that search parties be sent to the Solomon Islands. Denham had been given instructions to find out what had happened to Boyd should an opportunity arise. So, when Denham was told in Fiji that the crew of an American whaler had seen trees with Boyd's name carved into them on Guadalcanal, he did not hesitate to investigate.[11]

Denham's month-long search provided confirmation that Boyd had been killed. No body was found but the stories he managed to elicit from the locals about those October days when Boyd was on the island convinced him that Boyd had been captured and killed. He also learned that the killer was dead. The only relic Denham obtained, and it was enough to confirm in his mind that Boyd was not alive, was a tomahawk with Boyd's name marked on it. The search for Boyd over, the *Herald* set sail for Sydney on 9 January 1855 and arrived in the port on 30 January.[12]

The next day, an article appeared in the *Sydney Morning Herald* detailing Denham's search for Boyd and the conclusions he had come to. That was no surprise. What came as a shock, however, was that on the same day, another article written by someone on the *Herald* who preferred to remain anonymous, appeared in Sydney's rival paper, *The Empire*, which severely criticized Denham's command, in particular, his conduct during the search for Boyd, accusing him of putting his men at risk and not taking care to victual the ship properly, with the result that most of the crew contracted scurvy. Two days later, another article appeared in the same paper, this time signed by E.S. Hill, which continued the attack on Denham.[13]

Denham was, apparently, very disturbed by the articles, particularly as he didn't know who had written them. On 20 April, MacGillivray presented Denham with a letter in which he complained that Denham had published an article in an issue of the *Nautical Magazine* of 1854 in which he presented as his own, observations made by MacGillivray on the island of St Paul's. In the conversation that ensued, MacGillivray, it was stated, declared himself to be the author of the article in the 31 January edition of *The Empire*.

Two days later, Denham told the whole story to Captain Stephen Fremantle, commander of HMS *Juno*, and the most senior officer in Sydney at the time. Fremantle decided to investigate the matter and convened an enquiry on 25 April on HMS *Herald*. It was held in the presence of Denham and another naval commander, but we know nothing of how the proceedings were arranged. What we do know is that Fremantle concluded that MacGillivray's behaviour was so heinous as to warrant instant dismissal from the service.[14]

Fremantle had terrible things to say about MacGillivray. These were related in graphic detail in a letter to Beaufort where Fremantle attacked MacGillivray in a most vicious and unrelenting manner, accusing him of endangering the voyage by poisoning the atmosphere with his attacks on the commander.[15] However, it should be pointed out, Fremantle himself was dismissed from the service a few years later.[16]

Not long after his dishonourable discharge, MacGillivray wrote to his wife and three children to join him in Sydney. They were in dire straits in London, living from hand to mouth. What kept them out of the workhouse was a handout of £6 per month from the famous shell collector and world traveller, Hugh Cuming, an old acquaintance and now sorry creditor of MacGillivray's – MacGillivray owed him almost £200.[17] In desperation, Williamina turned to Huxley, who raised the £50 – possibly from Sir

William Hooker – necessary to send the family to Sydney.[18] 'It is most lamentable', Huxley confided in Joseph Hooker, 'that a man of so much ability should have so utterly damned himself as MacGillivray has – but he is hopelessly Celtic.'[19]

Huxley was probably referring to the drinking which Philip Ruffle Sharpe, one of the *Rattlesnake*'s midshipmen, mentioned in his reminiscences of the return voyage:

> At times of an evening, we were often much amused by the soliloquies of our naturalist, McGillivray [sic], whose cabin was just outside the gun room. A clever, talented Scotchman: he used at nights to get 'fou' – and it was laughable at such times, to hear him, moralizing as he sat, contemplating himself in the looking-glass: somewhat after this fashion: – 'Ah! Jock, you're up to your old tricks again tonight – it will n'a do Jock: you've a wife and a bit bairnie, and you're fou: you must pull up Jock, or what will become of you', and so on.[20]

However it seems to have been his critical outspokenness rather than his drinking that brought about his dismissal from the Navy.

The MacGillivray family departed London on 2 December 1855 and arrived in Sydney on 2 March 1856.[21] Once the *Herald* affair was over, MacGillivray made a life for himself in Australia. He continued to travel and to work in natural history, becoming, in time, closely associated with the Australian Museum. His travels, between 1858 and 1861, took him to New Caledonia and New Hebrides, as well as to the Great Barrier Reef and the Torres Strait. He became an expert on sandalwood – the chief product of New Caledonia and New Hebrides – and wrote up his adventures in a series of well-received articles in the *Sydney Morning Herald* and *The Empire*. MacGillivray also continued to associate with James Wilcox, Bishop Stanley's private collector on the *Rattlesnake*, and, in 1864, moved to Grafton to work alongside him. His last few and surviving letters show MacGillivray in total command of his subject, full of confidence and collecting mammals and birds for museums in Sydney and Melbourne. He died from heart failure in a Sydney boarding-house in 1867, aged 46.[22] His children grew up in Australia where other family members from Scotland settled and flourished.

THOMAS HENRY HUXLEY stepped off the *Rattlesnake* in November 1850 into the scientific limelight. He knew something of what had happened to the various papers that were sent to London. He knew, for example, that his first learned contribution from the *Rattlesnake* voyage, the paper on *Physalia,* was read at the Linnean Society meeting; that his second paper, on *Diphyes,* had had the first instalment read at the same venue; that his *Trigonia* paper had been read at the Zoological Society by Edward Forbes; and that his crowning piece of research, the *Medusa* paper, had been read at the Royal Society and that its publication was forthcoming. What he didn't know was how the papers had been received.

One of the first people to greet him was Edward Forbes who overwhelmed him with news of his scientific success. He introduced Huxley to the elite of the British scientific community, who wined and dined and praised him. At the age of only twenty-six, and six months after leaving the *Rattlesnake*, he was elected a Fellow of the Royal Society. It seemed that the door to British science, still dominated by patronage and men of private means, was open to merit. But the £14 per year it cost him was hard for Huxley – it was about a month's salary. He was still in the Navy, on half-pay, while he completed the zoological researches he had pursued on the *Rattlesnake*.[23] The Admiralty wanted the work done but was totally unwilling to pay for its publication.[24] Instead of a book the results of his *Rattlesnake* researches appeared in scientific journals, in the *Annals and Magazine of Natural History*, and, even more prestigiously, in the *Philosophical Transactions of the Royal Society*.

Huxley needed properly paid work if he were to marry as he longed to do. He applied for the Chair of Natural History at the University of Toronto, which went to someone else, and for a chair in Sydney, which never materialized.[25] On 1 January 1852, Huxley wrote to Eliza Stanley, telling her about the success of MacGillivray's book. He also added that his own career was at rock bottom. He didn't know what to do. Should he keep trying for a chair? – there was another one going in Ireland – or, as he expressed it to Mrs Stanley, 'make my adieux to science altogether – and betake myself to the Bush.' 'I am getting very tired of my unsettled condition', he continued, '– and as science will do very well without me – I have a great mind to return the compliment and show that I can do without science.'[26]

However he continued to try. Throughout 1852 he wrote up and published further researches from the *Rattlesnake*. He received another year on half-pay from the Admiralty, supplementing it with any bits of translating and cataloguing he could get.

Two years after leaving the ship, he was still living from hand to mouth with no possibility of bringing Nettie over to London. He was in despair. But then he was awarded the Royal Society's Gold Medal and the 50 guineas that came with it. He continued struggling through 1853 when the Admiralty refused any more leaves of absence from the Service. On 1 January 1854, he wrote to Nettie to pray that he would never have as bad a year as the last.[27]

In April 1854 Huxley was dismissed from the Navy for disobeying orders to return to active service. As a civilian, fortunately, he could be funded by the Royal Society, which gave him £300 to finance his book.

Edward Forbes was called away, in May 1854, to the Chair of Natural History in Edinburgh and Huxley took over his lectures at the Government School of Mines in London. He taught a parallel course for the Department of Science and Art starting in mid-June, and in July he started lecturing at the London Institution. By autumn he could reckon on earning at least £500 a year. At last he could write to Nettie. 'So my darling pet come home as soon as you will – thank God I can at last say those words.'[28]

Nettie arrived in May of the following year and the couple were married in July. Huxley's scientific reputation and financial success grew apace. He became one of the most famous scientists and personalities of the second half of the nineteenth century, forever linked with the name of Charles Darwin and evolution. His life in science, forged on the voyage of the *Rattlesnake*, covered half a century. He died in 1895, aged 70.

FRANCIS BEAUFORT, the mastermind of the British scientific maritime survey, and the figure involved in the lives of so many people on the *Rattlesnake*, was knighted in 1848. He never did get the recognition he so justly deserved from the Admiralty. The sudden and tragic death of Owen Stanley must have been very painful for him. After the *Rattlesnake*'s return, Beaufort continued to send ships to survey the world's waterways, including HMS *Herald* to the Pacific, but most of his energies were taken up by organizing expeditions to the Arctic to search for Sir John Franklin and his two ships, last heard of in mid-1845. Beaufort retired as

Hydrographer in 1855, aged 80 years, after 26 years in the job. He died two years later.

CHARLES JAMES CARD returned to the South Seas in October 1851, serving on HMS *Calliope*. He continued serving on naval vessels until his retirement, as Paymaster, in 1885. He spent the last years of his life in Wareham, Dorset, where he died in 1903, aged 73.

ARTHUR PACKE's subsequent life is more mysterious. Nothing is known of him as far as his naval career is concerned. He went to Buenos Aires in 1856 and then Montevideo, to join his brother Vere, who had gone into the cattle business there. He died and was buried in Montevideo in 1857, aged 28.

JOSEPH DAYMAN, the *Rattlesnake*'s magnetical officer, had an illustrious naval career. After serving on the *Rattlesnake*, he served on ten other ships and was made Captain in 1863. During his career he was commended several times on his surveying work by Beaufort and the Secretary of State for the Colonies. He was involved in the laying down of the Atlantic telegraph cable, and received a gold watch from the Mayor of New York for this work. He died in 1868, aged 50, while on half-pay.

GEORGE INSKIP returned to the Pacific on HMS *Virago*, his next appointment. He pursued a naval career, though he did not reach the rank of Captain until 1874, at which point he retired. He was a magistrate in Plymouth and died in 1915.

CHARLES YULE got his promotion to Commander in 1851. He never went to sea again though. Beaufort employed him in completing Australian charts. After Beaufort's retirement Yule continued to work for the new Hydrographer, compiling volumes of the Australian Directory, the official publication giving sailing directions for the continent. Yule retired from the navy in 1864 and died in 1878, aged 69.

JOHN THOMSON, by contrast, continued as a naval surgeon. After a stay of four years in Edinburgh, he returned to the sea in 1854 and continued to serve on naval vessels until 1869, eventually retiring at the rank of Staff Surgeon. He had a great interest in photography, which he first learned about in 1846, before the *Rattlesnake* set sail. There is no evidence that he had a camera with him on the ship, but he did take a photograph of Huxley in March 1850 when the *Rattlesnake* was in Sydney. It's possible that he bought or borrowed a camera there. After retiring, he became Vice-President of the Edinburgh Photographic Society. He and Huxley corresponded for several years following the *Rattlesnake*'s return. Thomson died in 1892.

JAMES WILCOX remained in Australia and married the woman he had met earlier in the *Rattlesnake*'s voyage. The couple lived in Sydney where Wilcox set himself up as a natural history dealer. In 1855, they moved to Grafton, on the Clarence River. He remained committed to natural history throughout the rest of his life, having many of Australia's leading natural scientists as colleagues and friends. He died in 1881, aged 58.

OSWALD BRIERLY left Sydney on HMS *Meander* the day after the *Rattlesnake*, and returned to London in August 1851. He quickly sought the company of the social elite, attending, amongst other functions, the Cowes Regatta. He was back at sea in 1854, and continued voyaging, sketching and painting on many ships over the next 16 years. He was appointed marine painter to Queen Victoria in 1874, having accompanied members of the Royal Family on several voyages to Norway, the Mediterranean and Australia. He became a member of the Royal Watercolour Society in 1880. A year later he was appointed curator of the Painted Hall at Greenwich and was awarded a knighthood in 1885. He held one large show of his work during his life, in 1887, in London. He died in 1894, aged 77. Apart from a small number of magazine articles on the canoes of Australia, he never published a word about his Twofold Bay and his *Rattlesnake* experiences, or his meeting with Barbara Thompson and her account of the Muralag people, though he clearly had intended to do something someday.

REVEREND ROBERT KING remained in Australia where he followed an ecclesiastical career. In 1867 he became a canon and the following year principal of Moore Theological College, where he remained for ten years. He returned to parish ministry and eventually, in 1881, became an archdeacon. King remained in this position until 1895, when he retired. He died in 1897 aged 74.

ELIZA STANLEY regained her strength during the voyage and in London. She kept up a small correspondence with both Thomson and Huxley for a number of years. Eliza Stanley died in 1901. The brooch, which she presented to Thomson as a gift for his wife, is in the possession of the National Library of Australia.

BARBARA THOMPSON's movements once she left the *Rattlesnake* are not well recorded. She married another ship's captain, James Adams, in November 1851, in the Scots Church in Sydney where MacGillivray had been married. In 1876, she married another man named John Simpson. She died in 1916, though there was some confusion at her death about her real age – to the best of our knowledge she was 87 years old. The story of her time on Muralag was told, for the first time, by MacGillivray in a chapter in the published narrative of the voyage. (On 8 April 1850, an extract from the journal of a passenger on the *Sir John Byng*, which brought provisions to the *Rattlesnake* in October 1849, was published in London in *The Times* giving his account of the first meeting with Barbara Thompson.) Until David Moore published his transcription of Brierly's journals in 1977, MacGillivray's chapter remained the only factual account. The reason for the relative silence about Barbara Thompson may be that, in a sense, her story was not sensational enough. Other tales of women kept captive by 'native' people, such as those of Eliza Fraser, and the white woman of Gipps Land, provided a much more threatening and hostile picture of the Aboriginal people.[29] Barbara's experience of being rescued and looked after was not what people wanted to hear. The most well-known fictionalized account was written by Ion Idriess, and published under the title *Isles of Despair*, in 1947. *The Sun* newspaper in Sydney published two short, and somewhat sensationalized, articles about Barbara Thompson in 1975. In 1976, Patrick White published a book with the title *A Fringe of Leaves*, the phrase MacGillivray used to describe Barbara Thompson's state of undress. White's story certainly borrows elements from Barbara Thompson's tale, but it is not about her experiences, but rather those of Eliza Fraser, who was famously shipwrecked off Queensland in 1836 and was 'saved' from the Aborigines by a runaway convict. The most recent account appears in a chapter in Susan Geason's *Australian Heroines*, published in 2001.

JACKEY JACKEY received an inscribed brass breast-plate – the most elaborate kind – from Governor Charles FitzRoy on his return to Sydney from the search for Kennedy's remains – it is on deposit at the Mitchell Library in Sydney. What happened to him next is still a bit of a mystery. One version has it that he began to drift and drink and that he was burned to death, when he fell into a fire drunkenly, early in 1854, about 30 miles from Albury, on the New South Wales–Victoria border. Another version, far less dramatic, maintains that Jackey Jackey returned to his people in the district near the town of Singleton in the Hunter River Valley, New South Wales, and died there, possibly in the same year, 1854, from tuberculosis.[30]

THE NATURAL HISTORY COLLECTIONS of mammals, birds, reptiles, fish, insects and molluscs made by MacGillivray were deposited at the British Museum. Stanley's ethnographic collection of Torres Strait, New Guinea and Louisiade artefacts was catalogued by MacGillivray and deposited, likewise, at the British Museum. The Norwich and Ipswich museums received James Wilcox's collections. The Darnley Island mummy also found its way to the Norwich Castle Museum but was sold, with its head missing, to the Liverpool Museum in 1956, where it now resides.

THE *RATTLESNAKE* returned to sea in 1852 sailing to the opposite corner of the world, as part of the Franklin Arctic relief expedition. The ship was back in Plymouth in 1856, but the days of active service were over. The *Rattlesnake*'s final use was as a floating chapel at Newcastle-upon-Tyne, and soon thereafter, it was ordered to Chatham to be broken up, on the grounds that it was 'unfit for further service'. The ship's figurehead, however, was saved and remains in excellent condition to this day.

Acknowledgements

This book has been a labour of love but I could not have done it without the kindness and generosity of many individuals and institutions. I knew for some time that I wanted to write a book about the voyage of a scientific vessel in the nineteenth century, but it was not until my close friend David Hebb first told me about John MacGillivray and his long and subsequently difficult experience with the Admiralty that I was sent on the trail of the *Rattlesnake*.

The story I have written rests largely on unpublished material, journals, diaries, letters and reports. While much of it is scattered in public collections in the United Kingdom and in Australia, there are a few extremely valuable items that are in private hands. I would like to thank these individuals for their enormous generosity in sharing their material with me. David Richardson, who let me see and use John Thomson's letters and journal; Robert Boyle, who kindly lent me the Kennedy family letters; Lady Harrod, who invited me to read Ama and Carrie Boileau's diaries; and Patsy Grigg, who gave me access to the Deas Thomson correspondence. I would also like to thank Kay Barnett, a descendant of John MacGillivray, and Lyn Simpson, a descendant of James Wilcox, for generously inviting me to meet them and talk about their respective families; to David McGillivray for help on the MacGillivray clan; and Frank Mack and Maureen O'Shea who showed me around South Grafton where Wilcox lived, and where he and MacGillivray went into partnership dealing in natural history specimens. I would also like to thank Lord Stanley of Alderley who invited me to look at some of Owen Stanley's early sketchbooks; and to David Lambrick and Sue Long, who shared with me her knowledge of Port Essington and the Lambrick family.

To the staff of the many institutions where I found so much fascinating material, I wish to extend my warmest thanks. To the National Library of Scotland, and especially Sheila McKenzie who put me in touch with David Richardson; to the National Maritime Museum; to the United Kingdom Hydrographic Office, especially Adrian Webb and Sharon

Relph; to the Royal Botanic Gardens, especially Kate Pickard; to Imperial College, especially Hilary McEwan and Anne Barrett; to the Natural History Museum, especially Ann Datta, Carol Gocke and Susan Snell; to the Linnean Society, especially Gina Douglas; to the Museum of Archaeology and Anthropology, University of Cambridge, especially Anita Herle; to the Scott Polar Research Institute; to the Cheshire Record Office, Liverpool Record Office and the Record Office for Leicestershire, Leicester and Rutland; to the Royal Society; to the National Archives, Kew; to the Royal Geographical Society, especially Sarah Strong; to the Mitchell Library, State Library of New South Wales, especially Martin Beckett and Judy Nelson; to the National Library of Australia; to the John Oxley Library, State Library of Queensland, especially Kaye Nardella; to the Northern Territory Archive Service and the Northern Territory Library. Thanks also to Gill and Rick Croft, Clem Fisher, Stephen Foster, Susan Geason, Jill Hasall, Tony Irwin, Sara Joynes, Alan Lester, Luciana Martins, James McHugh, Stephen Plunkett, Bob Ralph, Helen Rozwadowski, Jane Samson, Larry Schaaf, Lynne Stumpe, Rebecca Ullrich, Alberto Vieira, Ian Wilkins and Adam Wilkinson, all of whom went out of their way to do special favours for me. To Bob Williams for information on Hutchinson Browne, to Brian Walsh and Jack Sullivan for help with Jackey Jackey and to Linda Rowe for talking me through Cape York.

For permission to use and quote from manuscript material in their possession, I would like to thank the following: The Cheshire Record Office; Imperial College, Library Archives and Special Collections; The Linnean Society; The Liverpool Record Office; The National Library of Australia; The National Maritime Museum; The National Archives; The Record Office for Leicestershire, Leicester and Rutland; The Royal Botanic Gardens; The Royal Geographical Society; The Royal Society; The Scott Polar Research Institute; The State Library of New South Wales; The State Library of Queensland; The Trustees of the Natural History Museum; and The United Kingdom Hydrographic Office.

At UMIST, my former institution, I would like to thank a number of people for their help and kindness. To Barbara Keeling of the Joule Library for cheerfully retrieving obscure material from far and wide; to Barrie Dale, Dale Littler and Jill Rubery for supporting this project and the time I devoted to it; and to Katia Tarasova for putting up with me.

Financial assistance to support the research was kindly made available by the British Academy and the Royal Society.

Many individuals, friends and colleagues, gave their precious time to me, to talk about my project and, especially, to read what I had written. I would like to thank them all. They are Richard Allen, Marina Carter, Adrian Desmond, Maria Lepowsky, Pedro Lowenstein, and Nigel Rigby; to Henry Volans at Faber and Faber for seeing the problems and how to fix them; to Janet Browne, Cathy Crawford, Eric Hirsch and Ludmilla Jordanova, who have heard me going on about the *Rattlesnake* for years, for their friendship, support and patience. And to Julian Loose, my editor at Faber and Faber, who not only listened to me and read my work, but most importantly believed in me and the book from the start.

As I said, I couldn't have written this book without all these people, but there is one person, more than anyone else, who has been with me throughout this whole long episode and who has given me everything that has made it possible. My partner Dallas heard me out, read everything I wrote, commented, edited, helped me re-write, and, despite all that, still managed to be good-humoured and loving. I dedicate this book to her.

J.G.

Bibliography

Allen, D. E., 'Huxley's Botanist Brother-In-Law', *Archives of Natural History* 11 (1983), 191–3.

Allen, David Elliston, *The Naturalist in Britain: A Social History*. Harmondsworth, Penguin, 1978.

Allen, Jim, 'The Archaeology of Nineteenth-Century British Imperialism: An Australian Case Study', *World Archaeology* 5 (1973), 44–60.

Allen, Jim, 'Port Essington –A Successful Limpet Port?', *Historical Studies* 15 (1972), 341–60.

Allen, Jim and Corris, Peter, eds., *The Journal of John Sweatman: A Nineteenth Century Voyage in North Australia and Torres Strait*. St Lucia, Queensland, University of Queensland Press, 1977.

Allen, Richard B., 'Passing Through a Perilous Transition: Capital, Labor, and the Transformation of the Mauritian Economy, 1810–1860', unpublished paper, 2001.

Allen, Richard, B., 'The Slender, Sweet Thread: Sugar, Capital and Dependency in Mauritius, 1860–1936', *Journal of Imperial and Commonwealth History* 16 (1988), 177–200.

Altick, Richard Daniel, *The Shows of London*. Cambridge, Massachusetts, Harvard University Press, 1978.

Angus, Max, *Simpkinson de Wesselow: Landscape Painter in Van Diemen's Land and the Port Philip District*. Hobart, Tasmania, Blubber Head Press, 1984.

Bach, John, 'The Maintenance of Royal Navy Vessels in the Pacific Ocean, 1825–1875', *The Mariner's Mirror* 56 (1970), 259–73.

Barker, Francis, Hulme, Peter and Iversen, Margaret, eds., *Cannibalism and the Colonial World*. Cambridge, Cambridge University Press, 1998.

Barley, Nigel, *White Rajah*. London, Little, Brown, 2002.

Barnes, John, 'Philip Carpenter 1776–1833', *The New Magic Lantern Journal* 3 (1984), 8–9.

Barrett, Paul H. ed., *The Collected Papers of Charles Darwin*. Chicago, Chicago University Press, 1977.

Bartlett, Christopher John, *Great Britain and Sea Power, 1815–1853*. Oxford, Clarendon, 1963.

Bartram, Lady Alfred, *Recollections of Seven Years Residence at the Mauritius or Ile de France, By a Lady*. London, James Cawthorn, 1830.

Bateson, Charles, *Gold Fleet for California: Forty-Niners from Australia and New Zealand*. Sydney, Ure Smith, 1963.

Bauss, Rudy, 'Rio de Janeiro, Strategic Base for Global Designs of the British Royal Navy, 1777–1815' in Symonds, Craig L., *New Aspects of Naval History*. Annapolis, Maryland, Naval Institute Press, 1981, 75–89.

Bauss, Rudy, 'The Critical Importance of Rio de Janeiro to British Interests, With Particular Attention to Australia in Her Formative Years, 1787–1805', *Journal of the Royal Australian Historical Society* 65 (1979), 145–72.

Beaglehole, J. G. ed., *The Journals of Captain James Cook on His Voyages of Discovery: The Voyage of the Endeavour 1768–1771*. Cambridge, Hakluyt Society, Cambridge University Press, 1955.

Beale, Edgar, *Kennedy of Cape York*. Adelaide, South Australia, Rigby, 1970.

Beale, Edgar, *Kennedy, The Barcoo and Beyond 1847*. Hobart, Tasmania, Blubber Head Press, 1983.

Beale, Edgar, 'Kennedy's Weymouth Bay Camp', *Journal of the Royal Australian Historical Society* 48 (1962), 230–34.

Beaton, P. C., 'A Martyr to Science', *Good Words* 9 (1868), 425–29.

Beechey, F. W., 'Hydrography' in Herschel, John Frederick William, ed. *A Manual of Scientific Enquiry*. London, John Murray, 1851, 52–107.

Bell, Gerda E., *Ernest [sic] Dieffenbach: Rebel and Humanist*. Palmerston North, New Zealand, The Dunmore Press, 1976.

Bernardin de Saint-Pierre, Jacques-Henri, *Paul and Virginia*. Translated from the French and with an Introduction by John Donovan. London, Peter Owen, 1982.

Bethell, Leslie, *The Abolition of the Brazilian Slave Trade: Britain, Brazil and the Slave Trade Question 1807–1869*. Cambridge, Cambridge University Press, 1970.

Bethell, Leslie and Carvalho, José Murilo de, 'Brazil from Independence to the Middle of the Nineteenth Century' in Bethell, Leslie, *The Cambridge History of Latin America. Volume III. From Independence to c. 1870*. Cambridge, Cambridge University Press, 1985, 679–746.

Boileau, Ama, 'Diary for 1846', LHC.

Boileau, Carrie, 'Diary for 1850', LHC.

Bowden, Ross, 'Maori Cannibalism: An Interpretation', *Oceania* 55 (1984), 81–99.

Boyd, Mark, *Reminiscences of Fifty Years*. London, Longmans, Green, 1871.

Bradlow, Frank Rosslyn, *Pictorial Album of Cape Town with Views of Simon's Town, Port Elizabeth, and Graham's Town*. Cape Town, C. Struik, 1966.

Bradshaw, T., *Views in the Mauritius, or Isle of France*. London, Published for the Proprietor by James Carpenter and Son, 1832.

Branagan, D. F., 'Phillip Parker King: Colonial Anchor Man' in Wheeler, Alwyne and Price, James H., eds., *From Linnaeus to Darwin: Commentaries on the History of Biology and Geology*. London, Society for the History of Natural History, 1985, 179–93.

Brock, W. H., 'Ernst Dieffenbach's Comments on the State of Chemistry in Britain in 1846', *Ambix* 47 (2000), 121–34.

Broeze, Frank J. A., 'British Intercontinental Shipping and Australia, 1813–1850', *Journal of Transport History* 4 (1978), 189–207.

Broeze, Frank J. A., 'Distance Tamed: Steam Navigation to Australia and New Zealand From Its Beginnings to the Outbreak of the Great War', *Journal of Transport History* 10 (1989), 1–21.

Browne, Janet, *Charles Darwin: Voyaging*. London, Pimlico, 1996.

Browner, Stephanie, 'Ideologies of the Anesthetic: Professionalism, Egalitarianism and the Ether Controversy', *American Quarterly* 51 (1999), 108–43.

Burkhardt, Frederick and Smith, Sydney, eds., *The Correspondence of Charles Darwin. Volume 3 1844–1846*. Cambridge, Cambridge University Press, 1987.

Calley, Graham, *The Pumpkin Settlements: Agriculture and Animals in Australia's First Northern Colonies*. Darwin, Northern Territory, Historical Society of the Northern Territory, 1998.

Cameron, J. M. R., *Letters from Port Essington, 1838–1845*. Darwin, Northern Territory, Historical Society of the Northern Territory, 1999.

Cameron, James, 'The Northern Settlements: Outposts of Empire', in Statham, Pamela, ed., *The Origins of Australia's Capital Cities*. Cambridge, Cambridge University Press, 1989, 271–91.

Cannon, Walter, F., 'Scientists and Broad Churchmen: An Early Victorian Intellectual Network', *Journal of British Studies* 4 (1964), 65–88.

Card, Charles James, 'Diary Kept on Board H.M.S. *Rattlesnake* 1847 to 1850', John Oxley Library, State Library of Queensland, OMR 97.

Carr, Julie E., *The Captive White Woman of Gipps Land: In Pursuit of the Legend*. Carlton South, Victoria, Melbourne University Press, 2001.

Carron, William, *Narrative of an Expedition Undertaken Under the Direction of the Late Mr. Assistant Surveyor E. B. Kennedy, for the Exploration of the Country Lying Between Rockingham Bay and Cape York*. Sydney, Kemp and Fairfax, 1849.

Cawood, John, 'Terrestrial Magnetism and the Development of International Collaboration in the Early Nineteenth Century', *Annals of Science* 34 (1977), 551–87.

Chadwick, Owen, *Victorian Miniature*. Cambridge, Cambridge University Press, 1991.

Chang, Hsin-pao, *Commissioner Lin and the Opium War*. Cambridge, Massachusetts, Harvard University Press, 1964.

Clark, James, *The Sanative Influence of Climate*. London, John Murray, 1841.

Clarke, C. G. Drury, 'Captain John Clements Wickham, R.N.: His Antecedents and Descendants', *Journal of the Royal Historical Society of Queensland* 12 (1984), 1–25.

Coltheart, Lenore, 'Australia Misère: The Northern Territory in the Nineteenth Century', unpublished Ph.D. dissertation, Griffith University, 1982.

Conrad, Robert Edgar, *World of Sorrow: The African Slave Trade to Brazil*. Baton Rouge, Louisiana, Louisiana State University Press, 1986.

Cook, Andrew, 'Alexander Dalrymple and the Hydrographic Office', in Frost, Alan and Samson, Jane, eds., *Pacific Empires: Essays in Honour of Glyndwr Williams*. Carlton South, Victoria, Melbourne University Press, 1999, pp. 53–68.

Cossart, Noël, *Madeira: The Island Vineyard*. London, Christie's Wine Publications, 1984.

Creed, Barbara and Hoorn, Jeanette, eds., *Body Trade: Captivity, Cannibalism and Colonialism in the Pacific*. New York, Routledge, 2001.

Crisswell, Colin M., *Rajah Charles Brooke: Monarch of All He Surveyed*. Kuala Lumpur, Oxford University Press, 1979.

Crowther, W. E. L. H., 'Dr. E. S. P. Bedford and His Hospital and Medical School of Saint Mary's, Van Diemen's Land', *The Medical Journal of Australia* (8 July 1944), 25–31.

Crowther, W. E. L. H., 'The Introduction of Surgical Anæsthesia in Van Diemen's Land', *The Medical Journal of Australia* (8 November 1947), 561–70.

Cumpston, J. H. L., *Thomas Mitchell: Surveyor General & Explorer*. Melbourne, Oxford University Press, 1954.

Dance, Peter S., *Shell Collecting: An Illustrated History*. London, Faber and Faber, 1966.

Darwin, Charles, *The Voyage of the 'Beagle'*. London, Dent, 1959.

David, Andrew, *The Voyage of HMS Herald*, Carlton, Victoria, Melbourne University Press, 1995.

Davidson, René, *Whalemen of Twofold Bay*. Eden, N.S.W., Privately Printed, 1988.

Dawson, L. S., *Memoirs of Hydrography*. Eastbourne, Henry W. Keay, 1885.

Day, Archibald, *The Admiralty Hydrographic Service 1795–1919*. London, H.M.S.O., 1967.

Deacon, Margaret, *Scientists and the Sea 1650–1900: A Study of Marine Science*. London, Academic Press, 1971.

Deerr, Noël, *The History of Sugar*. London, Chapman and Hall, 1949–50.

De Falbe, Jane, *My Dear Miss Macarthur: The Recollections of Emmeline Maria Macarthur, 1828–1911*. Kenthurst , N.S.W., Kangaroo Press, 1988.

De França, Isabella, *Journal of a Visit to Madeira and Portugal (1853–1854)*. Funchal, Junta Geral do Distrito Autónomo de Funchal, 1970.

Desmond, Adrian, *Huxley: From Devil's Disciple to Evolution's High Priest*. London, Penguin, 1998.

Desmond, Adrian and Moore, James, *Darwin*. London, Michael Joseph, 1991.

De Vries-Evans, Susanna, *Conrad Martens on the Beagle and in Australia*. Chapel Hill, Brisbane, Pandanus Press, 1993.

Diamond, Marion, *The Sea Horse and the Wanderer: Ben Boyd in Australia*. Carlton, Victoria, Melbourne University Press, 1988.

Driver, John, *Letters from Madeira in 1834*. Liverpool, Privately Published, 1838.

Duyker, Edward, *An Officer of the Blue: Marc-Joseph Marion Dufresne, South Sea Explorer, 1724–1772*. Carlton, Victoria, Melbourne University Press, 1994.

Earle, Peter, *Sailors: English Merchant Seamen 1650–1775*. London, Methuen, 1998.

'The Eight Stones' 1. *Nautical Magazine* (1837), 456–8.

'The Eight Stones' 2. *Nautical Magazine* (1843), 100–102.

Ellis, William, *Three Visits to Madagascar During the Years 1853–1854–1856*. London, John Murray, 1858.

Eltis, David, *Economic Growth and the Ending of the Atlantic Slave Trade*. New York, Oxford University Press, 1987.

Farber, Paul Lawrence, 'The Development of Taxidermy and the History of Ornithology', *Isis* 68 (1977), 550–66.

Featherstone, Donald, *Victorian Colonial Warfare: Africa*. London, Cassell, 1992.

Fisher, Clemency, 'Frederick Strange', unpublished entry for the *New Dictionary of National Biography*.

Fisher, Clemency, ed., *A Passion for Natural History: The Life and Legacy of the 13th Earl of Derby*. Liverpool, National Museums & Galleries on Merseyside, 2002.

Fisher, John R., 'British Veterinary Surgeons, The Australian Agricultural Company and the Early Years of the Indian Horse Trade', *Veterinary History* 9 (1997), 126–39.

Fitzpatrick, Kathleen Elizabeth, *Sir John Franklin in Tasmania 1837–1843*. Carlton, Victoria, Melbourne University Press, 1949.

Forbes, Edward, 'Letters from J. MacGillivray, Esq., Naturalist to H. M. Surveying Ship Rattlesnake, Capt. Stanley, R.N.', *The Annals and Magazine of Natural History* 2 (1848), 21–32.

Foster, Michael and Lankester, E. Ray, *The Scientific Memoirs of Thomas Henry Huxley*, volume 1. London, Macmillan, 1898.

Foster, Stephen G., *Colonial Improver: Edward Deas Thomson, 1800–1879*. Carlton, Victoria, Melbourne University Press, 1978.

Foster, William C., *Sir Thomas Mitchell and His World 1792–1855: Surveyor-General of New South Wales 1828–1855*. Sydney, The Institution of Surveyors N.S.W. Incorporated, 1985.

Friendly, Alfred, *Beaufort of the Admiralty: The Life of Sir Francis Beaufort, 1774–1857*. London, Hutchinson, 1977.

Gale, Robert, 'Journal Kept in H.M.S. *Rattlesnake* from 1846 to 1850', NMM/MSS/76/094.0 and NMM/MSS/76/094.1.

Gardner, George, *Travels in the Interior of Brazil: Principally Through the Northern Province*. London, Reeve Brothers, 1846.

Gilliard, Ernest Thomas, *Birds of Paradise and Bower Birds*. London, Weidenfeld & Nicolson, 1969.

Goodman, Jordan, 'Making Imperial Space: Settlement, Surveying and Trade in Northern Australia in the Nineteenth Century' in Killingray, David, Lincoln, Margarette and Rigby, Nigel, eds., *Maritime Empires: British Imperial Maritime Trade in the Nineteenth Century*. Woodbridge, Suffolk, Boydell, 2004, 128–41.

Goodsir, John, 'On the Anatomy of *Amphioxus lanceolatus*', *Transactions of the Royal Society of Edinburgh* 15 (1844), 247–63.

Gough, Barry M., 'Sea Power and South America: The "Brazils" or South American Station of the Royal Navy 1808–1837', *American Neptune* 50 (1990), 26–34.

Gough, Barry M., 'Specie Conveyance from the West Coast of Mexico in British Warships c. 1820–1870: An Aspect of the *Pax Britannica*', *The Mariner's Mirror* 69 (1983), 419–33.

Gould, John, 'A Brief Account of the Researches in Natural History of John M'Gillivray, Esq.' in Jardine, W. ed. *Contributions to Ornithology*. London, Reeve, Benham & Reeve, 1850, 92–105.

Gould, John, 'On New Species of Mammalia and Birds from Australia', *Proceedings of the Zoological Society of London* 17 (1849), 109–112.

Gould, John, 'On the Family *Procillaridae*, with Description of the New Species', *Annals and Magazine of Natural History* 8 (1844), 360–68.

Graden, Dale T., 'An Act "Even of Public Security": Slave Resistance, Social Tensions, and the End of the International Slave Trade to Brazil, 1835–1856', *Hispanic American Historical Review* 76 (1996), 249–82.

Graham, Gerald S., *Great Britain in the Indian Ocean: A Study of Maritime Enterprise 1810–1850*. Oxford, Clarendon, 1967.

Gregory, Desmond, *The Beneficent Usurpers: A History of the British in Madeira*. Rutherford, New Jersey, Fairleigh Dickinson University Press, 1988.

Grove, Richard H., *Green Imperialism: Colonial Expansion, Tropical Island Edens and the Origins of Environmentalism, 1600–1860*. Cambridge, Cambridge University Press, 1995.

Henningsen, Henning, *Crossing the Equator*. Copenhagen, Munksgaard, 1961.

Henry, David, 'Carpenter & Westley', *New Magic Lantern Journal 3* (1984), 8–9.

Herschel, John Frederick William, 'Meteorology' in Herschel, John Frederick William, ed. *A Manual of Scientific Enquiry*. London, John Murray, 1851, 280–336.

Herschel, John Frederick William, ed. *A Manual of Scientific Enquiry*. London, John Murray, 1851.

Historical Records of Australia. Series 1. Sydney, The Library Committee of the Commonwealth Parliament, 1914–1925.

Hogan, James Francis, *The Gladstone Colony: An Unwritten Chapter on Australian History*. London, T. Fisher Unwin, 1898.

Holland, Julian, 'Diminishing Circles: W.S. Macleay in Sydney, 1839–1865', *Historical Records of Australian Science* 11 (1996), 119–47.

Holman, James, *Travels in Madeira, Sierra Leone, Teneriffe, etc. etc.*. London, George Routledge, 1840.

Hordern, Marsden, *Mariners are Warned! John Lort Stokes and H.M.S. Beagle in Australia 1837–1843*. Carlton, Victoria, Melbourne University Press, 1989.

Hordern, Marsden, *King of the Australian Coast: The Work of Phillip Parker King in the Mermaid and Bathurst 1817–1822*. Carlton, Victoria, Melbourne University Press, 1997.

Horner, Frank, *Looking for Lapérouse: D'Entrecasteaux in Australia and the South Pacific, 1792–1793*. Carlton, Victoria, Melbourne University Press, 1995.

Hoskins, Janet, *Headhunting and the Social Imagination in Southeast Asia*. Stanford, California, Stanford University Press, 1996.

Howell, Brenda M., 'Mauritius, 1832–1849: A Study of a Sugar Colony', unpublished Ph.D. dissertation, University of London, 1951.

Hughes, Robert, *The Fatal Shore*, London, Collins Harvill, 1987.

Humanitas, 'Australian Surveys – Torres Strait', *Nautical Magazine* (1838), 200–202.

Huxley, Julian, ed., *T. H. Huxley's Diary of the Voyage of H.M.S. Rattlesnake*. Garden City, New York, Doubleday, Doran & Company, 1936.

Huxley, Leonard, *Life and Letters of Thomas Henry Huxley*. London, Macmillan and Co., 1900.

Huxley, Thomas Henry, 'Examination of the Corpuscles of the Blood of *Amphioxus lanceolatus*' in *Report of the Seventeenth Meeting of the British Association for the Advancement of Science Held at Oxford in June 1847*. London, John Murray, 1848.

Huxley, Thomas Henry, 'On the Anatomy and the Affinities of the Family of the *Medusæ*', *Transactions of the Royal Society* (1849), 413–34.

Huxley, Thomas Henry, 'Science at Sea', *Westminster Review* 61 (1854), 98–119.

Huxley, Mrs. Thomas Henry, 'Pictures of Australian Life, 1843–1844', *Cornhill Magazine* 31 (1911), 770–81.

Inskip, George Hastings, 'Diary kept on H.M.S. *Bramble*, 1849–1850', NLA/MS3784.

Iredale, Tom, 'The Last Letters of John MacGillivray', *Australian Zoologist* 9 (1937), 40–63.

Ireland, John, *The Shipwrecked Orphans: A True Narrative of the Shipwreck and Sufferings of John Ireland and William Doyley, Who Were Wrecked in the Ship Charles Eaton, On an Island in the South Seas.* London, [1838?].

Jobst, Keith, *A Pioneer Family of Queensland.* Brisbane, CopyRight, 1997.

Johnson, Robert Eugene, *Sir John Richardson: Arctic Explorer, Natural Historian, Naval Surgeon.* London, Taylor and Francis, 1976.

Johnston, Ross and Gregory, Helen, 'Choosing Brisbane' in Statham, Pamela, ed., *The Origins of Australia's Capital Cities.* Cambridge, Cambridge University Press, 1989, 235–51.

Johnston, Ross and Gregory, Helen, 'Brisbane: Making It Work' in Statham, Pamela, ed., *The Origins of Australia's Capital Cities.* Cambridge, Cambridge University Press, 1989, 252–68.

Jukes, Joseph Beete, *Narrative of the Surveying Voyage of H.M.S. Fly; Commanded by Capt. F. P. Blackwood in Torres Strait, New Guinea, and other Islands of the Eastern Archipelago, 1842–1846, Together with an Excursion into the Interior of the Eastern Part of Java.* London, T. & W. Boone, 1847.

Karasch, Mary, 'Rio de Janeiro: From Colonial Town to Imperial Capital (1808–1850)' in Ross, Robert and Telkamp, Gerard J. eds., *Colonial Cities: Essays on Urbanism in a Colonial Context.* Dordrecht, Martinus Nijhoff Publishers, 1985, pp. 123–51.

Karasch, Mary C., *Slave Life in Rio de Janeiro 1808–1850.* Princeton, New Jersey, Princeton University Press, 1987.

Keegan, Timothy, *Colonial South Africa and the Origins of the Racial Order.* Charlottesville, Virginia, University Press of Virginia, 1996.

Kennedy, Paul M., *The Rise and Fall of British Naval Mastery.* London, Allen Lane, 1976.

Kenworthy, Joan M. and Walker, J. Malcolm, *Colonial Observatories and Observations: Meteorology and Geophysics.* Occasional Publication No. 31, Department of Geography, University of Durham, 1997.

Kerr, Joan, ed., *The Dictionary of Australian Artists: Painters, Sketchers, Photographers and Engravers to 1870.* Melbourne, Oxford University Press, 1992.

King, Reverend Robert Lethbridge, 'Journal of a Voyage in H.M.S. *Rattlesnake*', ML/ML MSS.673/4.

Koebel, William Henry, *Madeira, Old and New.* London, G. Bell, 1909.

Lambert, Andrew, *The Last Sailing Battlefleet: Maintaining Naval Mastery 1815–1850.* London, Conway, 1991.

Langham-Carter, R. R., 'Farmer Peck's Inn', *Bulletin of the Simons Town Historical Society* 14 (1986), 24–7.

Larsen, Anne, 'Equipment for the Field' in Jardine, Nicholas, Secord, James A. and Spary, Emma C., eds., *Cultures of Natural History.* Cambridge, Cambridge University Press, 1996, 358–77.

Larsen, Anne Laurine, 'Not Since Noah: The English Scientific Zoologists and the Craft of Collecting, 1800–1840', unpublished Ph.D. dissertation, Princeton University, 1993.

Lawrence, Sarah and Staniforth, Mark, *The Archaeology of Whaling in Southern Australia and New Zealand*. Gundaroo, N.S.W., The Australasian Society for Historical Archaeology and The Australian Institute of Maritime Archaeology, 1998.

Le Cordeur, Basil and Saunders, Christopher, *The War of the Axe, 1847*. Johannesburg, The Brenthurst Press, 1981.

Legassick, Martin, 'The State, Racism and the Rise of Capitalism in the Nineteenth-Century Cape Colony', *South African Historical Journal* 28 (1993), 329–68.

Lester, Alan, '"Otherness" and the Frontiers of Empire: the Eastern Cape Colony, 1806–c.1850', *Journal of Historical Geography* 24 (1998), 2–19.

Lester, Alan, Nel, Etienne, and Binns, Tony, *South Africa, Past, Present and Future: Gold at The End of the Rainbow?*. Harlow, Longman, 2000.

Lestringant, Frank, *Cannibals: The Discovery and Representation of the Cannibal from Columbus to Jules Verne*. Berkeley, California, University of California Press, 1997.

Lewis, Michael, *The Navy in Transition 1814–1864: A Social History*. London, Hodder and Stoughton, 1965.

Lowe, Richard Thomas, *A History of the Fishes of Madeira*. London, J. Van Voorst, 1843–60.

Lowe, Richard Thomas, *Primitiæ Faunæ et Floræ Maderæ et Portus Sancti : sive Species quædam novæ vel hactenus minus rite cognitæ Animalium et Plantarum in his Insulis degentium breviter descriptæ*. Cambridge, 1831.

Lubbock, Adelaide, *Owen Stanley, R.N., 1811–1850, Captain of the Rattlesnake*. Melbourne, Heinemann, 1968.

Ly-Tio-Fane Pineo, Huguette, *In the Grips of the Eagle: Matthew Flinders at Ile de France, 1803–1810*. Moka, Mauritius, Mahatma Gandhi Institute, 1988.

Ly-Tio-Fane, M., 'Pierre Poivre et l'expansion française dans l'Indo-Pacifique', *Bulletin Economique Française d'Extrème Orient* 53 (1967), 453–511.

Macaulay, James, 'Notes on the Physical Geography, Geology, and Climate of the Island of Madeira', *Edinburgh New Philosophical Journal* 29 (1840), 336–75.

MacGillivray, John, 'Notes on Australian Natural History', *The Zoologist* 4 (1846), pp.1485–91.

MacGillivray, John, 'Letter to J. B. Jukes dated 16 October 1849', *Nautical Magazine* (1850), 236–7.

MacGillivray, John, 'Sketch of the Natural History of Such Portions of the Louisiade Archipelago and New Guinea, As Were Visited by H.M.S. 'Rattlesnake', June to September, 1849', *Journal of the Royal Geographical Society* 21 (1851), 15–18.

MacGillivray, John, *Narrative of the Voyage of H.M.S. Rattlesnake: Commanded by the Late Captain Owen Stanley, During the Years 1846–1850*. London, T. & W. Boone, 1852.

Macmillan, Allister, *Mauritius. Illustrated. Historical and Descriptive, Commercial and Industrial. Facts, Figures, & Resources*. London, W. H. & L. Collongridge, 1914.

Manchester, Alan K., *British Preeminence in Brazil, Its Rise and Decline: A Study in European Expansion*. Chapel Hill, North Carolina, University of North Carolina Press, 1933.

Markham, Robert Alfred Derrick, *A Rhino in the High Street: Ipswich Museum – The Early Years*. Ipswich, Ipswich Borough Council, 1990.

Martins, Luciana L., 'A Naturalist's Vision of the Tropics: Charles Darwin and the Brazilian Landscape', *Singapore Journal of Tropical Geography* 21 (2000), 19–33.

Martins, Luciana L. and Abreu, Mauricio A., 'Paradoxes of Modernity: Imperial Rio de Janeiro, 1808–1821', *Geoforum* 32 (2001), 533–550.

McAllan, Ian A.W., 'John Gilbert's Missing Months', *Memoirs of the Queensland Museum*. 35 (1994), 155–79.

McConnell, Anita, *No Sea Too Deep: The History of Oceanographic Instruments*. Bristol, Hilger, 1982.

McConnell, Anita, 'Six's Thermometer: A Century of Use in Oceanography' in Sears, Mary and Merriman, Daniel, eds., *Oceanography: The Past*. New York, Springer-Verlag, 1980, 252–65.

McInnes, Allan, 'The Wreck of the "Charles Eaton"', *Journal of the Royal Historical Society of Queensland* 11 (1983), 21–50.

McKenna, Mark, *Looking for Blackfellas' Point: An Australian History of Place*. Sydney, University of New South Wales Press, 2002.

McWilliam, James Ormiston, *Report on the Fever at Boa Vista. Presented to the House of Commons, In Pursuance of Their Address of the 16th March 1847*. London, T.R. Harrison, 1847.

Menhennet, David, 'International Bestseller: *Paul and Virginia* by Bernardin de Saint-Pierre', *The Book Collector* 38 (1989), 483–502.

Mezzadri, Tarq A., *150th Anniversary of the Death of Father Angelo Bartolomeo Confalonieri, 9 June 1848*. Darwin, Northern Territory, Dante Alighieri Italian Cultural Society, 1998.

Mitchell, Thomas Livingstone, 'Account of the Recent Exploring Expedition to the Interior of Australia', *Journal of the Royal Geographical Society* 7 (1837), 271–85.

Mitchell, Thomas Livingstone, *Journal of an Expedition into the Interior of Tropical Australia, In Search of a Route from Sydney to the Gulf of Carpentaria*. London, Longman, Brown, Green and Longmans, 1848.

Milton, John, *The Edges of War: A History of Frontier Wars (1702–1878)*. Cape Town, Juta & Co, Ltd, 1983.

Minchinton, Walter, 'Britain and Madeira to 1914' in *Colóquio Internacional de História da Madeira 1986*. Funchal, Governo Regional da Madeira, Secretaria Regional do Turismo, Cultura e Emigraçao, Direcçao Regional dos Assuntos Culturais, 1989, 498–521.

Moore, David R., *Islanders and Aborigines at Cape York*. Canberra, Australian Institute of Aboriginal Studies, 1979.

Morrell, Jack and Thackray, Arnold, eds., *Gentlemen of Science: Early Years of the British Association for the Advancement of Science* Oxford, Clarendon, 1981.

Morris, P.A., 'An Historical Review of Bird Taxidermy in Britain', *Archives of Natural History* 20 (1993), 241–55.

Mostert, Noël, *Frontiers: The Epic of South Africa's Creation and the Tragedy of the Xhosa People*. London, Jonathan Cape, 1992.

Murchison, Roderick I., 'Address to the Royal Geographical Society', *Journal of the Royal Geographical Society* 14 (1844), xlv–cxxviii.

Nash, Roy, *Scandal in Madeira*. Lewes, Book Guild, 1990.

Needell, Jeffrey D., *A Tropical Belle Epoque: Elite Culture and Society in Turn-of-the-Century Rio de Janeiro*. Cambridge, Cambridge University Press, 1987.

Nicholson, Ian, *Via Torres Strait*. Nambour, Queensland, Roebuck, 1996.

Nixon, Frederick Robert, *Sketches in Mauritius*. Port Louis, Mauritius, V. Devaux, 1848.

Owen, Richard, 'Zoology' in Herschel, John Frederick William, ed., *A Manual of Scientific Enquiry*. London, John Murray, 1851, 357–415.

Packe, Arthur, 'Private Journal Aboard H.M.S. *Rattlesnake* and H.M.S. *Bramble*, 1846–57', ROLLR/DE1672/15.

Pearson, Michael, 'Shore-Based Whaling at Twofold Bay', *Journal of the Royal Australian Historical Society* 71 (1985), 3–27.

Pearson, Michael, 'The Technology of Whaling in Australian Waters in the 19th Century', *Australian Historical Archaeology* 1 (1983), 40–54.

Phelts, Bev, 'Did Water Defeat the British on the Northern Territory Coast?: Why Did the Three British Colonies Fail?', unpublished paper, 2001.

Pike, Nicholas, *Sub-Tropical Rambles in the Land of the Aphanapteryx*. London, Sampson Low, Marston, Low, & Searle, 1873.

Plunkett, Stephen J., 'Ipswich Museum Moralities in the 1840s and 1850s', unpublished paper, 2001.

Porter, James G., *A Family of Islands*. Moorooka, Brisbane, Boolarong Press, 2000.

Prestwich, Joseph, 'Tables of Temperatures of the Sea at Different Depths Beneath the Surface', *Philosophical Transactions of the Royal Society* 165 (1875), 587–674.

Pridham, Charles, *England's Colonial Empire: An Historical and Statistical Account of the Empire; Its Colonies and Dependencies. Volume 1. The Mauritius and Its Dependencies*. London, T. and W. Boone, 1849.

Priestley, Susan, 'Melbourne: A Kangaroo Advance' in Statham, Pamela, ed., *The Origins of Australia's Capital Cities*. Cambridge, Cambridge University Press, 1989, 216–232.

Pryer, G., 'Angelo Bernardo Confalonieri' in Carment, David, Maynard, Robyn, and Powell, Alan, *Northern Territory Dictionary of Biography. Volume One: To 1945*. Darwin, Northern Territory, NTU Press, 1990, 58–60.

Quoy, Jean René Constant and Gaimard, Paul, *Voyage de découvertes de l'Astrolabe, executée par ordre du roi, pendant les années 1826–1827–1828–1829, sous le commandement de M. J. Dumont d'Urville. Zoologie*. Paris, J Tasu, 1830–1833.

Ralph, Robert, 'John MacGillivray – His Life and Work', *Archives of Natural History* 20 (1993), 185–95.

Reece, Bob, 'The Australasian Career of George Windsor Earl', *Journal of the Malaysian Branch of the Royal Asiatic Society* 65 (1992), 39–67.

Rehbock, Philip F., 'The Early Dredgers: "Naturalizing" in British Seas, 1830–1850', *Journal of the History of Biology* 12 (1979), 293–368.

Reid, Brian, 'Malaria in Nineteenth Century British Military Settlements', *Journal of Northern Territory History* 3 (1992), 41–54.

Rimmer, Gordon, 'Hobart: A Moment of Glory' in Statham, Pamela, ed., *The Origins of Australia's Capital Cities*. Cambridge, Cambridge University Press, 1989, 97–117.

Rimmer, W.G., *Portrait of a Hospital The Royal Hobart*. Hobart, Tasmania, Royal Hobart Hospital, 1981.

Riviere, Lindsay, *Historical Dictionary of Mauritius*. London, Scarecrow, 1982.

Robinson, Philip, 'Traduction ou trahison de *Paul et Virginie*: l'exemple de Helen Maria Williams', *Revue d'Histoire Littéraire de la France* (1989), 843–55.

Roget, I. L., 'Her Majesty's Marine Painter, Sir Oswald Brierly', *Art Journal* 50 (1887), 129–34.

Rouillard, Guy, *Le Jardin des Pamplemousses 1729–1979: histoire et botanique*. Les Pailles, Mauritius, General Printing & Stationery Company, 1983.

Samson, Jane, 'An Empire of Science: The Voyage of HMS *Herald*, 1845–1851', in Alan Frost and Jane Samson, eds., *Pacific Empires: Essays in Honour of Glyndwr Williams*. Carlton South, Victoria, Melbourne University Press, 1999, pp. 69–85.

Sauer, Gordon C., *John Gould The Bird Man: Correspondence, Volume 3*. Mansfield Centre, Connecticut, Maurizio Martino, 1999.

Sauer, Gordon C., *John Gould The Bird Man: Correspondence, Volume 4*. Mansfield Centre, Connecticut, Maurizio Martino, 2001.

Saunders, Suzanne, 'Malaria: Its Effect on the Early European Settlement of the Northern Territory', *Journal of Northern Territory History* 1 (1990), 1–14.

Savours, Ann, *The Search for the Northwest Passage*. London, Chatham, 1999.

Savours, Ann and McConnell, Anita, 'The History of the Rossbank Observatory, Tasmania', *Annals of Science* 39 (1982), 527–564.

Schaffer, Kay, *In the Wake of First Contact: The Eliza Fraser Stories*. Cambridge, Cambridge University Press, 1995.

Sharpe, Philip Ruffle, 'Jottings of Past Years', Book I and II, NMM/SHP1 and NMM/SHP2.

Shaw, Alan, 'The Founding of Melbourne' in Statham, Pamela, ed., *The Origins of Australia's Capital Cities*. Cambridge, Cambridge University Press, 1989, 199–215.

Shineberg, Dorothy, *They Came for Sandalwood*. Carlton, Victoria, Melbourne University Press, 1967.

Silva, Fernando Augusto da, and Meneses, Carlos Azevedo da, *Elucidário Madeirense*. Funchal, Secreteria Regional da Educação e Cultura, 1978.

Spillett, Peter G., *Forsaken Settlement: An Illustrated History of the Settlement of Victoria, Port Essington, North Australia 1838–1849*. Melbourne, Landsdowne, 1972.

Stanley, Arthur Penrhyn, *Memoirs of Edward and Catherine Stanley*. London, J. Murray, 1879.

Stanley, Edward, *Address Delivered on Board H.M.S. 'Rattlesnake'*. London, William Clowes and Sons, 1850.

Stanley, Owen, 'On the Lengths and Velocities of Waves', *Report of the Eighteenth Meeting of the British Association for the Advancement of Science Held at Swansea in August 1848*. London, John Murray, 1849.

Stokes, John Lort, *Discoveries in Australia*. London, T. & W. Boone, 1846.

313

Stubbings, H. G., 'H. M. S. *Rattlesnake*', *Journal of the Royal Naval Scientific Service* 19 (1964), 149–53.

Sullivan, Jack, *A Fortunate Liaison: Dr Adoniah Vallack and Jackey Jackey*. Paterson, N.S.W., Paterson Historical Society, 2003.

Thomson, Charles Wyville, *The Depths of the Sea*. London, Macmillan and Co., 1873.

Thomson, John, 'Journal Kept on Board H.M.S. *Rattlesnake* 1848', DRC.

Thomson, Keith Stewart, *HMS Beagle: The Story of Darwin's Ship*. New York, W.W. Norton, 1995.

Tizzard, T. H., *List of British Discovery & Survey Vessels From The Earliest Time to 1900*. London, H.M.S.O., 1900.

Toussaint, Auguste, *Port Louis: A Tropical City*. London, George Allen & Unwin, 1973.

Townsend, Norma, 'Memoir of a Minor Mariner: Thomas Beckford Simpson and New South Wales, 1839–1853', *The Great Circle* 5 (1983), 105–115.

Tredgold, Arderne, *Bay Between the Mountains*. Cape Town, Human & Rousseau, 1985.

Tremewan, Peter, *French Akaroa: An Attempt to Colonise Southern New Zealand*. Christchurch, New Zealand, University of Canterbury Press, 1990.

Van Arsdel, R., 'The Westminster Review' in Houghton, W. E., ed., *The Wellesley Index to Victorian Periodicals 1824–1900 Volume 3*. Toronto, University of Toronto Press, 1979, 529–58.

Webster, John, *The Last Cruise of 'The Wanderer'*. Sydney, F. Cunninghame, [1854?].

Wellings, H. P., *Eden & Twofold Bay: Discovery, Early History and Points of Interest 1797–1965*. Eden, N.S.W., Eden Killer Whale Museum, 1996.

Wellings, H. P., *Shore Whaling at Twofold Bay*. Eden, N.S.W., Privately Printed, 1964.

Wells, William Henry, *A Geographical Dictionary or Gazetteer of the Australian Colonies*. Sydney, W. & F. Ford, 1848.

White, Robert, *Madeira, Its Climate and Scenery*. London, Cradock & Co., 1851.

Whittell, H. M., 'Frederick Strange', *Australian Zoologist* 11 (1947), 96–114.

Wilde, William Robert, *Narrative of a Voyage to Madeira, Tenerife and Along the Shores of the Mediterranean*. Dublin, W. Curry and Co., 1840.

Winsor, Mary P., *Starfish, Jellyfish, and the Order of Life: Issues in Nineteenth-Century Science*. New Haven, Connecticut, Yale University Press, 1976.

Winter, Alison, 'Ethereal Epidemic: Mesmerism and the Introduction of Inhalation Anaesthesia to Early Victorian London', *Society for the History of Medicine* 4 (1991), 1–27.

Wood, Fanny Anne Burney, *A Great-Niece's Journals*. London, Constable, 1926.

Woolfall, S. J., 'History of the 13th Earl of Derby's Menagerie and Aviary at Knowsley Hall, Liverpool (1806–1851)', *Archives of Natural History* 17 (1990), 1–47.

Abbreviations

BC	Boyle Collection, Private.
BPP	British Parliamentary Papers.
CRO	Cheshire Record Office, Chester.
DL	Dixson Library, State Library of New South Wales, Sydney
DRC	David Richardson Collection, Private.
DTP	Deas Thomson Papers, Private.
HRA	Historical Records of Australia
IC	Imperial College, London.
LHC	Lady Harrod Collection, Private.
LRO	Liverpool Record Office, Liverpool.
LS	Linnean Society, London.
ML	Mitchell Library, State Library of New South Wales, Sydney.
NHM(A)	Natural History Museum, Archives, London.
NHM(Z)	Natural History Museum, Zoology Library, London.
NLA	National Library of Australia, Canberra.
NMM	National Maritime Museum, Greenwich.
PRO	Public Record Office, Kew.
RBG	Royal Botanic Garden, Kew.
RGS	Royal Geogrpahical Society
ROLLR	Record Office for Leicestershire, Leicester and Rutland, Leicester.
RS	Royal Society, London.
SPRI	Scott Polar Research Institute, Cambridge.
UKHO	United Kingdom Hydrographic Office, Taunton.

Notes

Substantive manuscript material, such as journals and diaries, and published works, which were widely used in the preparation of this book, are listed in the notes with shortened titles. A full record for each of these items can be found in the Bibliography. The full bibliographical record for other manuscript material, such as correspondence and reports, and for a few lightly used materials, is given in the notes.

CHAPTER I

1 Cook, 'Alexander Dalrymple'.
2 Day, *The Admiralty* and Dawson, *Memoirs*.
3 *The Times*, 24 December 1836, p. 3.
4 *The Times*, 31 August 1837, p. 6 and Ireland, *The Shipwrecked*.
5 *The Times*, 31 August 1837, p. 3.
6 Minutes, 12 December 1836, RGS/Council Minute Book, 1830–41/210.
7 Humanitas, 'Australian'.
8 Friendly, *Beaufort*.
9 Day, *The Admiralty*, p. 52.
10 Bartlett, *Great Britain* and Lambert, *The Last*.
11 Desmond and Moore, *Darwin* and Browne, *Charles Darwin*.
12 Quoted in Friendly, *Beaufort*, p. 255.
13 Savours, *The Search*.
14 Beaglehole, *The Journals*.
15 Hordern, *King*.
16 Tizzard, *List of British*, Dawson, *Memoirs* and Broeze, 'British'.
17 Stokes, *Discoveries, vol. 1*, pp. 6–16.
18 Cameron, *Letters*, p. 2–7.
19 Stokes, *Discoveries, vol. 1*, pp. 359–60.
20 Stokes, *Discoveries, vol. 2*, pp. 437.
21 Hordern, *Mariners* and Thomson, *HMS Beagle*.
22 UKHO/MB3/335–6.
23 UKHO/MB3/409–10.
24 UKHO/MB3/412.
25 Jukes, *Narrative*.
26 UKHO/LB12/127.
27 Beaufort to Blackwood, 29 April 1843, UKHO/LB11/154.
28 UKHO/SL29/76 and 77.
29 Beaufort to Blackwood, 31 May 1844, UKHO/LB12/70.

CHAPTER II

1 Cannon, 'Scientists'; Morrell and Thackray, *Gentlemen*.
2 Tremewan, *French Akaroa*.
3 Fitzpatrick, *Sir John Franklin*.
4 Beaufort to Stanley, 24 October 1844, UKHO/LB12/209–10; Beaufort to Stanley, 11 November 1844, UKHO/LB12/225; Beaufort to Stanley, 8 December 1845, UKHO/LB13/242.
5 Owen to Mary, 29 January 1846, NMM/XSTA1/6.
6 Owen to Mary, 29 January 1846, NMM/XSTA1/4.
7 Dawson, *Memoirs*, I, pp. 94–5.
8 Owen to Mary, 28 January 1846, NMM/XSTA1/5.
9 Beaufort to Vidal, 7 March 1846; UKHO/LB13/333.
10 Vidal to Beaufort, 11 March 1846, UKHO/SL13b.
11 Owen to Mary, 8 April 1846, NMM/XSTA1/21 and Gale, 'Journal'.
12 Owen to Mary, 15 April 1846, NMM/XSTA1/22.
13 Carrie Boileau, 'Diary' and Ama Boileau, 'Diary'.
14 Chadwick, *Victorian*, pp. 58–74 and 121–5; Lubbock, *Owen Stanley*, pp. 159–68 and Ama Boileau, 'Diary'.
15 Owen to Mary, 28 January 1846, NMM/XSTA1/5.
16 Edye to Beaufort, 5 April 1846, UKHO/Pre-1857/E3.
17 Bartlett, *Great Britain*, p. 342.
18 Stubbings, 'H.M.S. *Rattlesnake*', pp. 149–150; Chang, *Commissioner Lin*, p. 209.
19 Beaufort to Sir William, 8 April 1846, UKHO/Pre-1857/E3.
20 Edye to Beaufort, 5 April 1846, UKHO/Pre-1857/E3; Samson, 'An Empire'.
21 UKHO/MB5/274.
22 Beaufort to Stanley, 11 May 1846, UKHO/LB13/406.
23 Lubbock, *Owen Stanley*, p. 169.
24 11 June 1846, UKHO/MB5/306.
25 Gale, 'Journal'.
26 Lubbock, *Owen Stanley*, pp. 175–6
27 Owen to Mary, no date, NMM/XSTA1/30.
28 Owen to Mary, 11 October 1846, NMM/XSTA1/39.
29 Owen to Mary, 19 July 1846, NMM/XSTA1/24.
30 Huxley, *Life and Letters*, p. 25.
31 Stanley to Herschel, 29 June 1846, RS/HS17:229.
32 Stanley to Miles, 18 October 1846, UKHO/SL15c.
33 Owen to Mary, 23 September 1846, NMM/XSTA1/34 and Stanley to Beaufort, 15 November 1846, UKHO/SL15c.
34 Gale, 'Journal' and PRO/ADM38/8835.
35 PRO/ADM2/1542/416 and PRO/ADM2/1659/258.
36 This can be found attached to PRO/ADM2/1659/258.
37 Desmond, *Huxley*, pp. 3–35.
38 Desmond, *Huxley*, pp. 34–37.

39 Desmond, *Huxley*, pp. 36–41; Johnson, *John Richardson*.

40 Huxley, *Life and Letters*, p. 25; Desmond, *Huxley*, p. 42.

41 Huxley, *Life and Letters*, p. 25.

42 Huxley, *Life and Letters*, p. 27.

43 PRO/ADM196/8/319.

44 Stanley to Thomson, 10 June 1846, DRC Letters.

45 John Thomson to Mary Arthur, 18 June 1846, DRC Letters.

46 Owen to Mary, 13 November 1846, NMM/XSTA1/51.

47 Stanley to Beaufort, 2 October 1846, UKHO/SL15c.

48 Owen to Louisa, 19 October 1846, CRO/DSA199.

49 Stanley to Becher, 20 October 1846, UKHO/SL15c.

50 Stanley to Beaufort, 15 November 1846, UKHO/SL15c.

51 Owen to Mary, 19 July 1846, NMM/XSTA1/24; Owen to Mary, 5 August 1846, NMM/XSTA1/25; Owen to Mary 17/19 October 1846, NMM/XSTA1/45 and Stanley to Ogle, 19 October 1846, UKHO/SL15f/10.

52 Owen to Mary, 17/19 October 1846, NMM/XSTA1/45.

53 Owen to Louisa, 19 October 1846, CRO/DSA199.

54 PRO/ADM2/1544/134–135.

55 Bartlett, *Great Britain*, pp. 187–8.

56 Stanley to Becher, 5 November 1846, UKHO/SL15c.

57 Stanley to Becher, 5 November 1846, UKHO/SL15c.

58 Stanley to Becher, 18 October 1846, UKHO/SL15c

59 Owen to Louisa, 4 November 1846, CRO/DSA199.

60 Stanley to Becher, 5 November 1846, UKHO/SL15c.

61 Stanley to Becher, 5 November 1846, UKHO/SL15c.

62 Stanley to Beaufort, 15 November 1846, UKHO/SL15c.

63 Stanley to Beaufort, 15 November 1846, UKHO/SL15c.

64 Stanley to Ogle, 14 November 1846, UKHO/SL15f/22–3 and Stanley to Beaufort, 15 November 1846, UKHO/SL15c.

65 Stanley to Beaufort, 15 November 1846, UKHO/SL15c.

66 Stanley to Becher, 5 November 1846, UKHO/SL15c.

67 Stanley to Becher, 8 November 1846, UKHO/SL15c.

68 Fisher, *A Passion*; Woolfall, 'History' and MacGillivray to Harley, 27 June 1846, ROLLR/13D56/7/fol.41.

69 The Australian observations were published in *The Zoologist*, vol. 4 (1846); Ralph, 'John MacGillivray'.

70 Hooker to Beaufort, 11 April 1846, UKHO/Pre-1857/H902.

71 Burkhardt and Smith, *Correspondence 3*, pp. 319–20; Bell, *Ernest [sic] Dieffenbach*; Brock, 'Ernst Dieffenbach's'. Dieffenbach had taken an enlightened view of native New Zealanders and respected their title to the land on which they lived, a view which his masters did not share and which they wished he would not make public. He paid no attention to them and, instead, made his views public in the published account of his experiences in New Zealand. There were also rumours of other kinds of disagreements but nothing very specific. News of Dieffenbach's difficulties had

spread within scientific circles in England. Darwin was unsure about the man.

72 Owen to Mary, 15 April 1846, NMM/XSTA1/22.

73 Huxley, *Life and Letters*, pp. 215–6.

74 In mid-July 1846, word was received that Thomas Edmonstone, who was out with HMS *Herald* on the western coast of South America as naturalist, had been accidentally killed by a gunshot at the end of January near Guayaquil. Seemann was ordered to take his place and set sail for Panama in September 1846 – Beaufort to Hooker, 15 July 1846, RBG/DC24/53; Beaufort to Kellett, 16 July 1846, UKHO/LB14/45.

75 MacGillivray to Harley, 27 June 1846, ROLLR/13D56/7/fol.41.

76 Stanley to Beaufort, 29 July 1846, UKHO/SL15c.

77 MacGillivray to Harley, 4 August 1846, ROLLR/13D56/7/fol. 54; Becher to MacGillivray, 28 October 1846, UKHO/LB14/169.

78 Miles to Stanley, 7 December 1846, UKHO/LB14/228.

79 Bishop Stanley to William Hooker, 29 July 1846, RBG/DC24/437; Markham, *A Rhino*; Plunkett, 'Ipswich'.

80 Owen to Mary, 4 October 1846, NMM/XSTA1/38 and Becher to Stanley, 9 October 1846, UKHO/LB14/144.

81 UKHO/MB5/398. The correspondence relating to the armaments issue can be found in PRO/ADM/1542, 1543 and 1544.

82 PRO/ADM2/1544/133.

83 Quoted in Lubbock, *Owen Stanley*, p. 179.

84 Mary to Louisa, 22 November 1846, CRO/DSA132/1.

85 PRO/ADM2/1544/152.

86 Mary to Louisa, 22 November 1846, CRO/DSA132/1 and PRO/ADM2/1544/152.

87 PRO/ADM2/1659/484–485.

88 Owen to Mary, 2 November 1846, NMM/XSTA1/48 and Owen to Mary, 16 November 1846, NMM/XSTA1/52.

89 Owen to Mary, 16 November 1846, NMM/XSTA1/52.

90 Packe, 'Private Journal'.

91 Gale, 'Journal' and Lubbock, *Owen Stanley*, p. 183.

92 Henry, 'Carpenter & Westley'; Barnes, 'Philip Carpenter' and Altick, *The Shows*, pp. 219–20.

93 Owen to Mary, no date, NMM/XSTA1/19; Mary to Louisa, 28 November 1846, CRO/DSA 132/1 and Lubbock, *Owen Stanley*, p. 182.

94 Bishop Stanley to Owen Stanley, 25 December 1847, CRO/DSA200.

95 PRO/ADM2/1544/201–202.

96 Lewis, *The Navy*, pp. 212, 244 and Gough, 'Specie'.

97 Owen to Mary, 22 November 1846, NMM/XSTA1/54.

98 Packe, 'Private Journal' and Lubbock, *Owen Stanley*, p. 180.

99 Packe, 'Private Journal' and Mary Stanley to Louisa Stanley, 28 November 1846, CRO/DSA132/1.

100 UKHO/MB6/13.

101 The revised memorandum is in PRO/ADM2/1544/207–16; the original, i.e. without mention of specie shipment, is in UKHO/MB6/1–4.

102 Stanley to Becher, 5 November 1846 and Stanley to Beaufort, 15 November 1846, UKHO/SL15c.
103 Stanley had been told to take Denison with him in early October – Owen to Mary, 5 October 1846, NMM/XSTA1/41; also Owen to Mary, 6 August 1846, NMM/XSTA1/26.
104 King, 'Journal', pp. 1–2.
105 Stanley, *Address*, p. 5. He was both Bishop of Norwich and President of the Linnean Society from 1837 to 1849.
106 Stanley, *Address*, p. 7.
107 King, 'Journal'.
108 Huxley, *T.H. Huxley's Diary*, p. 8.

CHAPTER III

1 John Thomson to Mary Thomson, 20 December 1846, DRC Letters
2 PRO/ADM 196/8/319.
3 King, 'Journal', p. 10.
4 King, 'Journal', p. 10.
5 MacGillivray to Harley, 1 May 1847, ROLLR/13D56/8/12.
6 King, 'Journal', p. 10; Beaufort to Stanley, 28 November 1846, UKHO/LB14/211 and 'The Eight Stones'(1), p. 457.
7 'The Eight Stones'(2).
8 Stanley to Beaufort, 26 December 1846, UKHO/SL15c.
9 McConnell, *No Sea*, pp. 25–31.
10 King, 'Journal', p. 11.
11 King, 'Journal', p. 13.
12 MacGillivray, *Narrative*, v.1, p. 11.
13 Huxley, *T.H. Huxley's Diary*, p. 10.
14 Holman, *Travels*, p. 29; MacGillivray, *Narrative*, v.1, p.11; White, *Madeira*, pp. 167–8 and Silva and Meneses, *Elucidário*, vol. 3, pp. 98–99.
15 There were probably about the same number of British visitors annually as there were residents – Silva and Meneses, *Elucidário*, vol. 2, p. 161.
16 Koebel, *Madeira*.
17 Gregory, *The Beneficent*, pp. 21–23, 125; Cossart, *Madeira*, pp. 23–71, 179–81 and Minchinton, 'Britain and Madeira'.
18 Clark, *The Sanative*, p. 272.
19 A number of books, not unlike contemporary guidebooks, appeared during the first half of the nineteenth century, telling visitors about what they would expect on the island, places to visit, costs of upkeep, things to do, and so on. Early examples included Driver, *Letters* and Wilde, *Narrative*. A comprehensive guide first appeared in 1851 – White, *Madeira*.
20 De França, *Journal*, p. 62.
21 De França, *Journal*, p. 143.
22 For example, *Primitiæ* and *A History*.

23 Gregory, *The Beneficent*, pp. 82–4. The Lowe affair is described in some detail in Nash, *Scandal*, pp. 38–51.

24 Gregory, *The Beneficent*, p. 84.

25 Gregory, *The Beneficent*, p. 85 and Nash, *Scandal*, pp. 66–110.

26 Gregory, *The Beneficent*, p. 85 and Nash, *Scandal*, pp. 123–127.

27 Charles Edward Stanley to Catherine Stanley, 2 November 1846, CRO/DSA 198.

28 De França, *Journal*, p. 81.

29 Packe, 'Private Journal' and Owen to Mary, 19 July 1846, NMM/XSTA1/24.

30 Wood, *A Great-Niece's Journals*, p. 186.

31 John Thomson to Mary Thomson, 20 December 1846, DRC Letters.

32 Packe, 'Private Journal'.

33 John Thomson to Mary Thomson, 20 December 1846, DRC Letters.

34 King, 'Journal', pp. 16–17 and Cossart, *Madeira*, pp. 38–40.

35 Packe, 'Private Journal' and Cossart, *Madeira*, p. 179.

36 Catherine Stanley (Mother) to Owen Stanley, 26 July 1847, CRO/DSA79.

37 John Thomson to Mary Thomson, 20 December 1846, DRC Letters.

38 There was some discussion at the time about how the Curral was formed. An oceanic volcanic eruption was strongly suspected – Macaulay, 'Notes'.

39 MacGillivray, *Narrative*, v.1, p. 14.

40 King, 'Journal', p. 17; MacGillivray, *Narrative*, v.1, p. 13 and 337.

41 John Thomson to Mary Thomson, 20 December 1846, DRC Letters.

42 John Thomson to Mary Thomson, 20 December 1846, DRC Letters.

43 Forbes, 'Letters', p. 21.

44 Forbes, 'Letters', p. 21.

45 Forbes, 'Letters', p. 21 and MacGillivray to Harley, 1 May 1847, ROLLR/13D56/8/12.

46 King, 'Journal', p. 9 (Friday 11 December 1846) and John Thomson to Mary Thomson, 20 December 1846, DRC Letters.

47 Stanley to Beaufort, 26 December 1846, UKHO/SL15c.

48 Huxley, *T.H. Huxley's Diary*, p. 13.

49 Packe, 'Private Journal'.

50 King, 'Journal', p. 21.

51 Packe, 'Private Journal'.

52 Lubbock, *Owen Stanley*, pp. 21, 85.

53 Stanley's sketches of Rio when on HMS *Ganges* and *Forte* are in the National Maritime Museum, London, and in the National Library of Australia, Canberra, and those on HMS *Britomart* are in the Mitchell Library, Sydney, and the Tasmanian Museum and Art Gallery, Hobart.

54 Beaufort to Stanley, 28 November 1846, UKHO/LB14/212.

55 Owen to Mary, 4 November 1846, NMM/XSTA1/49 and 22 November 1846, NMM/XSTA1/54.

56 Gale, 'Journal'.

57 King, 'Journal', p. 22.

58 Larsen, 'Equipment'.

59 MacGillivray, *Narrative*, v.1, p. 27.

60 King, 'Journal' p. 22.

61 Huxley, *T.H. Huxley's Diary*, p. 8.

62 Huxley, *T.H. Huxley's Diary*, p. 8.

63 Huxley, *T.H. Huxley's Diary*, pp. 8–9.

64 Desmond, *Huxley*, p. 43.

65 Desmond, *Huxley*, pp. 56–7.

66 Huxley, *Life and Letters*, p. 28 and Huxley, 'Examination'.

67 Huxley, *Life and Letters*, p. 27.

68 Huxley, *T.H. Huxley's Diary*, p. 14.

69 Huxley, *T.H. Huxley's Diary*, p. 13; Darwin, *The Voyage*, pp. 4–5 and Barrett, *The Collected Papers*, pp. 199–203. Darwin read a paper in which he discussed the composition of this dust – largely microscopic plant and animal organisms – at a meeting of the Geological Society in London on 4 June 1845. It was subsequently published in the Society's Journal in the following year.

70 McWilliam, *Report*.

71 Packe, 'Private Journal'.

72 Thomson, 'Journal' and Huxley, *T.H. Huxley's Diary*, p. 15.

73 King, 'Journal', p. 26 and Packe, 'Private Journal'.

74 Forbes, 'Letters', p. 22.

75 King, 'Journal', p. 25.

76 John MacGillivray to James Harley, 1 May 1847, ROLLR/13D56/8/12 and John MacGillivray to John Gould, 6 February 1848, ML/FM4/2231.

77 Thomson, 'Journal'.

78 Thomson, 'Journal'.

79 MacGillivray, *Narrative*, v.1, pp. 14–15.

80 King, 'Journal', p. 24.

81 Henningsen, *Crossing*.

82 Thomson, 'Journal'.

83 Huxley, *T.H. Huxley's Diary*, p. 17 and King, 'Journal', p. 24.

84 King, 'Journal', p. 24.

85 Sharpe, 'Jottings'.

86 John MacGillivray to James Harley, 1 May 1847, ROLLR/13D56/8/12.

87 Huxley, *T.H. Huxley's Diary*, p. 17.

88 Thomson, 'Journal' and King, 'Journal', p. 36.

89 John Thomson to Mary Thomson, 24 January 1847, DRC Letters.

90 King, 'Journal', p. 35.

91 Huxley, *T.H. Huxley's Diary*, p. 17 and Winsor, *Starfish*, pp. 74–5.

92 Huxley, *Life and Letters*, p. 32.

93 Huxley, *T.H. Huxley's Diary*, p. 17.

94 Huxley, *Life and Letters*, p. 31.

95 John MacGillivray to James Harley, 1 May 1847, ROLLR/13D56/8/12.

96 MacGillivray, *Narrative*, v.1, pp. 17–18.

97 John Thomson to Mary Thomson, 24 January 1847, DRC Letters.

98 Darwin, *The Voyage*, pp. 17–36 and Martins, 'A Naturalist's Vision'.

99 Karasch, 'Rio de Janeiro', p. 138. The 1849 census, an accurate one, showed Rio to have a population of 205,906.

100 Bethell, *The Abolition*, pp. 27–61.

101 Graden, 'The End'; Eltis, *Economic Growth*, pp. 243–4 and Bethell and de Carvalho, 'Brazil'.

102 Manchester, *British*, pp. 220–63.

103 Kennedy, *The Rise*, p. 171. These squadrons accounted for 40% of the total number of British warships stationed in foreign parts.

104 Bauss, 'Rio de Janeiro'; Bauss, 'The Critical Importance'; Gough, 'Sea Power' and Bach, 'The Maintenance'.

105 Bethell, *The Abolition*, pp. 318–19.

106 Packe, 'Private Journal'.

107 Stanley to Beaufort, 1 February 1847, UKHO/SL15c.

108 Gale, 'Journal'.

109 Forbes, 'Letters', p. 22.

110 King, 'Journal', pp. 38–45.

111 Bishop Stanley to Owen Stanley, 29 January 1848, CRO/DSA 200.

112 Huxley, *T.H. Huxley's Diary*, p. 18.

113 Allen, *The Naturalist*, p. 130.

114 Owen, 'Zoology', pp. 378–9.

115 Larsen, 'Not Since Noah', pp. 167–8.

116 Rehbock, 'The Early Dredgers'.

117 Rehbock, 'The Early Dredgers', pp. 323–4; Allen, *The Naturalist*, pp. 207–8.

118 Quoted in Rehbock, 'The Early Dredgers', pp. 326–7.

119 The Rua do Ouvidor was not just European but Europe itself, specializing in everything French – Needell, *A Tropical*, pp. 161–6.

120 MacGillivray, *Narrative*, v.1, p. 21.

121 MacGillivray, *Narrative*, v.1, p. 22 and Forbes, 'Letters', p. 23.

122 Forbes, 'Letters', p. 23. Goodsir's analysis and drawings of *Amphioxus* was published in 1844, 'On the anatomy'.

123 King, 'Journal', p. 41.

124 Forbes, 'Letters', p. 23.

125 Huxley, *Life and Letters*, pp. 32–3. The source of the rumour was John Edward Gray of the British Museum who was unhappy with MacGillivray's conduct during the voyage of HMS *Fly* in Australia – Allen, 'Huxley's Botanist' and, for example, J E Gray to Lord Derby, 8 July 1846, LRO/920DER(13)/1/69/87.

126 John MacGillivray to James Harley, 1 May 1847, ROLLR/13D56/8/12.

127 John MacGillivray to James Harley, 1 May 1847, ROLLR/13D56/8/12.

128 Huxley, *T.H. Huxley's Diary*, p. 18.

129 Gale, 'Journal'.

130 Thomson, 'Journal'.

131 Conrad, *World of Sorrow*, pp. 25–32.

132 Karasch, *Slave Life*, p. 66.

133 Karasch, *Slave Life*, pp. 185–213.

134 Earlier European visitors to Rio had similar reactions – Martins and Abreu, 'Paradoxes', p. 545; Darwin, *The Voyage*, p. 22 and Gardner, *Travels*, p. 5, for examples of these.

135 John Thomson to Mary Thomson, 24 January 1847, DRC Letters.

136 John MacGillivray to James Harley, 1 May 1847, ROLLR/13D56/8/12.

137 King, 'Journal', p. 44.

138 King, 'Journal', p. 45; Thomson, 'Journal' and Packe, 'Private Journal'.

CHAPTER IV

1 King, 'Journal', p. 45; Forbes, 'Letters', p. 24 and MacGillivray, *Narrative*, v.1, pp. 24-5.

2 Beaufort to Stanley, 28 November 1846, UKHO/LB14/212.

3 Stanley to Beaufort, 9 April 1847, UKHO/SL15c.

4 McConnell, 'Six's Thermometer'.

5 MacGillivray, *Narrative*, v.1, p. 25 and McConnell, *No Sea*, pp. 22-4.

6 Prestwich, 'Tables of Temperatures', pp. 671-2.

7 Beechey, 'Hydrography'; Herschel, 'Meteorology'; Beaufort, *General Instructions for the Hydrographic Surveyors of the Admiralty*, UKHO/Oa51(a)/15; Thomson, *The Depths*, pp. 288-9 and Deacon, *Scientists*, pp. 292-4.

8 The observations are in MacGillivray, *Narrative*, v.1, pp. 329-30.

9 Lewis, *The Navy*, p. 170 and Earle, *Sailors*, pp. 145-58.

10 King, 'Journal', p. 46 and Gale, 'Journal'.

11 Gould, 'A Brief Account', pp. 94-5.

12 Farber, 'The Development' and Morris, 'An Historical'.

13 MacGillivray to Gould, 12 May 1847, NHM(Z)/Z MSS Gou B.

14 Forbes, 'Letters', p. 24.

15 The details of what happened are recounted in King, 'Journal', pp. 49-50 and in John Thomson to Mary Thomson, March 1847, DRC Letters.

16 Forbes, 'Letters', p. 25.

17 Forbes, 'Letters', p. 25.

18 Huxley, *T.H. Huxley's Diary*, pp. 20-21.

19 Huxley, *T.H. Huxley's Diary*, p. 22.

20 Huxley, *T.H. Huxley's Diary*, p. 22.

21 King, 'Journal', p. 55.

22 Packe, 'Private Journal'.

23 King, 'Journal', pp. 53-4.

24 John Thomson to Mary Thomson, March 1847, DRC Letters.

25 Forbes, 'Letters', pp. 25, 27.

26 Huxley, *T.H. Huxley's Diary*, p. 23.

27 Bradlow, *Pictorial Album*, p. 40.

28 Beaufort to Stanley, 28 November 1846, UKHO/LB14/215 and Dawson, *Memoirs I*, p. 58.

29 Tredgold, *Bay*, p. 131.

30 Lester, 'Otherness' and Legassick, 'The State'.

31 Lester, Nel and Binns, *South Africa*, pp. 117-120; Milton, *The Edges* and Featherstone, *Victorian*.

32 Mostert, *Frontiers*, pp. 868–9 and Keegan, *Colonial*, pp. 215–18.

33 Mostert, *Frontiers*, pp. 869–90 and Le Cordeur and Saunders, *The War*, pp. 15–25.

34 BPP 1847-8, XL 479 (54).

35 Stanley to Robert Were Fox, 6 April 1847, RS/MS710/110.

36 Stanley to Robert Were Fox, 6 April 1847, RS/MS710/110.

37 Stanley to Beaufort, 9 April 1847, UKHO/SL15c.

38 Gale, 'Journal'.

39 King, 'Journal', p. 61.

40 Huxley, *Life and Letters*, p. 33.

41 Huxley, *T.H. Huxley's Diary*, p. 25.

42 LS/General Minute Book, no. 6, 21 November 1848 and 5 December 1848.

43 Huxley, *T.H. Huxley's Diary*, p. 25.

44 Huxley, *T.H. Huxley's Diary*, p. 23.

45 Huxley, *T.H. Huxley's Diary*, p. 23.

46 MacGillivray to Harley, 1 May 1847, ROLLR/13D56/8/12 and Forbes, 'Letters', p. 27.

47 John Thomson to Mary Thomson, March 1847, DRC Letters and Packe, 'Private Journal'.

48 King, 'Journal', p. 57.

49 Stanley to Beaufort, 9 April 1847, UKHO/SL15c.

50 The sign read as follows:

> Multum in parvo; pro bono publico
> Entertainment for man and beast in a row.
> Lekker kost as much as you please,
> Excellent beds without any fleas.
> Nos patriam fugiamus – now we are here,
> Vivamus, let us live by selling beer,
> On donne à boire et à manger ici;
> Come in and try it whoever you be.

See King, 'Journal'; Tredgold, *Bay*, pp. 129–35 and Langham-Carter, 'Farmer Peck's'.

51 Stanley Letter Book, 9 April 1847, UKHO/SL15f.

52 Forbes, 'Letters', p. 27.

53 Packe, 'Private Journal'.

54 MacGillivray, *Narrative*, v.1, p. 330.

55 Stanley to Beaufort, 7 May 1847, UKHO/SL15c and King, 'Journal', p. 63.

56 Beaufort to Stanley, 31 July 1847, UKHO/LB14/434.

57 Deacon, *Scientists*, pp. 285–6.

58 MacGillivray, *Narrative*, v.1, p. 31.

59 Stanley, 'On the Lengths' and Herschel, *A Manual*,

60 King, 'Journal', p. 65.

61 Huxley, *Life and Letters*, p.33 and Winsor, *Starfish*, p. 76.

62 Beaufort to Bishop of Norwich, 26 April 1847, UKHO/LB14/354.

63 Beaufort to Stanley, 13 and 30 April 1847, UKHO/LB14/356–7.

64 Beaufort to Stanley, 31 July 1847, UKHO/LB14/433–4.
65 Beaufort to Stanley, 31 May 1848, UKHO/LB15/211.
66 Deerr, *The History*, pp. 198–203, Allen 'The Slender', p. 195 and Howell, 'Mauritius', pp. 257–9.
67 Allen, 'Passing' and personal communication, 12 April 2002.
68 BPP 1849 XXXVII [280–ll], p. 194.
69 Riviere, *Historical Dictionary*, p. xxxiii, Toussaint, *Port Louis*, p. 91 and MacGillivray to Harley, 1 May 1847, ROLLR/13D56/8/12.
70 MacGillivray, *Narrative*, v.1, p. 34.
71 Forbes, 'Letters', p. 29.
72 Forbes, 'Letters', p. 29.
73 Huxley, *Life and Letters*, p. 34.
74 Huxley, *T.H. Huxley's Diary*, p. 26.
75 Packe, 'Private Journal'.
76 Grove, *Green Imperialism*, pp. 184–99 and Ly-Tio-Fane, 'Pierre Poivre'.
77 Rouillard, *Le Jardin*, pp. 35–9.
78 MacGillivray, *Narrative*, v.1, p. 36.
79 Nixon, *Sketches*, n.p.
80 Menhennet, 'International', p. 490.
81 Robinson, 'Traduction' and Bernardin de Saint-Pierre, *Paul and Virginia*, p.9.
82 Huxley, *Life and Letters*, p. 34.
83 Bartram, *Recollections*, pp. 167–8.
84 Bartram, *Recollections*, p. 168.
85 Bradshaw, *Views*, n.p.; Pridham, *England's*, p. 211; Pike, *Sub-Tropical*, p. 82; Ellis, *Three Visits* and Macmillan, *Mauritius*, p. 130.
86 Huxley, *Life and Letters*, p. 35.
87 Huxley, *Life and Letters*, p. 34.
88 MacGillivray to Harley, 1 May 1847, ROLLR/13D56/8/12; MacGillivray, 'List of Molluscs', NHM(Z)/Zoology/MiscColl/Z890M and MacGillivray, *Narrative*, v.1, pp. 34–5.
89 Ly-Tio-Fane Pineo, *In the Grips*.
90 Owen Stanley to Mary Stanley, 9 March 1846, NMM/XSTA1/15.
91 Huxley, *T.H. Huxley's Diary*, p. 34.
92 King, 'Journal' and Huxley, *T.H. Huxley's Diary*, pp. 32–5.
93 Forbes, 'Letters', p. 28.
94 Sharpe, 'Jottings', pp. 7–8.
95 Forbes, 'Letters', p. 28.
96 Forbes, 'Letters'.
97 Gomm to Earl Grey, 22 May 1847, PRO/CO167/282/117.
98 Stanley to Beaufort, 17 May 1847, UKHO/SL15c.

CHAPTER V

1 Robert King to William Hooker, 27 April 1847, RBG/DC73/doc. 221.

2 Gale, 'Journal' and King, 'Journal'.

3 Huxley, *T.H. Huxley's Diary*, p. 25.

4 Gale, 'Journal'.

5 Huxley, *T.H. Huxley's Diary*, p. 31.

6 MacGillivray, *Narrative*, v. 1, p. 330.

7 Gale, 'Journal'.

8 Gale, 'Journal'.

9 King, 'Journal' and MacGillivray, *Narrative*, v.1, p. 330.

10 Gale, 'Journal'.

11 Gale, 'Journal'.

12 MacGillivray, *Narrative*, v.1, p. 40.

13 MacGillivray, *Narrative*, v.1, p. 40 and Forbes, 'Letters', p. 29.

14 Stanley to Beaufort, 14 June 1847, UKHO/SL15c.

15 Forbes, 'Letters', p.29 and Gould, 'A Brief Account', pp. 94–96.

16 Gould, A Brief Account', p. 96 and Gould, 'On the Family'.

17 King, 'Journal'.

18 Huxley, *T.H. Huxley's Diary*, p. 31 and Packe, 'Private Journal'.

19 King, 'Journal'.

20 Huxley, *T.H. Huxley's Diary*, p. 31.

21 King, 'Journal'.

22 Gale, 'Journal'.

23 Forbes, 'Letters', p. 29.

24 Gale, 'Journal' and King, 'Journal'.

25 King, 'Journal'; Gale, 'Journal' and Huxley, *T.H. Huxley's Diary*, p. 35.

26 PRO/ADM38/8835.

27 King, 'Journal'.

28 Gale, 'Journal'.

29 Huxley, *T.H. Huxley's Diary*, p. 35.

30 Huxley, *T.H. Huxley's Diary*, p. 60.

31 Rimmer, *Portrait*, p. 9.

32 John Thomson to Mary Thomson, 20 July 1847, DRC Letters and Rimmer, 'Hobart', p. 99.

33 Rimmer, 'Hobart'.

34 Charles Stanley to Catherine Stanley, 13 March 1847, Eliza Stanley to Catherine Stanley, 24 March 1847 and Charles Stanley to Catherine (Mrs Edward) Stanley, 13 July 1847, all in CRO/DSA 198.

35 Sharpe, 'Jottings'.

36 Savours and McConnell, 'The History', p. 528; Kenworthy and Walker, *Colonial*, and Cawood, 'Terrestrial Magnetism'.

37 Savours and McConnell, 'The History', p. 535.

38 John Thomson to Mary Thomson, 20 July 1847, DRC Letters and Rimmer, 'Hobart', p. 99.

39 Forbes, 'Letters', p. 29.

40 King, 'Journal'.

41 Crowther, 'Dr. E.S.P. Bedford', and Rimmer, *Portrait*, pp. 61–7.

42 Browner, 'Ideologies' and Winter, 'Ethereal'.

43 Crowther, 'The Introduction', p. 567.

44 King, 'Journal'.

45 Gale, 'Journal'.

46 Gale, 'Journal'.

47 Gale, 'Journal'.

48 Packe, 'Private Journal'.

49 King, 'Journal'.

50 King, 'Journal'.

51 Huxley, *T.H. Huxley's Diary*, p. 61.

52 MacGillivray to Gould, 6 and 12 February 1848, NHM(Z)/Z MSS GOU B/2.

53 Gale, 'Journal'.

54 Huxley, *T.H. Huxley's Diary*, p. 61.

55 Huxley, *T.H. Huxley's Diary*, p. 61.

56 Gale, 'Journal'.

57 Packe, 'Private Journal'.

58 Huxley, *T.H. Huxley's Diary*, p.61.

59 John Thomson to Mary Thomson, 30 September 1847, DRC Letters.

60 Beaufort to Stanley, 30 November 1847, UKHO/LB15/56.

61 Packe, 'Private Journal'.

62 Packe, 'Private Journal'.

63 Stanley to Beaufort, 9 August 1847, UKHO/SL15c and Stanley to Charles Tyers, 28 August 1847, NLA/MS264/1.

64 Stanley to Beaufort, 25 August 1847, UKHO/SL15c.

65 Beaufort to Stanley, 31 July 1847, UKHO/LB14/434.

66 Allen and Corris, *The Journal*, p. 186.

67 Allen and Corris, *The Journal*, p. 186 and *The Shipping Gazette and Sydney General Trade List*, 24 July 1847, p. 551.

68 Stanley to Beaufort, 9 August 1847, UKHO/SL15c.

69 Packe, 'Private Journal' and Stanley to Charles Tyers, 28 August 1847, NLA/MS264/1.

70 Allen and Corris, *The Journal*, p. 187.

71 Allen and Corris, *The Journal*, p. 189.

72 Allen and Corris, *The Journal*, p. 189.

73 Allen and Corris, *The Journal*, p. 189.

74 Allen and Corris, *The Journal*, pp. 189–90.

75 Beaufort to Stanley, 31 July 1847, UKHO/LB14/434.

76 Beaufort to Stanley, 31 July 1847, UKHO/LB14/434 and Yule to Beaufort, 27 March 1847, UKHO/SL15c.

77 Stanley to Beaufort, 9 August 1847, UKHO/SL15c.

78 Stanley to Beaufort, 9 August 1847, UKHO/SL15c.

79 Beaufort to Stanley, 31 July 1847, UKHO/LB14/434.

80 Packe, 'Private Journal'.

81 Stanley to Charles Tyers, 28 August 1847, NLA/MS264/1.

82 Beaufort to Stanley, 29 February 1848, UKHO/LB15/136.
83 John Thomson to Mary Thomson, 23 August 1847, DRC Letters.
84 Huxley, *Life and Letters*, p. 37.
85 John Thomson to Mary Thomson, 20 July 1847, DRC Letters.
86 John Thomson to Mary Thomson, 30 September 1847, DRC Letters.
87 Huxley, *T.H. Huxley's Diary*, p. 61.
88 IC/HA/HP62.1.
89 Huxley, 'Pictures', pp. 779–81.
90 Desmond, *Huxley*, p. 72.
91 Huxley, 'Pictures', p. 781.
92 IC/HA/HP62.1.
93 Branagan, 'Phillip Parker King'.
94 Fisher, 'British Veterinary Surgeons'.
95 Huxley, *T.H. Huxley's Diary*, p. 61.
96 IC/HA/HP62.1.
97 Huxley, *T.H. Huxley's Diary*, p. 62.
98 Huxley, *T.H. Huxley's Diary*, p. 64.
99 Fisher, 'Strange'; Whittell, 'Frederick Strange' and Sauer, *John Gould vol. 3*, p. 274.
100 Sauer, *John Gould vol. 3*, pp. 317, 438 and McAllan, 'John Gilbert's', p. 156.
101 Kay Barnett, personal communication.
102 Sauer, *John Gould vol. 4*, p. 209.
103 Huxley, *Life and Letters*, p. 37.
104 Huxley, *T.H. Huxley's Diary*, pp. 65–6.
105 LS/General Minute Book 6.
106 IC/HA/HP34.38.
107 MacGillivray to Forbes, 1 February 1848, ML/FM4/2231/42.
108 Forbes, 'Letters', p. 30 and Sauer, *John Gould vol 4*, pp. 148 and 161.
109 MacGillivray, 'Notes', pp.1486–89.
110 Forbes, 'Letters', p. 30.
111 Forbes, 'Letters', p. 30.
112 Quoy and Gaimard, *Voyage*, vol. 3, pp. 464–7.
113 Forbes, 'Letters', p. 31.
114 Foster and Lankester, *Scientific Memoirs*, pp. 6–9.
115 Forbes, 'Letters', p. 31.
116 NHM(Z)/Z890M.
117 Packe, 'Private Journal'.
118 Bishop Stanley to Owen Stanley, 29 January 1848, CRO/DSA199.
119 Gale, 'Journal'.
120 Gale, 'Journal'.
121 Stanley to Charles Tyers, 28 August 1847, NLA/MS264/1.
122 Lubbock, *Owen Stanley*, p. 88.
123 Lubbock, *Owen Stanley*, p. 88.
124 Clarke, 'Captain'.
125 De Falbe, *My Dear*.

126 Sharpe, 'Jottings', p. 10.

127 Sharpe, 'Jottings', pp. 10–11.

128 *Sydney Morning Herald*, 6 September 1847.

129 Gale, 'Journal'.

130 Gale, 'Journal'.

131 Gale, 'Journal'.

132 HRA, vol 25, pp. 738–9.

133 Wells, *A Geographical*, pp. 72–85.

134 Stanley to Yule, 9 October 1847, UKHO/SL15f/69.

135 Packe, 'Private Journal'.

136 Angus, *Simpkinson* and Kerr, *The Dictionary*, pp. 726–7.

137 Charles Stanley to Catherine Stanley (mother), 13 July 1847, CRO/DSA198.

138 Roget, 'Her Majesty's', p. 130.

139 Diamond, *The Sea Horse*, p. 26.

140 Boyd, *Reminiscences*, p. 94.

141 Crisswell, *Rajah Charles Brooke* and Barley, *White*.

142 Any gentleman who owned a yacht exceeding 10 tons in weight could qualify for membership.

143 Diamond, *The Sea Horse*, p. 34.

144 Diamond, *The Sea Horse*, p. 57.

145 Wellings, *Eden*, p. 38; Davidson, *Whalemen*, p. 26.

146 Brierly, 'Journal', 27 December 1842, ML/A545.

147 Wellings, *Eden*, pp. 8–9.

148 Diamond, *The Sea Horse*, p. 99.

149 Diamond, *The Sea Horse*, pp. 102–3.

150 Packe, 'Private Journal'.

151 Stanley to Beaufort, 2 October 1847, UKHO/SL15c.

152 Pearson, 'Shore-Based Whaling'; Pearson, 'The Technology' and Lawrence and Staniforth, *The Archaeology*.

153 Wellings, *Shore Whaling*.

154 Brierly, 'Reminiscences', ML/A546.

155 Stanley to Deas Thomson, 1 October 1847, UKHO/SL15f/58.

156 Gale, 'Journal'.

157 Packe, 'Private Journal'.

CHAPTER VI

1 Both sets of instructions are in UKHO/MB6/1–11. They were repeated, for the most part, by MacGillivray in the opening pages of his published account of the voyage: see MacGillivray, *Narrative*, v.1 pp. 2–10.

2 Hordern, *King*, pp. 156–85.

3 Nicholson, *Via Torres Strait*, pp. 154–9.

4 UKHO, MB6/1–4.

5 UKHO, MB6/6.

6 UKHO, MB6/6–7.

7 Friendly, *Beaufort*, p. 329.

8 Friendly, *Beaufort*, p. 15.

9 UKHO, MB6/7.

10 Broeze, 'Distance'.

11 BPP, 1851 XXXV, 152–3 and UKHO/MB5/359–60.

12 BPP, 1851 XXXV, 140.

13 Johnston and Gregory, 'Choosing Brisbane' and Johnston and Gregory, 'Brisbane'.

14 Johnston and Gregory, 'Choosing Brisbane' and MacGillivray, *Narrative*, v.1, p. 44.

15 Johnston and Gregory, 'Choosing Brisbane', p. 247.

16 Owen Stanley to Edward Deas Thomson, 1 November 1847, UKHO/SL15f/64–66.

17 Gale, 'Journal'.

18 Gale, 'Journal'.

19 Stanley to Beaufort, 28 November 1847, UKHO/SL15c.

20 Hughes, *The Fatal Shore*, pp. 551–2 and Hogan, *The Gladstone Colony*.

21 BPP, 1847–8 XLIII, 567–71 and Jobst, *A Pioneer Family*.

22 BPP, 1847–8 XLIII, 571.

23 BPP, 1847–8 XLIII, 569.

24 Stanley to Edward Deas Thomson, 28 November 1847, UKHO/SL15f/68–9 and Stanley to Beaufort, 28 November 1847, UKHO/SL15c.

25 MacGillivray to Forbes, 1 February 1848, ML/FM4/2231/34.

26 MacGillivray to Forbes, 1 February 1848, ML/FM4/2231/34.

27 Packe, 'Private Journal'.

28 MacGillivray to Forbes, 1 February 1848, ML/FM4/2231/34.

29 Stanley to Edward Deas Thomson, 28 November 1847, UKHO/SL15f/69 and Stanley to Beaufort, 28 November 1847, UKHO/SL15c.

30 Beaufort to Stanley, 30 November 1847, UKHO/LB15/57.

31 UKHO/MB5/5–6.

32 John MacGillivray to Edward Forbes, 1 February 1848, ML/FM4/2231/42.

33 John MacGillivray to Edward Forbes, 1 February 1848, ML/FM4/2231/42.

34 John MacGillivray to Edward Forbes, 1 February 1848, ML/FM4/2231/42.

35 John MacGillivray to Adam White, 10 May 1847, NHM(A)/DF205/4/241.

36 MacGillivray, *Narrative*, v.1, p. 45.

37 Forbes, 'Letters', pp. 32–3, NHM(Z)/Zoology Library/Miscellaneous Collections/Z890M, and MacGillivray, *Narrative*, v.1, p. 45.

38 MacGillivray, *Narrative*, v.1, pp. 48–9.

39 MacGillivray to Forbes, 1 February 1848, ML/FM4/2231/31.

40 MacGillivray to White, 22 January 1848, ML/FM4/2231/29.

41 MacGillivray to Forbes, 1 February 1848, ML/FM4/2231/32.

42 MacGillivray to Hooker, 13 February 1848, ML/FM4/2231/52–3.

43 MacGillivray to Hooker, 13 February 1848, ML/FM4/2231/53.

44 MacGillivray, *Narrative*, v.1, p. 48 and MacGillivray to Forbes, 1 February 1848, ML/FM4/2231/33.

45 MacGillivray, *Narrative*, v.1, p. 48.

46 John Thomson to Mary Thomson, 29 October 1847, DRC Letters.

47 Huxley, *T.H. Huxley's Diary*, p. 67.

48 MacGillivray, *Narrative*, v.1, p. 57.

49 MacGillivray to Forbes, 1 February 1847, ML/FM4/2231/36.

50 MacGillivray, *Narrative*, v.1, pp. 55, 57.

51 John Thomson to Mary Thomson, 28 November 1847, DRC Letters.

52 UKHO/Remark Books/H.M.S. *Rattlesnake*.

53 Hordern, *King*, pp. 168–70 and Porter, *A Family of Islands*, pp. 17–18.

54 MacGillivray to Forbes, 1 February 1848, ML/FM4/2231/37–8.

55 MacGillivray to Forbes, 1 February 1848, ML/FM4/2231/37–8.

56 John Thomson to Mary Thomson, 19 January 1848, DRC Letters and Stanley to Beaufort, 24 January 1848, UKHO/SL15c.

57 Stanley to Beaufort, 24 January 1848, UKHO/SL15c and Card, 'Diary'.

58 MacGillivray to Forbes, 1 February 1848, ML/FM4/2231/40.

59 MacGillivray to Forbes, 1 February 1848, ML/FM4/2231/41.

60 Card, 'Diary'.

61 Card, 'Diary' and Huxley, *T.H. Huxley's Diary*, pp. 69–70.

62 Card, 'Diary'.

63 Huxley, *T.H. Huxley's Diary*, p. 71.

64 Card, 'Diary'.

65 Stanley to Beaufort, 24 January 1848, UKHO/SL15c.

66 Beaufort to Stanley, 31 May 1848, UKHO/LB15/210 and John Thomson to Mary Thomson, 20 January 1848, DRC Letters.

67 John Thomson to Mary Thomson, 20 January 1848, DRC Letters.

68 MacGillivray to Forbes, 1 February 1848, ML/FM4/2231/44–5.

69 Huxley, *T.H. Huxley's Diary*, p. 66.

70 Huxley, *T.H. Huxley's Diary*, p. 66.

71 Huxley, *T.H. Huxley's Diary*, pp. 74–5.

72 Huxley, *T.H. Huxley's Diary*, p. 75.

73 Shaw, 'The Founding' and Priestley, 'Melbourne'.

74 The State of Victoria was formally brought into being in 1851.

75 Stanley to Beaufort, 13 March 1848, UKHO/SL15c. A report on the lighthouses, written by Stanley, was printed in *The Nautical Magazine and Naval Chronicle* in vol. 17 (1848), pp. 449–53.

76 NHM(Z)/Z890M and Sauer, *John Gould vol. 3*, p. 213.

77 Stanley to Beaufort, 15 March 1848, UKHO/SL15c.

78 Huxley, *T.H. Huxley's Diary*, pp. 76–8 and Card, 'Diary'.

79 Huxley, *T.H. Huxley's Diary*, p. 78.

80 Huxley, *T.H. Huxley's Diary*, p. 78.

81 Huxley, *T.H. Huxley's Diary*, p. 82.

82 Holland, 'Diminishing Circles'.

83 Stanley to Beaufort, 28 April 1848, UKHO/SL15c.

84 Becher to Bishop Stanley, 20 September 1848, UKHO/LB15/334 and Huxley, 'On the Anatomy'.

85 Huxley, 'On the Anatomy', p. 429.

86 Huxley, 'On the Anatomy', p. 413.

87 Huxley, 'On the Anatomy', p. 413.

88 Huxley, *Life and Letters*, p. 38.

89 Huxley, *T.H. Huxley's Dairy*, pp. 82–3.

90 Card, 'Diary'.

91 Card, 'Diary'.

CHAPTER VII

1 Beale, *Kennedy, the Barcoo*, pp. 12–13.

2 Beale, *Kennedy, the Barcoo*, pp. 19–26.

3 HRA, vol. 23, pp. 245–7 and Murchison, 'Address', xcvii–ciii.

4 Beale, *Kennedy*, p. 54.

5 Cumpston, *Thomas Mitchell*, p. 172; Beale, *Kennedy, the Barcoo*, p. 25 and Mitchell, 'Account'.

6 Cumpston, *Thomas Mitchell*, p. 173.

7 Cumpston, *Thomas Mitchell*, p. 189.

8 Beale, *Kennedy*, p. 73.

9 Mitchell, *Journal*, pp. 406–11.

10 Cumpston, *Thomas Mitchell*, p. 195.

11 Quoted in Beale, *Kennedy, the Barcoo*, p. 45.

12 Beale, *Kennedy*, pp. 101–3.

13 Beale, *Kennedy, the Barcoo*, p. 54.

14 Beale, *Kennedy*, pp. 112–38.

15 Beale, *Kennedy, the Barcoo*, p. 56.

16 Beale, *Kennedy, the Barcoo*, p. 57.

17 Beale, *Kennedy*, pp. 139–40; Beale, *Kennedy, the Barcoo*, p. 58 and Edmund Kennedy to Colonel Thomas Kennedy, 27 February 1848, BC/KP/P/2/31.

18 Foster, *Colonial*, pp. 99–100.

19 Edmund Kennedy to Colonel Thomas Kennedy, 27 February 1848, BC/KP/P/2/31 and HRA, vol. 26, p. 282.

20 Blackwood and Juke's opinions on Port Essington took the form of reports to Sir George Gipps, Governor of New South Wales, on 18 September 1845 and 22 October 1845, which were then enclosed with his despatch to the Colonial Office in London. The reports can be found reprinted in Cameron, *Letters*, pp. 154–5 and 160–5. MacGillivray was more daring. He berated the settlement in an article published in the *Sydney Morning Herald*, 15 October 1845.

21 Cameron, *Letters*, pp. 168–9.

22 Cameron, *Letters*, pp. 168–9.

23 Beaufort to Yule, 30 September 1846, UKHO/LB14/133.

24 Beale, *Kennedy*, p. 140.

25 HRA, vol. 26, p. 282.

26 Stanley to Beaufort, 24 January 1848, UKHO/SL15c.

27 Stanley to [family], 7 April 1848, CRO/DSA199.

28 Beale, *Kennedy*, p. 141 and Murchison, 'Address', p. cii.

29 Stanley to Beaufort, 7 April 1848, UKHO/SL15c.

30 Stanley to [family], 7 April 1848, CRO/DSA199 and Edmund Kennedy to Colonel Thomas Kennedy, BC/KP/P/2/32

31 Stanley to Beaufort, 7 April 1848, UKHO/SL15c.

32 Stanley to [family], 7 April 1848, CRO/DSA199.

33 ML/ZDL Spencer 191. The draft instructions were passed to Stanley as an attachment to a letter from Deas Thomson, the Colonial Secretary, and then from Stanley to Beaufort: Thomson to Stanley, 11 April 1848 and Stanley to Beaufort, 28 April 1848, UKHO/SL15c.

34 Stanley to Thomson, 12 April 1848, UKHO/SL15c.

35 Stanley to Thomson, 12 April 1848, UKHO/SL15c.

36 ML/ZDL Spencer 191.

37 *The Shipping Gazette and Sydney General Trade List*, 11 March 1848, 1 April 1848, 8 April 1848, 22 April 1848.

38 Beale, *Kennedy, the Barcoo*, p. 92.

39 Beale, *Kennedy*, p. 145.

40 Beale, *Kennedy*, p. 146.

41 HRA, vol. 26, p. 440.

42 Thomson to Stanley, 11 April 1848, UKHO/SL15c.

43 Gale, 'Journal'.

44 Stanley to [family], 7 April 1848, CRO/DSA199.

45 Stanley to Beaufort, 28 April 1848, UKHO/SL15c.

46 Stanley to Beaufort, 28 April 1848, UKHO/SL15c.

47 *Sydney Morning Herald*, 26 April 1848.

48 *Sydney Morning Herald*, 26 April 1848.

49 *Sydney Morning Herald*, 26 April 1848.

50 Stanley to Thomson, 29 April 1848, UKHO/SL15f.

51 *The Shipping Gazette and Sydney General Trade List*, 29 April 1848, p.102.

52 Diamond, *The Sea Horse*, pp. 104–5.

53 Brierly, 'Journal', 26 February 1848, ML/A503.

54 Brierly, 'Journal', 10 March1848, ML/A503. Before leaving Boyd Town for good, Brierly went to Sydney, where he remained from 22 March to 5 April to wind up his affairs: *The Shipping Gazette and Sydney General Trade List*, 25 March 1848, p. 78 and 8 April 1848, p. 90.

55 McKenna, *Looking*, p. 133.

56 Stanley to Beaufort, 6 May 1849, UKHO/SL15e.

57 Packe, 'Private Journal'.

58 Thomson, 'Diary'.

59 Card, 'Diary'.

60 Stanley to Beaufort, 30 May 1848, UKHO/SL15c.

61 Thomson, 'Diary'.

62 Card, 'Diary'.

63 Huxley, *T.H. Huxley's Diary*, p. 97.

64 Brierly, 'Journal', ML/A505.

65 Brierly, 'Journal', ML/A505.

66 Brierly, 'Journal', ML/A505.

67 MacGillivray, *Narrative*, v.1, p. 80.

68 Brierly, 'Journal', ML/A505.

69 Card, 'Diary'.

70 Beale, *Kennedy*, p. 154 and MacGillivray, *Narrative*, v.2, p. 120.

71 None of the sources give a name to the island, and they contradict one another as to which island it might have been. Thomson said it was the most northerly of the island group (fits Timana); Brierly called it 'a very pretty little island' (fits Timana), without saying anything more about its location; Card thought it was the largest of the group, nearest to Dunk Island (fits Bedarra), while Packe reported that the *Rattlesnake* was 'at anchor under the lee of the Southernmost Family Island' (Wheeler or Coombe). Timana is closer to the shore than any other of the Family Islands. James Porter, an expert on the islands, has no doubt that it was Timana – Porter, *A Family*.

72 Stanley to Deas Thomson, 26 May 1848, DTP.

73 Stanley to Deas Thomson, 26 May 1848, DTP.

74 Brierly, 'Journal', ML/A505.

75 Stanley to Beaufort, 30 May 1848, UKHO/SL15c.

76 Beale, *Kennedy, the Barcoo*, p. 63.

77 Huxley, *T.H. Huxley's Diary*, p. 104.

78 Thomas Huxley to Henrietta Heathorn, 11 June 1848, IC/HA/HH/23.

79 Huxley, *T.H. Huxley's Diary*, p. 105 and Thomas Huxley to Henrietta Heathorn, 11 June 1848, IC/HA/HH/23.

80 Stanley to Deas Thomson, 30 June 1848, ML/ML Doc. 1127.

81 Owen Stanley to Edward Stanley, 26 May 1848, CRO/DSA 199.

82 Stanley to Deas Thomson, 26 May 1848, UKHO/SL15f.

83 Stanley to Beaufort, 30 May 1848, UKHO/SL15c.

84 Sharpe, 'Jottings'.

85 MacGillivray, *Narrative*, v.1, p. 106.

86 Card, 'Diary'.

87 MacGillivray, *Narrative*, v.1, p. 94.

88 Dance, *Shell Collecting*, pp. 189–218.

89 John Thomson to Mary Thomson, 23 April 1848, DRC Letters.

90 John Thomson to Mary Thomson, 29 October 1848, DRC Letters.

91 John Thomson to Mary Thomson, 24 May 1848, DRC Letters.

92 Sauer, *John Gould vol. 3*, p. 307.

93 MacGillivray, *Narrative*, v.1, p. 90. Gould thought that it was one of the most beautiful birds in the world, a velvety black with metallic green – Gould, 'On New Species', p. 111.

94 MacGillivray, *Narrative*, v.1, p. 114.

95 MacGillivray to Hooker, 27 May 1848, ML/FM4/2231/56.

96 MacGillivray to Hooker, 27 May 1848, ML/FM4/2231/57.

97 MacGillivray to Hooker, 27 May 1848, ML/FM4/2231/56.
98 MacGillivray to Forbes, 2 April 1849, ML/FM4/2231/58.
99 Huxley, *T.H. Huxley's Diary*, p. 96.
100 Huxley, *T.H. Huxley's Diary*, p. 99.
101 Huxley, *T.H. Huxley's Diary*, p. 111.
102 Thomas Huxley to Henrietta Heathorn, 2 July 1848, IC/HA/HH/35.
103 Thomas Huxley to Henrietta Heathorn, 2 September 1848, IC/HA/HH/37.
104 Card, 'Diary'.
105 John Thomson to Mary Thomson, 29 October 1848, DRC Letters.
106 Huxley, *T.H. Huxley's Diary*, p. 107.
107 Shineberg, *They Came*.
108 The preceding paragraphs are base on Card, 'Diary', Packe, 'Private Journal', Brierly, 'Journal', ML/A505 and Huxley, *T.H. Huxley's Diary*, pp. 107–8
109 Stanley to Deas Thomson, 30 June 1848, ML/ML Doc. 1127.
110 Packe, 'Private Journal'.
111 Card, 'Diary'.
112 Packe, 'Private Journal'.
113 Packe, 'Private Journal'.
114 Packe, 'Private Journal'.
115 Packe, 'Private Journal'.
116 Yule to Beaufort, 27 March 1847, UKHO/SL15c and Stanley to Beaufort, 28 April 1848, UKHO/SL15c.
117 Sauer, *John Gould vol. 3*, p. 307.
118 Card, 'Diary'.
119 Stanley to Ramsay, 7 April 1848, UKHO/SL15f/85.
120 Stanley to Ramsay, 7 April 1848, UKHO/SL15f/85.
121 Card, 'Diary'.

CHAPTER VIII

1 MacGillivray to Forbes, 14/24 May 1849, ML/FM4/2231/89.
2 Card, 'Diary' and Packe, 'Private Journal'.
3 Card, 'Diary'.
4 Packe, 'Private Journal'.
5 Card, 'Diary'.
6 Card, 'Diary'.
7 Card, 'Diary'.
8 Packe, 'Private Journal'.
9 John Thomson to Mary Thomson, 29 October 1848, DRC Letters.
10 John Thomson to Mary Thomson, 5 March 1849, DRC Letters.
11 Brierly, 'Journal', ML/A535 and McKenna, *Looking*, pp. 120–134.
12 Moore, *Islanders*, p. 29.
13 Moore, *Islanders*, p. 30.
14 Moore, *Islanders*, p. 31.

15 Packe, 'Private Journal', John Thomson to Mary Thomson, 29 October 1848, DRC Letters.

16 Moore, *Islanders*, p. 27 and MacGillivray, 'Journal'.

17 Moore, *Islanders*, pp. 42–3.

18 Moore, *Islanders*, p. 44.

19 Moore, *Islanders*, pp. 45–6.

20 Moore, *Islanders*, p. 46.

21 Moore, *Islanders*, p. 48.

22 Card, 'Diary'.

23 Card, 'Diary'.

24 Thomas Huxley to Henrietta Heathorn, 18 October 1848, IC/HA/HH/37.

25 Nicholson, *Via Torres Strait*, p. 128.

26 John Thomson to Mary Thomson, 30 January 1849, DRC, i.e. Thomson Letters, and Thomas Huxley to Henrietta Heathorn, 26 December 1848, IC/HA/HH/40.

27 Card, 'Diary'.

28 Brierly, 'Journal', ML/A501, for a description.

29 Card, 'Diary'.

30 *The Shipping Gazette and Sydney General Trade List*, 30 September 1848, p. 235 and 7 October 1848, p. 242.

31 Card, 'Diary' and Stanley to Yule, 2 November 1848, UKHO/SL15f/117.

32 Stanley to Vallack, 1 November 1848, UKHO/SL15f/116.

33 Card, 'Diary'.

34 Packe, 'Private Journal'.

35 Packe, 'Private Journal'.

36 Packe, 'Private Journal'.

37 Packe, 'Private Journal'.

38 Yule to Stanley, 16 January 1849, UKHO/SL15d.

39 Packe, 'Private Journal'.

40 Packe, 'Private Journal'.

41 Yule to Stanley, 16 January 1849, UKHO/SL15d.

42 Stanley to Beaufort, 31 January 1849, UKHO/SL15c.

43 Stanley to Beaufort, 31 January 1849, UKHO/SL15c.

44 Cameron, 'The Northern' and Goodman, 'Making'.

45 Cameron, *Letters*, p. 7; Reece, 'The Australasian'; Allen, 'Port'; Allen, 'The Archaeology' and Coltheart, 'Australia'

46 Cameron, *Letters*, p. 7.

47 Spillett, *Forsaken*, pp. 19–24.

48 Spillett, *Forsaken*, pp. 26–7.

49 Spillett, *Forsaken*, pp. 56–62.

50 PRO/ADM7/766/275–6.

51 Cameron, *Letters*, pp. 138–49.

52 MacGillivray, *Narrative*, p. 155.

53 *Sydney Morning Herald*, 15 October 1845, also reprinted in Cameron, *Letters*, pp. 155–60.

54 Gale, 'Journal'.

55 Gale, 'Journal'.

56 Stanley to Beaufort, 31 January 1849, UKHO/SL15c.

57 Stanley to Beaufort, 31 January 1849, UKHO/SL15c.

58 MacGillivray to Hooker, 2 May 1849, RBG/DC74/101; Sauer, *John Gould Vol. 4*, p. 307; NHM(Z)/Z890M and MacGillivray, 'Collection of Mammalia and Birds', NHM(Z)/Z GOU B/6.

59 MacGillivray, *Narrative*, p. 157 and Spillett, *Forsaken*, p. 149.

60 MacGillivray, *Narrative*, pp. 157–8; Mezzadri, *150th Anniversary* and Pryer, 'Confalonieri'.

61 John Thomson to Mary Thomson, 30 January 1849, DRC Letters.

62 Huxley, *T. H. Huxley's Diary*, p. 114.

63 What went wrong at Port Essington and, for that matter, at the previous attempts at settlement in northern Australia has been subject to much recent research. Examples include Reid, 'Malaria', Calley, *The Pumpkin* and Phelts, 'Did Water'.

64 Huxley, *Life and Letters*, pp. 43–4.

65 Huxley, *T. H. Huxley's Diary*, p. 115.

66 Thomas Huxley to Henrietta Heathorn, 23 November 1848, IC/HA/HH/39.

67 Thomas Huxley to Henrietta Heathorn, 1 November 1848, IC/HA/HH/38.

68 Huxley, *T. H. Huxley's Diary*, pp. 116–7.

69 Huxley, *T. H. Huxley's Diary*, p. 118.

70 Brierly, 'Journal', ML/A502.

71 Brierly, 'Journal', ML/A502.

72 MacGillivray, *Narrative*, p. 161.

73 John Thomson to Mary Thomson, 5 March 1849, DRC Letters.

74 Beaufort to Stanley, 31 May 1849, UKHO/LB16/125.

75 Allen and Corris, *The Journal*, pp. 55–6.

76 Allen and Corris, *The Journal*, p. 128.

77 Allen and Corris, *The Journal*, p. 129.

CHAPTER IX

1 *The Shipping Gazette and Sydney General Trade List*, 17 February 1849.

2 *The Shipping Gazette and Sydney General Trade List*, 24 February 1849.

3 Card, 'Diary'.

4 *Sydney Morning Herald*, 5 March 1849.

5 *Sydney Morning Herald*, 5 March 1849.

6 *Sydney Morning Herald*, 5 March 1849.

7 'Extract: From the Journal of the Brigantine *Ariel*', UKHO/SL15e.

8 'Extract: From the Journal of the Brigantine *Ariel*', UKHO/SL15e.

9 Card, 'Diary' and *Sydney Morning Herald*, 6 March 1849.

10 Card, 'Diary'.

11 MacGillivray, *Narrative*, pp. 162–3.

12 *Sydney Morning Herald*, 7 March 1849.

13 John Thomson to Mary Thomson, 5 March 1849, DRC Letters.

14 Bishop Stanley to Owen Stanley, 29 June 1849, CRO/DSA200.

15 Stanley to Beaufort, 10 March 1849, UKHO/SL15e.

16 'Exploratory Expedition under the Late Mr. Kennedy', ML/ZDL ADD142.

17 Owen Stanley to Louisa Stanley, 15 May 1849, CRO/DSA199.

18 Stanley to Tyers, 7 May 1849, NLA/MS264/2.

19 Card, 'Diary'.

20 Stanley to Deas Thomson, 17 April 1849, UKHO/SL15f/153.

21 De Vries-Evans, *Conrad Martens* and 'Conrad Marten's Account Book', 18 April 1849, DL MS142, f. 133.

22 Townsend, 'Memoir'.

23 *The Shipping Gazette and Sydney General Trade List*, 24 March 1849, p. 77.

24 *The Shipping Gazette and Sydney General Trade List*, 7 April 1849, p. 88 and 'Log book of the brig *Freak*', ML/A2619.

25 Gale, 'Journal'.

26 MacGillivray, *Narrative*, p. 257.

27 'Log book of the brig *Freak*', ML/A2619.

28 MacGillivray, *Narrative*, pp. 260–61.

29 MacGillivray, *Narrative*, pp. 264–72.

30 MacGillivray, *Narrative*, p. 275.

31 The letter to Stanley was published in the *Journal of the Royal Geographical Society*, volume 21, (1851), pp. 14–15.

32 Carron, *Narrative*.

33 Mitchell to Colonel Thomas Kennedy, 8 March 1849, BC/KP/P/6/11.

34 Mitchell to Colonel Thomas Kennedy, 10 March 1849, BC/KP/P/6/12.

35 Quoted in Foster, *Sir Thomas*, p. 436.

36 Quoted in Foster, *Sir Thomas*, p. 436.

37 Quoted in Foster, *Sir Thomas*, p. 438.

CHAPTER X

1 Owen Stanley to Louisa Stanley, 15 May 1849, CRO/DSA199.

2 Stanley to Beaufort, 3 April 1849, UKHO/SL15e.

3 Beaufort to Stanley, 31 March 1849, UKHO/LB16/71.

4 Stanley to Tyers, 7 May 1849, NLA/MS264/2.

5 MacGillivray to Hooker, 2 May 1849, RBG/DC74/101; Sauer, *John Gould Vol. 4*, p. 306 and Gilliard, *Birds*, pp. 22–3.

6 Stanley's fear about being eaten was not unusual, based as it was on stories circulating in Europe about voracious people living in and around the Pacific. Stanley didn't have to look too far for an example of a commander of an exploring expedition who ended up on the dinner table. The French naval captain, Marc-Joseph Marion du Fresne, suffered this fate in 1772 at the Bay of Islands, New Zealand, at the hands of Maoris – Duyker, *An Officer*, pp. 153–63. Headhunters were also feared, as Stanley made clear. There is a wealth of literature on cannibalism (and headhunting) from

which one can piece together tales of cannibals and headhunters. See, for example, Barker, Hulme and Iversen, *Cannibalism*, Lestringant, *Cannibals*, Creed and Hoorn, *Body Trade*, Hoskins, *Headhunting* and Bowden, 'Maori'.

7 Owen Stanley to Louisa Stanley, 15 May 1849, CRO/DSA199.

8 Sauer, *John Gould Vol. 4*, p. 308.

9 Stanley to MacGillivray, 6 May 1849, UKHO/SL15f/167.

10 Sauer, *John Gould Vol. 4*, p. 308.

11 Beaufort to Stanley, 31 May 1849, UKHO/LB16/125.

12 Card, 'Diary' and Huxley, *T. H. Huxley's Diary*, p. 132.

13 Stanley to Tyers, 22 December 1849, NLA/MS264/3.

14 Card, 'Diary'.

15 Huxley, *T. H. Huxley's Diary*, p. 134.

16 Huxley, *T. H. Huxley's Diary*, p. 134.

17 Huxley, *T. H. Huxley's Diary*, p. 134.

18 Card, 'Diary'.

19 Inskip, 'Diary'.

20 Stanley to Tyers, 22 December 1849, NLA/MS264/3.

21 Stanley to Tyers, 22 December 1849, NLA/MS264/3.

22 Huxley, *T. H. Huxley's Diary*, pp. 134-5.

23 Card, 'Diary'.

24 Inskip, 'Diary'.

25 Huxley, *T. H. Huxley's Diary*, pp. 136-7.

26 Inskip, 'Diary'.

27 Card, 'Diary'.

28 UKHO/MB6/3.

29 UKHO/MB6/7-8.

30 Murchison, 'Address', pp. lviii–lix.

31 Horner, *Looking*, pp. 179–81.

32 UKHO/LB16/125, 339.

33 UKHO/MB6/10 and UKHO/LB15/210.

34 UKHO/MB3/413.

35 Stanley to family, 3 June 1849 and onwards, CRO/DSA199.

36 Huxley, *T. H. Huxley's Diary*, p. 139.

37 Stanley to family, 3 June 1849 and onwards, CRO/DSA199.

38 Card, 'Diary'.

39 Stanley to family, 3 June 1849 and onwards, CRO/DSA199.

40 Brierly, 'Journal', A507.

41 Brierly, 'Journal', A507.

42 Stanley to family, 3 June 1849 and onwards, CRO/DSA199.

43 Stanley to family, 3 June 1849 and onwards, CRO/DSA199.

44 Card, 'Diary'.

45 Card, 'Diary' and Inskip, 'Diary'.

46 Huxley, *T. H. Huxley's Diary*, p. 142.

47 Stanley to family, 3 June 1849 and onwards, CRO/DSA199.

48 Huxley, *T. H. Huxley's Diary*, p. 143.

49 MacGillivray, 'Sketch' and NHM(Z)/Z890M.

50 MacGillivray, *Narrative*, p. 190.

51 Huxley, *T. H. Huxley's Diary*, p. 144 and MacGillivray, *Narrative*, p.189.

52 Huxley, *T. H. Huxley's Diary*, p. 144.

53 MacGillivray, *Narrative*, p. 217.

54 MacGillivray, *Narrative*, pp. 190–1.

55 Inskip, 'Diary'.

56 Card, 'Diary'; MacGillivray, *Narrative*, pp. 191–5; Brierly, 'Journal', ML/A507 and
   Huxley, *T. H. Huxley's Diary*, pp. 145-7.

57 Card, 'Diary' and Stanley to family, 3 June 1849 and onwards, CRO/DSA199.

58 Stanley to family, 3 June 1849 and onwards, CRO/DSA199.

59 Stanley to family, 3 June 1849 and onwards, CRO/DSA199.

60 MacGillivray, *Narrative*, pp. 198–201.

61 Stanley to family, 3 June 1849 and onwards, CRO/DSA199 and MacGillivray,
   Narrative, p. 210.

62 MacGillivray, *Narrative*, pp. 210–14 and MacGillivray, 'Sketch'.

63 UKHO/OD81.

64 MacGillivray, *Narrative*, p. 223.

65 MacGillivray, *Narrative*, p. 229.

66 UKHO/OD81/96.

67 Yule to Stanley, 4 July 1849, UKHO/SL15d.

68 Dayman to Stanley, 6 July 1849, UKHO/SL15e and Card, 'Diary'.

69 Stanley to family, 3 June 1849 and onwards, CRO/DSA199.

70 Card, 'Diary'.

71 Stanley to Beaufort, 17 October 1849, UKHO/SL15e.

72 Card, 'Diary'.

73 UKHO/MB2/405.

74 UKHO/OD81/99.

75 Huxley, *T. H. Huxley's Diary*, p. 163.

76 Huxley, *T. H. Huxley's Diary*, p. 141.

77 Huxley, *T. H. Huxley's Diary*, p. 151.

78 Stanley to family, 3 June 1849 and onwards, CRO/DSA199.

79 Stanley to family, 3 June 1849 and onwards, CRO/DSA199.

80 Huxley, *T. H. Huxley's Diary*, p. 153.

81 Huxley, *T. H. Huxley's Diary*, p. 154.

82 Stanley to family, 3 June 1849 and onwards, CRO/DSA199.

83 Card, 'Diary'.

84 Huxley, *T. H. Huxley's Diary*, p. 165.

85 Huxley, *T. H. Huxley's Diary*, p. 165.

86 Stanley to family, 3 June 1849 and onwards, CRO/DSA199.

87 Huxley, *T. H. Huxley's Diary*, p. 165.

88 Huxley, *T. H. Huxley's Diary*, p. 166.

89 Card, 'Diary'.

90 Stanley to family, 3 June 1849 and onwards, CRO/DSA199.

91 Huxley, *Life and Letters*, p. 25.

92 Card, 'Diary'.

93 Stanley to family, 3 June 1849 and onwards, CRO/DSA199.

94 MacGillivray, *Narrative*, pp. 259–66; Huxley, *T. H. Huxley's Diary*, pp. 170–2; Card, 'Diary' and Brierly, 'Journal', ML/A511.

95 MacGillivray, *Narrative*, pp. 262–3.

96 MacGillivray, *Narrative*, p. 262.

97 Card, 'Diary'; Packe, 'Private Journal'; Brierly, 'Journal', ML/A511; MacGillivray, *Narrative*, pp. 266–7 and Huxley, *T. H. Huxley's Diary*, pp. 172–3.

98 Packe, 'Private Journal'.

99 Packe, 'Private Journal'.

100 Card, 'Diary'.

101 Stanley to family, 3 June 1849 and onwards, CRO/DSA199.

102 Stanley to family, 3 June 1849 and onwards, CRO/DSA199.

103 Stanley to family, 3 June 1849 and onwards, CRO/DSA199.

104 Gould, 'A Brief Account', p. 102.

105 Huxley, *T. H. Huxley's Diary*, p. 181.

106 Stanley to family, 3 June 1849 and onwards, CRO/DSA199.

107 Yule to Stanley, 4 September 1849, UKHO/SL15d.

108 Card, 'Diary'.

109 Inskip, 'Diary'.

110 Huxley, *T. H. Huxley's Diary*, p. 184.

111 Stanley to family, 3 June 1849 and onwards, CRO/DSA199.

112 Card, 'Diary'.

113 Owen Stanley to Miss Tunno, 5 October 1849, CRO/DSA199.

114 Owen Stanley to Miss Tunno, 5 October 1849, CRO/DSA199.

115 Jukes, *Narrative*, vol. I, p. 291.

116 MacGillivray, *Narrative*, p. 292.

117 Huxley, *T. H. Huxley's Diary*, p. 187.

118 MacGillivray, *Narrative*, pp. 297–8.

119 Stanley to family, 3 June 1849 and onwards, CRO/DSA199.

120 Stanley to family, 3 June 1849 and onwards, CRO/DSA199, MacGillivray, *Narrative*, pp. 299–300 and Card, 'Diary'.

CHAPTER XI

1 Quoted in Huxley, 'Science at Sea', p. 109.

2 Stanley to ?, 1 March 1850, CRO/DSA199.

3 Stanley to Beaufort, 16 October 1849, UKHO/SL15e.

4 Stanley to Beaufort, 16 October 1849, UKHO/SL15e.

5 Stanley to family, 3 June 1849 and onwards, CRO/DSA199 and Owen Stanley to Miss Tunno, 5 October 1849, CRO/DSA199.

6 Stanley to family, 3 June 1849 and onwards, CRO/DSA199.

7 John Thomson to Mary Thomson, 9 October 1849, DRC Letters.

8 Gould, 'A Brief Account', p. 103.

9 Hepburn to Harley, 5 December 1843, ROLLR/13D56/6/23.

10 Brierly, 'Journal', ML/A507.

11 Huxley, *T. H. Huxley's Diary*, p. 175.

12 Inskip, 'Diary'.

13 Card, 'Diary'.

14 Card, 'Diary'.

15 Moore, *Islanders*, p. 60.

16 Desmond, *Huxley*, p. 123.

17 Thomas Huxley to Henrietta Heathorn, 6 October 1849, IC/HA/HH/71.

18 Thomas Huxley to Henrietta Heathorn, 6 October 1849, IC/HA/HH/71.

19 Owen Stanley to Bishop Stanley, 16 October 1849, CRO/D3113 and Lubbock, *Owen Stanley*, p. 258.

20 Owen Stanley to Bishop Stanley, 16 October 1849, CRO/D3113.

21 Stanley to Deas Thomson, 11 February 1850, UKHO/SL15f.

22 Moore, *Islanders*, p. 76.

23 Moore, *Islanders*, p. 77.

24 Moore, *Islanders*, p. 77.

25 Moore, *Islanders*, p. 77.

26 Inskip, 'Diary'.

27 Gale, 'Journal'.

28 Huxley, *T. H. Huxley's Diary*, pp. 188, 191.

29 Owen Stanley to Mary Stanley, 16 October 1849, CRO/DSA199.

30 Moore, *Islanders*, p. 80.

31 Gale, 'Journal'.

32 Owen Stanley to Mary Stanley, 16 October 1849, CRO/DSA199.

33 Inskip, 'Diary'.

34 Inskip, 'Diary'.

35 Owen Stanley to Mary Stanley, 16 October 1849, CRO/DSA199.

36 Owen Stanley to Mary Stanley, 16 October 1849, CRO/DSA199.

37 Card, 'Diary'.

38 Card, 'Diary'.

39 Stanley to Beaufort, 16 October 1849, UKHO/SL15e.

40 Owen Stanley to Bishop Stanley, 16 October 1849, CRO/D3113.

41 MacGillivray, 'Letter', pp. 236–7.

42 In recording Barbara Thompson's story, the native names were spelled in many, but not grossly, different ways. Muralag and Kaurareg are the accepted forms.

43 Moore, *Islanders*, p. 191. There is no extant record of Barbara Thompson being asked directly whether she had been married to a Kaurareg man. Brierly recorded her saying to another Kaurareg woman 'I had no husband or children to cook for.' Stanley was certain she was never married and wrote that to his sister and his friend, the surveyor, Charles Tyers – Owen Stanley to Mary Stanley, 16 October 1849, CRO/DSA199 and Stanley to Tyers, 22 December 1849, NLA/MS264/3. Huxley and

other eyewitnesses make no mention of this aspect of Barbara Thompson's experience. MacGillivray, on the other hand, wrote in the published narrative of the voyage that Boroto 'took possession of the woman as his share of the plunder; she was compelled to live with him . . .' – MacGillivray, *Narrative*, p. 302. When he first wrote to Joseph Jukes about Barbara Thompson, he did not say anything about her being Boroto's possession. Rather, he wrote the following: '. . . she states that on only one occasion was any improper liberty attempted by the men, – she was fortunately saved by a friend, (a friend of ours) who soundly thrashed the intending ravisher, an old man well known to us.' – MacGillivray, 'Letter', p. 237. Several months later, in February 1850, however, when he wrote to John Gould about birds, he mentioned Barbara Thompson and remarked that 'one of [the natives] claimed her as his property, and treated her as his gin ever afterwards . . .' – Sauer, *John Gould Vol. 4*, p. 401.

44 This account is based on a number of sources where what Barbara Thompson told the *Rattlesnake* people from the time she was encountered on Cape York to her return to Sydney was recorded. The sources are: Moore, *Islanders*, passim, Huxley, *T. H. Huxley's Diary*, pp. 188–91; Inskip, 'Diary'; Card, 'Diary' and Owen Stanley to Bishop Stanley, 16 October 1849, CRO/D3113.

45 Moore, *Islanders*, p. 197. The preceding account is based on Moore, *Islanders*, pp. 186–97.

46 Moore, *Islanders*, p. 147.

47 Owen Stanley to Mary Stanley, 16 October 1849, CRO/DSA199.

48 Owen Stanley to Mary Stanley, 16 October 1849, CRO/DSA199.

49 Card, 'Diary'.

50 Inskip, 'Diary'.

51 Inskip, 'Diary'.

52 Sauer, *John Gould Vol. 4*, p. 400.

53 Moore, *Islanders*. His journals remained unpublished, lying in the Mitchell Library in Sydney, until David Moore transcribed and published this outstanding ethnography.

54 Moore, *Islanders*, pp. 129–35 and Huxley, *T. H. Huxley's Diary*, pp. 196–99.

55 This is now in the Department of Ethnography, British Museum.

56 Moore, *Islanders*, p. 138.

57 Owen Stanley to Mary Stanley, 16 October 1849, CRO/DSA199.

58 MacGillivray, *Narrative*, vol. 2, p. 46.

59 Huxley, *T. H. Huxley's Diary*, p. 203 and MacGillivray, *Narrative*, vol. 2, p. 46.

60 MacGillivray, *Narrative*, vol. 2, pp. 47–8; Huxley, *T. H. Huxley's Diary*, pp. 203–5 and Card, 'Diary'.

61 Inskip, 'Diary'.

CHAPTER XII

1 John Thomson to Mary Thomson, February 1850, DRC Letters.

2 Stanley to family, 1 March 1850, CRO/DSA199.

3 Robert King to Catherine/Mary Stanley, 14 March 1850, CRO/DSA199.

4 John Thomson to Mary Thomson, February 1850, DRC Letters.

5 Stanley to family, 1 March 1850, CRO/DSA199.

6 Robert King to Catherine/Mary Stanley, 14 March 1850, CRO/DSA199.

7 Robert King to Catherine/Mary Stanley, 14 March 1850, CRO/DSA199.

8 Stanley to family, 1 March 1850, CRO/DSA199.

9 Owen Stanley to Mary Stanley, 19 February 1850, CRO/D3113.

10 King to Beaufort, 19 March 1850, UKHO/SL19a/35.

11 Owen Stanley to Mary Stanley, 19 February 1850, CRO/D3113.

12 Stanley to family, 1 March 1850, CRO/DSA199.

13 Stanley to family, 1 March 1850, CRO/DSA199 and John Thomson to Mary Thomson, February 1850, DRC Letters.

14 Bateson, *Gold*.

15 Card, 'Diary'.

16 Spillett, *Forsaken*, pp. 166–8.

17 Robert King to Catherine/Mary Stanley, 14 March 1850, CRO/DSA199.

18 Owen Stanley to Mary Stanley, 19 February 1850, CRO/D3113.

19 Stanley to Tyers, 22 December 1849 and 5 March 1850, NLA/MS264/3.

20 Stanley to Deas Thomson, 11 and 15 February 1850, UKHO/SL15f/189–90.

21 Stanley to Keppel, 15 February 1850, UKHO/SL15f/193.

22 Owen Stanley to Mary Stanley, 19 February 1850, CRO/D3113.

23 Owen Stanley to Edward Stanley, 16 October 1849, CRO/D3113.

24 Owen Stanley to Mary Stanley, 19 February 1850, CRO/D3113.

25 Stanley to family, 1 March 1850, CRO/DSA199.

26 John Thomson to Mary Thomson, February 1850, DRC Letters and Thomas Huxley to George Huxley, 27 April 1849, IC/HA/HP31.52.

27 UKHO/MB7/57–8.

28 Beaufort to Stanley, 31 January 1850, UKHO/LB16/339.

29 Stanley to family, 1 March 1850, CRO/DSA199.

30 Robert King to Catherine/Mary Stanley, 14 March 1850, CRO/DSA199.

31 King to Beaufort, 19 March 1850, UKHO/SL19a/35.

32 16 March 1850.

33 MacGillivray, *Narrative*, vol. 2, p. 85 and Huxley, 'Science at Sea' p. 103. In the twentieth century, another story began to surface, that Stanley had committed suicide. This has been repeated in serious works many times, most recently in 1993 – Ralph, 'John MacGillivray' – though there is not a shred of evidence for it.

34 Stanley, *Memoirs*, p. 126 and King to Beaufort, 19 March 1850, UKHO/SL19a/35.

35 *The Shipping Gazette and Sydney General Trade List*, 16 March 1850, p. 76.

36 Packe, 'Private Journal'.

37 *Sydney Morning Herald*, 16 March 1850.

CHAPTER XIII

1 Yule to Beaufort, 21 March 1850, UKHO/SL15e.

2 Eliza Stanley to Phillip Parker King, 14 November 1850, ML/MSS 7048/5.

3 MacGillivray, *Narrative*, vol. 2, p. 86.

4 This account is based on Sharpe, 'Jottings', Inskip, 'Diary' and *The Shipping Gazette and Sydney General Trade List*, 4 May 1850, p. 131.

5 Sharpe, 'Jottings'.

6 John Thomson to Mary Thomson, 1 October 1850, DRC Letters.

7 MacGillivray, *Narrative*, vol. 2, pp. 86–116; Sharpe, 'Jottings' and Inskip, 'Diary'.

AFTERWORD

1 Yule to Beaufort, 5 November 1850, UKHO/SL15e.

2 Becher to MacGillivray, 7 November 1850, UKHO/LB17/135–6 and MacGillivray to Hooker, 26 November 1850, RBG/DC30/97.

3 Huxley to Thomson, 31 March 1851, DRC Letters.

4 Huxley, *T.H. Huxley's Diary*, p. 285.

5 *The Literary Gazette, And Journal of Science and Art*, no. 8822, 20 December 1851, pp. 891–3 and *The Examiner*, 27 December 1851, pp. 820–22.

6 Hooker to Beaufort, 1 January 1852, UKHO/Pre-1857 Letters/M972.

7 Huxley, *T.H. Huxley's Diary*, p. 285 and Huxley to Eliza Stanley, 1 January 1852, CRO/DSA92A.

8 Huxley to Eliza Stanley, 24 January 1852, CRO/DSA92A.

9 Huxley to Eliza Stanley, 23 and 28 February 1853, CRO/DSA92A.

10 Van Arsdel, 'Westminster', p. 547.

11 Huxley, 'Science at Sea', p. 98.

12 Huxley, 'Science at Sea', p. 99.

13 Huxley, 'Science at Sea', p. 108.

14 Huxley, 'Science at Sea', p. 112.

15 Huxley, 'Science at Sea', p. 112.

16 Huxley, 'Science at Sea', p. 113.

17 Huxley, 'Science at Sea', p. 105.

18 Huxley, 'Science at Sea', p. 104.

19 Huxley, 'Science at Sea', p. 112.

20 Huxley, 'Science at Sea', p. 105.

21 Huxley, 'Science at Sea', p. 106.

22 Huxley, 'Science at Sea', p. 108.

23 Huxley, 'Science at Sea', p. 100.

24 Huxley, 'Science at Sea', p. 100.

25 Huxley, 'Science at Sea', p. 107.

26 Huxley, 'Science at Sea', p. 107.

27 Huxley, 'Science at Sea', p. 107.

28 Huxley, 'Science at Sea', pp. 108–9.

29 Huxley, 'Science at Sea', p. 109.

30 Huxley, 'Science at Sea', p. 103.

31 Huxley, 'Science at Sea', p. 112.

EPILOGUE

1 MacGillivray to Richardson, 20 November 1851, SPRI/MS1503/44/18.
2 MacGillivray to Beaufort, 12 January 1852, UKHO/Pre-1857 Letters/M969.
3 UKHO/Pre-1857 Letters/M936, M972.
4 Huxley to Eliza Stanley, 24 January 1852, CRO/DSA92A.
5 MacGillivray to Hooker, 14 February 1852, RBG/DC32/280.
6 MacGillivray to Hooker, 14 February 1852, RBG/DC32/280.
7 PRO/ADM7/851.
8 David, *The Voyage*, pp. 27–57.
9 Diamond, *The Sea Horse*, pp. 187–201.
10 Webster, *The Last*.
11 David, *The Voyage*, p. 115.
12 David, *The Voyage*, pp. 117–42.
13 'Report of an Enquiry upon Mr MacGillivray, 26 April 1855', NMM/FRE/205 and *Shipping Gazette and Sydney General Trade List*, 5 February 1855.
14 'Report of an Enquiry upon Mr MacGillivray, 26 April 1855', NMM/FRE/205.
15 Fremantle to Beaufort, 1 May 1855, UKHO/Pre-1857 Letters/F358.
16 David, *The Voyage*, p. 271.
17 Ralph, 'John MacGillivray', p.191.
18 Huxley to Joseph Hooker, 17 and 19 November 1855, IC/HA/HP2.196 and 2.110, and J.W. Mill to Hooker, 18 October 1855, RBG/DC35/315.
19 Huxley to Joseph Hooker, 17 November 1855, IC/HA/HP2.196.
20 Sharpe, 'Jottings'.
21 Milne to Hooker, 5 March 1856, RBG/DC74/108.
22 Iredale, 'The Last'; Beaton, 'A Martyr' and 'John MacGillivray: Natural History Notebook, 1855–66', ML/B944.
23 Huxley to Beaufort, 20 November 1850, UKHO/Misc L&P/24/1/C1 and IC/HA/HP32.(1).
24 Beaufort to Yule, 8 November 1850, UKHO/LB17/136–7.
25 Desmond, *Huxley*, pp. 157–61.
26 Huxley to Eliza Stanley, 1 January 1852, CRO/DSA92A.
27 Huxley to Henrietta Heathorn, 1 January 1854, IC/HA/HH259.
28 Huxley to Henrietta Heathorn, 30 July 1854, IC/HA/HH281.
29 See Carr, *The Captive* and Schaffer, *In the Wake*.
30 One version is in Beale, *Kennedy*, pp. 234–8 and another in Sullivan, *A Fortunate*, pp. 171–96. Sullivan discusses both these and other, less creditable stories.

Index